D1606449

Borderland on the Isthmus

AMERICAN ENCOUNTERS/GLOBAL INTERACTIONS

A series edited by Gilbert M. Joseph and Emily S. Rosenberg

This series aims to stimulate critical perspectives and fresh inter-
pretive frameworks for scholarship on the history of the imposing global presence of the United States. Its primary concerns
include the deployment and contestation of power, the construction and deconstruction of cultural and political borders, the fluid
meanings of intercultural encounters, and the complex interplay
between the global and the local. American Encounters seeks to
strengthen dialogue and collaboration between historians of U.S.
international relations and area studies specialists.

The series encourages scholarship based on multiarchival historical research. At the same time, it supports a recognition of the
representational character of all stories about the past and pro-
motes critical inquiry into issues of subjectivity and narrative. In
the process, American Encounters strives to understand the context in which meanings related to nations, cultures, and political
economy are continually produced, challenged, and reshaped.

Borderland
on the Isthmus

RACE,

CULTURE,

AND THE

STRUGGLE

FOR THE

CANAL

ZONE

Michael E. Donoghue

DUKE UNIVERSITY PRESS

Durham and London 2014

Designed by Amy Ruth Buchanan

Typeset in Quadraat and Quadraat

Sans by Graphic Composition, Inc.,

Bogart, Georgia

Library of Congress Cataloging-

in-Publication Data

Donoghue, Michael E.

Borderland on the isthmus : race,

culture, and the struggle for the canal

zone / Michael E. Donoghue.

pages cm — (American encounters/

global interactions)

Includes bibliographical references and index

ISBN 978-0-8223-5666-0 (cloth : alk. paper)

ISBN 978-0-8223-5678-3 (pbk. : alk. paper)

1. Panama Canal (Panama)—Social

conditions—20th century. 2. Panama

Canal (Panama)—Race relations—

20th century. I. Title. II. Series:

American encounters/global interactions.

F1569.C2D66   2014

972.87′5—dc23   2013045007

THIS BOOK IS

DEDICATED WITH LOVE

TO MY FATHER,

CHARLES DONOGHUE,

AND TO MY BROTHER, JOSEPH.

WE WILL SEE YOU BOTH

ON THE OTHER SIDE,

DAD AND JOEY.

Contents

Acknowledgments

A work of this scope required support from numerous institutions, grants, and individuals, all of whom distinguished themselves with their generosity. The University of Connecticut at Storrs supplied summer grants, predoctoral fellowships, and a doctoral research grant from the university's research foundation that proved crucial to the early stages of this project. The William F. Fulbright Overseas Research Grant program enabled me to spend a year plumbing the archives of Panama and interviewing scores of Panamanians, West Indians, and Zonians, without which this study would have been impossible. Five presidential libraries awarded me research and travel grants: the Harry S. Truman Library Institute, the Eisenhower World Affairs Institute, the John F. Kennedy Library Foundation, the Lyndon Baines Johnson Foundation, and the Gerald R. Ford Library Foundation. The Society of Historians of American Foreign Relations generously awarded me the Bernath Research Travel Grant and the W. Stull Holt Dissertation Fellowship. Marquette University, my new home, continued to fund this project generously with summer fellowships and research grants.

Numerous scholars in the United States offered advice and counsel during this project, including David Sheinin, Stephen Rabe, Mark Gilderhus, Gilbert Joseph, Emily Rosenberg, Blanca Silvestrini, Eileen Suárez Findlay, Darlene Rivas, Michael L. Conniff, Stephen Streeter, Doug Little, Mark Overmyer-Velasquez, James Howe, Gloria Rudolf, Luis Figueroa, Robert McMahon, Kyle Longley, Jana Lipman, John Lindsay-Poland, Marixa Llasso, Cornelia Dayton, Mark Lawrence, Alan McPherson, and Peter Szok. Elizabeth Mahan made all the facilities and talents of University of Connecticut's Latin American Studies Program available to me as well as her own sage and humane advice. I am also indebted to Laurietz Seda, MacGregor O'Brien, Steve Wille, and Augustana College and CEDEI's Summer in the Andes program for greatly improving my Spanish prior to research in Panama. In Panama I received generous aid from Professors Francisco Herrera, Alfredo Castillero Calvo, Alfredo Figueroa Navarro, Rubén Darío Carles, Miguel Antonio Bernal, and Marco Gandásegui. I am forever indebted to my personal guides to Panamanian history, culture, and geography: Osvaldo Jordan Romeros, Joyce Isveth Mendoza, Daira Arias, Belsi de Medina, Maria Carazo, and "Hans" Etienne Parisis.

I wish to express my deep appreciation and thanks to the following library and archival staffs in the United States: the National Archives, the Library of Congress, the Washington National Records Center, the Homer Babbidge Library at the University of Connecticut, the John Hay and John D. Rockefeller Jr. Libraries at Brown University, the Georgetown University Library, the Yale University Library, The Raynor Memorial Libraries at Marquette, and the U.S. Army Military History Institute. Archivists who made important contributions to this work include Liz Safly and Dennis Bilger at the Truman Library, David Haight at the Eisenhower Library, Megan Desnoyers at the Kennedy Library, Regina Greenwell and Michael Parrish at the Johnson Library, Helmi Raaska and Geir Gundersen at the Ford Library, Michael Wasche at the Washington National Records Center, and John Taylor, Fred Romanski, and Milton Gustafson at the U.S. National Archives. For help with the book's images from the Panama and Canal Zone Collection at the University of Florida's George A. Smathers Libraries, I want to thank Laurie Taylor. For his superb work in creating the maps of the Zone-Panama borderland, kudos to Bill Nelson.

I also wish to express my appreciation to the talented staffs and archivists in the Republic of Panama. These include Griselda Añino de Valdes, Apolinar Guerrero, Darixa Ruiz, and especially Ida Cecilia Mitre at the Biblioteca Nacional; Xiomara de Robleta at the Archivos del Ministerio de Relaciones Exteriores; Carlos Arrellano Rodríquez, Gilberto Marulanda, Elvia Williams, and Rosario Carrera at the Instituto del Canal y Estudios Internacionales at the Universidad de Panamá; Rolando Cochez, Adolfo Vallarino, Lorena Riba, Miguel Montague, and Gisela Lammerts van Bueren at the Centro de Recursos Tecnícos (Biblioteca del Autoridad del Canal de Panamá); and Albert Brown, Lee Amberths, Earl Barber, Sam Edwards, and Pablo Prieto at the Archivos y Recuerdos del Autoridad del Canal de Panamá in Corozal.

The warmth and generosity of the people of Panama proved indispensable to this study that rested so much on understanding the culture and rhythms of the republic. The scores of Panamanians whom I interviewed greatly enriched this study. All their names are too numerous to record here and are in the notes but I would like to especially acknowledge Frank Azcarraga,

Helen Escobar, José Espino, Enrique Cantera, Rodrigo Mendoza, Miguel J. Moreno, Porfirio Sánchez, Antonio Stanziola, Rolando Sterling Arango, and Rimksy and Fulvia Sucre. The West Indian community in Panama especially welcomed my work. I want to thank Cecil Haynes, George Barnabas, Lester Leon Greaves, Vincente Williams, Lindolph Leon Ashby III, and Gilberto Alls for their help and their memories and critiques of the old Zone. I also received great guidance, hospitality, and aid from the Zonian community in both Panama and Florida. The Elks Club in Balboa served for a time as my unofficial residence, as did Niko's Café in Balboa, haunt of the diehard Zonies. The retired U.S. military society in Panama also proved welcoming at the VFW in Curundu and later at Albrook as well as at the Balboa Yacht Club. I would like to single out Captain Joseph "Jody" Chamberlain, Luke Palumbo, Tom Carey, Edgardo Tirado, Carl "Tortuga" Tuttle, Tony and Anne Tiblier, Dave Sherman, Don Philips, Doug Philips, James Reid, Nina Kosik, Angela (Lee) Azcarraga, George Gershow, John Coffey, Mary Coffey, Rolando Linares, John McTaggart, Jason and Leo Critides, Bob Thrush, Robin and Peter Moreland, Tom McLean, Skip Berger, the entire Homa family, Larry Liberty, Wayne Bryant, Daniel Cooper, Art Mokray, John and Lucy Haines, Trina Clark, Pablo Eastman, Marvin Wainwright, and Vic Malent for their support and friendship.

My advisory committee at Storrs proved invaluable with their expert counsel, organizational ideas, and superb editing advice. Thomas G. Paterson's enduring inspiration as a writer, scholar, teacher, and mentor permeates this entire work. J. Garry Clifford's encyclopedic knowledge of sources, his sharp editing of my prose, his encouragement, and his good humor provided the bedrock of this study. Finally, Frank Costigliola's immeasurable intellectual curiosity, collegial generosity, and pluralistic approach to foreign relations history infused every page of this study. My new colleagues at Marquette University, including my chair, James Marten, and my colleagues Steve Avella, Irene Guenther, Laura Matthew, Tim MacMahon, Daniel Meissner, Michael Wert, Alison Efford, and Kristen Foster, were also a great source of inspiration. The editing and art staff at Duke University Press, especially Valerie Millholland, Miriam Angress, and Christine Choi, helped me immeasurably with their patience and expertise. The anonymous readers of the manuscript offered superb advice on improving the structure and content of this study.

Family and friends supplied vital sustenance throughout this long but fruitful process. Deborah Kisatsky and Shane Maddock were the two best friends a historian could ever have—kind, giving, and full of enthusiasm for my work. Ted Kryla and John and Karen St. Lawrence sustained my spirits back home in Providence, my hometown. Historians at Storrs always treated me more like a colleague than a student, and I want to thank Richard D. Brown, Kent Newmeyer, Bill Hoglund, Bruce Stave, Ed Wherle, and Marvin and Diane Cox for their encouragement and ideas as I worked my way through this project. My sister, Eileen, and my brothers, Kevin and Stephen, provided spiritual reservoirs that I could always draw upon. My parents, Charles and Jane Donoghue, inspired me with a love of learning, reading, and laughter that all found redemption in this work.

This book is dedicated to my recently deceased father, Charles, and to my younger brother, Joseph, whom we lost while I was away conducting research in Panama. Joey's spirit lives on in the harsh beauty at the heart of this study of human frailty and wounded aspirations.

Introduction

For the first half of the twentieth century, the Panama Canal Zone was arguably the most important overseas possession of the United States. In addition to its geostrategic and economic value, the Canal held a symbolic primacy in the minds of many Americans as a mark of their technological and national superiority. But the establishment of the territorial enclave around the Canal under the 1903 Hay–Bunau-Varilla Treaty had other consequences. It forged an imperial borderland across the isthmus of Panama that would have profound ramifications for all of its inhabitants, from a wide variety of backgrounds and walks of life. The interactions, conflicts, and accommodations among the various peoples who strove for survival and ascendance within the vortex of this borderland, from World War II until the Carter-Torrijos treaties, form the subject of this study.

The American inhabitants of the enclave, the Zonians, established their dominance early in the century, as did their coequal partners in the Canal project, the U.S. military. But throughout this process, these groups experienced friction, resistance, and troubles from the host nation of Panama and the various subaltern peoples drawn to the excavation. The gargantuan size of the project attracted workers from all over the world, especially a large contingent of West Indian laborers who formed the backbone of the workforce. The racial discrimination that these workers endured, combined with the national chauvinism that Panamanians and other Latinos experienced from American borderlanders, quickly ignited conflicts over race and identity along the Zone boundaries that would intensify in the decades after World War II.

In July 1939, two months before the war, the U.S. Senate finally ratified the 1936 Hull-Alfaro Treaty that ended the official U.S. protectorate over Panama, which included the right to eminent domain and unilateral intervention practiced by Washington for thirty-six years. This accord proved a turning point in the greater development of competing Panamanian institutions and projects in relation to the United States, with the eventual goal to eject the colossus from the isthmus.[1] The international conflict of World War II launched even more important global and local shifts, which put the entire rationale behind the Zone's existence under attack. These included decolonization, a resurgence in local nationalism and demography, and the rejection of racism inspired by the U.S. and global civil rights movements.[2] Besides the central issues of cultural identity, always at odds in this and other borderlands, additional points of contention arose over smuggling, crime, sex and drug trafficking, and jurisdictional authority. Panamanians, and a host of other non-U.S. citizens, showed a propensity early on to ignore the boundaries of the Zone, and in so doing to challenge the social, political, and economic status quo established by the enclave's powerful founders.

The Canal Zone formed four distinct landed borders, two fifty-mile-long boundaries that ran east and west of the Canal across rural regions, and two urban frontiers, one to the north that faced the transit city of Colón, the other to the south that abutted the capital, Panama City. But the contact zones of these boundaries extended far into the urban sectors of these cities and deep into the interior regions of Panama and the Zone. This peculiar Zone-Panama borderland held sway across the entire transisthmian corridor, bringing divergent peoples, economies, and cultures into alliances, dependencies, and confrontations typical of oppositional border regions long studied by anthropologists, political scientists, and historians.[3]

The Panama Canal Zone was unique in that it encompassed a *noncontiguous* imperial borderland, unlike those more famous imperial frontiers that stretched across North America during the colonial and early national periods, toward the Great Lakes and Ohio Valley with French Canada, or astride the Spanish borderlands in northern Florida and the current Southwest.[4] Most imperial borderlands throughout history have been *contiguous*, joined territorially to a larger imperial heartland, such as the Russian borderlands of the tsarist era that stretched into Eastern Europe, the Caucasus, Central Asia, and Siberia, or the Roman borderlands along the Rhine and the Danube.[5] But history provides us with numerous examples of noncontiguous imperial borderlands: Hadrian's Wall across northern England, Gibraltar at the southernmost tip of Iberia, the Suez Canal Zone in Egypt, Singapore at the end of the Malaysian peninsula, and the present-day U.S.-Cuban borderland at Guantánamo.[6]

What made the Zone-Panama borderland especially unique was that it operated in such a rich, cosmopolitan milieu among the Panamanian,

American, Barbadian, Jamaican, Kuna, Chinese, Hindu, Jewish, Arab, and Latin American populations that peopled the Zone, Colón, Panama City, and their environs. This complex mix of peoples living astride an international transportation hub complicated the reactions and contestations that emanated throughout the region in response to U.S. belligerence, Panamanian resistance, and joint and competing projects for political, cultural, and economic aggrandizement. All the aforementioned groups constantly engaged in "crossing borders" throughout this process, entering into relationships of mutual interest, hostility, and ambivalence with those from the "other side." The intersection of different cultures, hierarchies, and mores at the borders brought these conflicts into sharp relief, forged new syntheses, and provided fruitful case studies for analyzing the day-to-day operation of the American Empire in Panama.[7]

Several distinguished historians of U.S. foreign relations—Walter LaFeber, Michael L. Conniff, and John Major—have ably analyzed the larger strategic, political, and economic structure of U.S. dominance on the isthmus. Their work has emphasized high-status actors and events, as well as key economic indices and political developments. But less scholarly research has focused on the Zone as a *borderland*, with its unique social and cultural impacts on U.S.-Panamanian relations.[8] Historians have not sufficiently studied the complex interplay between the various peoples at the margins who lived within and along the enclave's frontiers. *Borderland on the Isthmus* seeks to address these encounters and provide both a social history of the American Empire in Panama and an analysis of the Zone and its frontiers as sites of contestation over race, identity, gender, and power. A borderlands approach to analyzing the Zone-Panama corridor provides a revealing lens for exploring such conflicts and what they tell us about the players, their beliefs, illusions, and goals, as well as issues of gender and power, all of which could change at a moment's notice, simply by stepping across an artificial line.

Panamanians expressed their opposition and accommodation to the Zone not just in official policies, protests, and demonstrations but in everyday forms of resistance and acquiescence. They often embraced aspects of American culture and the economic opportunities that the Zone offered, even as they rejected U.S. colonialism. Likewise U.S. military personnel and canal workers stigmatized Panamanians as inferiors during the week, then sought pleasure on weekends in the nightclubs, festivals, and brothels of Colón and Panama City. The Zone borderland became a microcosm of the strains of postwar America and Panama, as well as a mirror for the projection of U.S. power, culture, and ideology abroad.

Within the Latin American context, the Zone stood as the ultimate symbol of Yankee hegemony and racism toward blacks and Latinos. Constituting a population of over fifty thousand administrators, technicians, canal workers, soldiers, and their dependents, plus nine thousand workers who lived on the other side of the line, the enclave constituted one of the largest U.S. overseas communities from World War II through 1979.[9] No serious discussion of American imperialism (or arguments over whether it ever existed) can proceed without considering the Zone-Panama borderland, its inhabitants, its internal and external conflicts, and its significance to U.S.–Latin American relations and the formation of the American Empire.

Debates over the Canal Zone abound. Was working for the Panama Canal Company similar to life in a company town, a huge plantation, a socialist state, a Jim Crow society, a military base, a tropical utopia, or a combination of all of these? Was the Zone-Panama borderland a colony, an enclave, or a state within a state? The different perspectives of the Zonian and U.S. military communities, of the West Indian labor force, and of neighboring Panama all brought varied responses to these questions at the borders. In *Zone Policeman 88* (1913), a primary source memoir, Harry A. Franck portrayed the Zone as a turn-of-the-century Euro-American colony with a unique U.S. civilizing mission and strong cultural hostility toward the locals. John and Mavis Biesanz, in their sociological study, *The People of Panama* (1955), portrayed the Zonians as a highly regimented yet essentially middle-class, paternalistic community that kept its distance from Panamanians and discriminated against the West Indian workforce. Herbert and Mary Knapp, in *Red, White, and Blue Paradise* (1984), a personal account with many journalistic and secondary sources, defended the Zone community against charges of extreme racism, jingoism, and privilege. The Knapps viewed the Zonians as hardworking, dedicated Americans concerned more with job security and enjoying a workers' paradise than with the dictates of empire. Their study also took a critical view of Panamanian cultural, social, and political mores.

Historical change and processes are not adequately tracked in these studies through the use of archival documents, personal papers, oral histories, and court, company, and military records that were employed in this volume. Julie Greene in *The Canal Builders* (2009) has expertly explored the formative years of the Canal Zone using many of these sources, with a particular emphasis on the Canal as a canvas for Progressive-era labor and reform struggles. But her study concentrates understandably on the construction years, as does David McCullough's earlier, celebratory *The Path between* the Seas (1977). In *Seaway to the Future: American Social Visions and the Construction of the Panama Canal* (2008) Alexander Missal analyzes the influence of Progressive-era writers in creating a utopian discourse regarding the Canal and their hopes for a model, futuristic society. Because of their earlier focus, none of these works analyzed the post–World War II Zone when the enclave and the reasons for maintaining it came under such intense national and international pressure.

Two pioneering works, Verna Newton's *The Silver Men* (1984) and Michael L. Conniff's *Black Labor on a White Canal* (1985), brought much needed scholarly attention to the hitherto neglected role of West Indians in shaping the Canal project and subsequent Panamanian society. Noel Maurer and Carlos Yu's *The Big Ditch* (2011) provides a superb economic history of the Panama Canal which argues that Washington decided to build and later transfer the Canal largely on the basis of a cost-benefit analysis. But much more than mere dollars and cents was at stake for Americans, West Indians, and Panamanians in the cultural borderland that developed between them.

In contrast, viewing the Zone as an imperial borderland refocuses the often ignored centrality of local agency in the formation of identity politics on the isthmus that drove so many related processes. *Borderland on the Isthmus* investigates the colonial nature of the Zone and its frontiers by comparing and contrasting this imperial frontier with key features of other postwar colonies and borderlands in Africa and Asia. This work supports the notion of the Zone-Panama corridor as a locus of intercultural and overlapping societies influenced by local traditions, colonial innovations, metropolitan authority, and "intercultural politics of race, identity, and gender."[10]

While this study relies on many state archival sources, a wide variety of periodicals, newspapers, pamphlets, novels, films, and other popular culture materials were also employed to provide a street-level or bottom-up history of the lived experience of the borderland. Central to this approach and to the thick description methodology used to decipher the many encounters among Panamanians, U.S. citizens, West Indians, and Kuna are scores of oral interviews I conducted.[11] It is important to note that all those interviewed brought their own unique perspectives and discourses to the many controversial topics of this study. While oral histories provide a fascinating window into the social and cultural life of the Zone and its neighboring Panamanian barrios, these interviews also have their limitations and should be approached with care. White Zonians, for instance, were well aware that the racism so commonplace in the Canal Zone in the 1940s–1960s was no longer socially acceptable when these interviews were conducted in 2001–8. Zonians frequently tended to look back on the enclave with nostalgia, exaggerating its sublimities and minimizing its injustices.

Similarly Latin Panamanians who grew up in the shadow of the Zone and its humiliation of Panamanians sometimes hyperbolized its cruelties. Older service workers and Panamanian taxi drivers who benefited from the Zone expressed a certain longing for the good times of the enclave, and so amplified its benefits to Panama, partly in hopes of securing a better tip from the author. In contrast, retired West Indians expressed fear of condemning the racism of the old borderland too vociferously, as they worried it might affect their U.S. pensions and relations with Panamanian neighbors when this book was published. Romanticized memories, hurtful biases, and economic fears naturally influenced remembrances of this imperial frontier, as is the case with most historical memory.[12]

The structure of this study is based on identity groups and themes rather than chronology. The first chapter serves as an introduction to the work and to the central theoretical framework of the Zone and its frontiers as a *borderland* where various influences and interactions reached out and impacted everyday life on either side of the line. This chapter takes a longer historical view, back to 1903 and as far forward as 1999, as it traces the peaks and valleys of the Zone's sway within the republic, as well as increases in Panamanian influence upon the enclave. Chapter 2 analyzes the central categories of race and national identity in conflict throughout the borderland in the post–World War II period, with special focus on the Zonians, the term used to describe U.S. civilian canal workers and their families. Changing notions of identity and race emerged from World War II that would profoundly question the enclave's once comfortable ascendance. Chapter 3 examines various modes of West Indian identity that arose in response to U.S. discrimination and continued Panamanian hostility. West Indians found themselves in an especially perilous position within the postwar borderland as local nationalism surged and generational strife erupted within their own ranks. Eventually these challenges in identity politics, combined with the global decolonization struggle, led many West Indians to transfer their loyalty, however grudgingly, from the United States to Panama.

Chapter 4 probes the highly charged gender relations within the Zone-Panama borderland. Sexual interaction and the mutability of gender constructions both complicated and exacerbated U.S.-Panamanian everyday associations across borders. U.S. sexual violence repelled Panamanians, while intermarriage, concubinage, and a regulated sex industry that mushroomed from the World War II troop buildup pulled Panamanians and U.S. citizens into mutual webs of intimacy. Chapter 5 examines the history of the U.S. military on the isthmus, its unique culture and relationship with the Panamanian people, National Guard, and elites. The central role of the U.S. military as armed guardians of the borderland put them in competition with technocratic, middle-class Zonians who felt that their operation of the Canal merited a loftier authority. Their rivalry constituted a hallmark of the borderland's postwar history, as did changing local perceptions of the U.S. military from World War II antifascist heroes to the chief instrument of a resented occupation.

Chapter 6 explores the often ignored role of crime throughout the borderland, which at least some Panamanians and West Indians viewed as a form of resistance. With its provocative presence beside the poorest slums of Panama, the U.S.-run enclave provided a tempting target for Panamanian criminals, who through theft, contraband, and drug trafficking fought their own private wars against the Zone. The postwar growth in population and poverty intensified this struggle, which included surprising alliances, dependencies, and cooperation that both united and divided communities on either side of the line. The contrast between the U.S. and Panamanian justice systems complicated these encounters. While the political nature of such crime is difficult to gauge, the popular perception that much of it embodied a patriotic defiance against the *gringos* can be established in several cases. Finally, an epilogue draws the larger conclusions of this study. The two conflicted societies—actually five or six, if one counts the principal divisions within them—formed an often antagonistic borderland culture at various intersections, an in-between land neither fully Panamanian, West Indian, nor Zonian. The question of U.S. empire is also addressed, with insights gleaned from a century of conflict and accommodation along the borders of the transisthmian corridor.

BORDERLAND ON THE ISTHMUS

The Changing Boundaries and Frontiers of the Panama Canal Zone

A strange sight occurred during the warm January nights along Fourth of July Avenue, the border that divided the U.S.-controlled Canal Zone from the Republic of Panama. On January 12, 1964, the U.S. military officially closed down the border following four days of bloody anti-American riots over a disputed flag-raising at a U.S. high school in the Zone. A few nights after the lockdown, North American and Panamanian witnesses saw groups of local prostitutes gather clandestinely near the cyclone fence that ran along the borderline. Simultaneously small groups of U.S. soldiers began lining up along their side of the Zone's wire barrier. In the thick brush the prostitutes knelt and fellated the GIs through the chain-link apertures. Just days before, these same soldiers had shot down Panamanian snipers and protesters and had been fired upon themselves by Panamanian militants in the crowds.[1]

These incidents of sex through a border fence, which occurred nightly until U.S. officials lifted the travel ban in March 1964, spoke volumes about the Canal Zone's sexual hunger for Panama. They are also a telling image of the U.S.-Panamanian relationship. From this graphic interaction we can better understand the indignation that many Panamanians felt about their country's relationship with the United States. We can also better appreciate what a complex site of conflict and accommodation an imperial borderland represents. Complicating this image is that a significant portion of the soldiers along the fence were probably Puerto Ricans, as in the 1960s this ethnic category made up nearly a third of the GIs in Panama. Most of the prostitutes along the fence were likely Colombians, Venezuelans, and Dominicans, as they composed a majority of the guest-worker prostitutes working in Panama City and Colón.[2]

The geographical, economic, and cultural frontiers of the Canal Zone shifted throughout the U.S. century in Panama, 1903–99. This chapter examines how and why they changed over time and the effect such transformations had on the lives of ordinary U.S. and Panamanian citizens who lived within this borderland. It will focus especially on the importance of the borders and boundaries of the Zone. The Zone helped shape the economy, demographics, and social relations of transisthmian Panama, particularly after World War II. This borderland not only provided jobs and economic opportunities for Panamanians but also encouraged familial bonds, dependencies, and psychic fears. As one older Panamanian stated, "It still bothers me to walk across that street into the old Zone. I know the *gringo* police aren't there anymore, but I still hesitate a little when I walk across, you know."[3] Such a revelation illustrates Foucault's notion of the dispersal of power that power resides not just in the state's official instruments of coercion but also in the consciousness of those subjected to that power.[4]

The Canal Zone also encompassed a mass of internal boundaries and divisions besides its landed frontiers with the republic. These proved important for several reasons. At first glance in 1940, the Zone appeared monolithic and invulnerable. But like so many European colonies in Africa and Asia, the Zone comprised a mass of contradictions and complexities, a "house divided against itself." Its internal fissures help explain its demise in the postwar era, when external Panamanian pressures, sociopolitical changes in the U.S. metropolis, and internal complaints emanating from the Zone itself coalesced to delegitimize the enclave. Panamanian opponents of the Zone grew adept at playing off the various factions that lived on the U.S. side of the border to achieve their own nationalist ends.

The Zone Borderland's Contribution to Panama's Development

Many Panamanians reviled the Canal Zone as a kind of Frankenstein, born of the Mephistophelian deal with the United States in 1903. This powerful entity had to be constantly wrestled down and beaten back, as it displayed a remarkable resiliency and thirst for hegemony. According to this nationalist critique, Panamanians managed to drive the stake through this monster's heart only on December 31, 1999, as the Zone still lived on for more than twenty years after the 1977 Carter-Torrijos treaties, albeit as the Panama Canal Area.[5]

This interpretation of colonialism as a demonic force offers insights, but it also distorts the totality of the relationship. For despite the Zone's obstruction to Panama's sovereignty, the republic derived considerable benefits from its bargain with the Devil, though never in the proportions that the republic's founders had hoped. The Canal Zone provided between one half and one fifth of Panama's gross domestic product from 1904 through 1979, and even as late as the 1990s U.S. military spending alone accounted for about 5 percent of GDP, some $255 million. Tens of thousands of Panamanians worked either directly or indirectly for the Canal Zone in every year of its existence.[6] But the vast majority of these Latin and West Indian Panamanians, as we shall see, were never fairly compensated for their labor compared to the white U.S. workers. And the infamous (in Panama anyway) U.S. commissary system of the Zone prevented Panamanian merchants from sharing in the economic largesse of the enclave, as imported, duty-free goods from the United States cut locals out of a bonanza of potential sales.[7]

As in other Latin American states, a fairly high percentage of Panamanian students attended U.S. colleges and universities, but tuition costs and discrimination on the isthmus prevented poorer Panamanian children from attending Canal Zone schools and its junior college for decades. Thousands of U.S. citizens and Panamanians intermarried over the past century, including GIs who lifted numerous Panamanian women out of poverty. But these same servicemen routinely abandoned their girlfriends and mixed-nationality children and were often abusive toward their common-law and official wives. While the United States built railroads, highways, roads, and bridges across the country, it did so primarily for its own economic and wartime needs, not Panama's. U.S. Canal Zone health officials virtually eliminated yellow fever and malaria from the transisthmian corridor, where these diseases had ravaged the locals for centuries. But this was done primarily to facilitate the excavation of the U.S. Canal and not to save the lives of Panamanians, many of whom continued to live in want and suffer from a variety of diseases in the interior regions of the country throughout and after construction.[8]

In contrast, postwar foreign aid and U.S. military civic action built hospitals and clinics throughout the isthmus and distributed emergency food and medical services to victims of disasters. U.S. engineers from the Canal Zone installed the water and electrical systems that brought improved quality of life to hundreds of thousands of Panamanians. But Panamanians paid for their U.S.-supplied water, as stipulated in the original 1903 treaty. The republic also escaped the ravages of runaway inflation, so common in Latin America, through its use of the U.S. dollar as its national currency. The strong U.S. military presence may have spared this small nation the bloody, internal conflicts that wracked most of its Central American neighbors, but U.S. troops intervened numerous times in Panama, including in the violent and destructive 1989 invasion. Thanks in part to U.S. investment and the prosperity engendered by the Canal and its adjacent Free Zone in Colón, Panama ranks fifth in per capita income among all Latin American and Caribbean nations. Yet despite these U.S. contributions, Panama continues to suffer from the second worst maldistribution of income in the hemisphere and from substantial poverty. And regardless of the aforementioned benefits, Panamanians endured a century of foreign domination that included armed interventions, cultural denigration, and personal humiliations difficult to quantify.[9]

This long colonial relationship also encompassed countless interactions between ordinary people who forged bonds and enmities along the borders of the Zone. As one Kennedy administration memo described the relationship, "The United States presence in the Zone is to Panamanians an overpowering factor . . . which governs their daily lives in a hundred different ways." A 1958 Canal Zone U.S. employee handbook explained, "International relations are put on an individual basis on the Isthmus, for when you cross certain streets you find yourself within the boundaries of another nation." However, the sharply different power status between the citizens of the mightiest nation on earth and those of a small Latin American country inevitably affected the character of these interactions.[10]

Defining the Borders

Political scientists and historians of borders have long noted that such physical intersections of states, peoples, and cultures are key sites and symbols of national power. Borders mark and delimit state sovereignty and the rights of individual citizenship. But more important, borders constitute processes, not static institutions. Peoples at the borders, on either side of a demarcated boundary, frequently shape, distort, or influence official policy through their own agency in conflicts and accommodations with those from the other side.[11]

Neither the U.S. Canal Zone nor Panama ever effectively controlled contraband, political refugees, sexual relations, drug trafficking, identity politics, and crime along the border, despite their purported efforts to do so. James R. Prescott in his classic work, *Political Frontiers and Boundaries*, noted that *boundaries* are the actual lines that demarcate state territories. For the most part, boundaries follow the opening of *frontiers*, the vanguard of an expanding state that marks the fluid areas of contact between two peoples or between a settled and a less populated land. A *border* is the area immediately adjacent to a state's boundary. According to Prescott, a *borderland* denotes a transitional zone of varying depth on either side of a *boundary*, an area porous and open to a variety of social, cultural, and economic interplay. The U.S.-Mexican borderland from Tijuana in the west to Brownsville in the east is the one most studied by U.S. scholars.[12]

These terms—*borders, boundaries,* and *frontiers*—are not only geographical but also psychological constructs. The common expression "beyond the pale" was originally a military term, referring to the moat and palisade built around twelfth-century Dublin by its Norman conquerors to fortify the town from the "barbarous Irish." Much later the term took on a metaphorical meaning, referring to behavior outside accepted norms. Similarly "crossing borders," in addition to the physical act of traversing a state-sanctioned boundary, connotes entering into a different milieu, culture, or mind-set, with all the attendant fears, attractions, and possibilities.[13]

A History of the Zone Borderland's Changing Boundaries and Frontiers

The original zone of U.S. influence in Panama evolved along the site of the Panama Railroad, constructed from 1850 to 1855 and often known as "the Yankee Strip." Built as a shorter route to the U.S. Pacific Coast following the 1849 California gold rush, the railway first brought Panamanians into large-scale contact with Americans. The later French and U.S. canal construction projects followed the route of the rails for practical reasons as its tracks provided transportation for heavy equipment, workers, and supplies.[14]

During negotiations with Colombia in 1902 prior to the November 1903 Panamanian Revolution, U.S. diplomats envisioned a smaller, less expansive canal zone. The January 1903 Hay-Herrán Treaty, initialed by U.S. Secretary of State John Hay and Colombian Foreign Minister Tomás Herrán, called for a ten-kilometer-wide rather than a ten-mile-wide enclave. This U.S.-Colombian canal zone would have been only around 340 rather than 558 square miles and had a finite life span of one hundred years, not the perpetuity of U.S. rights in the later Zone. The treaty also called for mixed U.S.-Colombian courts. But the Colombian legislature rejected the treaty, hoping to gain greater monetary concessions from Washington. Frustrated U.S. leaders then opted for a "Panama solution" to their canal problem: they backed a Panamanian secessionist revolt against Bogotá.[15]

Days after the successful revolution, Secretary Hay opened negotiations with Frenchman Philippe Bunau-Varilla, chief engineer under Ferdinand de Lesseps's failed canal project and envoy of the new Panamanian government. Bunau-Varilla altered both the territorial and the temporal dimensions of the Zone in favor of Washington to ensure rapid congressional passage of the treaty. Therefore from its earliest inception as a territory of the imagination rather than a geographical reality, the Canal Zone was open to negotiation, interpretation, and manipulation—all classic characteristics of a borderland.[16]

In the early years of the construction and protectorate era (1903–39), the U.S. Zone held the entire Panamanian nation in thrall as a virtual colony of the United States. In 1912, at the height of the construction effort, the total number of U.S. workers, troops, and tourists, plus foreign laborers and their families, over 100,000, equaled a third of Panama's population of 336,000. At this juncture Panama often appeared as much a North American as a Latin American state. Nine times between 1904 and 1925 U.S. troops exercised their right of unilateral intervention in Panama, suppressing disturbances and expanding the Zone's frontiers of influence across the entire country. During World War I U.S. forces took possession of various tracts of land and islands for defense bases under Article II of the treaty, giving only the barest notification of their actions to the republic.[17]

The 1936 Hull-Alfaro Treaty ended this unilateral right of U.S. intervention and eminent domain. In addition the treaty returned control of Panama City and Colón's port and water facilities to the republic and restricted purchases from U.S. commissaries to Panama Canal and Railroad employees. The Acción Comunal movement, a nationalist regeneration party led by the middle-class Arias brothers, Harmodio and Arnulfo, spearheaded this populist effort to end the U.S. protectorate. Acción Comunal had broad support from younger, educated Panamanians angered over the flouting of Panamanian sovereignty and arrogant U.S. troop behavior throughout the isthmus.[18]

The frontiers of the Zone's influence shrank briefly under pressure from the nationalist firebrand Arnulfo Arias and his Panameñismo movement. Inaugurated as president in 1940, Arias enacted a Spanish-only program, aimed at the West Indian and commercial neighborhoods that bordered the Zone. Under his orders, local officials and telephone operators refused to speak English to North Americans. Arias insisted that all street and store signs also be in Spanish, irritating U.S. shoppers in the terminal cities. The popular president attempted, in effect, to take back the borderland, that region of mixed U.S.-Panamanian influences, at least on the Panamanian side of the line. He viewed Americanization that emanated from the Zone as a threat to sovereignty and the Panamanian way of life. Arias's "culture war," as well as his fascist sympathies and racist policies toward ethnic and religious minorities, alarmed both Washington and the liberal-minded Panamanian oligarchy (who also feared Arias's populism). In October 1941 both helped engineer his overthrow.[19]

The international crisis of World War II temporarily upended Panamanian nationalist gains and led to the greatest expansion of the Canal Zone's frontiers. U.S. troop levels in Panama rose from thirteen thousand to sixty-seven thousand by January 1943 to protect the Canal from the threat of Nazi submarines and Japanese bombers. Besides more troops, the Zone imported twenty-two thousand Central American and West Indian laborers to work on the Third Locks Project, designed to provide a wider set of locks for larger ships. These laborers also worked on the numerous U.S.-funded road projects that included the Transistmica Highway and sections of what later became the Pan-American Highway. Additional tens of thousands of U.S. service personnel flooded World War II Panama when they disembarked from the thousands of war vessels that transited the canal in support of Allied campaigns in Europe and the Pacific.[20]

On furlough these U.S. soldiers, sailors, and marines thronged the streets of Colón and Panama City until they resembled American base towns. In their wild, legendary carousing on Bottle Alley, Cash Street, Río Abajo, and J Street, U.S. servicemen ran roughshod over taxi drivers, bar furniture, Panamanian police, and Panamanian women, to the point that they threatened civil order. Panamanian officials received so many complaints of U.S. assaults on women that they established a special protective system. Panamanian and Latina prostitutes wore distinctive gold-plated ankle bracelets so that U.S. servicemen could discern more easily who was a prostitute and who was simply a local woman out shopping on the Avenida Central.[21]

Far more threatening to Panama's sovereignty in the eyes of nationalists was the widespread wartime base expansion. In all, Washington established 134 military installations, from small radar sites to large training grounds like the nineteen-thousand-acre Río Hato airbase. Patriotic Panamanians began to see these sites as "little Canal Zones" sprouting up all over the countryside with U.S. flags, military checkpoints, and adjacent red-light districts. On two occasions when President Ricardo Adolfo de la Guardia happened upon these defense sites in his limousine, U.S. Army sentries halted him at gunpoint. According to one widely told story, de la Guardia tried to explain to the guard that he was the president of Panama, but the corporal replied that he "didn't care if he was the 'King of Spickland,' if he didn't know the password he couldn't drive onto the base."[22]

At the height of World War II, with these 134 "little zones," the original 558-square-mile Canal Zone, scores of brothel "red zones," plus the two large United Fruit "banana zones" in western Panama, the original Zone borderland appeared on the verge of overwhelming Panama. On any given day from 1942 to 1945, approximately 150,000 U.S. service personnel (permanently stationed or on maritime leave), U.S. citizens, and foreign laborers lived on the isthmus—a quarter of Panama's population of 622,000. Panama seemed destined to become "Zonia," the name for the forty-ninth state proposed by one jingoistic American who favored the republic's incorporation into the Union.[23]

Although the World War II era threatened Panamanian nationalism, it also prompted an economic boom. The flow of dollars from the U.S. garrison, troops in transit, and construction, plus the burgeoning black market in smuggled goods, all fueled the greatest economic good times in Panama's history. Ironically this bonanza also expanded the borderland's fiercest future enemy, the small but important Panamanian middle class.[24] The war opened up significant economic possibilities for thousands of Panamanians, rich and poor. During 1941–45 bar owners and *artistas* (prostitutes and entertainers) reaped large profits. The owner of the Happyland nightclub, Lucho Donadio, reportedly wept upon hearing of Hiroshima and the sudden end to the war. Due to Panama's humidity, Donadio dried out his money on sunny days from a clothesline on his third-story porch above the club. Optimistic even after the late 1940s downturn, he assured friends, "Just wait until the Americans start the Third World War, then we'll really have it made!" But the Third World War never came, and in 1959 the Happyland went bankrupt.[25]

The immediate postwar recession hit Panama hard, as did nationalist disillusionment over hopes that Washington might relinquish the Zone. Panamanians cheered the U.S. grant of independence to the Philippines in 1946 and the end of the British Empire in India in 1947. But the Pentagon dashed local aspirations when it failed to live up to the May 1942 U.S.-Panamanian base treaty. That accord stipulated that all U.S. bases outside the Zone must revert to Panama "one year after the cessation of hostilities."[26] Instead the Pentagon withdrew from 98 of the original 134 bases yet retained the other 36. Simultaneously Washington negotiated a treaty extension that sought ninety-nine-year leases on Río Hato as well as twelve other sites outside the Zone. On December 12, 1947, patriotic frustration exploded when opponents of the agreement learned that the Panamanian Assembly might ratify it despite Foreign Minister Ricardo J. Alfaro's objections. Four days of anti-government and anti-U.S. riots rocked Panama City and Colón. Under such pressure, legislators repudiated the treaty. By the end of January 1948, the U.S. military had closed its last base outside the Zone, with the exception of a Punta Paitilla radar station. The wartime crisis of the "little zones" ended with a nationalist victory and a retreat of the Zone's military frontiers back to the borders of the enclave.[27]

In 1948 Panama also completed construction of its own airport and ended another humiliating dependency on the borderland. Prior to the 1949 debut of international service at Tocumen Airport, Panama relied upon the Zone's Albrook Air Force Base as its sole international hub. First-time visitors to Panama experienced confusion when they landed at an airport that flew only U.S. flags. "Is this Panama?" a British couple asked their taxi driver Porfirio Sánchez in 1947. "Not yet," he quipped, explaining that they would cross the Zone border in a few minutes.[28]

In 1951, under economic pressure, the U.S. Canal administration reorganized into the Panama Canal Company, which ran transit operations, and the Canal Zone government, which managed civil affairs. For the first time canal tolls alone would finance the enclave's operation without subsidies from Congress. Effective July 1, 1951, this reorganization had far-reaching implications. Fiscal restraints forced a trimming of both the U.S. and Panamanian workforce. U.S.-rate civilian employees, the so-called Zonians, fell from a World War II high of 8,550 to 3,327 in 1979, the last year of the Canal Zone.[29] In March 1953, close on the heels of this reorganization, President José Antonio Remón demanded a new treaty from Washington. A former National Guard commander and kingmaker in Panamanian politics, Remón had long collaborated with the *yanquis*. But even as loyal an ally as he proved susceptible to patriotic pressure for reform in U.S.-Panamanian relations.[30]

The 1955 Eisenhower-Remón Treaty contained key changes for the boundaries of the enclave. For the first time, under nationalist pressure, the U.S.-run Zone ceded small sections of its territory back to Panama: the town of New Cristobal astride Colón, the Hotel Washington, the Colón Hospital, the Panama Railroad station in the capital, and the U.S. Army base in Punta Paitilla. The Zone also relinquished sanitary controls in the terminal cities. U.S. negotiators agreed to build a new $20 million suspension bridge over the canal on the Pacific side to facilitate the flow of Panamanian traffic across the borderland, replacing the old Thatcher Ferry. The Zone further pledged to close down its cattle farm, slaughterhouse, dairy, and ice-cream factory and promised to buy Panamanian products as replacements provided that they met "U.S. health standards."[31]

Despite these concessions in the treaty, the Zone's Caribbean Command scored a comeback of sorts in reacquiring Río Hato, whose disposition in December 1947 had sparked such widespread anti-yanqui violence. But Panama won other victories in the 1955 treaty as Panamanian frontiers of economic and cultural influence reached inside the Zone. For the first time Panama gained the right to tax the income of its West Indian citizens who worked and lived in the enclave. Panamanians and West Indians who labored for the Zone but lived outside it lost their commissary privileges. In 1956, in accordance with the treaty, segregated Zone colored schools began teaching West Indians a Panamanian curriculum in Spanish for the first time. No longer did West Indian Panamanians begin each school day with the Pledge of Allegiance and the singing of "The Star Spangled Banner." Instead they sang the Panamanian national anthem, an unnerving portent for white Zonians who drove by the schools in their cars.[32]

On July 28, 1956, President Gamal Abdel Nasser of Egypt nationalized the Suez Canal, ringing in a new era in Zone-Panamanian relations. Though conducted eight thousand miles away, Nasser's act enthralled Panamanian nationalists. In May 1958 Panamanian students organized Operation Sovereignty. Led by activists such as Alquino Boyd and Ernesto Castillero, young Panamanians charged across the Zone's fairly open boundaries and planted fifty small Panamanian flags in the enclave. Operation Sovereignty represented, on one level, a serious protest against U.S. empire and, on another, a giant high school prank. Zone officials were especially irked at their impotence in preventing Panamanians from simply walking in en masse and, at least symbolically, taking over.[33]

On November 3, 1959, following a Panamanian Independence Day celebration, Panamanians crossed the boundaries again in another symbolic attempt to take back the borderland. Canal Zone policemen permitted a prearranged group of protesters carrying a Panamanian flag and led by ex–Foreign Minister Aquilino Boyd to enter the Zone. On the banks of the canal at Miraflores, Boyd made a brief speech predicting that one day his nation's flag would fly over the entire Zone. Waving another flag, fifty university students tried to join the demonstration near the Tivoli Hotel, but the U.S. police blocked their entrance. Burgeoning numbers of protesters began hurling rocks and bottles at the U.S. police and firemen.[34] Fire hoses, police dogs, tear gas, and clubs drove the demonstrators back to the Panamanian side of the border. Other groups of Panamanians retaliated by attacking the nearby U.S. embassy and tearing its flag. The riots soon spread to Colón, where protesters demolished several U.S. facilities. Finally the Panamanian National Guard intervened to quell the riots. U.S. troops also deployed and set up barbed-wire barricades to lend a tangible definition to the boundary.[35]

In the wake of the 1959 uprisings that had caused some ninety U.S. injuries, Zone authorities made a momentous decision: to construct an eight-foot-high, barbed-wire-topped fence along the Zone border in the more congested areas of Panama City. This decision marked a turning point in Zonian-Panamanian relations. The fence said to Panamanians, "This territory is ours. Stay out—and on your side of the line!" In 1939 the U.S. military had erected a fence around the Quarry Heights Military Reservation near the border. Earlier fence sections rose beside U.S. facilities in Ancon to deter thieves. But in December 1959 officials added several more sections, enclosing nearly the entire Fourth of July border with a chain-link barrier a mile and a half long.[36]

Such a move could not have occurred at a worse moment: a reenergized nationalist movement gathered steam in Panama, inspired in part by the Cuban Revolution's victory over U.S. neocolonialism. The fence provided precisely the hated symbol that Panamanian patriots, radicals, and *fidelistas* required. After August 1961 they renamed it "the Berlin Wall," voicing their contempt toward U.S. hypocrisy on the "right to free travel" for Eastern Europeans. The fence also galled the Panamanian poor who lived alongside it in the borderland barrios of Chorrillo, Calidonia, and San Miguel since it made access more difficult to the Zone that they depended on for their livelihoods.[37]

Supreme Crisis in the Borderland

January 9–12, 1964, when Zonian students raised a lone U.S. flag at Balboa High School in violation of the 1963 Kennedy-Chiari flag accord, they provoked a social uprising that ignited the most serious confrontation of the borderland. The Panamanian poor in the capital and Colón erupted in an orgy of anti-American and anti-oligarchic violence that ended with twenty-five deaths and hundreds of seriously wounded. Panamanian protesters attempted to tear down sections of "the Berlin Wall" during the uprising, as if to erase forever the internal frontier that divided their nation. In their postmortems on the riots, U.S. officials praised the utility of the Zone's infamous fence without acknowledging that it was as much a cause of the riots as the flag imbroglio that received the most publicity.[38]

Twenty-one Panamanian deaths in the 1964 uprising transformed the border section of the Canal Zone in the capital from Fourth of July Avenue to the Avenida de los Martires. European and U.S empire builders had long derived enormous mythic power from their ability to name the conquered geography of their colonies in Africa, Asia, and Latin America. When the border of the Zone was renamed to honor sacred Panamanian blood spilled by Yankee murderers instead of Uncle Sam's birthday, the enclave suffered a psychological blow from which it never recovered.[39]

Following these deadly January clashes that also cost the lives of four GIs, U.S. officials closed the border to U.S. military and civilians for several weeks, declaring Panama off-limits. This embargo provoked an economic emergency for local businesses in the borderland that depended on U.S. cash flow for survival. In addition to restaurants, bars, nightclubs, cinemas, bodegas, taxis, shops, and nightclubs, Panamanian brothels, drug dealers, shoe-shiners, street vendors, and news boys all suffered grave losses from the shutdown. Constituent complaints pressured the Chiari administration to resume diplomacy and reopen la frontera for "normal business."[40]

In his work on the U.S.-Mexican border, Oscar J. Martínez adopted the concept of "borderland milieus" that can be applied to this phase of Zone-Panama relations. According to Martínez, the most desirable borderland model is that of "integrated borderlands," in which no barriers exist to the free flow of goods and people and their states enjoy relationships of equity, trust, and respect. This utopia never existed between Panama and the Canal Zone. Martínez's second model of "interdependent borderlands" better describes the Zone and Panama. Within this milieu a cross-national economic, social, and cultural system operates, though the two polities maintain key separations of function at their adjacent boundaries. Martínez's third model is the "coexistent borderlands," when neighboring states reduce tensions to manageable levels, but only very limited interactions transpire. Such a paradigm describes the Zone borderland following the crisis of early 1964.[41]

Sexual Crisis in the Borderland

The Zone lockdown, which included the U.S. Southern Command, quickly disrupted the borderland's sexual equilibrium. U.S. military officials decided to resolve the crisis by busing Panamanian women, among them prostitutes, into the Zone until normal border interaction could be restored. But enterprising U.S. soldiers and local prostitutes made their own arrangements to subvert the lockdown by having nightly sex at the boundary fence. Panamanian nationalists also sabotaged Southern Command's "busing solution." On the Colón side of the canal in late January 1964, Panamanian protesters stopped one bus that they judged to be carrying prostitutes, dragged out their occupants, and shaved their heads before jeering onlookers. These punishments served as both public theater and political education similar to that conducted against sexual collaborators in France in 1944.[42]

Relations in the borderland did not return to normal until March 1964. Panamanian maids and laborers, however, continued to enter the enclave days after the riots, despite the prohibitions on travel for U.S. citizens. "We only lost our maids for one day," one Zonian told a U.S. reporter. In April 1964 President Lyndon Johnson and President Roberto Chiari restored diplomatic relations. In September 1965 Washington agreed to negotiate a new treaty with Panama that would gradually terminate the Zone and give Panama a larger voice and profit share in canal operations. In the summer of 1967 diplomats from both sides presented the negotiated treaties to their respective legislatures. But neither government could garner sufficient support for the accords and subsequently shelved them. These failed treaties eventually served as a blueprint for the successful Carter-Torrijos treaties of 1977.[43]

The Borderland and Panama's New Military Regime

In October 1968 the Zone-Panama borderland suffered another crisis when the Panamanian National Guard overthrew the eleven-day-old government of President Arnulfo Arias. Guard fears over the dismissal of key officers by Arias sparked the takeover that led to twenty-one years of military rule. U.S. Southern Command, headquartered in the Zone, played an indirect role in the coup, as it had trained, equipped, and helped raise the status of the National Guard as part of its cold war containment strategy. Arias, a longtime agitator against the Zone, fled across its border seeking political asylum. In the next few weeks scores of Panamanians followed his example, until more than two hundred refugees lived in the enclave. This snafu created the surreal condition of a Panamanian colony living within the U.S. colony that lived within Panama. The Canal Zone had long served as a refuge for Panamanian political exiles seeking immunity from arrest. This phenomenon reached another peak toward the end of General Manuel Noriega's reign, when from 1987 until the U.S. invasion scores of local political refugees sought asylum on U.S. military bases, including presidents Eric Arturo Delvalle and Guillermo Endara. After the invasion these same bases held thousands of Panamanian Defense Force prisoners.[44]

U.S. officials normally gave political refugees quarters in the Tivoli Guest House and in Zone jails. But from 1968 to 1969 so many opponents of the junta arrived that authorities had to place refugees with volunteer Zonian families. This policy created tense scenes when Panamanian nationalists and Zonians, neither of whom liked one another, cohabitated in close quarters. Colonel Omar Torrijos played a secondary role in the 1968 coup initiated by Colonel Boris Martínez, but after surviving a countercoup by rival officers in December 1969, Torrijos emerged as the nation's strongman. Torrijos sought popular support by addressing the economic polarization of Panamanian society. He demonized the Panamanian oligarchy and the U.S. Canal Zone as "the twin heads of the serpent." When in 1970 Southern Command's fifteen-year lease of its Río Hato base expired, Torrijos reaped political capital at the reversion ceremony. Following an elaborate flag-exchange ritual, he claimed that never again would Americans occupy sacred Panamanian soil. With the transfer of Río Hato, Southern Command's last military frontier receded to the Zone's actual boundaries.[45]

In 1971 Torrijos began a program of protest at the Canal Zone borders and in Latin American forums, and in 1973 at the United Nations, elevating the Panamanian conflict with the Zone to the global anti-imperialist struggle. Although a sincere nationalist, Torrijos also used his very public hostility toward the Zone to deflect attention from his "revolutionary" government's failure to abolish oligarchic power or hold free elections, as it had long promised. In August 1972, as part of a goodwill counteroffensive against Torrijos, David Parker, the Canal Zone's governor, offered to remove the fence along the Zone border that Panamanian nationalists had long decried. Parker admitted, "Panamanians view it as a Berlin Wall and a barrier to mutual trust."[46]

But Torrijos surprised Zone officials when he opposed dismantling the fence. He expressed concerns over an ongoing strike and student demonstrations that might prove difficult to control without the barrier. Zone officials were mystified. But Torrijos appreciated the symbolic import of the border fence far better than his U.S. counterparts. To remove that marker of "Yankee imperialism" just when the general pressed his global campaign against the Zone might weaken his crusade. Indeed parts of the fence remain today as reminders of the knife that once cut through Panama's heart.[47]

In the mid-1970s Torrijos and the Gerald Ford administration moved closer to an accord that would extricate the United States from the isthmus. Diplomacy proceeded at a snail's pace, prolonged by Zonian recalcitrance, U.S. congressional obstructionism, and a presidential campaign in which one candidate, Ronald Reagan, claimed that the Canal Zone was as much a part of the United States as Louisiana or Alaska. Torrijos and an army of Panamanian demonstrators kept up the pressure at the Zone borders, gradually wearing down the U.S. will to retain an imperial borderland that had long since lost its strategic value. Threats of guerrilla war, canal sabotage, and another explosion like the one in January 1964 gradually took their toll on U.S. resolve.[48]

In 1977 the new Jimmy Carter administration decided that improved relations with Latin America held more importance than maintaining the privileges of a few thousand U.S. workers in an area no longer paramount to Washington's interests. A crucial part of the thorny negotiations settled on borders: Just how much real estate did the United States require for canal defense and operations until December 31, 1999, the agreed-upon, final U.S. departure date? Ironically negotiations over this new "transitional zone" came back full circle to the January 1903 Hay-Herrán Treaty, worked out before the Panamanian Revolution. Like that earlier U.S.-Colombian zone, the new Panama Canal Area would be much smaller, retain no U.S. sovereignty, and have a limited life span.

Indeed two years after President Carter and General Torrijos signed their famous treaties on October 1, 1979, the original Zone officially ended, surrendering 58 percent of its territory to the republic. But another kind of zone, more strictly military than its predecessor, lived on until December 31, 1999. Gradually, in stages, during the 1980s–1990s the remaining 42 percent of the land passed to Panama as the last of the U.S. bases closed, one after another. At all points in these recessions of the Zone's frontiers Panamanian nationalists and individuals influenced the U.S. retreat from the isthmus.[49]

The Demographic Pull of the Borderland

The first major demographic impact of the Zone on the republic was urbanization after 1940: the movement of tens of thousands of rural Panamanians into the borderland cities of Panama City and Colón. While employment opportunities were not the only cause for this population shift, the chance to work in and around the Zone proved a powerful magnet for new migrants, especially during the World War II boom and postwar period. The U.S. construction in 1962 of the Maurice Thatcher Memorial Bridge (later renamed

1.1. Official Zonian publications favored apolitical images of happy, "innocent," country-folk Panamanians rather than the more politicized urban dwellers who increasingly opposed the U.S. presence. Courtesy of *Panama Canal Review* in the Panama Canal Museum Collection, George Smathers Library, University of Florida, http://ufdc .ufl.edu/pcm.

the Bridge of the Americas) across the Pacific end of the waterway facilitated the flow of motorized transport from the interior to the capital. Panama changed from a country in which two-thirds of the populace lived in the countryside in 1940 to a nation where two-thirds lived in cities by 1980.[50]

Most of these migrants settled in the capital, whose population rose from 118,000 in 1940 to 784,000 by 1980, a third of the nation's inhabitants. Here *campesinos* entered into the economic purview of the Zone. Only the most privileged among them worked for the Panama Canal Company, the Canal Zone government, or the U.S. Armed Forces. But thousands of others labored in the underground or indirect economy connected to the borderland: washing the cars of U.S. citizens; polishing the boots of soldiers; hawking street food and drinks; selling sex, drugs, and newspapers; smuggling contraband; and performing myriad other extralegal activities. Stealing from the Zone and its inhabitants also proved a growth industry in these years, and crime rates rose in Colón and in the borderland barrios of Chorrillo and Calidonia.[51]

The Zone's presence also helped shape and distort the urban sprawl at either end of the transisthmian corridor. Without the establishment of the Canal Zone, which blocked the more natural suburbanization south of Colón and north of Panama City, urban expansion would have spread out like a concentric fan from these coastal ports. Instead the boundaries of the Zone forced development to the east and west of Panama City and Colón, creating an elongated metropolis in the capital that still plagues its residents to this day. The results fostered a lightly populated Canal Zone with very dense Panamanian populations at either end of the enclave, a peculiarly warped urban development pattern.[52]

Gendered and Cultural Frontiers

The expanding frontiers of the Canal Zone in the 1940s and 1950s also included gendered frontiers. Panamanian women from all over the country migrated to the capital and Colón to work as domestics in the Zone and as waitresses and barmaids in the restaurants and nightclubs of the terminal cities. Some Panamanian women and Latinas also toiled in the sex industry, fed by the Zone's military bases. They labored as artistas, bar girls, and freelance streetwalkers in Bottle Alley in Colón and the Río Abajo and Chorrillo sections of the capital.[53]

Young Panamanian women from the towns west of Panama City, such as Arraiján and Chorrera, and even as far as Veraguas and Los Santos donned their best dresses and makeup and traveled by bus each weekend to the Zone. There they attended USO and NCO club dances in hopes of meeting a husband or boyfriend among the GIs. Although this activity predated World War II, it increased during the war and postwar periods, right up to the December 1999 final base closures. Commonly referred to as "gate girls" because they lined up in front of the entrances to U.S. bases, these young women were a fixture of the Zone's and nearby Panama's social life. As late as the 1990s U.S. soldiers married these women at the rate of fifty per month, though such unions typically surged when troop levels were at their highest, such as during World War II and following the 1989 U.S. invasion.[54]

One of the ironies in this migration of Panamanian gate girls to the Zone every weekend in the postwar era was that it took place simultaneously with a weekend migration of some U.S. citizens from the Zone into the Panamanian interior. In the 1950s–1970s increasing numbers of Zonians began buying country homes in the interior. As they acquired greater wealth, these second- and third-generation Zonians, the U.S. descendants of the original "ditch diggers," decided to purchase property in the republic since the 1903 treaty forbade private land ownership in the enclave. For these Zonians, born and bred in the borderland, Panama, not the United States, had become home.[55]

During the 1970s even some recent U.S. hires purchased homes in the interior, as they sought to escape the conformity and boredom of the Zone or simply because they "fell in love with Panama," its lush tropics, beaches, and cool hill country, its laid-back lifestyle. Zonians bought these weekend or retirement homes all over the republic, from Santa Clara, Coronado, Chitre, and El Valle to Volcán and Boquete in the western province of Chiriquí. Zonians hired Panamanian servants and caretakers for their estates and frequented nearby Panamanian restaurants and shops, extending the economic reach of the borderland deep into the interior.[56]

Many newspaper articles in the postwar era criticized the racist, chauvinist Zonian who derided Panama and never left the enclave. He certainly existed in large numbers. But few examined the small but significant group of Zonians who preferred to spend their weekends and leisure time in Panama rather than in the Zone or the United States. A minority of Zonians in fact chose to retire in Panama beginning in the early 1950s, when new regulations forbade U.S. retirees from living in the enclave.[57]

This curious cross-migration of Zonians wanting to be "weekend Panamanians" and Panamanian women wanting to spend their weekends in the Zone speaks to the complexities of the social and cultural forces that swirled about the borderland. The ultimate goal or fantasy of many Panamanian women who flocked to the bases was to become a U.S. citizen, whether or not they were aware of the consequences. The dream of Zonian weekend warriors in Panama was to retire and live out their golden years, not in the United States but in the republic. This process of transculturation, though limited to a minority of Zonians, follows a familiar imperial paradigm of colonists becoming "more like the natives" and natives "more like the colonists." But most Zonians, even those who retired in Panama, still cherished their U.S. identity, despite their fondness for the *tranquilidad* of the rural isthmus.[58]

The cultural and economic frontiers of the borderland stretched as far to the east as the San Blas islands off the Caribbean coast of Panama's easternmost province, Darién. Besides the more significant *mestizo* migration from the western interior into the transit cities, the Zone also attracted Kuna Amerindians. These Kuna (or San Blas, as North Americans called them) developed a special relationship with the U.S. military. As far back as the construction days, North Americans viewed these Amerindians as unspoiled, natural creatures, in contrast to the "corrupted," mixed-race Panamanians. The Kuna developed a fascination for North Americans as well. These indigenous sold their artifacts, baskets, and mola textiles in the Zone. Their young men labored in the military barracks as janitors, shoe-shiners, and mess workers. Their hostility toward the Panamanian state made them ideal workers on U.S. bases that emphasized security and the dangers of espionage. Unlike nationalist Latin Panamanians, the Kuna viewed the Zone as a protective wall that blocked Panamanian expansion into their homeland. Long resistant to the Panamanian national project and rebel separatists in the 1920s, the Kuna were the only ethnic group in Panama to vote against the 1977 Carter-Torrijos treaties. The U.S. cultivation of this special relationship with the Kuna exemplified the divide-and-conquer strategy that many imperial borderlanders have utilized throughout history to maintain power.[59]

The Internal Boundaries of the Canal Zone

The boundaries of the Canal Zone also signified internal demarcations of geography, social groups, and behavior. The most important internal boundaries of the Zone were those of race and nationality. The Canal Zone was a segregated society from the first years of its operations until its last day, September 30, 1979. In the early twentieth century the Zone imported over forty thousand black West Indian laborers and tens of thousands of their dependents to build the canal. Throughout the U.S. excavation, the Isthmian Canal Commission paid white, U.S. skilled and managerial workers in gold and West Indian and other foreign laborers lower wages in silver. The United States built segregated housing in separate "gold" and "silver" towns" throughout the Zone, with gold and silver schools, commissaries, clubhouses, gymnasiums, lavatories, even drinking fountains.[60]

After 1948, in response to the Truman administration's civil rights reforms, the Canal government referred to these separate communities as "U.S.-rate" and "local-rate" towns, although the popular parlance of "gold towns" and "silver towns" persisted through the 1970s. Following the 1955 Eisenhower-Remón Treaty, in a further effort to disguise their segregated nature, local-rate towns received another euphemism, "Latin American communities," even though the majority of their inhabitants were English-speaking West Indians who, after the 1955 accords, became "Antillean Panamanians" as the Panamanian government moved to assimilate them.[61]

The gold towns of Ancon, Balboa, and Diablo on the Pacific side of the Canal Zone and Cristobal, Gatun, and Margarita on the Atlantic side evolved into sites of safety and comfort for white U.S. citizens. In their psychological geography such communities constituted Wilderesque "our towns" rather than the silver towns of La Boca, Paraiso, Rainbow City, Silver City, and Red Tank that in their eyes denoted blackness, inferiority, and the threat of crime. Gamboa, home of the Canal's Dredging Division, was located toward the center of the enclave, between the transit cities. Blacks and whites lived in close proximity there, unlike in other Zone villages. West Indians resided in the "Dust Bowl" adjacent to the U.S.-rate community. Zone authorities built a wall down the center of the Gamboa commissary, where both black and white employees purchased foodstuffs and clothing, whites on one side and blacks on the other, with separate entrances and exits. Rod Carew, the perennial American League batting champion in the 1970s, remembered with bitterness his experiences growing up in segregated Gamboa.[62]

West Indians learned through experience the hard nature of the Zone's internal boundaries. When in the 1940s–1950s black youths from Gamboa's Dust Bowl wandered into the white section to use its playground facilities, white youths sometimes stoned them and drove them back with racial epithets. West Indians also learned to stay out of the gold towns after sundown. Canal Zone Police routinely picked up any black caught roaming about a gold town in the evening for vagrancy or suspicion of burglary. "You better have a dam good reason for bein' in a town like Balboa at night," one West Indian recalled. "You better be workin' for a whyte family or have an appointment with a whyte mon or you goin' ta jail."[63]

These internal racial boundaries changed over the years, as the Zone government moved black West Indians about "like reservation Indians," as one silver worker remembered. In 1953 Zone officials closed down Red Tank for demographic reasons, as the black population declined in the 1950s due to hiring cutbacks and U.S. policies of moving West Indians into Panama. In 1956 the Zone government moved West Indians from the silver town of La Boca, supposedly for safety reasons, due to its location near fuel storage tanks at the southern entrance to the Canal. But shortly after the West Indians' relocation, officials tore down the old wood-and-screen housing and built concrete homes in La Boca for white Zonians. U.S. authorities never removed the "dangerous" fuel tanks. West Indians still claim that they were pushed out of La Boca because its location caused an undesirable transit of blacks through the white town of Balboa. Others assert that the Zone government acceded to cruise ship officials who disliked the sight of a dilapi-

1.2. The Canal Zone Police chief of Gamboa oversees the distribution of Christmas toys by a white Santa to West Indian children. Note that some children appear delighted, but that their parents, who lived in the substandard segregated housing of Gamboa's "Dust Bowl" under the rule of the feared Zone police, seem less pleased. Courtesy of *Panama Canal Review* in the Panama Canal Museum Collection, George Smathers Library, University of Florida, http://ufdc.ufl.edu/pcm.

dated black town at the Canal's entrance, with "niggers fishing and hanging out their underwear."[64]

Ethnic Boundaries in the Borderland

The local-rate town of La Boca also spoke to the boundaries of nationality within the Zone. Thousands of laborers from dozens of nations, besides the West Indies, came to work on the Panama Canal: Spaniards, Greeks, Italians, Indians, Chinese, Colombians, Salvadorans, and Hondurans. The majority of these non-U.S. citizens were placed on the "silver roll" along with the West Indians and housed in "silver" quarters. U.S. officials strove to separate these nationalities in housing to avoid conflicts. But fights and occasional riots broke out among the rivals. With the cancellation of the last great U.S.

construction effort, the Third Locks project in 1942, the Zone ceased recruiting non-U.S. workers from overseas. Many non-Caribbean "silver rollers" either moved to Panama after their contracts expired or gradually worked their way onto the "gold roll" by attaining U.S. citizenship through intermarriage or U.S. military service.[65]

Still, the complexities of the Zone's ethnic boundaries intensified in at least one aspect following World War II. In 1949 the Pentagon established the U.S. Army Caribbean School (renamed the School of the Americas in 1963) at Fort Gulick near the Atlantic side of the Zone. This institution trained Latin American militaries for hemispheric defense against communist subversion and leftist insurgencies. Soldiers from more than twenty Latin American nations trained there. In the 1950s, during border clashes between their countries, Ecuadorian and Peruvian students in the school's dormitories fought savage fistfights. Argentine cadets wrestled with and broke chairs over the heads of Chilean officers. While on weekend furloughs, virtually all Latin national groups battled Panamanian National Guardsmen in the bars and bordellos of Colón. Following a fierce donnybrook in the MacArthur Bar between Brazilian and Argentine cadets, one U.S. officer complained that the Latin American students should have stayed on base over the weekend "to finish their homework instead of starting international incidents."[66]

In addition to these temporary Latin American "students" in the Zone, Chinese immigrants to Panama also worked in the enclave and on surrounding bases. They had permission from the Zone government since 1906 to grow vegetables and fruits in some fourteen truck gardens that provided the enclave's population with fresh produce, sparing Zonians the need to enter Panama for such foods. Like many minority groups in Panama, the Chinese had a more sympathetic view of the Zone and its American inhabitants than the majority population. Often victims of discrimination from Latin Panamanians and isolated from the networks of Panamanian nepotism, the Chinese, like the Kuna, saw the Zone as a refuge and Americans as protectors. During construction hundreds of Chinese worked in the Zone, and scores of them did so for generations afterward. During World War II, when they faced legal discrimination in the republic, Chinese found work on U.S. bases both in and beside the Zone, baking bread, cooking food, and washing laundry for GIs and Zonians. Their memories of Americans, as Lok C. D. Sui has shown, proved more positive than those held by Panamanians from the same era. Diasporic Chinese worked in numerous colonial and borderland settings where their transnational identities and political neutrality served them well in niche occupations. They developed a near monopoly over the bodega and laundry trade in the republic and along the Zone-Panama frontier, where they formed a key minority group among isthmian borderlanders.[67]

Military-Civilian Boundaries

After race and nationality, the most significant internal boundary of the Canal Zone was the sharp division between the military and civilian communities. The boundaries that set the U.S. military apart from the Zone and Panama were not just social and cultural but physical and geographic. Throughout the Zone's history the U.S. military deployed forces on some twenty-seven military bases that were demarcated by barbed-wire fences and guarded gates. Most entrants to the bases had to show a military pass or worker ID to enter. Even for U.S. civilians with passes, many sites were restricted to service personnel only. These military bases and training areas encompassed 68 percent of the land in the Canal Zone; only 3.6 percent of the land was reserved for Zonian and local-rate town sites.[68]

The American military had its own separate facilities and society on the Zone: schools, housing, post exchanges (PXs), golf courses, gymnasiums and swimming pools, officer and NCO clubs, dances, and cocktail parties. They maintained a certain distance from the civilian Zonians that became mutual. A rivalry prevailed between the two groups as to who was most important: the military as armed guardians of the borderland or the Zonians as the technicians of the Canal. The largely middle-class Zonians did not mind their daughters dating military officers, but they frowned upon relationships with lower-class enlisted men. These social divisions and class distinctions ebbed and flowed over time. Enlisted men knew how Zonians felt about them and labeled them "draft dodgers" for their military exemption status and "crybabies" for their constant complaints against any threat to their "precious company privileges." The U.S. military maintained better social relations with the Panamanian borderland community than did most Zonians, which also set them apart and even marked them as suspicious among some in the dominant social group.[69]

Even the civilian U.S. community had jurisdictional boundaries: the Cristobal District on the Atlantic side and the more populous Balboa District on the Pacific side. In any given year from 1940 to 1979 roughly three-quarters of the Zone's civilian community lived on the Pacific side, while only a quarter lived along the Atlantic. Atlantic-siders developed something of an inferiority complex, referred to as the "Atlantic Side Syndrome," over the size and influence of their community and its distance from the seat of administrative power in Balboa. Still, they prided themselves on coming from "the good side of the canal," where people worked and socialized "more like a family" and everyone was friendly, laid-back, and got along better with the nearby Panamanian, Chinese, Arab, and Jewish communities of Colón. Supposedly free of the backstabbing politics of the pretentious Pacific side, inhabitants of Cristobal and Margarita ridiculed their rival district for its "Snob Hill" or "Big Shot Hill," references to Ancon Hill and Balboa Heights, site of the governor's mansion and top administrative offices. "The cops were such jerks on the Pacific side that they would even arrest *one another* for drunk driving," an Atlantic-sider recalled, describing a breach of etiquette unheard of on the Caribbean coast.[70]

Pacific-siders, by contrast, considered the Atlantic side the "boondocks" or the "sticks," a site of sand fleas, too much rain, and dangerous, largely black Colón. "If you constantly screwed up or couldn't write out a ticket correctly," a former Canal Zone Police officer remembered, "they sent you to the Atlantic side. I mean, we all started out there as rookies, but if you couldn't get to the Pacific after a few years, you had to be a real dope. But then again a few guys liked it over there. Less pressure, I guess." A fierce sports rivalry added to this division. The annual football games between the Balboa High School Bulldogs and the Cristobal High Tigers (known as the Palm Bowl) were the Super Bowls of the Canal Zone.[71]

Company transfers from one side of the Zone to the other created traumatic experiences. "I hated it when they made us move to the Pacific side," remembered schoolteacher Sue Stabler. So parochial was the world of the Canal Zone that the two favorite Zonian newspapers, the *Star and Herald* and the *Panama American*, frequently announced visits by families or individuals from the Atlantic to the Pacific side (or vice versa) in their society pages, as if they had journeyed from London to New York. In fact the distance from Cristobal to Balboa was forty-five miles.[72]

U.S. Employee Boundaries

Another internal boundary between U.S. civilians "on the Zone" underscored the distinction between those who worked for the Panama Canal Company or the Canal Zone government (the Zonians) and those civilians who worked for the U.S. Department of Defense (DOD) on military bases. "If you didn't work for Pan Canal down here, you weren't worth shit," a former defense worker remarked. DOD workers were not considered Zonians, white U.S. descendants of the original excavators. Defense workers lived in DOD housing in communities like Curundu, Corozal, and Coco Solito, generally viewed as inferior to Zonian town sites. Many of these defense workers expressed a profound animosity toward the Zonians. "They thought they were the kings of the mountain down here. They really looked down on us."[73]

Other lower-status employee groups who lived in the gold or U.S.-rate towns were U.S. citizens of Latin American descent and gold workers of foreign birth, most from Latin America but several from Europe and Asia as well. The Zone, like neighboring Panama with its long history as a cosmopolitan transit hub, contained a greater diversity than its popular image suggested. Scores of U.S. civilian workers were married to Colombian, Venezuelan, Chilean, Mexican, Dominican, and of course Panamanian women. According to the 1970 Canal Zone census, of the 10,573 people who lived in the U.S.-rate towns, some 26 percent were foreign-born (most of whom had acquired U.S. citizenship). Of the 2,765 foreign-born U.S.-rate workers, two-thirds were Panamanian, but fully a third came from a variety of other countries. Few of these Americans compromised by foreign birth or foreign marriage held the same status as the Zonians or even U.S.-born canal workers recruited from the States.[74]

Gendered Enclaves within the Borderland

Gendered boundaries also divided identity and social activity along the borderland. U.S. men who worked for the canal hunted, golfed, drank, and fished together at the various Zone clubs, several of which had male-only memberships. Zonian males fired their pistols and rifles at Gatun Gun Club. They gambled at poker, billiards, gin, and shuffle ball at the Elks Club and American Legion and in the casinos and racetracks of Panama. A considerable number of the Zone's male inhabitants, be they soldiers or civilians, drank and whored in Panama on a regular basis.[75]

With some important exceptions, Zonian women in the postwar era adhered to what Elaine Tyler May has called a cult of cold war domesticity. North American women tended to their husbands and children in their homes and socialized at various philanthropic and educational clubs, engaging in nurturing activities. Zonian wives with blue-collar husbands enjoyed a lifestyle, complete with servants and plentiful leisure time, reserved for upper-middle-class or well-to-do women in the States. In contrast, West Indian women sacrificed attention to their own children in order to raise the white children of the Zonians. "I spent more time with dem than with my own," one recalled. "I knew some of them better than my own." Such behavior followed a pattern of gender, race, and class relations in European colonies and borderlands analyzed by Ann Laura Stoler, Ronald Hyam, and other postcolonial scholars. Nonetheless, after World War II increasing numbers of U.S. women in the Zone did work, unlike some of their counterparts in European colonies.[76]

Zonian women also challenged their domestic roles in the Canal Zone by participating in typically male activities. Part of this mixed-gender persona related to the frontier nature of the enclave, the fact that it formed an overseas military post ringed by what many regarded as a "hostile" population of color. It should be stressed, however, that apprehension over violent Panamanian threats, such as the 1959 and 1964 riots, occurred rarely. Canal Zone women never faced the kind of prolonged bloody insurgency, with all its sexual fears, that British women in Kenya or French women in Algeria endured in the postwar era. Rather cognizant of the threat that juvenile delinquency posed to its truncated society, the Zone government sponsored many sports activities for Zonian boys and girls "to keep them occupied and out of trouble (read Panama)." The fearless Canal Zone tomboy, swimming, shooting, hiking, and riding, thus became a cultural archetype of the borderland, along with the traditional cotillion coming-out princess and society grand dame. This tomboy or "tomwoman" even had an appropriate sobriquet, celebrated in Canal Zone publications: the "Ama-Zonian."[77]

Borderland on the Isthmus

The Zone-Panama corridor fit many classic characteristics of a borderland throughout its seventy-five-year existence. But its frontiers came under their greatest political and social stress following World War II. A key section of this mixed cultural borderland ran along the Zone boundary with the densely populated neighborhoods of the capital. In the early 1960s, the midpoint of this study, it curved in a mile-and-a-quarter arc from the approaches to the Bridge of the Americas to the east and then north to the Panama Railroad terminal at Ancon. Traveling along this boundary from the bridge, one viewed on the left the Quarry Heights Military Reservation—headquarters of U.S. Southern Command—Ancon proper, with its courthouse, church, school, and private residences; the Shaler Triangle and the Tivoli Guest House; and finally the Ancon Laundry and the Little Theatre, with the railroad station opposite. On the right slumped Chorrillo, a sprawling Panamanian ghetto where wooden buildings topped with rusted tin roofs dripped water onto

1.3. Rifle practice for an Ama-Zonian. Young U.S. women in the Canal Zone frequently embraced a tomboy persona, given the bounty of outdoor pursuits available to them in their tropical paradise. The ability of all U.S. citizens to wield firearms also held value in an enclave that felt increasingly besieged by hostile local nationalists in the postwar era. Courtesy of the *Panama Canal Review* in the Panama Canal Museum Collection, George Smathers Library, University of Florida, http://ufdc.ufl.edu/pcm.

trash-strewn alleys; the Instituto Nacional, hotbed of Panamanian nationalism; a strip of modern shops that served Zone clientele; the Pan American Airways Building; the Panamanian Legislative Palace; the San Miguel slum; and finally the commercial section of the Avenida Nacional. At the center of this arc stood the intersection of Fourth of July Avenue with J Street, a key crossing point for the Zone-Panama border.[78]

This specific borderland provided the most incendiary flashpoints of the postwar Zonian-Panamanian conflict. But for generations it also marked the area most open to interaction and bartering, where U.S. service personnel, Zonians, West Indians, Chinese, Kuna, and Latin Panamanians intermingled, argued, drank, fought, had sex, shopped, traded marijuana, bought

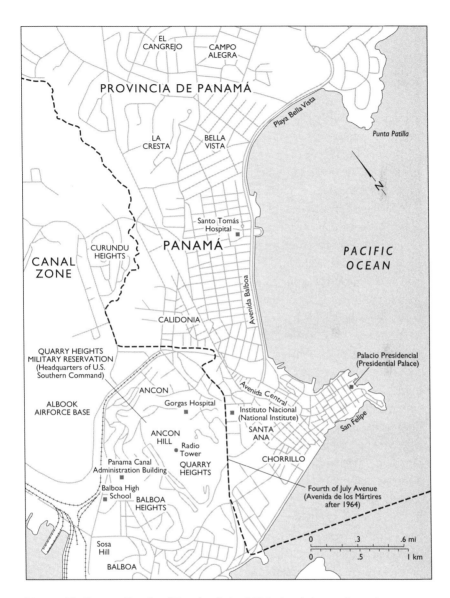

Map 1.1. The Panama City–Canal Zone borderland. This sharply interactive region where the capital city of Panamá abutted the U.S. Canal Zone constituted the main urban borderland at the Pacific end of the Canal. It was a site of much conflict and socioeconomic interchange. The various streets that intersected the Fourth of July Avenue (later the Avenue of the Martyrs) on a west–east trajectory led to the Panamanian barrios of Calidonia and Chorrillo and included J Street near the Instituto Nacional and, farther south, Balboa Road, that all fed into the commercial districts and red zones of Panama's largest city.

lottery tickets, and swapped contraband. One Panamanian pedestrian, Rodrigo Mendoza, remembered being deluged with a "shower of hams" (*lluvía de jamones*) when he walked along the American boundary line one night in 1962. A West Indian contrabander mistook him for his partner and kept hurling commissary hams over the fence, two of which struck Mendoza on the shoulder. "It really is true what they say about the Zone," he thought. "There the living is so good that hams fall from the sky!"[79]

On the Zonian side of this border there was little commerce, mostly the institutions of power and officialdom. On the Panamanian side were cantinas, Chinese bodegas and laundries, beer gardens, bordellos, and shops with Spanish names yet adorned with signs that advertised Coca-Cola, White Horse Whiskey, Bulova watches, Esso gasoline, Pall Mall cigarettes, Wurlitzer organs, Westinghouse refrigerators, Coppertone lotion, and Orange Crush. Signs proclaimed "Welcome," "Open," and "English Spoken Here." They announced their wares as linens, shirts, hamburgers, pizza, and coffee. Here pulsed the urban heart of the Zone-Panama borderland where the lingua franca of Spanglish predominated among many residents.[80]

Along with the U.S.-Mexico border, the Zone-Panama borderland marked one of the few places where a First World polity abutted a Third World country, where a Protestant work ethic and legal and moral code confronted a more open Catholic, Latin American society. The most famous military checkpoint in Panama City, located on Balboa Road before it intersects with the Fourth of July, was called "the Limits." It constituted a cultural as well as a geographic divide, for beyond it stood Panama, a country allegedly without limits, where gambling, prostitution, strip shows, and cockfighting were legal, where Caribbean music filled the air and Panamanians shouted, danced, and argued in the streets. While technically illegal, drugs were plentiful and "if one's chin reached the bar, Panamanian bartenders would serve you a drink." West of the Limits stood the Zone, with its three legal code books full of rules and regulations that forbade every infraction from playing the radio too loudly to "unauthorized sleeping."[81]

Cultural exchange existed alongside stark differences. GIs and well-to-do Panamanian youths raced their Thunderbirds and Camaros up and down the Avenida Nacional. Jazz, Motown, and rock and roll as well as *musica tipica* sounded from radios and record players in much of the borderland. In some of the West Indian blocks, trick-or-treaters sought candy on Halloween night and Christmas trees adorned windows at *navidad*. U.S. movies played at various cinemas, and natives wore American-style sneakers, jeans, and shorts.

1.4. Davey Crockett in the jungle. A Zonian boy from the mid-1950s demonstrates that borderland's larger connections to the imperial metropole and its popular culture. U.S. citizens and their children were enraptured with Disney's resurrection of Crockett as an American icon whose last stand at the Alamo signaled the heroism needed to prevail in the cold war. Courtesy of the *Panama Canal Review* in the Panama Canal Museum Collection, George Smathers Library, University of Florida, http://ufdc.ufl.edu/pcm.

The cultural power of the U.S. Zone was visible along sections of the borderland, though much less so in the Panamanian interior.

For all this, the U.S. side of the border defined itself starkly as a site of order, cleanliness, and efficiency in its physical organization and legal codes. Many of the Zone's inhabitants saw Panama, in contrast, as a place of chaos, litter, and corruption but also a site of passion, pleasure, and *fiesta*. Panama held many charms for North Americans—its food, its women, its music, its Carnaval celebrations—but most failed to take it seriously as a nation. Panama was a "pair o' dice," as one Zonian put it, not a North American heaven. While Panama was an exciting place to visit, it was best to live in the Zone. For many U.S. inhabitants, the republic still represented the jungle, with all its associations of disorder and fecundity, even into the postwar era. One of the most costly U.S. endeavors throughout the borderland encom-

1.5. The weekly DDT spraying of the Canal Zone neighborhoods had its roots in the construction period (1904–14), when thousands perished from yellow fever and malaria. Such efforts also alluded to fears of neighboring Panama "contaminating" the purity of the clean and orderly Zone. Courtesy of the *Panama Canal Review* in the Panama Canal Museum Collection, George Smathers Library, University of Florida, http://ufdc.ufl.edu/pcm.

passed holding back that jungle by constantly spraying insecticides and herbicides, hacking at underbrush, and mowing U.S. lawns. Zonian school kids let out of classes would actually run behind the weekly DDT-spraying trucks to breathe in that sweet smell of U.S. success. (This may account for higher Canal Zone cancer rates.)[82]

The Lure of the Panamanian Jungle

Holding back the psychological jungle of Panama, however, proved more difficult. When in 1906 President Theodore Roosevelt toured the Zone, he forbade the use of hammocks in the enclave. TR viewed U.S. citizens dozing in hammocks as slipping into "Latin degeneracy." But overstressed Zone officials never codified this regulation. By World War II hundreds of Zone homes boasted hammocks in their backyards, and the practice of siesta on the weekends became common. Although North Americans who came to

Panama in the early twentieth century mostly drank bourbon and scotch, by World War II rum was their favorite libation. *Ceviche, sanchocho,* and *corbina,* traditional Panamanian dishes, were also among their favorite fare.[83]

On weekends disgruntled Zonian men felt the lure of Panama as a sexual frontier and slipped across the border to sample the brothels that had grown so extensive due to the World War II troop buildup and postwar urban surge. Even U.S. high school boys headed for the red-light districts to relieve the stress of final exams or unrequited puppy love. They opted for the more authentic thrills of the Grut Azul (Blue Goose), the Villa Amor, or the Ancon Inn, whose matchboxes read, "A PARADISE FOR SOLDIERS, BACHELORS, AND MARRIED MEN, TOO!" Zonian high school girls were attracted to Panamanian boys from the better families of the isthmus whose attendance in U.S. high schools increased in the postwar era. These young men taught Zonian girls how to dance *salsa, meringue, cumbias,* and *tamboritas.* Some Zonian girls acted on their feelings for these youths. Sue Stabler, a young Zonian girl in the 1960s, recalled her romance with a Panamanian boy and with "all things Panamanian." These experiences were also a part of the Panamanian jungle that U.S. officials strove to restrain.[84]

Crossing the Borders

After World War II Panamanians who crossed borders into the Zone often expressed their own fears and anxieties. The U.S.-administered Zone completely surrounded Colón, Panama's second largest city, on the Caribbean side of the canal. Until the United States established the Colón Corridor in the early 1950s, it was impossible to enter or leave Colón without traversing the Zone. Similarly it was impossible to drive out of Panama City toward the western interior of Panama or into Panama City from the west without crossing the Canal Zone.[85]

Panamanian drivers generally slowed to a crawl upon entering the enclave, as they strove to obey the strict speed limits and confusing traffic laws. The Canal Zone Police rigorously enforced these rules, partly to maintain order but also to discourage Panamanian "intruders." "Oh, if you were Panamanian, you could drive through all right. But your car better be damned near perfect and you had better be driving just right," one former Canal Zone policeman recalled.[86] Panamanians' lack of Canal Zone plates and the dilapidated state of their cars immediately gave away their nationality, as did the darker hue of their faces. Before 1943, when all of Panama changed to the U.S. system, navigating the roads of the Canal Zone proved even more difficult for Panamanians. They had to switch from driving on the left side of the road to the right, sometimes in European cars with steering wheels on the right.[87]

For inhabitants of Panama, where police rarely enforced traffic laws and laissez-faire road chaos remained the rule, the traffic regulations of the Zone seemed perverse. One Panamanian priest recalled being pulled over and ticketed in the late 1960s for going thirty-five miles per hour in a thirty-mile-an-hour zone while driving to give the last rites to a friend. In Panama, and in many parts of the United States, this same priest would have received a police escort, not a ticket.[88]

Entering the Zone on foot caused similar apprehension for many Panamanians who did not work for the Canal and were unaccustomed to its laws and geography. Despite few checkpoints, signs, or barriers, these Panamanians' bodies tightened when they "crossed the line." They tread carefully and their expressions hardened. The Canal Zone Police, or *los hijos de putas* (sons of whores), as the Panamanian poor referred to them, issued summonses for jaywalking, spitting on the sidewalk, and littering even a single gum wrapper. Zone Police often challenged unfamiliar Panamanian interlopers and demanded identification. Panamanians frequently experienced a sense of dread at their approach. "It was funny to watch Panamanians, who were normally so easygoing, get so uptight when they walked into the Zone," a retired U.S. soldier recalled.[89]

For the U.S. inhabitants of the Zone, military or civilian, the effect of leaving the enclave and entering Panama was markedly different. No Panamanian policeman ever challenged a U.S. citizen who crossed the border. As these Americans sauntered toward the red-light district, the bars, brothels, and casinos, their bodies relaxed, their expressions grew carefree. Gone was the stifling conformity and regulations of the Zone. But the Panamanians they passed, headed in the opposite direction, felt constrained.[90]

The Blind Borderline

West Indian canal workers and working-class Panamanians sometimes referred to the Zone border as the "blind boundary line" since its lack of physical markers from 1903 to 1959 served their extralegal activities well.[91] Some Panamanians, especially those from the interior who were unfamiliar with the transit cities, literally did not know whether they were in Panama or the Canal Zone at times. The famed Panamanian attorney Woodrow De Castro once commented, "The border is so irregular not even educated persons know exactly where it runs." This was particularly true in Colón, where the ill-defined boundary ran through a warren of side streets and alleys near New Cristobal.[92]

Canal Zone Police on the Pacific side recognized the boundary as the middle of Fourth of July Avenue. In 1973 a Zone policeman, Carlos Tirado, arrested a U.S. soldier for drunk and disorderly conduct near the middle of the avenue. "You can't arrest me," the GI protested. "I'm still in Panama! Only a guardia or an MP can arrest me here!" "No, you're not; you're on this side of the middle of the street, so you're in the Canal Zone," Tirado told him. But before Tirado could apprehend him, the soldier sprinted across Fourth of July to the Panamanian side. "Arrest me now, you sonofabitch! I'm in Panama now!" That the Panamanian-born Tirado had become a U.S. citizen after military service in Vietnam added to this encounter's complexities, for one might ask, "On which side of the street did Tirado belong?"[93]

The arrest and trial of one Panamanian "trespasser" in 1968 gave special cogency to the blind boundary line. U.S. District Court Judge Guthrie Crowe castigated Alfonso Bowen, who was partially blind and claimed to have wandered into the Zone inadvertently. "Your physical condition is no excuse for not knowing where you are," Crowe declared, a classic example of what West Indians and Panamanians called "Canal Zone justice."[94]

Poaching at the Borders

Along the Zone's remote rural boundaries, only sporadic U.S. patrols operated. Several Panamanian farmers living near Lake Madden, Lake Gatun, Paja, Chilibre, Agua Buena, Santa Rosa, or Emperador routinely grew crops on Zone lands or cut timber there. Reports of this activity elicited Zone Police patrols that either warned off or arrested infiltrators. Policemen "on bush patrol" from the Atlantic side would even scout Lake Gatun in riverboats, looking for suspected Panamanian "squatters" on the scores of tiny islands in the man-made, U.S.-controlled, lake.[95]

The District Court of the Canal Zone dealt firmly with these rural poachers, viewing them as a danger to the watershed so necessary for the operation of the locks. In June 1958 the court told one timber cutter, José Leocadio Meña, "The Canal Zone cannot permit its lumber and its properties here to be stolen by people who are irresponsible and do not correctly check its accurate location." Ignoring Meña's protests, Judge Crowe told him, "You may not know where the boundaries are but the fact that you were convicted just a short time ago of cutting timber in the Zone . . . makes it doubly your respon-

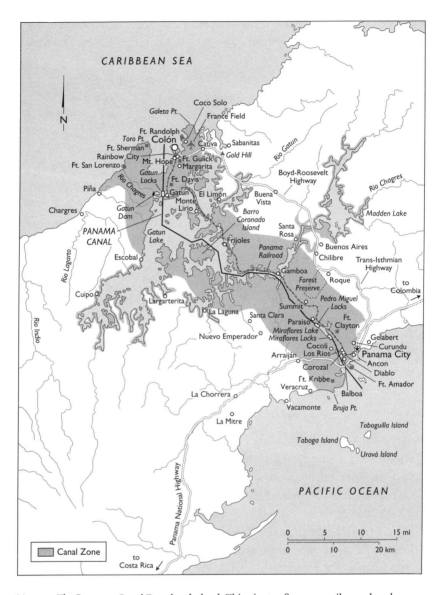

Map 1.2. The Panama–Canal Zone borderland. This giant 558-square-mile canal enclave cut across the entire isthmus of Panama in a northwesterly direction, bisecting the republic. What previous historians and cartographers often failed to emphasize was that in addition to the numerous U.S. towns and bases of the Zone and its two large urban frontiers with Colón and Panama City, the enclave also impacted dozens of smaller towns and islands along the rural regions of the Zone, where Panamanians engaged in "illegal" farming, immigration, timber poaching, trade, contraband, and police interactions with inhabitants from the U.S. side of the line.

sibility to determine where Canal Zone lumber lies and where it doesn't." Crowe sentenced Meña to sixty days in the U.S. penitentiary in Gamboa. But timber cutting and the illegal cultivation of crops continued. This indifference to the power of the Zone among rural Panamanian borderlanders replicated a traditional form of resistance, of squatting and poaching, frequently exerted against wealthy Panamanian landowners by isthmian campesinos.[96]

Racial and Ethnic Boundaries

Maintaining the racial order of the Zone also affected the flow of individuals across its boundaries. A daily procession of West Indian and Latin Panamanian domestics and laborers entered the Zone early each morning and exited late in the afternoon, like the Palestinian workers in Israel or the black South African laborers in Cape Town during apartheid. In the 1960s–1970s nearly nine thousand Panamanian canal workers alone, most of them of West Indian descent, made this trek daily. When Zone Police recognized an individual, the transient entered unmolested. But police in dark sunglasses questioned black and brown strangers, whom they arrested on trespassing charges or drove to the border with orders to "get back to Panama."[97]

The borderland's "mango wars" provided another locus of exclusion. During mango season, hungry Panamanian boys from Chorrillo sprinted across the boundary line to gather these ripe, fallen fruits from the plentiful trees along the U.S. border. Many Zonians did not eat mangoes and left them to rot on the ground. Zone Police would chase these boys for "stealing" the fruit (technically U.S. property), especially those bolder youngsters who trespassed into the Zone's residential sections to gather mangoes from individual homes. Often such encounters became serious business, with arrests and imprisonments, but on most occasions they were a game played by both sides. Panamanian onlookers would laugh and cheer when grinning youths carrying shirts full of mangoes outran overweight gringo police. Probably the most famous of these "mango boys" was the future five-time world champion boxer, Roberto Durán.[98]

The Canal Zone Police also apprehended poorer Panamanians of color who crossed the border to visit friends and relatives who lived in the silver towns. Some of these trespassers had committed petty offenses or thefts in the Zone in the past. When convicted, such offenders were officially barred from the Zone for a period of three to five years. Thus through their extraterritorial judicial system, U.S. authorities retained the power to "deport" Panamanians from a part of their own country.[99]

1.6. West Indian and Latin Panamanian workers referred to as "silver" and later "local-rate" laborers line up for inspection of their IDs by Canal Zone policemen before entering the U.S.-run enclave. U.S. security concerns over border control increased when rising crime and nationalist protest spilled over from the republic into the once pristine Zone. Courtesy of the *Panama Canal Review* in the Panama Canal Museum Collection, George Smathers Library, University of Florida, http://ufdc.ufl.edu/pcm.

Not so for lighter-skinned, more affluent Panamanians. Their complexion usually provided a passport into the enclave. The Zone Police were less likely to question these elite Panamanians of European descent, some of whom attended U.S. high schools in the enclave and were the sons and daughters of important officials. Nor did the police harass members of the Panamanian oligarchy who drank, golfed, and hobnobbed at Zone or U.S. military clubs. "I used to go into the Zone all the time, especially at night to date the girls. I never had any problem," one well-to-do Panamanian and graduate of Balboa High recalled.[100]

The Subversive Economy at the Borders

As in all borderlands, contraband posed a major problem along the Zone-Panama nexus. The "locational ambiguity" of borderlands, their porosity, and the de facto dual citizenship of their inhabitants enable some borderlanders to earn their living transporting goods from one polity to another. This was certainly the case in Panama, where constant contraband exposed the hollowness of Zonian assurances to limit the smuggling of duty-free commissary goods. But contraband also served as a social lubricant between otherwise hostile Americans and Panamanians. In the 1960s–1970s, during an era of deteriorating U.S.-Panamanian relations, the illicit drug traffic from Panama into the Zone and from Panama into the United States emerged as a major concern for Washington. Narcotics provided a more serious form of contraband that, unlike commissary smuggling, Zone officials and the U.S. Drug Enforcement Agency could not tolerate. By the late 1980s obsession with cocaine trafficking provided one of the U.S. motivations for violent invasion.[101]

During the construction era the Isthmian Canal Commission first established the commissary system to ensure an adequate supply of fresh, hygienic, and reasonably priced food and necessities for canal workers. The host nation's economy lacked the resources to feed and clothe the 100,000 workers and dependents that flocked to the enclave. To the disgust of Panamanian merchants, Canal Zone governor George Goethals (1907–17) maintained this exclusionary system even after construction ended. The Zone had already established a state within a state in Panama and, as the commissary system matured, an economy within an economy. So many Panamanians bought low-priced, duty-free goods from U.S. commissaries during the century's first three decades that Foreign Minister Ricardo J. Alfaro insisted on restricting these sales as a minimal concession in his negotiations with U.S. Secretary of State Cordell Hull in the 1930s.[102]

But large-scale smuggling in commissary goods continued even after the 1955 Eisenhower-Remón Treaty that limited their purchases to employees of the Canal Company and Zone government who lived inside the Zone. Unlike most Latin American ruling classes, the Panamanian oligarchy composed a commercial, not a landed, elite who objected strongly to this loss of business. The Zone agreed to employ more contraband-control officers to address their concerns, but these officers never stopped more than a fraction of the trade.[103]

The greatest obstacle to controlling smuggling derived from the benefits it accrued to both buyers and sellers. Increased sales, whether to U.S. or Panamanian customers, boosted commissary profits. Only Panamanian shop owners, never popular in Panama or in the Zone, lost out. Zonians habitually purchased extra commissary goods, then sold them at cost or donated them to their Panamanian servants and acquaintances, earning no profit but cementing useful dependencies and friendships. Among the greatest offenders, U.S. servicemen bought food, nylons, clothing, and jewelry from PXs for the families of their Panamanian girlfriends. DOD workers, who had higher rates of intermarriage with Panamanians than Zonians, purchased items for their Panamanian wives' families.[104]

Due to a discriminatory wage system, West Indians earned about one-third of what Zonians made. Many of them supplemented their meager incomes by selling commissary goods to fellow West Indian relatives and friends who lived across the line. West Indians felt unfairly targeted by contraband officers, who questioned them outside commissaries and in cars and buses whenever they found them loaded down with shopping bags beyond their personal or family needs.[105]

Contraband reigned supreme during Christmas season. Zone shoppers, black and white, would routinely toss five large turkeys and five giant hams into their shopping carts. Control officers and police could only throw up their hands in resignation, as it was impossible to arrest the entire population that week, particularly since so many of the culprits were close friends—and it was Christmas, after all. Just about everyone in the borderland became involved in some way in this smuggling. Zone policemen would load their trunks with commissary beer, then drive across the line and sell it in Panama for extra money. "The worse the beer was, the more the Panamanians loved it: Hamms, Old Milwaukee, Schlitz, Pabst. As long as Americans drank it, Panamanians figured it had to be the best," recalled retired Canal Zone policeman Pablo Prieto. The small but important American business colony that lived in Panama, highly critical of the commissary system when it hurt their concerns, would ask Zonian friends to pick up difficult-to-find products, such as Heinz ketchup, for them. Even Panamanian officials who criticized the commissary system in speeches had their U.S. military or Zonian friends procure commissary items for them on occasion.[106]

Comic aspects emerged from this activity. A former Canal Zone policeman remembered a Christmas collection of canned goods for Panama's poor at St. Mary's Catholic School in the Zone. Just as the nuns prepared to drive the goods to Panama in their station wagon, one of the Zonian children cried out, "Hey, wait a minute! That's all contraband! All those canned goods come from the commissary and you're taking them to Panama!" Embarrassed nuns hesitated for a moment but decided to donate the cans to the poor anyway, promising that they would seek forgiveness in confession the following Friday.[107]

Narcotics Trade in the Borderland

Drug smuggling constituted the second leading source of contraband across the Zone-Panama border in the postwar era. In the 1940s and 1950s the U.S. military were the primary consumers. Marijuana proved the most popular drug, although military and Zone Police occasionally arrested soldiers and Panamanian dealers in possession of cocaine, morphine, and heroin. In the 1960s–1970s both the number of narcotics arrests and the use of harder drugs increased in the Zone, a reflection of changing social and cultural attitudes toward drugs among U.S. citizens. Increased military consumption of hard drugs reflected the global problem of low service morale due to the Vietnam War. Equally troubling for Canal Zone authorities was the growing drug use among Zonian teenagers.[108]

As with commissary contraband, drug smuggling involved numerous social networks. Kuna Indians grew marijuana in Darién and smuggled it onto U.S. military bases. The unique access Kuna enjoyed both to U.S. bases and to the production of marijuana made them ideal runners. They were also exempt from U.S. prosecution because Zone judges typically handed arrested Kuna over to their chiefs for "tribal justice." West Indian employees of the Panama Canal Company likewise had more opportunities to bring drugs into the Zone than many Latin Panamanians, who lacked access to the enclave. The Zone's airfields provided additional entry and exit points, as did the scores of merchant ships that docked at the Canal's harbors each year.[109]

Still, the most risk-free way for GIs and young Zonians to buy drugs was simply to walk or drive into Panama and purchase them from street dealers

and acquaintances. Though technically illegal, drugs abounded in the barrios of Panama City and Colón. And if a Panamanian National Guardsman
did arrest a U.S. soldier or civilian for possession, a small cash bribe resolved
most arrests. In the 1970s the Nixon and Ford administrations exerted pressure on the Torrijos government to cooperate in eradicating drug traffic to
the United States.[110] Ironically the Panamanian officer charged with stamping out drugs in this era was none other than Colonel Manuel Noriega, who
later became Panama's ruler and a major trafficker.[111]

Summary

In September 1977 the Carter administration concluded a controversial
agreement, built upon the spade work of past administrations, that ended
the Zone borderland forever. The new accords recognized Panama's sovereignty over all its national territory, terminated the Zone's old borders, and
surrendered 60 percent of its former territory, including an estimated $2 bil-
lion worth of facilities, to Panama on October 1, 1979. The remaining 40 percent of the old Zone continued as a jointly administered territory, designated
for canal operations and military bases under a status-of-forces agreement
like those with other U.S. allies. Unlike in the old Zone, Panamanians could
travel freely across most parts of this "canal area" that lacked U.S. gover-
nance, police, and courts. Military bases and key sections of the Canal's operation imposed the only restrictions. On the first day in October 1979, tens
of thousands of cheering Panamanians ran across the Avenue of the Martyrs,
violating a contested boundary that no longer existed. Once known as "the
country with five frontiers," a reference to the Zone borderland, Panama had
returned once again to a nation of four frontiers: its two landed borders with
Costa Rica and Colombia and its two ocean coasts.[112]

Still, Panamanian concern over the breadth of its sovereignty continued.
After the 1989 U.S. invasion, critics from both nations questioned the true
purpose of the operation that overthrew the Noriega regime and cost the
lives of several hundred innocent Panamanians. The most suspicious observers judged the U.S. invasion a pretext to restore some kind of "new Zone"
to maintain U.S. hegemony. But Washington met the central obligation of
the 1977 treaty by terminating the last U.S. frontier on December 31, 1999.
Cleaning up abandoned munitions and environmental contamination on
U.S. bases, however, remained unfulfilled promises. Authorities actually arranged a hasty handover ceremony more than two weeks before the official
transfer, on December 14. Part of the reason for this rested with the troubled

legacy of the old borderland, site of so many anti-American riots and protests. The Zone's militant enemies, the university students, the communists, and the Torrijosistas, did not have time to prepare large protests for this surprise early ceremony.[113]

The Panama Canal Zone began as a territorial entity designed "for the construction, maintenance, and protection" of a transoceanic canal. But the enclave quickly expanded from its technical function to an internal colony, an instrument of domination and co-optation that forged a unique pan-American borderland that spread its influence across the republic. As the focal point of U.S. Caribbean hegemony, the Zone facilitated coups and interventions all throughout the region, allegedly to assure its strategic integrity. But the greatest battle for or against the Zone was not conducted at those distant outposts or, for that matter, at the U.S. State Department or the Panamanian Presidential Palace. Rather this struggle was fought, negotiated, reconciled, and reframed every day in the streets and alleyways of Panama City, Balboa, Colón, and Cristobal and along the jungle sections of the borderland's remotest frontiers.

In the postwar era Panamanians, North Americans, West Indians, Kuna, Chinese, and the descendants of laborers from twenty nations participated in and shaped this evolution of conflict and accommodation. The process included students, soldiers, drug dealers, "gate girls," lottery vendors, shoe-shine boys, bartenders, mango thieves, ketchup smugglers, prostitutes, maids, and National Guardsmen. Panamanian and U.S. scholars have devoted much analysis to the treaties negotiated between the two nations that established the relationship's parameters, but at the center of the contest for Panama's soul were these everyday conflicts and alliances along the boundaries of the "fifth frontier."

RACE AND IDENTITY IN THE

ZONE-PANAMA BORDERLAND

Zonians Uber Alles

Near midnight on February 24, 1946, a twenty-five-year-old North American woman walked home alone from the Balboa Railroad station to her parents' home in Ancon on the Pacific side of the Zone. Daughter of one of the canal's division chiefs, she had just returned from Cristobal after a railroad trip across the isthmus. A relative planned on meeting her at the station but erroneously thought she would arrive later that evening. As the young woman walked in the darkness, a truck loaded with "silver" workers finishing up the second shift drove by. One of the truck's riders, Lester Leon Greaves, who worked at the U.S. engineer depot at Corozal, eyed the woman closely, then asked the driver to drop him off at the next corner.[1]

Greaves, a twenty-year-old black Panamanian of West Indian descent, waited in the nearby bushes for the American woman to pass. When she did, he seized her and threw her down in the tall grass near Roosevelt Avenue, close to the Canal Administration Building. There, according to police documents, he put his hand over her mouth to stifle her cries, tore off her panties, and raped her. Before fleeing the scene, Greaves also robbed his victim of $24 from her pocketbook. Badly hurt and in a state of shock, the woman staggered to nearby Gorgas Hospital, where she reported the rape to doctors and later to the Canal Zone Police.[2]

In a critical error during his struggle with the woman, Greaves dropped his wallet, which contained his worker ID. Finding this document, Canal Zone Police notified authorities in Panama, who picked up Greaves the next night near his Río Abajo home and extradited him to the Canal Zone. On that first night, however, all available Canal Zone Police had scoured the Zone in search of a young black man who fit the victim's description, resulting in a frightening night for the Zone's West Indian workforce. While electric with tension, Greaves's trial in U.S. District Court at Balboa on April 2 proved anticlimactic. Having already given a full and remorseful confession, Greaves pled guilty before Judge Bunk Gardner and waived his right to a jury trial. "Don't fret for me," he told his tearful relatives and friends. Gardner's sentencing of Greaves would reverberate for decades throughout the Panamanian nationalist struggle and U.S.-Panamanian race relations. Gardner, a native of Kentucky, sentenced Greaves to fifty years at Gamboa Penitentiary for the crime of rape, the maximum sentence allowable under the Canal Zone Code. Greaves would later protest his innocence and become a symbol of U.S. racial discrimination in the Zone-Panama borderland. Pardoned in 1962 by President John F. Kennedy, Greaves returned to a normal life after sixteen years of hard labor at Gamboa. He married, raised a family, and even worked again briefly in the Zone.[3]

But in early 1946 Greaves's rape case sent shock waves through the Zone and nearby Panama. The brutal violation of a young U.S. white woman by a black Panamanian fed into the worst Zonian fears and exposed the stark racial and national divisions that operated along the borderland. In the postwar years, under increasing pressure from Panamanian nationalism, the global decolonization movement, and the U.S. civil rights struggle, the apartheid system of the Zone gradually weakened, despite the intransigence of U.S. officials, military leaders, and Zonians who strove to maintain it. To understand more fully the emotions unleashed by Greaves's crime and subsequent imprisonment, it is necessary to explore the conflicting notions of race and identity at work in this post–World War II borderland, for the Greaves case provided one of those seminal events that cast all three communities in broad relief and pitted elements of the principal ethnic and national groups against one another.

Race and U.S. Identity in the Zone Borderland

As scholars of anthropology and sociology have long noted, race and identity are social constructs that change over time, rather than static, innate, or biological categories. Human culture plays a fundamental role in their formations and transformations. Constructions of U.S. race and identity in the Zone borderland date back to the early excavation days (1904–14), when white U.S. officials, workers, and soldiers first arrived in Panama in large numbers. Earlier antecedents emerged during the Panama Railroad construction period (1850–1855). Conflicts over identity, ethnicity, and race are particular features of imperial borderlands where people from different backgrounds come into constant daily contact. Those on the imperial or "more advanced" side of a borderland tend to view those from "the other side" as inferior in racial or ethnic merit. This race thinking is in fact central to the operation of most borderlands. A pervasive myth from the canal construction era claimed that the majority of U.S. workers were Deep Southerners, who brought with them a Jim Crow mentality and peculiar white identity that re-created the American South in the Zone. Southerners did encompass a significant minority of U.S. canal personnel (around 32 percent, as determined by the 1912 census and other documents), but they were never the majority. Southerners did constitute a majority of the U.S. Army and Navy officers and the NCO corps stationed in the Zone in the early twentieth century (around 54 percent). But a more accurate interpretation of the U.S. "geographic influence" on the Zone was that these Southerners, as well as their fellow Northerners and Midwesterners, generally shared the same white supremacist ideology that fit contemporary U.S. attitudes on race and nation. This ideology derived from a "Euro-American history of thinking about difference, rather than a concept of describing an objective reality that is independent of a social context," as Peter Wade noted in his studies of race and ethnicity in Latin America.[4]

The North American founders of the Zone in Washington and Panama embraced late nineteenth-century Darwinian race theories and a belief in *Plessy v. Ferguson* segregation. For the founders of the enclave a "natural" hierarchy positioned white Anglo Saxons atop a pecking order destined to rule over Southern and Eastern Europeans, "mongrelized" Latin Americans, Asians, indigenous peoples, and, at the bottom of the scale, black Africans. Besides economic and strategic primacies, such racist rankings provided turn-of-the-century expansionists with a "moral" justification for extending U.S. sway over the Caribbean, Central America, and the Philippines.[5]

The "gold" and "silver" racial segregation of the Canal Zone found its basis in the U.S.-built Panama Railroad's pay practices (1850–55), adopted in an era of Manifest Destiny and Anglo-Saxonist race thinking. The canal builders continued this custom of paying Antilleans in silver and their own white managers and foremen higher salaries in gold. The Zone's strict separation of races in housing, education, commissaries, and public accommodations derived from this gold and silver pay system that eventually replicated segregation in the U.S. South with important qualifications. Canal Zone officials initially separated workers on the basis of nationality, not race. Thus authorities relegated Spanish, Italian, and Greek contract laborers who might otherwise be considered white to the silver roll along with the forty thousand West Indian workers imported to build the canal.[6]

Later apologists for the Zone's Jim Crow system pointed out that such racist ideology was universal at the turn of the century. But the graphic nature of this racial segregation shocked Panamanians, who, while they practiced their own, more subtle brand of discrimination, rejected the idea of a de jure separation based on skin color. Such divisions appeared alien and perverse in a multiracial polity where interracial relations abounded.[7]

As Michael Hunt has shown, turn-of-the-century popular imagery of Latin America transformed the former "mongrelized" courtesan "south of the border" into a willing maiden seeking U.S. guidance and protection. U.S. officials similarly viewed Panama, or at least their designated section of it, as a frontier in need of "racial taming." Fortunately for U.S.-Panamanian relations, the Zone quickly transformed itself into a "controlled" frontier, one that eschewed the violence so prominent during railroad construction (1850–55) and along contiguous U.S. borderlands in North America. But the U.S. sense of racial and societal superiority persisted from the earliest U.S. travelers to Panama until the end of the Zone in 1979. During and following the 1977–78 Carter-Torrijos Treaty negotiations, a number of Zonians predicted the inevitable collapse of canal operations once Americans ceased running the waterway. Edward "Ted" Scott, a columnist for the *Panama American*, actually predicted that the Panamanians would close down the Canal once they had control and turn its giant locks into public swimming pools.[8]

Besides the majority Latin Panamanians, West Indians formed an additional "other" for forging a U.S. imperial identity in Panama. While U.S. citizens often held Barbadians and Jamaicans in higher esteem than Panamanians of Hispanic descent, whites also stigmatized these island laborers as lazy, superstitious, and childish, creatures of brawn, not brains. U.S. complaints of West Indians' unreliability, fighting, and lack of work ethic flourished during the early construction period, though by the time of the waterway's completion, North Americans grudgingly acknowledged the Antillean contribution to the excavation.[9]

In contrast to the huge numbers of West Indians, only 357 Panamanian laborers took part in the Canal's construction. The isthmian population was too small to support the tens of thousands of workers required for the gargantuan project, and the majority of Panamanian campesinos operated outside the cash economy, eking out a living as subsistence farmers. Still, this Panamanian "non-participation" fueled derogatory U.S. images of a weak and indolent native population, allegedly lacking in ambition and uninterested in progress.[10]

Besides race, religion formed another key indicator of Zonian identity throughout the borderland. The overwhelming majority of U.S. officials, workers, and soldiers who first came to Panama were Protestants. A U.S. Protestant majority continued in the Zone until its demise in 1979, though their numbers declined markedly as more Catholics worked in the Zone in the postwar years. Just as turn-of-the-century America was a predominantly Protestant nation in culture and ideology, so too did the Canal Zone embody a Protestant enclave in its obsession with progress, order, and public morality.[11]

During construction Zone officials relegated Catholic migrants—Spaniards, Italians, and Latin American workers—to the silver roll on the basis of nationality. Still, Catholic workers, including Americans, suspected religious discrimination as a cause of their subordination. As a consequence in 1914 Catholic Zonians founded St. Mary's Church and in 1949, after much resistance from the Zone government, established the first parochial grammar school in the enclave. Catholic Zonians formed their own social clubs, such as the Catholic Youth Organization and the Knights of Columbus, in reaction to the Zone's YMCA, Masons, Redmen, and Strangers Clubs that prohibited Catholic membership. Some postwar Catholics complained about religious discrimination in promotions and appointments within the canal organization. The Zone never boasted a Catholic governor, and membership in the all-Protestant Masons purportedly boosted career advancement. Protestant kids referred to Catholic students as "St. Mary's fairies." While this taunt may have been a slur after the school's opening, it later became a comic tease by public school Zonians toward private school Catholic kids. Gradually the religious stigma against Catholics waned. But a Protestant ideology formed the bedrock of Zonian identity in relation to Catholic Panama.[12]

What Constituted a Zonian?

Social change after World War II impelled Zonians to reexamine their identity in ways that might have appeared alien to construction-era workers. For the first time, questions even arose as to who or exactly what was a Zonian. U.S. citizens living along the borderland used various terms to describe themselves over the years: Zoners, Zonites, Zonies, Zoniacs, Zonelanders, and, the most common, Zonians. Besides the Spanish word *Zonietas*, Panamanian nationalists employed less flattering sobriquets: Ku Klux Zonians, Zonakazes, Zonaladrones (or Zone thieves), and, the worst, Nazonians. By the postwar era, the U.S. community in Panama had matured and developed a sense of its own history. The 1950s witnessed the establishment of the Isthmian Historical Society, the dedication of the huge monument to chief engineer and later Canal Zone Governor George Goethals in 1954, and the Theodore Roosevelt Centenary held in Balboa in 1958. (Zonians were disappointed that so few Panamanians attended, but as one Panamanian remarked, "That's like wondering why more Indians didn't show up for the Custer Anniversary.")[13]

The most exclusive definition of Zonian identity applied only to those U.S. employees of the Panama Canal Company and Canal Zone government who had been born in the Canal Zone. Therefore to be a "true Zonian" one had to be at least second-generation. By 1960 this definition described fewer than a fifth of the enclave and barred U.S. military personnel, civilian defense workers, and canal workers born in the States. Some U.S. inhabitants never accepted such a strict definition of Zonehood. But several families, such as the Allens, Cottons, Cronins, Coffeys, Dillons, Doyles, DuVals, McIlheneys, and Moores, prided themselves on their ancestral links to the "ditch diggers." (West Indians referred to them as "the foremen of the ditch diggers," since few U.S. citizens actually wielded a shovel, though many operated the important steam shovels.)[14]

To Panamanian inhabitants of the borderland, every white U.S. national who lived in the enclave and was not in military uniform was a Zonian. Zonians were simply "those damned *gringos* over there that have everything and think they are better than us." Indeed fine distinctions proved complex when U.S. soldiers would return after a tour of duty to get a job with the Canal Company or when DOD workers would transfer to canal jobs. For canal workers recruited from the United States, the distinctions between "old-timers" (i.e., veteran Zonians) and "new comers" proved embittering. In 1945 one disgruntled worker wrote, "Yes, folks, I am homeward bound. But by choice. I can no longer stand them any longer. . . . Of course you all know who I mean by *them*. They are the quaint old-timers. They don't have much to say; they just grumble. You see, they are mad at us new comers. We upset their whole existence."[15]

This hostility between old-timers and newcomers, actually between *borderlanders* and *mainlanders*, repeated itself over the generations. True Zonians were, after all, *creoles*, while the U.S.-born in the Zone were *peninsulares* of a sort, with the key distinction that most lacked the power and social status of the creoles, a condition that was reversed in the old Spanish Empire. High officials, such as Canal Zone governors (practically U.S. viceroys) sent down from the States, more closely resembled the peninsulares of old. Not one of the twenty appointed governors had been born in the Zone, and several engendered considerable local (Zonian) hostility like their Spanish "predecessors." When in the early 1960s Walter Boltin, a postal employee from New Jersey, first arrived to work at the Cristobal Post Office, he was surprised by the animosity. "'If you don't like it here there's a boat leaving every week' was the common refrain. These guys were really cold to me and criticized everything I did. It was a helluva place to break into as a new guy." George Wheeler, a new U.S.-born hire on the Canal Police Force, experienced similar attitudes. "I was the only 'gringo' in the academy in 1971," he remembered. "The others were one Panamanian, and five goddamned Zonians. Those bastards really put me through the ringer. I used to tell Panamanians, 'I don't blame you for hating these sonsabitches [the Zonians] 'cause I hate 'em even worse than you do!'"[16]

In 1968, when engineer Phil Bonk arrived to work at the Dredging Division, he recalled a different reception perhaps due to his skilled status: "I got here a week early and my boss took me around the Zone to all the different clubs 'to show me the ropes.' We basically got plastered every day starting at ten in the morning. Having worked in the States, I couldn't get over how relaxed the atmosphere was down here plus all the benefits they gave you. We used to call it the 'executive package.'"[17]

Still to this day some former U.S. workers, such as George Wheeler, maintain emphatically that they were not Zonians, as if to set themselves apart from the chauvinistic mind-set of the Zone-born who, through their arrogant behavior toward the local population, allegedly "screwed up" or "lost" the Canal. Sue Stabler, who descended from a "ditch-digger" family, expressed this wistfully when she said, "All the things that made the Zone so wonderful were the very things that eventually destroyed it." She was referring to the enclave's exclusivity, insularity, and racial and national privilege.[18] But as Walter Boltin noted about most U.S. civilians in the enclave, regardless of their origins, "the longer you lived here, the more Zonian you became."[19]

Family Life on the Zone

Zonians most frequently praised their side of the borderland as "a great place to raise kids." In this respect Zonians saw themselves as maintaining a 1950s Ozzie-and-Harriet lifestyle long after the decade had ended. Community life that focused around the particular town where Zonians lived, be it Ancon, Balboa, Diablo, Gamboa, Margarita, or Cristobal, held powerful sway. The clubhouse, commissary, church, school, lodge, and athletic facilities were key sites of socialization. This sense of community also centered around the company divisions where individuals worked: the Dredging Division in Gamboa, the Electrical and Locks Divisions in Gatun, the Mechanical Division in Balboa, and the Industrial Division in Cristobal.[20]

Journalists who explored Zonian identity often denigrated the whole area as one giant "company town," which, to an extent, it was. But a more accurate appraisal of the Zone for whites was that it consisted of numerous "small company towns," each with its own ambience and idiosyncrasies. When categorizing one another, U.S. citizens frequently used these socio-geographical distinctions. Such-and-such a person was a "Curundu boy," a "Gamboa girl," a "Colón boy," or a "Gatuner," each of which had its own meaning. The company division where one worked signified identity as well. "My family were all 'dredgers,'" one Zonian boasted. "All my family worked the locks at Gatun. My Dad was a lockmaster, and I was a mule operator, and my uncle was a security guard there for a while," another said with pride. Clannishness and nepotism developed among these town and division mates. At larger social functions they often sat, ate, drank, and joked together. One Zonian remembered a pilot's wife admonishing her child not to play with children whose fathers were not pilots during a summer cruise back to the United States. But in such a small community, friendships and alliances frequently transcended these workplace-town boundaries.[21]

In such a claustrophobic environment, gossip predominated. U.S. wives waiting in line at the "commy" exchanged the latest on whose husband had been drunk and abusive, whose child had gotten into trouble with the police, or who was sleeping with whom. At the "clubby" or clubhouse, families talked about who had gotten an undeserved promotion through favoritism, who was vying for which job, and whose newly arrived wife or husband "was a pain in the ass." The intimacy of such a confined community as the Zone, where people practically lived on top of one another in multi-unit housing and partitioned office spaces, led to the sharing of lots of private information. "It was impossible for anyone to have an affair, a fight, or to screw up down here without everybody knowing about it the next morning. Sometimes within hours of it happening!" a Zonian remembered. The Canal Police knew all the "secrets" of the Zone and, while imbibing off-duty, spread the dirt on troubled or comic individuals. Gossip also centered on feared policy changes, particularly during crises, such as the 1947, 1959, and 1964 anti-

American riots or when negotiations for a new U.S.-Panamanian treaty were under way.[22]

Ultra-Americans in the Borderland

A significant group of postwar Zonians pictured themselves as ultra-Americans. As government workers tied to a defense site and surrounded by a nation that they perceived as hostile and inferior, they formed a deeply conservative community. Following the 1964 riots and during the Carter-Torrijos Treaty process, U.S. newspapers flew reporters to Panama who wrote disparagingly of the Zonians' "luxurious, privileged lifestyle, manicured lawns," and "racially segregated society." "Take us to see the *Afrikaaners!*" they told an annoyed Richard Koster, a longtime American resident in Panama. "This place had major problems, but there were no *Afrikaaners* here," Koster recalled. Yet Zonians with roots in the South and like-minded Northerners formed what collectively became known as the "Canal Zone rednecks." How large a group the "rednecks" comprised is difficult to tell, but like any vocal minority they maintained an influence out of proportion to their numbers. Former Zonian and science fiction writer Carl Posey noted that they could "fabricate racial epithets that would make one cringe." Redneck representation on the Canal Zone Police Force exacerbated community relations in the borderland for generations.[23]

Edgardo Tirado, a retired policeman, recalled at least two "hard-core" Zone cops who boasted of their membership in a Canal Zone Ku Klux Klan. One night in the early 1970s one of them showed Tirado his mail-ordered Klan uniform over drinks at his apartment. Some West Indians feared and talked about a Zone Klan, though there is no documentation of its existence. Still, the portly redneck Zonian in his overhanging Hawaiian shirt and shorts, hunting, drinking, and whoring in the borderland, formed a cultural archetype that still echoes in Panamanian memories of the Zone.[24]

Interactions with the "Other"

An alternative to Zonian exclusivity and racism might have been more borderland interactions with the "other," that is, with Latin and West Indian Panamanians. To an extent this mingling occurred, but with sharp qualifications. The golden age of Zonian-Panamanian socialization commenced during Prohibition. As a strict government reservation, the Canal Zone forbade the sale of alcohol within its borders except for 3.2 percent beer. Thus during the 1920s and early 1930s hundreds of thirsty Zonians left the enclave every night to seek out the bars and nightclubs of the capital and Colón. Zonian social clubs, such as the Century, the Miramar, and the Chagres Club, actually moved from the Zone to Panama during this period so that their members could imbibe hard liquor. As a byproduct of this search for alcohol, Zonians and the U.S. military formed more friendships and acquaintances with Panamanians than before, though largely with upper- and middle-class Panamanians seeking contacts with higher-status Zonians and with Panamanian service workers who commingled with them at various watering holes. Zone mechanics liked to drink in the Florida Club, Al's Place, the MacArthur Bar, El Limite, José El Abandonado, and Bilgray's Tropic Bar with working-class Panamanians from the barrios of El Chorrillo, Calidonia, and Colón, many of whom made a living serving the Zone through their labor and shop sales. Most of these clubs and bars, however, quickly acquired a reputation as American hangouts, as was the case of the Good Neighbor Bar in Curundu. The World War II bonanza in Panama that began with troop reinforcements in the late 1930s revitalized this "Prohibition party" and continued a fairly high level of social interaction.[25]

But the end of World War II brought key changes to borderland social relations. Panamanian elites often commented on this shift after the war. "I don't know what happened. We used to be such good friends before," one well-to-do Panamanian woman explained, "but after the war, everything changed. They retreated into the Zone and never wanted to come out—like turtles." While this statement simplifies U.S. postwar behavior, its insights are significant. Security concerns during the war led to tighter entry controls for foreign nationals who included Panamanians. In the 1950s cold war threat perceptions reinforced this attitude of sealing off the Zone, as did increased urban crime and political dissent in Panama.[26]

By the late 1940s the Zone had grown more institutionalized. A second and even third generation of Zonians worked and lived there. The early adventurous spirit of the canal builders had faded. The Zone government, its various departments, unions, and civil service codes, established a paternalistic, "company town" structure with ever more benefits and privileges for its workers. These included new cinder-block housing in the late 1940s–1950s to replace original wooden quarters. Officials built an array of modern, more upscale clubhouses with adjoining movie theaters, bowling alleys, athletic fields, basketball courts, and swimming pools. Newly constructed commissaries boasted a wider selection of services and goods, though still limited in comparison to the States. Voluntary associations also upgraded their lodge facilities. The mid-1950s witnessed the arrival of 60-cycle electricity, followed by television, and later in the decade, the true conqueror of the tropics, air-conditioning.[27]

An increasing array of television shows and motion pictures after 1955 from Caribbean Command Television linked Zonians to popular U.S. culture. The force and combination of this upgrading resulted in the postwar Zone requiring Panama less for distraction and social life than the prewar Zone had. The enclave steadily developed all the comforts of home that stateside suburbanites cherished. With so many attractions available in the Zone, why journey to "messy, chaotic" Panama, particularly after anti-U.S. riots demonstrated the republic's apparent hostility toward the enclave? A substantial minority of Zonians liked "messy, chaotic" Panama on the weekends and at night. But increasingly the majority of Zonians, as well as many U.S. military dependents, retreated to the agreeable routines of the Zone, of drinking, golfing, and socializing mostly with other Americans. And if they did "cross over" into Panama, these Americans rarely penetrated more than a few blocks from the boundary line, safely ensconced in a heavily Americanized border region.[28]

The English language proved a key determinant of this insularity. The entire structure of the Zone made Spanish superfluous for English-speaking U.S. citizens and West Indians, who composed the main groups there. Zonians studied Spanish in grammar and high school, but their failure to speak the language daily with their neighbors across the line resulted in an almost total lack of fluency among the majority. Those who did speak Spanish were the minority of Americans with Latin American spouses or relatives or those who spent considerable time in Panama and enjoyed the company of Panamanian friends. Zone professionals, such as teachers, doctors, lawyers, and history or culture buffs, made up most of this latter group.[29] James Reid, a Ford sales manager in Panama, married to a Colombian wife, remembered the animosity he encountered when he first tried to speak Spanish in the Zone's Balboa Elks Club: "I asked the bartender for a *whisky escoces* [scotch], and all the Americans at the bar looked at me like I was insane. 'What the hell are you doing?' one of them told me. 'We speak English here!' I couldn't believe it, but to them, this place was U.S. territory, the fifty-first state, even though Panama was just a mile down the road."[30] Thus while the tendency toward separation occurred early in the Zone, it worsened considerably after World War II.[31]

Panamanians, many of whom admired aspects of U.S. society, its modernity, technological innovation, and democratic ideals, recognized this

Zonian drive for exclusion and resented it. Their anger increased following the U.S. triumph in World War II, glorified in Allied propaganda as a victory of democracy over racist fascism. In 1946, shortly after the Greaves case, an embittered Panamanian wrote an open letter to the Zonians: "We like Americans. . . . We, however, strongly object to the abuse of privileges freely given, to the forceful imposition of a lower standard of living, to being barred from commercial advantages offered by the Canal . . . to the indifference, the lack of cooperation in all things Panamanian. In short, we object to all those things that set us apart from the 'Americans' and make us feel like strangers in our own land. We want to be given the opportunity of being like them, of living like them, of playing like them. We want to grow closer to them instead of being set apart by them."[32]

This letter spoke powerfully of the attraction-repulsion syndrome so many Panamanian borderlanders felt toward the Zone and the United States. The U.S. military community, more sympathetic to the Panamanian viewpoint, seconded these criticisms: "What, dear God, gives every American abroad the notion that he or she is so completely superior to the inhabitants of the area in which the American happens to be?. . . . Zonites laughingly deride Panama's efforts at Democratic government. . . . Loss of friendship abroad comes from these characters roaming around in our midst. . . . I once saw a Mexican boy refused service at a diner in Olathe, Kansas. What would happen I wonder if an American were told that he was not good enough to soil a plate in a Panamanian establishment?"[33]

After World War II Americans conducted their own internal debate over racism in a society that proclaimed itself leader of "the free world." The late 1940s witnessed Jackie Robinson's entry into Major League Baseball and President Harry S. Truman's integration of the U.S. military. Try as it might, the Zone could not remain isolated from such social change. But the push for racial progress also inspired a strong reaction. In 1948, a year when both U.S. and global race reform appeared ascendant, the victorious National Party in South Africa enacted apartheid. That same year the cold war heated, obstructing progress toward integration by associating civil rights protest with communist agitation. Rumors of federally enforced racial reforms troubled the Zone, as did scuttlebutt about the imposition of the federal income tax and even the termination of the 25 percent tropical differential. "Are we to be dragged down to a fish head and rice level of existence?" one indignant Zonian wrote in 1946, implying that under such conditions white U.S. citizens might be forced to live "like Panamanians."[34]

Cognizant of civil rights pressures at the conclusion of the war, President

2.1. West Indian "silver" laborers working under their "gold" Zonian foreman. This racial and national hierarchy of labor in the Zone favored white American Zonians over West Indian and Latin Panamanian workers of color, who often earned one-third the wages of their white foremen and fellow white workers. Courtesy of the *Panama Canal Review* in the Panama Canal Museum Collection, George Smathers Library, University of Florida, http://ufdc.ufl.edu/pcm.

Truman appointed retired Brigadier General Frank McSherry to conduct a study of the segregated labor, schools, and housing in the Zone. Released on June 1, 1947, the McSherry Report condemned racial discrimination and called for the abolishment of Jim Crow and the two-tier wage system. But Zone and U.S. military officials in Panama strongly resisted the report's recommendation that a single-wage system be implemented due to additional costs and the threat to U.S. supremacy.[35]

In place of the unequal gold-silver payroll, administrators established an unequal payroll using a U.S. rate and a local rate that continued to pay West Indians and Panamanians about one-third to one-half of what white Zonians received, often for similar work. Nepotism, the all-white AFL unions, and the "good ol' boy" system of the Zone blocked upward mobility and training to Latin and West Indian Panamanians for higher-paid, skilled jobs. Veteran West Indian workers complained about training recently hired whites who quickly became their supervisors and earned three times their pay. The gold

2.2. The racial and national divides of the Canal Zone are reflected in this photo of the all-white members of Balboa High School's football all-stars. Courtesy of the *Panama Canal Spillway* in the Panama Canal Museum Collection, George Smathers Library, University of Florida, http://ufdc.ufl.edu/pcm.

and silver signs gradually came down near Balboa and Cristobal, the entry ports of the Zone, where visiting dignitaries might take offense. But blacks and whites continued to use separate facilities, in most cases right up until the 1970s.[36]

The Zonian school system was largely lily-white until 1979. A striking feature in the photos of students gathered about their flag at Balboa High School on the eve of the 1964 riots is the near total absence of blacks in an enclave where a quarter of the population was West Indian. In the 1950s–1960s, when the modern civil rights movement erupted in the U.S. South, many Zonians sided with the forces of racial entrenchment, not liberation. Following the 1963 March on Birmingham, Dee Collins, a Zonian from an old construction-era family, wrote a letter in defense of "Bull" Connor: "People discriminate all the time. You discriminate when you buy a certain brand of food, accept a college, join a club, take a religion, or choose a friend. . . . My quarrel is not with a people's right to achieve civil equality but in the methods being used to achieve this goal. Allegations of discrimination do not give any group the right to select which laws they will obey. . . . Personally, I have friends from many races but I do not want a government decree telling [me] who I must associate with. . . . P.S. To alleviate a distortion of the truth, police dogs are not turned loose to bite as they please but are held by leach [sic] and it becomes the mob's prerogative to move or else."

Collins's arguments proved similar to those of the South's white middle class that privileged the rule of law over a larger moral justice. Collins's attitude represented a significant body of Zonian thought that recognized the link between agitation over Southern segregation and Panamanian protests over inequality in the borderland: "Panamanians apparently share, along with the Irish and other small ethnic national groups, that bundle of complexes which is forever producing great oratory, meaningless martyrdom, and so little constructive action. Some outer force is always responsible for their lack of greatness. Here apparently the old who have become bitter at the lack of justice blame the U.S. The young who despair of ever obtaining the Golden Fleece blame the U.S. . . . The politicians who wish to turn attention from their own failings blame the U.S. And everybody speaks patriotically about national pride."[37]

While a minority, some liberal members of the U.S. community did press for more enlightened attitudes. As early as 1956, during the Montgomery bus boycott, one Zonian, calling himself "Fair Play," wrote, "Do not graft the thinking of Alabama onto the Canal Zone. . . . There are many . . . among us who feel that they [Panamanians of color] should be allowed into our schools—and in our commissaries, and service centers. This is certainly a new day and age." Yet despite these admirable sentiments, the Zone remained a Jim Crow enclave throughout its existence. Not until 1973 did the Zone Elks Clubs induct black members. Panamanians, with some exceptions, usually those of lighter hue or on the gold roll, rarely gathered in U.S. clubhouses or attended U.S. schools. In 1956 in order to avoid the possibility of future school integration, Zone officials created the "Latin American School" system. West Indian students who had formerly attended "colored" (later renamed "local-rate") schools adopted a Spanish curriculum. Zone officials acted as if Panama had forced this policy upon them, but in their internal memos they clearly applauded this initiative as a device to evade *Brown v. The Board of Education* and to ensure that "U.S.-rate" schools would remain overwhelmingly white.[38]

After the early 1960s the U.S. military finally began deploying African Americans to Panama in significant numbers. (The Panamanian government had long forbidden their presence.) Thereafter the children of black service personnel attended Balboa and Cristobal High Schools. But these children always constituted a small minority. The sons and daughters of Panama's upper classes attended U.S. high schools in the Zone, where they made up 5 percent of enrollment. For this privilege they paid tuition beyond the reach of ordinary (read: colored) Panamanians. Most of these students came from leading isthmian families, a reflection of Panama's own racial hierarchy that linked wealth and status to light skin and European heritage.[39]

The Role of Associations and Clubs in U.S. Identity Formation

Benedict Anderson defined the nation as a political community that is "imagined as both inherently limited and sovereign." Limitations of race and nationality certainly constructed strict boundaries around Zonian identity in Panama. Exclusive voluntary associations played a key role in fortifying this distinctiveness since construction days. Social organizations, such as the YMCA, the Masons, the Odd Fellows, the Moose Lodge, the Elks, and more patriotic clubs like the Veterans of Foreign Wars (VFW) and the American Legion, reinforced U.S. pride and sense of belonging for Americans living thousands of miles from home. Since most of these clubs boasted charters that limited membership to white U.S. males, they further defined U.S. identity as white, masculine, and heroic. After 1947, surrounded by locals whom many considered hostile, Zonians may have looked to these lodges as rallying sites to reify their patriotism and notions of national superiority. "Getting together like we did definitely made us feel more American and unified as a group," one veteran Zonian recalled.[40]

Zone clubs adorned their halls with flags, bunting, pictures of U.S. historic and sports heroes, and American battlefields. While a U.S. citizen in the States might join two or three fraternal organizations, it was quite common for Zonians to be members of twelve to fifteen different clubs. Zonian professionals formed more nuanced bird-watching, stamp, book, bottle, photography, and butterfly-collecting organizations that permitted women members.[41] High school and club football served to reinforce American martial values. More than any other sport, baseball enshrined U.S. identity, with its values of teamwork and organization seamlessly wed to individual heroism. The Panama Baseball League flourished on the Zone and included pro, semipro, and amateur players. The New York Yankees journeyed to Panama during the 1940s and 1950s for spring training and exhibition games that delighted Zonians, as their appearances connected the locals to the metropole. According to their own remembrances, Zonians liked to "keep busy," and their energetic participation in sports and hobbies were viewed by U.S. officials as healthy alternatives to the perceived depravity of Panama's sex and nightclub scene.[42]

During the postwar era Panama's two English-language dailies, the *Panama American* and the *Star and Herald*, also played a role in bolstering U.S. identity in the borderland. They devoted the bulk of their coverage to Zone news and important wire stories from the States, including stateside politics, the latest sports standings, and news of celebrities, crime, and fashion. The AP and UPI stories that U.S. editors chose for their editions also played a didactic role for the conservative Zone community: "Hapless Husband Loses Job, Gets Clobbered by Wife," "Narcotic Fiends Arraigned in Gotham," "Wife Asks for Divorce from Messy Mate Who Didn't Bathe," "Pervert Inquiry Gets Go Ahead in Senate," and "Black All-American Football Star Rapes White Woman."[43]

Murders and juvenile delinquency stories from the States as well as accounts of Panamanian violence and political corruption highlighted these editions. When reading such critiques of America and Panama, many Zonians perceived their enclave as a haven of normalcy in a degenerating world. "It was like a paradise down here—little crime, mostly small-scale stuff, no serious drug problems. Everyone looked out for one another's kids. We had a real sense of community, much stronger than back home," one U.S. resident mused. "The flag really meant something here. There was none of that anti-Vietnam [War] bullshit on the Zone," another recalled. In this way at least some Zonians perceived themselves as "more American" than their fellow citizens living in the States. Similarly British inhabitants in the Ulster borderland often saw themselves as more "British" than the Britons of London and Manchester.[44]

From as early as 1904 the enclave's founders expressed concerns over this need to preserve "American" identity in Panama. Early Zone officials established mandatory, extended U.S. vacations for their workers, first to maintain the health of whites living too long in the tropics, and second to ensure that Zonians did not "go native" from decades of living beside an alien and allegedly inferior culture. And so Zonians returned to the States every two years for three-month summer vacations. This arrangement also allowed children to accompany their parents and reconnect with U.S. social norms: "When we went back to the States every couple of summers, we caught up on the latest trends, the hottest records, the most popular TV shows and movies. Even stupid stuff like hula hoops and pet rocks. This happened too when we met new military kids just down from the States. They had all the latest stuff, coolest records and clothes. We were kind of backward in the Zone. Our TV was mostly reruns, and Zone theaters played a lot of older, classic movies."[45]

The Zone indoctrination of U.S. identity began early in U.S. schools. Teachers Herbert and Mary Knapp remembered Zone kids being so patriotic in the early 1960s that they reported their teachers to the principal if they forgot to start the Pledge of Allegiance or the singing of the national anthem. World War II and the cold war fortified the importance of such rituals and militarized fidelity. Zone boys and girls visited nearby U.S. military bases on Armed Forces Day, Army Day, and Flag Day and vied for "commander-for-a-day" honors, when one lucky boy would be appointed commander-in-chief of Southern Command for twelve hours. "Zone brats," as they called themselves, also had unique activities that delineated their special nature as "Zonian Americans." As boy and girl scouts, they trekked the Cruces Trail, retracing the steps of Henry Morgan's pirates during their 1671 sack of Panama. Their identification with Morgan, an earlier white Anglo conqueror of Panama, revealed where Zonian sympathies lay. After Christmas, Zonians held communal Christmas tree burnings, with some youths stealing other towns' dried-out trees (the Zone government imported them from the States) to increase the size and prestige of their own town's bonfire. U.S. children sang "Jungle Bells" at yuletide gatherings. Beginning in 1954 U.S. youngsters paddled in "ocean to ocean" *cayuco* races through the Canal. For several years U.S. officials barred Panamanian teams from participating in this regatta. After all, as every Zonian knew, the Canal was a U.S. possession, not a Panamanian waterway.[46]

Zonians of all ages paraded in and cheered for U.S. military processions every Fourth of July, Veterans Day, Armed Forces Day, and Victory over Japan Day. Such "all-American" commemorations connoted powerful links to the motherland. Like all colonial communities, the Zone embodied a truncated society where the need to connect to the metropolis and create corresponding institutions and cultural models waxed powerfully. The enclave's Theatre Guild typified this tendency, as it put on productions of *Oklahoma*, *South Pacific*, and *Camelot*.[47]

Postwar Zone clubhouses and cafeterias served up hearty doses of Americana: hamburgers, hot dogs, french fries, potato salad, baked beans, barbecued ribs, grilled cheese sandwiches, and an American chop suey–style dish called "Johnny Mazzotti." Zonians gathered at their clubhouse soda fountains to imbibe root beer floats and banana splits. Adults sat in company cafeterias where they drank Maxwell House and smoked Marlboros. While some Zonians grew to love Panamanian cuisine—*sancocho, ceviche, arroz con pollo, ropa vieja, lengua,* and *corbina*—the menus of the clubhouses and cafeterias remained solidly North American, with some concessions to the local fare. The same process obtained in everyday purchases of U.S. brands from the commissaries, such as Jell-O, Coca-Cola, Spam, Colgate, Heinz, Armour, Budweiser, and Ivory.[48]

U.S. women waited eagerly for "boat days," when a fresh supply of items and clothing arrived from New York. A cachet developed over these U.S. products on both sides of the border. Only the more adventurous Zonian women bought Latin American products in Panama. Chinese truck gardens in the Zone allowed the purchase of fresh fruits and vegetables without having to cross the border. These Asian fruit vendors even brought their wares to individual Zone neighborhoods. Besides health concerns over "unsafe" or "contaminated" Panamanian goods, the use of local products may have connoted a lack of patriotism, a rejection of Zonian identity and pride.[49]

Popular Culture and U.S. Imperial Identity in the Borderland

In the postwar era each Zonian community movie theater played an array of westerns, film noir, and the foreign adventure films. Although they arrived several years late to the enclave, these films kept Zonians apprised of appropriate comportment and clothing styles, of popular expressions, and body language prevalent in the States. Besides valorizing U.S. lifestyles, physical looks, and ideology, U.S. films denigrated the characteristics of "others": Africans, Asians, and Latin Americans. Immediately after the war one movie in particular struck a nerve with Panamanian sensibilities.[50]

In late 1947 RKO released *Riff-Raff*, a low-budget potboiler starring Pat O'Brien, Walter Slezak, and Ann Jeffreys. The film portrayed an American adventurer in Panama searching for riches in a jungle oil field. The movie's title referred to the local populace, hence Panama's protest against its release. According to the film, which was set in the capital and the interior (though actually shot on RKO's back lot), Panama contained a sewer of humanity filled with loose women, thieves, con men, corrupt police, and treacherous half-breeds. The movie also constituted vintage film noir, as revealed in its advertisements: "A Dame Who Can Double-Cross You for a Dime . . . and a Map Worth Millions—That's What Pat's on the Look-out for in Danger-Filled Panama!" A B-movie fantasy, *Riff-Raff* demonstrated that U.S. stereotypes about Panama had not changed much since construction days. The government and several nationalist groups protested the film when it was released with especially bad timing right after the December 1947 anti-U.S. base riots.[51]

The Jungle and U.S. Identity in the Borderland

While the Panamanian jungle had appeared forbidding during the construction era, postwar Zonians confidently conquered and transcended its mysteries and danger. Hunting in the isthmian forest and frequent expeditions to the San Blas islands, where Zonian engineers gave gifts and broke bread with Kuna chieftains while sitting around their thatched *bohíos* smoking pipes, typified this "Jungle Jim" persona embraced by hardier Zonians. Before the war most Zonians displayed their disdain for the jungle by avoiding or eradicating it. But after the war many took a hands-on approach in mastering the forest. This explained the rise of hunting, hiking, botanical, and bird-watching clubs, as well as increased exploratory expeditions.[52]

In 1950 a Zonian couple adopted a "baby Tarzan," a mixed-race orphan child abandoned in Chiriquí. In 1956 Zonians cheered when fifteen-year-old Frank Corrigan, who became lost in the bush near Fort Sherman, emerged unscathed after two days of "living off the land." Postwar Zone parents came to see their "jungle cubs" as uniquely adaptive to this formerly hostile terrain. A 1957 *Panama Canal Review* article spotlighted the trend, showing ten-year-old Ricky and eight-year-old Scott Williams of Ancon playing in mango trees, climbing a coconut palm to gather *pipas*, feeding lemurs and lizards, and slumbering in bed with a baby ocelot. In such a manner even Zonian tots had become "lords of the Panamanian jungle."[53]

The "Socialist Identity" of the Zonians?

One of the great ironies of the postwar Zonian was that, while pro-American, conservative, and anticommunist, he or she embraced a unique, near socialist lifestyle. The Canal Zone prohibited free enterprise and home ownership, two bedrock principles of U.S. capitalism. From the excavation days onward, the Zone government, in direct contravention to trends at home, provided a range of benefits and services for its workers unheard of in the mother country and found only in utopian novels like Edward Bellamy's *Looking Backward* or Aldous Huxley's *Brave New World*. As one former Zone policeman put it, "People down here were provided for from the womb to the tomb." An ex-GI described it this way: "The Canal Company did everything down here but wipe their asses." Zonians received lifetime employment, full pensions after thirty years of service, paid health insurance, a 25 percent tropical differential, generous vacation time (including paid transportation to the States and back for their families *and for their cars*), duty-free shopping in commissaries,

2.3. Zone trekkers traverse the isthmus. Such outdoor activities, besides providing diversion for U.S. citizens, embodied an important identity for many Zonians as "masters" of Panama's natural environment, a role Americans had prided themselves on since excavating the Continental Divide earlier in the century. Courtesy of the *Panama Canal Spillway* in the Panama Canal Museum Collection, George Smathers Library, University of Florida, http://ufdc.ufl.edu/pcm.

low subsidized rents and utilities, free maintenance and grass cutting for their homes, and, if desired, free burial in a government-run cemetery. A popular joke went, "How many Zonians does it take to change a lightbulb? Two: one to call the Maintenance Division, and the other to make the rum cokes." The Zone government actually did send West Indian workers to replace lightbulbs for its tenants and also provided them with low-cost, government-run gas stations, movie theaters, clubhouses, barbershops, bowling alleys, soda fountains, coffee shops, and swimming pools. The

Zone even had its own "socialist" currency: the commissary coupon books of $5, $10, and $15 that residents used in lieu of cash from 1905 to 1952.[54]

This socialist nature of the enclave stood out in stark relief during the cold war. Zonians were team players and joiners rather than individuals and innovators, the more admired and "authentic" American types. Furthermore U.S.-style political democracy never operated in the Zone, not that all socialist societies are undemocratic. Zonians did not elect their governors; the U.S. president appointed them. The Zone sent no representatives to Congress. Zonians did elect deputies to civic councils, but these were strictly advisory boards that made recommendations or forwarded complaints. Thus the Zone government operated for its U.S. citizens as a kind of benevolent dictatorship. Authorities issued decrees like papal edicts and would call workers on the carpet for drinking too much or having an affair with a coworker's wife. While U.S. conservatives back home condemned the all-embracing state as the archenemy of mankind, Zonians thrived under an all-controlling welfare state that most regarded as beneficent.[55]

This cradle-to-grave security also had its drawbacks. While comfortable, no Zonian could ever achieve great wealth, a prized goal in U.S. society. All Zonians were renters and thus lost the property appreciation and tax benefits of home ownership, a bulwark of the U.S. middle class. But Zonians enjoyed exemption from federal income taxes from 1914 to 1951.[56] They paid no property or sales taxes. Low rents and lack of monthly mortgage payments freed up more money for socializing and boat and car ownership, but it also incited a tendency to overspend and a "live for today" attitude typical of other postwar colonial societies. In general, the Zone produced an organization-type man and woman who fit in and did not rock the boat. At weekend bottle parties, Zonians cut loose, though more in the manner of John Cheever's suburban functionaries who needed to get bombed to escape their corporate conformity. Heavy drinking, indulgence in prostitutes by bachelors, married men, and teenagers, and schoolboy pranks by adults marked the lifestyle of many Zonians. Yet the majority held to law-abiding, church-going, family-oriented life. Crime rates within the U.S. community remained very low.[57]

Like that of their fellow colonists in Africa and Asia, Zonians achieved legendary status with their drinking. "'Gamboa Golf Club'—it's a big joke," one Zonian wife complained in 1945. "Two hundred members but only forty of them play golf. Gamboa Bar would be more like it!" In the late 1970s a canal pilot who logged more years of service than any in the history of the Canal, Joseph "Jody" Chamberlain, rode a bicycle from bar to bar after the Canal Zone Police arrested him for drunk driving in Balboa and took away his driver's license. That is, until he fell off his bike drunk one night and broke his neck. "After that I had to walk to the bars," he recalled with a smile, "wearing this metal brace around my neck." This inordinate drinking suggests a deeper anxiety about their status, a homesickness common to colonists, though most Zonians recall their tippling as great fun and socialization. This activity shocked more moderate Panamanian drinkers and painted the Zonians as a bunch of foolhardy drunks.[58]

Conformity and lack of democracy in the Zone also forged a society of complainers. Zonians "beefed, bitched, and gossiped" about everything, often because they felt powerless to change the policies that ruled their lives. Canal workers actually published a secret samizdat newspaper, the *Undertow*, to express their anger at company dictates and double-dealing. Zonians regarded the State Department with particular ire since they, unlike most Americans, were subjected to its decisions on a very personal basis. The U.S. embassy came in for special odium. The idea of pampered, "college boy" diplomats criticizing Zonian chauvinism outraged the blue-collar mechanics. "They always complained about our privileges, but you want to see the way they lived," a retired Zonian bristled. "And they loved to shop in *our* commissaries too, after all their complaints about how unfair they were to the Panamanians!"[59]

Another irony of U.S. identity in the Canal Zone was its distinctive yet qualified egalitarianism. While the overall structure of the Zone rested on racial segregation of West Indians, as well as chauvinism toward Latin Panamanians, within the white Zonian community a remarkable sense of equality obtained.[60] White bosses and blue-collar workers mingled on the Zone in a manner rare within companies on the mainland. The differences between the highest paid officials and the lowliest white worker proved much smaller than in the United States. Shipping agents and construction contractor families, such as the Corrigans, the Morelands, the Doyles, and the Homas, proved the exception. They made considerably more money than the average Zonian yet generally downplayed their fortunes in a community that frowned on "uppity" behavior.[61]

Yet in spite of this, class differences did exist among Zonians. The highly paid canal pilots and their powerful union constituted a kind of aristocracy. Most pilots kept to themselves, and many thought little of the average Zonian. High officials made more money than the majority of workers and wielded more social and political power, though blue-collar Zonians called their line of better housing in the gold towns "dead peckerhead row."[62] Edgardo Tirado, a former Canal policeman, described the social hierarchy of

2.4. Some privileged Panamanian students gained "hands-on" experience working in Zone offices under U.S. direction as part of the effort to promote shared understanding between the two communities and grant Panamanians more jobs in the U.S. enclave due to pressure from Panama and Washington. Courtesy of the *Panama Canal Spillway*, in the Panama Canal Museum Collection, George Smathers Library, University of Florida, http://ufdc.ufl.edu/pcm.

the Zone as a racialized Monopoly game whose object was to get to the site of the governor's mansion and other top residences: "How to get to the top of Ancon Hill: that was the name of the game down here. And you could get there. If you were a Zonian, born and bred here, you had the best shot. They were like the original aristocracy. If you were hired in the States and came here, with enough brains and ambition you could do it too. Even if you were an outsider, say a soldier, you could retire and come back to work for the Canal and work your way up. Even some Panamanians could at least *get on* the Hill. Some from good families were on the gold roll. Or they could marry a *gringa*, get U.S. citizenship, and end up there. So a lot of people had a shot of moving up. Except for one guy, *the West Indian*. No, the only West Indian on Ancon Hill was a maid or a *machetero* [landscaper]."[63]

Purportedly those Zonians who could trace their ancestors back to the "ditch diggers" held more status in clubs and social activities and on civic councils. But by the 1960s–1970s college and engineering degrees counted more toward a higher civil service grade than nepotism and connections. By the early 1960s only 15 percent of U.S. employees were enclave-born Zonians. "Local hires," the children of Zonians, still received consideration when it came to employment, but increasingly under the dictates of the 1955 treaty (not really implemented until the 1960s) the Canal hired more qualified, U.S.-born personnel and trained Panamanian apprentices for a greater share of the Canal's prized gold-roll jobs. In 1950 Panamanians held only 4 percent of these U.S.-rate jobs. But as a result of growing momentum in the apprentice program concession to Panama by 1979, the last year of the Zone, they constituted 38 percent of the U.S.-rate workforce. (Most of these promotions occurred during the last decade of the enclave under mounting political pressure from Washington and Panama.) This increased Panamanian hiring in the 1970s heightened Zonian anxieties over a metropole-designed "sellout" of their privileged status.[64]

Narrow Range of U.S. Borderland Contacts

The colonial structure of the Zone also informed the range of social contacts between the two national communities in the postwar era. In their encounters Zonians tended to interact with two very distinct groups of Panamanians. The first included those who worked in the service sector that catered specifically to North Americans: bartenders, waitresses, taxi drivers, shoe-shine boys, street vendors, car washers, maids, landscapers, prostitutes, club musicians, and sales clerks at borderland shops favored by Americans. The second group, at the other extreme, comprised wealthier officials and businessmen and those who sought contacts with Zonians due to the U.S.-Panamanian political alliance, the cachet of associations with Americans, and their own business with the Zone. Despite their frequent snubs and gaffes, Americans still fascinated many well-to-do Panamanians. Having themselves been educated in the United States, many of these elite Panamanians spoke English and rubbed elbows with the more educated Zonians and U.S. businessmen in joint clubs, such as the American Society of Panama, the Isthmian Historical Society, and the Panama Lions Club.

Tellingly, the narrow range of these U.S.-Panamanian social contacts failed to include the largest sectors of the borderland's population. These groups composed the majority of Panama's urban and rural poor, the nation's working class, yeoman farmers, and the small but rising middle class. These professionals, government workers, small businessmen, and students emerged as key players in Panamanian politics and its nationalist aspirations.[65] Zonians, however, rarely interacted with them. U.S. citizens felt most

2.5. U.S. officials and President Roberto F. Chiari of Panama (on right) at a country fair. Maintaining good relations with Panamanian officials and communities proved essential in the borderland's operation, though by the 1960s rising Panamanian nationalism hindered such efforts. Courtesy of the *Panama Canal Review* in the Panama Canal Museum Collection, George Smathers Library, University of Florida, http://ufdc .ufl.edu/pcm.

comfortable with Panamanian servants and with Panamanian elites who chose not to voice their nationalism too boisterously. The danger of maintaining such a narrow range of contacts occurred when Zonians mistakenly thought that *they*, unlike their fellow citizens in the United States, "understood" Panama. It turned out that outside of servants, employees, and upper-class acquaintances, few Zonians knew any "real," that is, majority Panamanians. They mostly interacted with dependent Panamanians who told them what they wanted to hear, hence the Zone's initial incomprehension over the 1964 riots. In the postwar era the isolation of colonists from native societies' main political currents was a common phenomenon. Britons in Kenya expressed shock at the sudden appearance of the Mau-Mau; similarly in 1954 French *colons* in Algeria could not understand why the people they were supposedly helping, whom the colons regarded as Francophile and loyal, had suddenly turned against them.[66]

Ceremonial Encounters

During the postwar era numerous Zonians did interact with Panamanians at various ceremonial functions, ostensibly as a means of promoting positive neighborly relations. U.S. citizens elected Carnaval queens from Balboa and Cristobal High Schools and from other towns in the Zone. Enthroned on ornate floats, these blonde, blue-eyed U.S. queens rode in the large Panamanian Carnaval processions down the Via España in the capital. During tense periods in U.S.-Panamanian relations, locals sometimes booed U.S. queens, ruining the purpose of their participation. Until the 1964 riots Panamanians celebrated the Fourth of July as an official holiday, an act that cemented their long-standing alliance with Washington, if not with the Zone. Panama's November 3 Independence Day remained an official holiday in the Zone until the enclave's demise in 1979. While important on a symbolic level, these commemorations involved limited socialization. Bands and contingents tended to keep to themselves and, after events ended, returned to their respective communities. Carnaval celebrations in Las Tablas, Chitre, and other towns proved the exception as Panamanians embraced Zonians and just about anyone who journeyed to the interior during these four days of bacchanalian revelry.[67]

A significant minority of Zonians regularly partook in Panamanian *ferias* (country fairs). U.S. citizens also attended religious festivals, such as the Feast of Cristo Negro in Portobello and Semana Santa (Holy Week) in Las Tablas. Zonians bought *molas* and other Panamanian or Kuna handicrafts and clothing. Zonian men enjoyed wearing Panamanian hats and *mantuno* or *guayabera* shirts during Carnaval or other Panamanian holidays. A few Zonian women even wore *polleras*, the ornate, traditional Panamanian dresses, at these events. During these festivals and holidays Zonians consumed numerous Panamanian drinks and dishes. But after these parties ended, Zonians returned to their everyday U.S. lifestyles. "They played at being Panamanians during Carnaval and at the ferias," one Panamanian remarked bitterly. "They

2.6. U.S. Zonians don their Carnaval apparel. With their participation in their own and Panama's Carnaval celebrations, Zonians both transcended these isthmian rituals and put their own twist on the cultural interactions of the borderland. Courtesy of the *Panama Canal Spillway*, in the Panama Canal Museum Collection, George Smathers Library, University of Florida, http://ufdc.ufl.edu/pcm.

would do it a lot in the Zone too at their parties, where we could never go to, but were for those who wouldn't even dirty their feet by coming into our country—except for their beer gardens and to buy lottery tickets. They would have 'Panamanian Night' like 'Mexican Night' during Cinco de Mayo or 'Bastille Night' on the 14th of July. But what did it mean? They were still just a bunch of gringos."[68]

This "commingling with the natives" during traditional festivals marked a common imperial behavior. On one level, Zonians exhibited their superiority as anthropological observers or mimickers at such events. To quote Mary Louise Pratt, they became "monarchs of all they surveyed."[69] Zonians, in effect, monitored or transcended these events and often remarked on the quaint and picturesque nature of the rituals. Wearing native costumes became a way of literally "taking on Panamanian skins" for brief periods or of exoticizing Panamanians. Natives emerged as fascinating subjects for study rather than as equals or intimates. "They were thirty-year tourists," Panamanian lawyer José Menéndez characterized the Zonians at these events: "Most people are tourists for two weeks. They visit a country, they buy the hats and T-shirts, and take pictures. And then they go back to the cruise ship and it's over. But a Zonian was here for thirty years—until he got his pension. But they were still just tourists in Panama. Though a lot of them thought they owned the place. Most tourists don't think they own the countries that they visit."[70]

2.7. A Panamanian folkloric dance presentation in the borderland town of Aguadulce. U.S. Zonians occasionally attended such events for diversion and to understand more about the indigenous culture of Panama, some of which they replicated at their own social events. Courtesy of the *Panama Canal Spillway*, in the Panama Canal Museum Collection, George Smathers Library, University of Florida, http://ufdc.ufl.edu/pcm.

It should be noted that several U.S. inhabitants enthusiastically participated in Panamanian folk festivals and in joint historical, archaeological, and literary societies. Panamanians expressed admiration and respect for these Americans who professed a sincere interest in Panama's history and culture. Their encounters at these events also constituted the "contact zones" that Pratt has written on extensively. Moreover at ferias and carnavales North Americans found rural Panamanians friendlier than their urban brothers. *Interioranos* had little day-to-day contact with the Zone and lacked any personal or politically indoctrinated animosity toward the enclave. Variations on Panamanian national identity also operated in the rural provinces of the republic. In the far western state of Chiriquí, for instance, locals still celebrate a distinct regional identity as cattlemen and farmers, proudly fly the Chiriquí green and red flag, and complain about government corruption in the capital almost as much as the Zonians did.[71]

Fallen Zonians

The term *gone bushy* did not simply refer to an individual Zonian living in the interior like a *cholo* (an Indian or darker mestizo); it also encompassed taking on aspects of Panamanian lifestyle and perceived vices, such as wearing disheveled clothing or even marrying or living with a Panamanian woman. Entering into such relationships challenged cherished notions of U.S. identity. Since the Zone's founders viewed miscegenation as the root of Panamanian "degeneracy," early racist U.S. officials frowned on such unions. Housing authorities even established a special section for families of mixed marriages, either U.S.-Panamanian or U.S.–Latin American, in Ancon near Curundu that some Zonians referred to as "Squaw Hill." Initially Americans called their fellow citizens who married local women "squaw men." Curundu Flats, with its large population of civilian DOD workers, also housed many international and, in the eyes of at least some Zonians, interracial marriages. A common Zonian joke on this subject went, "Just because she's dark and she answers the door, doesn't mean she's the maid."[72]

John Morales, who had a Mexican American father and a Colombian grandmother, recalled growing up in a mixed-race "ghetto" in Curundu Flats derisively called "Jungle Glen." He remembered being insulted by fellow schoolchildren as a "spic," "Mexican," and a "greaser." At the same time he felt that the Canal Zone Police targeted him because he "looked Panamanian." Morales emphasized, "The Canal Zone was tough on us. We were treated like crap growing up here by the white kids," who frequently called him *bito*, a common epithet of Zonian youth, short for *chombito*, or "little nigger." Morales also noted that many of the most racist comments directed at Panamanians often came paradoxically from "mixed-race" children. These *panagringos* or *panahuchies*, as they were called, chose a U.S. identity, the signifier of power over a subordinated Panama. They thus reified their position within the U.S. community, especially during riots when a "Which side are you on?" mentality pervaded the borderland.[73]

By the 1970s international marriages became more accepted on the Zone, although the lighter skin and class status of the Panamanian partner eased social assimilation. Angela Lee came from an old Zonian family and married Frank Azcarrga, who was fair-skinned, the scion of a successful Panamanian musical family whose father, Lucho, was the favorite musician of the Zonians. Still, Angela faced some initial discrimination and coldness from some of her fellow Zonians for her marriage choice. English fluency aided social acceptance for Panamanian spouses. Americans who married *cholitas*, mixed-race Indian women from the countryside who barely spoke English, lacked the acceptance that Zonian men with middle-class, local wives enjoyed. Just how far tolerance extended often remained a mystery to the couples themselves. In 1947 Clarence McNeece married a Panamanian schoolteacher and always assumed that his fellow Americans accepted her until he overheard several of them chuckling about "his *cholita*," not realizing McNeece was sitting in a nearby toilet stall.[74]

Zonian Criminals

Criminality also marked a key threat to the U.S. borderlanders' hallowed identity. Such comportment ran counter to the Zonians' view of themselves as a moral, law-abiding people, in contrast to the "licentious" Panamanians. On May 3, 1943, Charles Gordon Scales and Carl Lee Johnson, two Americans hoping to cash in on the easy money of the World War II bonanza, broke into the Lux Theater on the Panamanian side of the borderland. There they beat two Panamanian janitors to death with an iron bar. The movie theater's safe that they cracked contained one dollar, not the $5,000 that the thieves had imagined. The Lux murder case ignited a storm of anti-Americanism in Panama during the crucial wartime alliance, when hundreds of U.S. warships transited the canal. Outraged Panamanian crowds surged outside police headquarters during Scales and Johnson's transfer to the Carcel Modelo and demanded, "Let us have them!" and "Give us the gringos!"[75]

In 1934 twenty-year-old Charles Scales and twenty-seven-year-old Carl Johnson came to the isthmus as U.S. soldiers. After he finished his hitch, Johnson went to work for the Zone in the Mechanical Division in Balboa. Scales, who had a criminal record for robbery before he joined the military, failed the Canal Company's background check. Upon his honorable discharge in 1940, he worked as a bartender in Panama. "Scales was definitely the worst of the two," a Zonian woman who knew both men recalled. "He was the leader, and Johnson was more of a follower." Scales lived in the Zone illegally, bunking in the apartments of various Zonian friends, including Johnson. Since he did not work for the Canal, Scales did not technically qualify as a Zonian, though he befriended many and spent much of his free time in the Zone.[76]

In 1942 Scales and Johnson started burglarizing buildings and apartments in the Zone and nearby Panama City. They led a gang of Canal Zone youths that also included Panamanian lookouts. The wartime blackout in Panama aided Scales and Johnson in their nighttime break-ins. World War II Panama offered easy pickings for robbers, who could net thousands in cash sticking up a single GI-favored nightclub. After a sensational trial in which the two partners turned on one another, the Panamanian court convicted both of first-degree murder and sentenced them each to twenty years, the maximum penalty in Panama, on the island penal colony of Coiba.[77]

Scales, Johnson, and their gang constituted the worst example of Zonians gone bad. Their community immediately recognized the import of the case. The Zonian journalist Brodie Burnham wrote, "Everybody appreciates that there are a few bad apples in every crop so there are bad actors in every country and nationality, but if Carl Lee Johnson and Jack Scales had to go around burglarizing places—and especially if they had to be so stupid and clumsy as to bash in people's brains—why the devil couldn't they have done it in their own United States or at least in the Canal Zone instead of crossing the line here and causing horror and sorrow in Panama and also embarrassing all the rest of us U.S. citizens." In his commentary Burnham exposed his own callousness toward Panamanians. By his account these savage murders to eliminate witnesses were more acts of stupidity than inhumanity.[78]

Scales and Johnson continued to embarrass the Zonians. Scales and a convicted Nicaraguan murderer escaped from Coiba in a daring episode straight out of Henri Charrière's *Papillon*. The desperados built a makeshift raft and braved shark-infested waters to reach the Contreras islands. They lived as castaways until picked up by a passing motor launch that alerted Panamanian authorities, who arrested the escapees and returned them to Coiba.[79] Scales and Johnson exited the scene in a blaze of gunfire if not glory. On September 28, 1946, the two Americans together with two Latin American prisoners launched a revolt against their guards, who shot all four convicts dead. Many Zonians had trouble swallowing the official version of the uprising. "They were marked men after what they did to those Panamanians at the Lux Theater," a Zonian recalled. No U.S. official questioned the inquest as they were no doubt relieved to see the convicts gone and the scandal over the Lux murders buried with them.[80]

The Lux Theater "massacre," as one Panamanian newspaper dubbed it, recalled the licentiousness of the "degenerate" or "fallen white," a disturbing figure in European colonies in Africa and Asia. Other "wayward" whites operated along the borderland. Leo J. Peltier, a U.S. citizen of Canadian birth and a former GI, broke into a number of homes on the isthmus following his 1944 dishonorable discharge there. A frequent guest at Gamboa Penitentiary, Peltier distinguished himself with his many escapes from Zone and Panama jails, his morphine addiction, robberies, check forgery, and generally schizo-phrenic behavior. Still, his white skin and "all-American looks" enabled him to run wild on the borderland for several years. He developed a knack for fooling Panamanian police with his expired U.S. military IDs, Spanish flu-ency, and his name-dropping of U.S. officials in an era when North Ameri-cans still overawed many Panamanians.[81]

More common examples of the "fallen white" in Panama were those U.S. citizens who bummed around the borderland, took up with Panamanian women, and, perhaps worst of all, refused to work. Panamanians referred to such individuals as *cholos blancos* (white Indians). The official report on one such fellow in 1950, an ex-serviceman, Chester Myers, read, "Following his termination, Myers was not gainfully employed in any capacity but continued to reside in Colón with a Negro woman." The Zone Police arrested Myers for vagrancy, begging, and loitering. They made repeated efforts to get him out of Panama, where he created an embarrassment by traipsing about the Caribbean entrance to the Zone with his outstretched palm, "behaving like a Panamanian."[82]

During the 1950s–1970s more Myers-like bohemians challenged the work ethic of the Zone. First U.S. beatnik travelers arrived in the late 1950s, followed by hippies in the 1960s–1970s. Some of these individuals passed through the borderland as part of their longer treks across Central America. They all posed a sticky problem for U.S. authorities, for while the Zone en-thusiastically welcomed U.S. tourists with fixed arrival and departure dates, bohemian and hippie troubadours threatened Zonian identity. These un-wanted borderlanders appeared like visitors from another planet, not the United States of Zonian imagination.[83]

The 1964 Uprising: Crisis of Borderland Identities

By the 1970s the proud imperial identity of the Zonians that had once domi-nated the borderland degenerated into an image of victimhood. This devolu-tion began with the cataclysmic 1964 riots. Larger actors and events impacted this debacle besides the decades of resentment in Zonian-Panamanian social relations. But the attitude of superiority by the enclave's inhabitants certainly helped fuel the formation of a militant *Panamanian* identity so evident in the student and activist leaders—and also in the thousands of working-class Panamanians who joined the fray. By their very mission, structure, and day-to-day operations imperial borderlands facilitate such oppositional iden-tity formation. On the political front, Zonian hatred of the conciliatory U.S.

ambassador Joseph S. Farland influenced his resignation in August 1963. The Zonians' earlier odium toward Governor William S. Carter, nicknamed "Flashbulb Willie" for his propensity to be photographed with Panamanian officials, also played a role in his resignation in early 1962. In contrast, Panamanians praised Farland and Carter for their willingness to engage in binational dialogue to bridge the gap between the two borderland communities.[84]

Farland supported the 1963 Kennedy-Chiari flag accord, in which the United States agreed to fly the Panamanian flag beside the U.S. flag at fifteen designated sites within the enclave. Flags proved powerful symbols of identity and patriotism for both sides. So many U.S. flags flew in the Zone, some 112 official ones, not to mention hundreds of private banners, that the Kennedy administration sought to limit their numbers first before it would honor the 1963 accord. Zone officials removed the U.S. flag from its lone pole at Balboa High School, as it was not one of the fifteen designated joint sites; they did so over Christmas vacation, hoping its absence would go noticed.[85]

But Balboa High represented a powerful cultural touchstone for patriotic Zonians. The school comprised a key locus of historical memory, where graduations, football victories, and ROTC rituals abounded. Stalwart U.S. children and their parents refused to sit still for a vacant flagpole or, perhaps worse, the shame of a foreign flag waving beside Old Glory. Indoctrinated into an uncompromising imperial identity for generations, U.S. students needed little encouragement to shinny up the pole (officials had removed the lanyards) and hoist the colors, in violation of the Kennedy-Chiari accords. They then maintained a "sacred vigil," along with their parents and supporters, beside the flag throughout the nights of January 7–8 to ensure that no U.S. authorities or Panamanians removed their banner. The nearby Elks, VFW, and American Legion sent hamburgers, coffee, and sandwiches to sustain the teenagers, who sang patriotic tunes into the night.[86]

Word spread quickly to neighboring Panama, only a thousand yards away, of the violation of the flag accord. On January 9 equally patriotic Panamanian students from the Instituto Nacional gathered at the border. The location of this highly nationalist school, called *el nido de águilas* (the nest of eagles), so close to the Fourth of July boundary heightened its fervid response. Instituto students age twelve to eighteen bore their school's unique Panamanian flag, with its crest and motto, like a sacred relic to the contested flag site. Their fathers had carried this same flag in the anti-U.S. base riots in 1947. Arguments continue to this day as to who started the scuffle when Panamanian youths attempted to raise their flag. Controversy even simmers as to whether Panamanian students had already torn their admittedly aged flag before it arrived at the school or whether U.S. students ripped it down its center. Canal Zone Police deliberately stood aside throughout the encounter instead of intervening to put an end to this unnecessary showdown. Through their inaction they revealed where their sympathies lay. The absence of the Canal Zone governor, Robert Fleming, who attended hearings in Washington, contributed to the indecisiveness of U.S. officials on the scene.[87]

Roughed up in the brawl that ensued and humiliated at their failure to hoist their colors, angry Instituto Nacional students carried their now "desecrated" flag back to Panama. The youths shouted slogans that proclaimed Panama's sovereignty over the Zone. When confronted by Zone Police, the youths hurled some trashcans and stoned Zonian cars and buildings. Rumors swirled throughout the nearby borderland streets of Chorrillo and Calidonia that the gringo police and Zonian rowdies had roughed up the children and trampled the republic's banner.[88]

In many ways, the terms *student* and *riots* in the commonly ascribed "Panamanian student riots" are misnomers because the event quickly escalated into a full-scale uprising against both the Zone and some elements of the Panamanian business community. The most striking features in the photographic record of the next four days are the numbers and ages of the participants. Overwhelming numbers of *adult* Panamanians, not just students, took part in the violence, most of them from the poorer barrios of the capital and of Colón. The scale of participation eventually included some thirty thousand. Had their numbers been only a few hundred or even a few thousand, the Canal Zone Police might have handled them, but the scale of Panamanian fury required SouthCom's commander, Lieutenant-General Andrew O'Meara, to deploy the fourteen thousand soldiers of the U.S. Army garrison, declare martial law in the Zone, and begin evacuating military dependents to the United States. The six-week-old Lyndon Baines Johnson administration suddenly confronted its first foreign policy crisis with an all-night meeting in the White House war room that included the decision to dispatch a carrier task force and marine landing detachment to Panama.[89]

Earlier that night, at 7:30, Canal Zone police shot and killed their first Panamanian demonstrator, Ascanio Arosemena, a twenty-year-old student at the Escuela Profesional. At that moment, Richard Koster wrote, "the twentieth century caught up with the Isthmus of Panama." By the time Arosemena died, Panamanian protesters had already set fire to the Ancon Laundry, the railway station, and the U.S. District Court judge's home and were rapidly moving on to the Pan American Airways and Braniff buildings, long symbols of U.S. corporate power. Panamanian snipers on their side of the border peppered GIs for the next few nights. Angry Panamanians tore down or mounted sections of the Canal Zone fencing and erected their flags on lamp-posts and barbed-wire. These flags, punctured with bullet holes and smeared with fresh blood, erased all doubts as to the strength of Panamanian nationalism after six decades of occupation. In all, twenty-one Panamanians and four U.S. soldiers died in the next four days; hundreds more suffered serious wounds on both sides. Many more might have died had the U.S. Army not exercised restraint in its use of live ammunition. Nonetheless fires and rifle shells reduced sections of the Zone-Panama borderland to pockmarked ruins.[90]

The funeral cortege of the Panamanian victims at the conclusion of the uprising marked one of the most stirring events in Panamanian history. An estimated one quarter of Panama City, upward of 100,000 Panamanians, attended the mass funerals. Unsympathetic Zonians noted that six of the twenty-one Panamanian "martyrs" died from asphyxiation at the Pan American Building fire, while presumably looting and vandalizing the facility. Official autopsy reports support this cause of death, but Zonians refused to accept the notion that vandalism of U.S. property could in any way constitute legitimate national resistance. It is also possible that some Panamanians died in the Pan Am Building after entering it to snipe and hurl projectiles at U.S. troops. At least two of the twenty-one Panamanian "martyrs" died from bullet wounds whose caliber was not in the U.S. arsenal, suggesting that they may have succumbed to stray Panamanian bullets. Several Panamanians insist that Zonian civilian vigilantes could have killed them. Some Zonians who lived near the contested border did man the fence with rifles and pistols to protect their homes.[91]

Initially the majority of Americans in the United States rallied around the flag and supported the U.S. troops and residents in the beleaguered Zone. These stalwarts appeared to be defending the Canal against nationalist and communist fanatics. But as more news reports filtered back from the borderland, Zonian students and their parents came in for criticism. Reporters labeled them the instigators of the riots for their long chauvinistic record in Panama and for the fiasco at Balboa High. As a result of the uprising, many Americans learned for the first time of the privileged lifestyle of U.S. residents on the isthmus, their segregated clubs and school system, and the strong, racially charged jingoism of their loudest spokesmen. The erosion of U.S. domestic support for the Zonians began with the 1964 uprising and would end on the Senate floor in April 1978, when legislators ratified the Carter-Torrijos accords.[92]

Other crises of borderland identity sprang from the uprising. In February 1964 the Zone government announced it would begin hiring forty Panamanian candidates for the Canal Zone Police to improve community relations and prevent such episodes from erupting again. Arthur Payne, a Zone administrator, and Richard Meehan, a Canal Zone cop, took the Zone government to court to prevent the hiring of foreign nationals as "first-class" policemen on the all-U.S., and nearly all-white, Canal Zone force. When mostly West Indians stepped forward to apply for these jobs (which paid U.S.-rate salaries), Joaquín Beleño, a Panamanian novelist and former champion of the imprisoned Lester Greaves, condemned the applicants as collaborators and traitors to the nation who would no doubt turn their guns on their fellow Panamanians while in U.S. uniform. Beleño accused criminal and low-life West Indians of taking advantage of the riots to loot Panamanian stores while real Panamanian heroes fought the U.S. military. These allegations alarmed West Indians in the Zone, fearful that they might face the ire of Latin Panamanians if and when Washington withdrew from the isthmus.[93]

The U.S. Fifth District Court in New Orleans eventually upheld the Zone government's right to hire whomever it pleased as policemen, regardless of nationality. This same court had dismissed Zonian Gerald Doyle's earlier lawsuit against President Eisenhower's decision in 1960 to fly a Panamanian flag in the enclave. Forty Panamanians were soon hired by the Canal Zone Police, to the dismay of many Zonians as well as their fellow officers, though the fact that most were West Indians, whom many Zonians saw as allies, facilitated their integration into the force. Among the Panamanians who joined was Ricardo Royo, a graduate of Balboa High and the younger brother of a future Panamanian president, Aristides Royo.[94]

On the eve of the Panamanian presidential election in May 1964, the most bizarre identity aftershock of the riots occurred. A rumor spread throughout the capital that the candidate and favorite, Arnulfo Arias, had secretly married Jane O'Meara, the teenage daughter of U.S. SouthCom commander General O'Meara, portrayed in local dailies as the bloodthirsty killer of twenty-one innocent Panamanians. The idea that this former Panamanian president and ardent nationalist had married a despicable gringa, daughter of a murdering yanqui general, threw the capital into a frenzy of *bochinche*, the Panamanian term for scandalous gossip. The newspaper *Guerra*, financed by Arias's presidential opponent, Marco Aurelio "the Rifleman" Robles, even published a photostat copy of the marriage license.[95]

While Arias vehemently denied this smear, the fact that it held such credence for several days spoke to the fevered state of identity crisis that swept the borderland in the wake of the revolt. U.S. military officials repudiated the forgery: General O'Meara's daughter had married no one. In any case Arnulfo lost the election, probably through fraud. The whole imbroglio touched on a sensitive subject in the wake of the riots: that of elite Panamanian connections to Americans. For several months oligarchs avoided entering the Zone for golf, cocktails, or fishing trips with Zonian and U.S. military friends. Any association with Americans after the riots incurred political suicide and the possibility of physical assault.[96]

Bishop Mark McGrath of Panama, the son of a Zonian father and upper-class Panamanian mother, came forward to condemn U.S. actions following the riots. McGrath, who had always occupied a precarious position as the borderland's foremost religious leader and panagringo, came out forthrightly on the Panamanian side of the conflict. Thereafter he always referred to himself as Marco McGrath and gave speeches and interviews only in Spanish (though with a heavy U.S. accent that many Panamanians disliked). "Even our bishop was half gringo back then!" one recalled with a smile.[97]

Panamanian national identity clearly coalesced and strengthened in the crucible of this borderland blood feud. Panamanian scholars and activists had long repudiated the popular Zonian notion of "the black legend," that Washington had "created" Panama through its support in 1903 for secession from Colombia. According to this chauvinistic view, Panamanians held no legitimacy as a people, when in reality the historical formation of a regional and cultural identity on the isthmus went back as far as the Spanish Empire. This process included many rebellions, and even a period from 1855 to 1886 when Panama ruled itself as a state within the Colombian federation. The celebration of Panamanian identity based on its unique rural culture, history, music, cuisine, and folkways, all linked to the natural beauty and geography of the isthmus, was central to the patriotic consciousness of virtually all Panamanians. The uprising against the Zone in 1964 deeply reified the wellsprings of this identification with a beleaguered and heroic nation.[98]

Imperial Coda: Zonians as Victims?

In January 1965 the Johnson administration began a twelve-year negotiation process with Panama that led eventually to the Carter-Torrijos treaties of 1977. Johnson started 1965 off on a bad note for the Zonians. He cut their tropical differential pay from 25 to 15 percent.[99] In 1972 General Omar Torrijos's military regime stunned the Zonians further by enacting a law that proclaimed all those born in the Canal Zone, regardless of parentage, to be

Panamanian citizens. This law affected hundreds of Zonians and threw into disarray the whole issue of national identity along the borderland. The law required that those Americans born in the Zone apply for Panamanian *cedulas* (identification cards) and Panamanian passports. Without these documents, Americans born in the Canal Zone could not leave Panama from the national airport.[100]

"We were all screwed up there for a while," a Zonian recollected. "I mean, we all knew we were Americans, but this law seemed to say we were also Panamanians, which went against everything we'd been taught since we were babies. I thought it was kind of cool to be a citizen of both countries. But if you admitted that to the older Zonies, they'd think you were Benedict Arnold." This issue of citizenship remained a serious matter for U.S. borderlanders. Prior to congressional legislation in 1937 that ended a technical dispute, children born in the Canal Zone to one or more American parents were U.S. nationals but not U.S. citizens until they completed State Department applications that confirmed their full citizenship status. Torrijos had resurrected these old fears from the early decades of the enclave regarding the identity of those born on the U.S. side of the line.[101]

Preoccupied with Southeast Asia and global grand strategy in its first term, the Nixon administration moved to settle the Canal's disposition in its second. The Kissinger-Tack accord in 1974 jump-started negotiations over the Canal's transfer. Zonian identity, once so strong and self-confident, buckled under the twin assaults of weakening domestic support and General Torrijos's bewildering tactics. Torrijos refused to accept the U.S. annuity check of $2.3 million for the use of the Zone, claiming that to take these funds legitimized U.S. control. Beginning in 1972 he held elections among the Panamanian inhabitants of the Zone (mostly West Indians) for representatives from the enclave, now known as "the tenth province." Such acts further complicated identity conflicts in an increasingly uncertain borderland.[102]

Zonians felt starkly isolated as their own government appeared to be moving against them. With the triumph of the Vietnamese, Angolan, and Mozambiquean independence movements in 1975, decolonization gathered steam and the Canal Zone looked more than ever like a white elephant. While many Zonians derided Torrijos's stratagems, community anxiety rose. This took the form of organized Zonian and congressional efforts to portray Torrijos as a communist due to his friendship with Fidel Castro. On the social level, the stress of living under constant denunciation may have played itself out through a decline in what many Zonians viewed as the moral values of the enclave. In the 1970s overindulgence in alcohol and drug use reached such a level that special congressional committees met to investigate these problems. For the first time reports of wife-swapping and swingers parties, fairly common in the British colonies and in some U.S. communities in this era, surfaced within the Zone. The counterculture of the 1960s–1970s had finally penetrated the enclave. Though still a minority, more Zonian teenagers smoked marijuana, wore long hair, and "turned off" from their parents. Thus the perceived moral rectitude of the enclave appeared to crack under pressure. "If the way you've always lived is going to end tomorrow, then why follow the rules anymore?" one Zonian recalled. "People were very depressed and bitter, especially with Jimmy Carter."[103]

In early 1977 the new Carter administration reinvigorated talks with Panama to break the Gordian knot of sovereignty. The previous year, Assistant Secretary of the Army Victor Veysey had told the Ford administration not to worry about the Zonian unions after a wage freeze because the canal workers were "all gutless sheep." Partly in reaction to these comments, and in response to worries over a "sellout" of the Canal, the waterway's pilots initiated sick-outs and slowdowns that backed up the lines in front of the Canal and cost shipping companies millions. But after four months they ended the sick-outs. Meanwhile treaty negotiations with Torrijos intensified. Zonians gathered in support of the pilot strikers, wearing T-shirts that read "Gutless Sheep" and "Baa-baa!" While comical, such demonstrations testified to the Zonians' overall weakness. As company men and bureaucrats dependent on the federal government, they made poor revolutionaries. The more fruitful strategy of lobbying Congress was where Zonians made strong inroads. Garnering broad conservative support, they nearly derailed the treaty in the Senate.[104]

Borderland Betrayal and Imperial Nostalgia

A sense of betrayal informed all Zonian resistance at this juncture. While some, such as Canal policeman William Drummond, tried to mobilize their community for popular protest, their efforts fizzled. Unlike European imperiums in Africa and Asia, the Canal Zone was never a settler colony; it constituted more of a strategic borderland like Gibraltar or Suez. All Zonians were renters. As such, they lacked the strong economic attachment to the enclave that plantation owners in Asia and Africa held toward their colonial homes. While a few Zonians created the Zone Liberation Organization (ZLO), it was more a propaganda device than a movement. No colonial terrorist organization such as the Organization of the Secret Army (OAS) in French Algeria emerged on the U.S. side of the border.[105]

Still, the 1978 treaty ratification hearings held Zonians spellbound. Every office and workshop in the enclave carried the coverage by television or radio, as did every *casa* and bodega on the other side of the line. The final vote and victory for the treaty on April 18, 1978, let the air out of the Zonians' last hopes. Simultaneous groans and cheers erupted on opposite sides of the Avenue of the Martyrs. A few bitter-enders spray-painted "Canal Zone Forever!" and "ZLO!" on building walls, but the Zonians knew the verdict was in: they had lost.[106]

Almost overnight a deep nostalgia enveloped the Zonian psyche that persists to this day. "In Memoriam" death notices for the Zone filled the *Canal Record*, a local periodical.[107] Some Zonians wore protest T-shirts to work that proclaimed in block letters "ZONIAN—ENDANGERED SPECIES." Most went about making preparations for their exodus; others devoted themselves to the fighting for treaty-enabling legislation that eventually granted most U.S. and many West Indian workers generous benefits, pension increases, and jobs in the federal system. The years 1978–82, when the Canal Zone Police finally disbanded, ending juridical protection for U.S. citizens, witnessed a steady flight of Zonians to Florida, Texas, California, Alabama, and Arkansas. A whole way of life evaporated before tear-filled eyes. According to Gorgas Hospital reports, numerous Zonians suffered depression and anxiety throughout this period. Divorced Zonians or those having affairs with others did not know where they stood or the eventual disposition and destination of their lovers and children. U.S. schoolteachers noticed the strain on Zone kids, who seemed listless and distracted in class.[108]

Nostalgia held powerful sway in the borderland's last days. On May 24, 1979, Zonians celebrated (or mourned) at one of their final formal dinners at the governor's mansion on Ancon Hill. Organizers called the party "A Sentimental Journey." Among the dishes served were Roosevelt Fruit Punch, Goethal's Chichita, DeLesseps Paté de Foie Gras, Stevens Assorted Raw Vegetables, Gaillard Baked Ham, and Panama Railroad Tropical Fruit Cup. Zonians dressed in turn-of-the-century Edwardian clothing.[109] To the music of "There's No People Like Show People" Zonians sang, "There's No People Like Zone People."[110] When the United States lowered its flag at numerous sites throughout the enclave on the night of September 30, 1979, Zonians gathered together and watched, crestfallen, almost unbelieving, especially when the giant flag came down on Ancon Hill, long the symbol of U.S. empire in the borderland.[111]

A major concern for departing Zonians centered on their dead. They mounted a concerted effort to exhume the remains of 1,300 Zonians in Mount Hope Cemetery, one of the territories about to be transferred to Panama, to Corozal, where the American Battle Monuments Commission operated a U.S. overseas cemetery. Zonians voiced fears that Panamanians would not maintain Mount Hope to "American standards" or might even desecrate their ancestors' graves. For generations the Zone had buried its whites in "gold" cemeteries and its West Indians and Panamanians in "silver" ones, carrying borderland segregation literally to the grave. Zonians published repeated notices in the *Canal Record* about the deadlines for exhumation: "Act quickly if you want to have your dear departed ones moved on time!"[112]

Summary

Not all Zonians retreated to the United States. Some remained, finding positions in the new Panama Canal Commission that operated as a joint U.S.-Panamanian agency until December 31, 1999, when Panama assumed complete control over the Canal. Many Zonians who moved early to the United States, not wishing to give up their former privileges and live under Panamanian law, regretted their decision. They tried to return when they learned that life in the new Panama Canal Area was not as bad as they had imagined. Hundreds of U.S. citizens continued to work in Panama as DOD employees, maintaining bases, facilities, and schools in Panama until the end of 1999.[113] Scores of retired Zonians live in Panama today and have accepted the change of sovereignty more graciously than the exiles in Florida, Texas, and California. Many have Panamanian spouses, mixed-nationality children, and close isthmian friends. Refugees in the States, however, still express an odd combination of nostalgia and bitterness over what they call "the old Zone." When entering Winn-Dixie supermarkets for the first time, several of them showed their commissary ID cards to security guards out of habit, to show that they were authorized to shop there, that they were not non-Zone-employed Panamanians.[114]

At their annual reunions, these exiles temporarily resuscitate the Zone with drink, song, Panamanian costumes, and isthmian folk dances. Retirees purchase Zone memorabilia, molas, guayabera shirts, pollera dresses, and Zone police souvenir mugs from convention sales events. Incongruously, now that they no longer live in Panama, retired Zonians embrace Panamanian dress, music, and material culture more than many had in the republic. They fortify old friendships with ceviche and cuba libres made with the Panamanian brands Seco Herrerano and Ron Cortez. Couples waltzed to the music of Lucho Azcarrga, the Zonians' favorite musician, who always played "Happy Days Are Here Again" at these reunions. But the magic of the old borderland is gone.[115]

For those Zonians and their children who live in Panama today, sentimentality for the enclave still intrudes on occasions. The borderland defined them and their personas. After 1999 many Zonians in Panama bought houses in their old communities where they had lived as children. Pride of place and accomplishment, the luxuriant fauna and flora in their gardens, draws them to familiar climes. Lori (Kent) Gibson and her husband, Jay, both from old Zone families, have Panamanian friends and participate in joint community programs like the annual Cayuco Regatta. But Lori admitted to a certain defensiveness and sensitivity over her Zonian ancestry. While talking to a Panamanian friend, she found herself reacting sharply to an offhand criticism of the Zonians. "You know," she told her friend, "I'm sick and tired of all this stuff about the Zonians. The thing that makes you mad is that you can be a Chiricano, you can be a Chorrerano, you can be from Bocas or from Veraguas, but the one thing you can never be is a Zonian!" Lori's Panamanian friend tried to calm her. Lori admitted being surprised at herself, wondering "where all that came from." But elements of her childhood identity remain. "Why would I want to move to Florida and become a nobody," she mused, "just another American, when here [in Panama] I'm somebody!" With these words she summed up the charm of Zonehood for generations of U.S. citizens along the "fifth frontier."[116]

RACE AND IDENTITY IN THE

ZONE-PANAMA BORDERLAND

West Indians Contra Todos

Albert Brown remembered fishing one afternoon as a boy in Lake Gatun in the early 1960s when three Southern GIs who had been drinking in the nearby Tarpon Club confronted him. Brown fished not just for pleasure but to help feed his West Indian family, who lived in harsh circumstances and appreciated his catch as a main course for dinner. "Look what we got here—a little nigger fisherman!" the GIs laughed as they approached Brown. Brown still remembers the fear that froze him momentarily until the soldiers were upon him. They stole his pail of fish, lifted him up, and threw him into the lake. When he tried to climb out, they just kept flinging him back in and laughed uproariously. After ten or twelve dunks, the GIs became bored with their bullying and staggered away. Brown remembered lying on the bank of the lake in tears, exhausted and trembling. He felt lucky to be alive. When he told his parents about the incident, they warned him not to mention it to Zone authorities or they might all get "into trouble." Brown later grew up to be an activist and a minister as well as an employee for the Defense Department and for the Canal Authority archives. Despite this assault and numerous other affronts, he also recalled feeling "safer" in the Zone than he did in Panama City, where in the tougher barrios, mestizo-majority Panamanians would taunt him and even hurl rocks and sticks at him, for reasons that, as a youth, he could never understand.[1]

One of the central clashes of race and identity along the Zone borderland pitted the black West Indian against the white Zonian. But the animosity of Latin Panamanians toward the Antillean community and its response played a key role in these racial and ethnic divides as well. Borderlands such as the one encompassed by the U.S.-controlled Canal Zone and Panama's transisthmian corridor are noteworthy, for the competition, interplay, and overlapping of national and racial identities. Struggles for dominance and survival marked these interactions. Such evolutions certainly unfolded for the Antillean community on both sides of the line with a special intensity as they composed a subaltern group regarded as inferior by both Panamanian and U.S. citizens. West Indians, as we shall see, both accommodated to and struggled against this assignation. An often contradictory process transformed their identities over time as they adopted different strategies to maintain their rights and cultural values in both Panama and the Zone. Part of this maneuvering in the first half of the twentieth century involved a level of collaboration with the dominant borderlanders, the Zonians, as a survival mechanism for obtaining jobs, housing, and security in an often hostile and danger-filled frontier.[2]

This denigration, at times demonization, of the black West Indian also encompassed one of the key dynamics of Panamanian identity politics, especially in this era. In their confrontations with Antillean immigrants and white Zonians, Latin Panamanians wrestled with the central question of what exactly constituted Panamanian citizenship. Each of the three groups served as a useful "other" to the remaining two in defining their own being, characteristics, and purpose on the isthmus. As the historian Michael Conniff has shown, Washington's use of West Indians as a privileged labor force in the Zone followed a "third nationality" labor strategy that many nineteenth- and twentieth-century colonial powers pursued. Britain's use of Indian workers in its African and Caribbean colonies proved another example. Washington, in effect, divided and dominated the Latin Panamanian majority in the borderland through its favoritism toward West Indian labor.[3]

It should be noted that the term *Latin Panamanian* is problematic as the non–West Indian native population on the isthmus encompassed a broad expanse of different racial and ethnic groupings: European-descent, mestizo, mulatto, indigenous, and more. Suffice it to say that those inhabitants of Panama who spoke Spanish as their principal language and practiced Catholicism as their official creed came to view their embrace of both as signifiers of their loyalty and conformity to the Panamanian state and majority culture. In 1941 the controversial president Arnulfo Arias provoked a serious identity crisis for Antillean borderers when he enacted his infamous constitution. Part of this xenophobic accord stripped West Indian immigrants and their children of Panamanian citizenship. Arias enjoyed widespread support during his first, abbreviated term in office (1940–41) for his national chauvinism that also removed citizenship and the right to own businesses from Jewish, Arab, Hindu, and Chinese minorities. The 1946 Panamanian Constitution, passed five years after Arnulfo's first overthrow, restored citizenship to West Indians and their children but failed to resolve entirely the status, aspirations, and identity of West Indians in the borderland.[4]

The Origins of West Indian Borderland Identities

West Indians composed over 66 percent of the Canal construction workforce and some 85 percent of all non-U.S. laborers. The first of these Antilleans who settled in the Zone-Panama corridor in 1904 identified themselves as British subjects and not as Panamanians or wards of the United States. These West Indians realized that they were not the most esteemed of British constituents, given their work as cane cutters on the plantations of Barbados and Jamaica. Their ancestors endured slavery for centuries, until British abolition in 1838, after which many continued to labor in the fields as low-paid cutters, tenant farmers, or sharecroppers. Still, it is one of the incongruities of imperialism that Afro-Antilleans from the British Caribbean took a certain pride in their association with the world's mightiest empire centered in London, with all its royal pageantry. They also appreciated the British educational system on their islands and the relative honesty and efficiency of British colonial officials. These Afro-Antilleans came as temporary laborers to the isthmus and initially planned to return to their British-controlled homelands after the Canal project ended. While the majority of the French canal workers (1880–89) hailed from Jamaica, some 95 percent of the forty thousand West Indian workers on the Canal emigrated from Barbados; with smaller contingents that came from other British Caribbean islands and the French islands of Guadeloupe, St. Lucia, and Martinique, and only forty-seven workers in the initial wave of immigrants from Jamaica.[5]

The city of Colón served as the great cultural and social center for West Indians in this period and would do so for decades to come. Famous for its French Caribbean architecture, brilliantly colored buildings, and scenic sea wall, Colón grew from a village of three thousand in 1900 to a town of over thirty thousand by the end of construction. The most famous families of the middle-class West Indian community established their homes in Colón; these included the Abrahams, the Archibolds, the Beebys, the Crowns, the Edwards, the Hoys, the Mackintoshes, the Moodys, and the Warehams. Doctors, teachers, lawyers, businessmen, and community leaders emerged from these families. George Westerman, another Colonese from this era, became an influential historian, labor activist, and publisher of the *Panama Tribune*, the principal West Indian daily on the isthmus.[6]

Colón operated very much as a borderland city, such as Tijuana or El Paso on the U.S.-Mexico frontier. During railroad construction days, it was particularly infamous for its violence and rebellions, stemming in part from its broad cultural mix and competition. While boasting a West Indian majority, the town, walled in almost entirely by the Canal Zone to the south yet projecting its wide northern vista to the Caribbean, contained a host of minorities: Arabs, Jews, Hindus, Chinese, Italians, and Spaniards. In the postwar era many of these minorities worked at the Colón Free Zone, a duty-free collection of warehouses established in 1948 to boost Panama's share of international trade at the Caribbean end of the Canal. The U.S.-run Zone was the city's other principal employer, with its harbor works and numerous facilities in Cristobal. A bevy of nearby U.S. military bases completed the rich cultural and labor mix of the city in the postwar era, where so many different peoples from various walks of life commingled. Colón still holds a special attachment for many West Indians as the entry point for their hopes and dreams on the isthmus, the place where they first settled during the early construction days and returned to so often in their lives. Though mired today in poverty and decay, the city's boast as the "Pearl of the Caribbean" lives on in West Indian historical memory.[7]

Despite the enormous contribution of the West Indian labor force, during his 1906 visit to the excavation site that began at Colón, President Theodore Roosevelt gave them limited attention. Instead he likened the U.S. white workforce, the Zonians, to soldiers in a great military campaign similar to the Grand Army of the Republic, the conquerors of the Confederacy. He authorized the creation of a military-style decoration that later became the Roosevelt Medal for U.S. workers who labored two years or more on the Canal's construction. Roosevelt Medal winners became a fraternity of first-generation builder-heroes whom later Zonians pointed to with pride. But only U.S. whites qualified for the medal. Non-U.S. citizens, such as the West Indians, were prohibited from receiving it, though they died at a rate of thirteen to one U.S. worker, since their dangerous pick-and-shovel work and explosive planting exposed them to cave-ins, mudslides, and gory deaths. Some 22,000 West Indians had perished during the French Project and over 5000 during the American phase of construction but not all from work accidents. The flimsy housing, spartan rations, and inferior health care that West

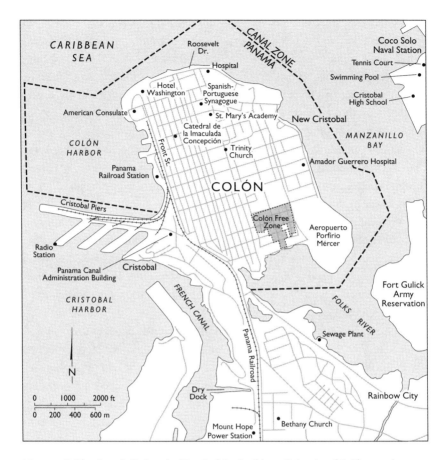

Map 3.1. Colón. Once hailed as the "Pearl of the Caribbean," the city of Colón was the bridgehead for West Indian settlement in the Panama Railroad strip (1850–55) and later the U.S. Canal Zone (1903–79). The latter entirely surrounded this transit city with facilities, bases, and towns. Myriad ethnic and religious minorities, foremost among them the West Indians, peopled this key port with its famous Free Trade Zone that was built after World War II.

Indians endured from 1904 to 1914 also contributed to their higher death, sickness, and infant mortality rates. The white American labor force, lionized in the U.S. press, lived in luxury compared to Antillean workers.[8]

The very year that Roosevelt toured Panama, the gold and silver pay system of the Canal hardened into an ugly segregation. In the first two or three years of construction, prized skills or U.S. citizenship occasionally trumped race, as over a hundred U.S. blacks and skilled or educated West Indians worked on the gold roll (though authorities forbade their use of gold commissaries and housing). However, the labor regime rapidly hardened along a strict color line. After 1906 U.S. officials forbade promotions of West Indians to the gold roll, no matter their skills or professions. By 1908 U.S. nationality and white skin converged as the prime markers of the gold roll, and Zone authorities pushed all West Indian craftsmen and professionals into the silver category. At the end of construction U.S. officials shipped U.S. black workers home. A handful of upper-class Panamanians received gold-roll jobs, mostly to cement the U.S.-Panamanian political alliance. Small gold and silver bars soon marked off the separate facilities of the Zone, but their effect of subordination on thousands of West Indians proved equal to the "colored" and "whites-only" signs in Georgia and Alabama.[9]

With the completion of the Canal, around a third of the West Indians returned to their islands; another third stayed on to work on Canal maintenance for the Americans in the Zone, and a final third moved into the Panamanian neighborhoods that straddled the U.S. enclave or labored on the banana plantations of Bocas del Toro and Chiriquí, the western provinces of the republic. Not all West Indians who worked for the Canal secured housing in the Zone. Several, along with their non-canal-employed brethren, settled in Colón or in Panama City in the borderland neighborhoods of El Chorrillo, Calidonia, San Miguel, and Río Abajo. The first generation of West Indian immigrants clung to many of the British-influenced aspects of their identities. They played cricket and soccer, drank tea, and worshiped as Methodists, Baptists, and Presbyterians. Afro-Antilleans celebrated English holidays such as Boxing Day and Guy Fawke's Day and toasted the king and queen on their birthday. Before World War II they also petitioned the British consul in Panama to resolve many of their problems, not Panamanian or U.S. officials.[10]

West Indians also embraced their African roots and their distinctive island identities, customs, and connections. Jamaicans and Barbadians frequently clashed during the U.S. construction era. U.S. bosses typically designated lighter-skinned Jamaicans as foremen and overseers, a favoritism that darker-skinned Barbadians resented. Some considered Jamaicans "too bossy, talky, and uppity." These class and color antagonisms continued when educated Jamaicans gained employment as teachers, doctors, dentists, and policemen in the Zone. "Dey was all con men, dem Jamaicans. Dey could talk a dog off a meat wagon and sell de whyte mon any piece a crop, too," a Barbadian remembered with some admiration. The fact that so many Jamaicans had journeyed to the isthmus earlier, during the French construction period, added to their sense of superiority over Barbadian greenhorns. Some conflicts between Jamaicans and Barbadians had their roots in the British imperial strategy of divide and conquer on the islands, when English authorities deliberately encouraged rivalries. French-speaking West Indians from Guadeloupe, Martinique, and Haiti constituted a smaller group within the Antillean community. These former French subjects retained an exotic aura for English-speaking West Indians, whose males often commented on the seductive beauty and wiles of "dem French girls from de islands."[11]

From their first days in Panama, Barbadians and Jamaicans strove to maintain their customs, diet, and culture on a largely Hispanic isthmus. They built Protestant churches, formed voluntary associations, founded banks and insurance co-ops, and published newspapers. Despite their grimy and perilous manual work, many West Indian men wore suits and bowler hats in the evenings. Some even dressed formally at work. When they attended religious services on Sundays, their wives sported calico, gingham, and brilliantly colored dresses. Their unique Caribbean cuisine included *bacalao* (salted cod), rice cooked in coconut milk, brown bread, *souse* (pickled pigs' feet with onions and cucumbers), *conkies* (steamed corn cakes), fried flying fish and *cou-cou* (an okra-based form of couscous), coconut bread, *puncha-crema* (a milk-based rum punch), rice and peas, ginger beer, and *sorrel*, a red-colored plant tea.[12]

While most were devout Protestants, some West Indians cherished African religious traditions as well. They consulted obeah men, shamans similar to practitioners of voudou or santería in Haiti and Cuba, even in the postwar era. After consulting a minister or Western-trained doctor, as insurance a West Indian might seek the advice of an obeah man when confronted with sickness, depression, or a legal or romantic problem. "An obeah mon could make a woman fall in love with you. He take a lock of her hair or some thread from her dress and he make a soup from dem things, and den when you drink it, dis girl she get big eyes for you. No, it is true!"[13]

West Indians also had their own colorful English dialect, called *bajan*, that they used to confound U.S. foremen and Latin Panamanians alike. Along with Spanglish, bajan was the second lingua franca of the borderland. West Indians would say "Park the car in de cool, mon," meaning "in the shade." An umbrella became "a house in hand"; a comb, a "hair rake"; a raincoat, a "tent"; a toothbrush, a "mouth broom." "He got mashed up bad in the coco bone" meant he got punched in the head. "Auntie-man" was their designation for a homosexual; "watchymon" for guard; "sky juice" signified rain; "pot-starver," a skinny dog; "propping-sorrow," staring into space; "goat-head," a dope; and "moses," a small rowboat or *cayuco*. Their favorite expression of disgust, "Rass!" (from "rasshole" or idiot), became part of the universal slang of the borderland. Even Zonian publications announced the late 1970s reductions-in-force with "Rass, I's Fired!" Baby-boomer Zonian children learned bajan from their West Indian maids and used it when speaking to one another, sometimes to deceive and infuriate their parents. The language reinforced West Indian identity and also proved subversive to the white-dominated power structure. Some U.S. bosses could not understand explanations in bajan from their West Indian charges and would simply throw up their hands and walk away in disgust when a job had not been completed right. Bajan particularly annoyed educated Panamanians who prided themselves on their English fluency but could not understand what on earth West Indians were saying when they spoke to them. Indeed one of the more fascinating transculturations of the Zone borderland emerged in the 1990s, when two Zonian youths formed a bajan reggae band called Shorty and Slim that is popular among Zonians in Panama today.[14]

In some ways the "protective" power of the United States both within the Canal Zone and in nearby urban Panama aided West Indians in preserving their culture on an unwelcoming isthmus. West Indians were also highly receptive to the popular U.S. culture that flowed through the Zone, more so than most Latin Panamanians who did not understand English and viewed Americans more as occupiers than protectors or employers. In other ways, however, the "guardianship" of the Zone proved a curse as it retarded the normal process of cultural synthesis on the isthmus for West Indians. Hindus, Chinese, Arabs, Jews, and a variety of European immigrants to Panama quickly learned to speak Spanish and adopted numerous Panamanian cultural practices and folkways. Many West Indians rejected such assimilation because they had no need to speak Spanish in the U.S.-administered Zone or in their Zone-bordered neighborhood, where so many worked and lived right across the street from the U.S. enclave.[15]

So-called colonial blacks, some referred to as *costeños* (who lived along the Caribbean littoral, where they had once worked plantations), others referred to as *negros nativos* (who gravitated toward urban centers), were originally brought to Panama from Africa as slaves during the Spanish imperial era. They were given Spanish names, taught Spanish, and converted to Catholicism. But the first two generations of U.S.-imported West Indians resisted such amalgamation into Panamanian society. They insisted on speaking mostly English and retaining their Protestant faiths, British customs, and loyalty toward the Americans who hired them in such large numbers for three times the pay that they could earn in Panama. As such, many Latin

Panamanians came to regard these West Indians as obstinate, even treacherous aliens. Their apparent alliance with the hated yanquis furthered the local hostility toward them. Catholic, Spanish-speaking costeños and negros nativos also viewed West Indians as outsiders even though both descended from similar African roots. The fact that numerous, better-paid West Indians dated and married mestiza Panamanians added a dollop of sexual resentment to these ethnocultural rivalries.[16]

While initially marginalized by the republic's citizens, West Indians would have significant influence on Panamanian popular culture. This proved especially true in music, such as reggae, calypso, reggae-rap (and another variation called reggaeton), and the drums or *tambores* in so much Panamanian music. The West Indian use of brilliant Caribbean colors in painting and murals is particularly striking on homes, hotels, seawalls, and the famous Diablos Rojos (Red Devils) that Panamanians call their public transit buses. Antilleans also brought elements of the African supernatural to isthmian storytelling and folktales and strongly impacted the Panamanian diet, as virtually all West Indian dishes became favorite fare for Latin Panamanians.[17]

Despite these cultural affinities, Latin Panamanians typically viewed West Indians as too fawning and submissive toward their U.S. bosses and indifferent to Panamanian nationalism. They called such Antilleans *tío toms* (Uncle Toms) for their apparent servility toward the gringos. Panamanians attributed the accommodating traits of West Indians to their historical legacy of plantation slavery and British colonialism. When President Arnulfo Arias, the personification of Panamanian machismo (his nickname was El Hombre, although he also carried the childhood sobriquet of "Fufu"), stripped West Indians of their Panamanian citizenship in 1941, he pleased Latin Panamanians but succeeded only in pushing Barbadians and Jamaicans closer to the Americans for protection. Arias felt compelled to take such measures as he viewed Panamanian national identity as disintegrating in a borderland crucible brimming with "disloyal foreigners" in the early decades of the U.S. protectorate.[18]

Many West Indians returned this political hostility of Latin Panamanians, regarding them as racist and untrustworthy. For nearly two generations after 1941 large numbers of West Indians refused to vote for Arnulfista candidates or for most other Latin Panamanians in a variety of offices. "I don't trust de Americans completely, and dey done many bad tings to us. But I trust dem a whole lot more than I do dese damn Panamanians!" one proclaimed angrily.[19] Carlos Jordan Romeros, an employee of the Zone, experienced this resentment when he was left in charge of a West Indian crew in the 1960s after his U.S. boss left their work site. When he tried to direct the West Indians in their work, one of them told him pointedly, "I don't take orders from de Latin mon. I only take orders from de whyte mon!"[20]

The Zone's "colored" school system aided this Americanization process that Latin Panamanians so begrudged. West Indian children learned subjects such as U.S. history, social studies, and civics, all in English. U.S.-paid teachers also taught West Indian children menial skills, such as sign painting, window washing, and shoe shining, unheard of subjects in the all-white Zonian schools but courses that helped prepare young West Indians for their future status on "de whyte mon's" side of the border. But the Canal Zone boundaries, so crucial to white Zonians in preserving their sense of identity, security, and mission, signified a largely artificial frontier to most West Indians, who repeatedly traversed it to visit their friends and relatives in the poorer neighborhoods astride the Zone. Despite their dependence on Americans for economic livelihood, most West Indians were far less wary of crossing borders than their more powerful stewards, the Zonians. As the favored workforce in the enclave, unlike many Latin Panamanians, they typically faced less Canal Zone Police scrutiny as well.[21]

Aspects of U.S. culture understandably made strong inroads among West Indians in the borderland, particularly since the dominant discourse proclaimed it as the world's finest. Indeed in some ways West Indians merely transferred their association with the former world's greatest power, the British Empire, to its successor, the United States. U.S. music, television, movies, and food quickly became popular among the Zone's Antilleans and in the West Indian neighborhoods along the line. Southern Command television staples such as *Gunsmoke, I Love Lucy, Bonanza, Perry Mason,* and even *All in the Family* found a receptive audience among postwar West Indians. They delighted in the foibles and stupidity of Archie Bunker, who reminded them of their own racist U.S. bosses, a mark of the important distinction between reception and diffusion in mass culture. West Indians also grew to love U.S. sports such as boxing, football, basketball, Triple Crown horseracing, and, most of all, baseball. West Indian "Panama" Al Brown, fighting out of Colón, became the republic's first world champion boxer in a heavily U.S.-influenced city that produced many outstanding pugilists. Following his retirement from the ring, Brown even worked as a clerk on the U.S. side of the borderland. Antilleans formed myriad baseball leagues and clubs that played throughout the silver towns from construction days through 1979. They produced several remarkably talented players who went on to play Major League Baseball: Rod Carew, Rennie Stennett, Fernando Ramsey, Webbo Clarke,

3.1. West Indian "silver" laborers did the dirty, arduous work within the Canal Zone and many of its environs. Courtesy of the *Panama Canal Review* in the Panama Canal Museum Collection, George Smathers Library, University of Florida, http://ufdc.ufl.edu/pcm.

3.2. West Indian Little League baseball teams in the Canal Zone reflected the racially segregated order of the enclave that stretched from cradle to grave. Courtesy of the *Panama Canal Spillway* in the Panama Canal Museum Collection, George Smathers Library, University of Florida, http://ufdc.ufl.edu/pcm.

Bill Haywood, Roberto Kelly, Bobby Prescott, Humberto Robinson, and Ray Webster.[22]

The Zone's demeaning system of segregation, however, wounded West Indian pride despite these accomplishments. Cecil Haynes, who established a record in working over seventy-one years for the Canal Zone, beginning as a fourteen-year-old office boy, recalled being passed over for promotions given to whites whom he had helped train. Haynes also had to endure being called "nigger" and "boy" in the earlier years of the Zone more times than he cared to remember. A particular humiliation that galled him was being compelled to address his white bosses' children as "mister" and "miss," while he was "a grown man in his forties and fifties." In 1946, the same year that the Greaves case heightened borderland racial tensions, the Canal Zone Police pulled a West Indian retiree out of line and reprimanded him for trying to borrow a penny from a Zonian in the Balboa Post Office to cover the postage for a letter to his daughter. The West Indian daily the *Panama Tribune* published a stinging rebuke at this outrage against a model retiree who had helped build the Canal in his youth. In 1952 the U.S. manager of the Balboa gas station where West Indian Vincente Williams worked as a teenager fired him "for addressing one of the Canal bosses in a familiar manner." Having drunk a few beers before he reported to his afternoon shift, Williams made the mistake of calling a Zone chief by his first name, as all the whites at the station did. Williams's white boss told him, "He's Mister Henderson to you, nigger—not Bob!" before firing him on the spot. As if this vicious bigotry were not enough, Haynes and many of his fellow West Indians endured the insult of *chombo* (the rough equivalent of *nigger*) from Latin Panamanians when they got into altercations with them on the other side of the line.[23]

"Colorism" in the Borderland: The West Indians' Plight

In addition to the segregation imposed by U.S. whites in the Zone, the Antillean community faced a more subtle yet important form of discrimination central to their identity struggles, that of the colorism. Colorism, the bias against darker-skinned people of color, constituted a traditional form of race-based prejudice that had long prevailed in Panama, tied to the racial hierarchies of the Spanish Empire. This skin-tone discrimination coexisted along with other, more egregious forms of racial subordination, such as the Zone's Jim Crow segregation. A form of this syndrome was even present within the West Indian community, as already mentioned, in the higher status and respect often accorded lighter-complexioned professionals in Antillean society. "Fair" or "clear" West Indians frequently, but not always, held leadership positions. African-descent populations that traced their origins to the diaspora of the slave trade and the widespread miscegenation that encompassed it, all dealt with this less apparent but still potent form of prejudice. The African American community in the United States is a prime example. The director Spike Lee emphasized the phenomenon of colorism in his controversial film *School Daze*, which traced the conflicts between lighter- and darker-skinned African Americans at an all-black college in the South.[24]

Race was never limited to two or three fixed categories in Latin America, as in Europe and the United States. Panamanians in particular had long recognized a dozen different classifications of race related to skin tone that fell short of negritude, among them, mestizo, mulatto, *morisco*, *moreno*, *cobrizo*, *trigueño*, *zambo*, *culiso*, and *amarillo*. These categories could be further specified through the insertion of the adjectives *oscuro* or *claro* for dark or light members of the above listed groupings. Some Panamanians were even more creative with precise racial ascriptions when referring to a woman as a *café-lechista* or a girl whose skin was the color of coffee with milk. Indeed only blacks from the West Indies who spoke English and practiced Protestantism were truly *negro* by Panamanian standards. Even Panamanians who had prominent African facial features, coarse hair, and very dark skin might still be considered mulatto, moreno, or even majority mestizo, provided they spoke Spanish, practiced Catholicism, and had Hispanic names. Culture, not skin color, often proved the key determinant of blackness in the borderland. But West Indians always found themselves inevitably at the bottom of this highly attenuated racial scale, even lower than costeños and negros nativos, who frequently looked like their doubles.[25]

Hair texture served as a key marker of inferiority in this racial pecking order. "El color es accidente pero el pelo no miente" (Color is accidental but the hair doesn't lie) expressed this prejudice, as did the ubiquity of Dominican beauty salons throughout the borderland that specialized in straightening African hair. Other Panamanian and Latin American inhabitants of the borderland also struggled with skin tone prejudice that alternated between *mestizaje*, a recognition and even pride of mixed-race identity, and *blanqueamiento*, the desire of people of color to whiten themselves or move closer toward cultural whiteness for social or economic advantage. Well into the postwar era the darker a Panamanian's complexion, the more likely he or she was to be a member of the poor and the working class, doing the arduous and disagreeable jobs of society. The lighter the skin tone, the greater were the odds for membership in the middle and upper classes. The whitest of Panamanians, with the so-called purest Spanish or European bloodlines, the *rabiblancos*, constituted the self-ordained elite.[26]

Broad exceptions certainly obtained within this racial pyramid. Panama, like all Latin American societies, never practiced anywhere near as rigid a race-based order as existed in the United States. The "one-drop rule" of the U.S. South, enshrined in state laws that required but a single drop of African blood to categorize an individual as negro, if applied to Panama might have made 50 percent or more of the population black. De jure segregation of public facilities never existed in Panama, but many darker-skinned Panamanians long complained of being barred from exclusive nightclubs and elite social clubs or of getting the cold shoulder when applying for loans or inquiring about housing in upscale (read: fairer-skinned) neighborhoods. West Indians felt especially vulnerable living under this hierarchy when they exited the segregated Zone and entered an uncertain borderland, as most of the isthmian population consigned them to the furthest end of the color spectrum from whiteness. As the darkest of isthmians, many lacked the "racial mobility" possessed by mestizos and mulattos, who could rise racially through intermarriage or economic or political success. "At least you knew where you stood in de Canal Zone. In Panama you was never sure," recalled a retired West Indian. "Everybody in Panama, no matter what dey color, had somebody dey could look down on, except us," another West Indian commented about a racial caste system whose prevalence resides in the shadowy corners of isthmian life that Panamanians still feel uncomfortable confronting.[27]

But this pervasive discrimination, fiercest in the Zone and still potent in postwar Panama, also served to unite Antilleans by identifying recognizable oppressors. Thus they began to see themselves more as West Indians than as Barbadians, Jamaicans, and Martinicans, despite the divisive elements of colorism within their own ranks. This double discrimination that West Indians faced hardened their resolve and survivalist mechanisms. While compliant on the surface, many maintained a tradition of covert resistance, typical of marginalized peoples, taking what they could grab, smuggling, bootlegging, bending the rules, and even stealing when opportunities presented themselves. A passive resentment on both sides of the borderland marked their social demeanor. But in the case of West Indian hero-outlaws like John Peter Williams, resistance proved far more overt.

The Origins of West Indian Resistance in the Borderland: A Seminal Case

The most spectacular model of West Indian defiance to the Zone-Panama power system emerged in the life and adventures of John Peter Williams. He set the standard for Antillean resistance against both "de whyte mon" and "de Latin mon" along a fractious frontier. In the early 1920s Williams launched a one-man crime wave, infuriating authorities on both sides of the border with his skills as a cat burglar and escape artist. Hailed as "the Robin Hood of the Canal Zone" in Panamanian newspapers, Williams represented the classic "social bandit" and would have an influence on the identity formation of militant West Indians throughout the twentieth century. While Latin Panamanians admired him less, his escapades offered them startling evidence of U.S. vulnerability, as he continually reduced the supposedly all-powerful Canal Zone Police to bumbling Keystone Kops.[28]

Born in 1899 in Panama City to Jamaican parents who had come to Panama in the 1880s to work on the French canal, John Peter Williams grew up in the working-class neighborhood of Calidonia, one of the mixed-race barrios that bordered the Zone on the Pacific side. Growing up on the hard streets there, he became an enterprising youth. He made an indirect living off the Zone, as many borderers of color did, working as a newsboy and later as a shoe-shine boy at the Ancon Clubhouse barbershop. As a teenager he devoured dime novels and detective stories, displaying a keen intelligence and desire to live out the adventures that these books contained. In 1918 he applied for a prized taxi license in the Zone, but he failed the driver's test that an apparently racist Zonian official administered to him.[29]

Williams later complained in a letter to the executive secretary of the Zone that the test demonstrator, a Mr. Cornell (his actual name was Charles F. Koerner), had treated him unfairly. When Williams asked Koerner if he was the demonstrator, Koerner replied, "That's right, and I'm gonna demonstrate you, boy!" According to Williams, Koerner abused him during the road test, asking him excessive and insulting questions. When a flustered Williams failed to answer one correctly, Koerner vacated the car and flunked the youth. Thus he denied Williams his dream of a Canal Zone taxi license. Koerner later admitted that he may have treated Williams "harshly on one occasion" but that his impatience with Williams rested upon "another matter al-to-gether. Williams," Koerner insisted, "interrupted a conversation between myself and two other white men."[30]

This early confrontation with Zone racism marked a turning point in Williams's life. Prior to his humiliation, like many West Indians, Williams had expressed an admiration for the Zone and for most Americans. A U.S. lawyer, Walter F. Van Dame, employed Williams as his office boy one summer. Another Zonian, Mr. Martin, who worked at the Panama City Waterworks, also took an interest in the youth and taught him how to drive. But after his failure to obtain his taxi license Williams's love for the U.S. enclave turned to hatred.[31]

This part of Williams's story has become mythic for older West Indians. Practically every one of them who worked in the borderland experienced similar emotional wounds and racial humiliation. "The words *nigger*, *boy*, *coon*, and *blackie* were used by whites as often as *if*, *and*, and *but* in those days," an older West Indian recalled. The first sentiments many West Indians and Panamanians felt toward North Americans were those of awe and admiration. The pattern of North Americans greeting such esteem with contempt proved central to the emotional history of the borderland.[32]

In response to his rejection in 1918, Williams embarked on a one-man war against the Zone. But despite the myth of his youthful innocence, even as a teenager he had been arrested for theft to support a flamboyant lifestyle at pool halls and bars. Therefore to present Williams's crimes solely as a response to U.S. racial injustice is simplistic. In fact in October 1918, five months after his celebrated rejection, Williams retook the Zone driving exam and passed it, receiving Canal Zone taxi license number 4315.[33]

From 1918 through 1920 Williams committed several high-profile break-ins in the Canal Zone and in Panama. He seemed to target individuals and institutions that symbolized U.S. power, robbing the Panama Railroad superintendent's home, the Zone's chief quartermaster's residence, the Ancon Post Office, U.S. District Judge John W. Hanan's home, and Police Captain E. P. Jessop's apartment. Operating alone or with Panamanian compatriots, Williams displayed a knack for the daring caper and the improbable escape. Frequently he eluded his police pursuers by retreating into the jungle sections of Las Sabanas near the border that became, in effect, Williams's "Sherwood Forest."[34]

Tabloid reports of his exploits referred to Williams as a "jungle man," reinforcing the stereotype of the rebellious Panamanian, particularly the Afro-Panamanian, as a creature of the forest and the night. This representation permeated police reports despite the fact that Williams was a city boy born in one of the capital's barrios. A similarity existed here between Williams and Henry McCarty, alias "Billy the Kid," the infamous New Mexican outlaw who was actually born in New York City.[35] But just as U.S. officials saw the law-abiding, eight-to-five Zonian as a sunshine town-dweller, they often characterized rebellious Panamanians as denizens of the jungle, engulfed in its nocturnal passions.[36]

Williams reinforced this jungle cat image by scaling mango trees from which he leaped onto Zonian porches during his burglaries. One of the most popular West Indian folktales surrounding Williams describes an occasion when he allegedly transformed himself into a banana tree to escape the Canal Zone Police after a burglary. Frustrated by his disappearance, the white police plucked several bananas from the tree, ate them, and discarded the peels on the ground before returning to their barracks. When Williams awoke later and purportedly assumed human form, he found himself lying naked on the ground with articles of his clothing strewn about in the exact locations where the police had dropped their banana peels. This story testifies to the West Indian belief in the supernatural and the hope that such otherworldly power might defeat the scientific, technological power of "de whyte mon."[37]

Williams also demonstrated apparent skill at exploiting divisions between the U.S. military and the Zonians. While the Canal Zone Police hunted him, he allegedly hid out on U.S. military posts, where he forged friendships with Puerto Rican soldiers through his bootlegging during these Prohibition years. It is possible that Puerto Rican recruits, victims of discrimination on U.S. bases and colonialism on their own island, may have sympathized with Williams. Williams also played Panamanian law enforcement off against the Zone constabulary, as he regularly fled across the border, exploiting the jurisdictional ambiguity of the Zone-Panama corridor. In this manner he operated within the still ill-defined spaces between the two emergent states.[38]

In September 1919, shortly after Williams's first arrest for burglary, the Canal Zone Police transported him to Ancon Hospital to be treated for syphilis. While awaiting a doctor in the hospital holding cell, Williams dismantled his cell lock, unscrewed the security screen on a nearby window, and climbed down the trestle. He then fled into the bush to resume his career. Zone authorities now viewed Williams as an escaped, syphilitic black burglar, amplifying his image of barbarism and contamination. Speculation as to how he got the screwdriver for his getaway filled the newspapers. Among the West Indian community the story soon spread that a sympathetic Barbadian janitor at the hospital slipped the tool to him while passing him in the corridor. This clandestine support fit the classic pattern of communal sympathy for the social bandit from his oppressed "countrymen." Zone Police had already arrested several Jamaican maids at homes that Williams burglarized on the suspicion that they supplied him with keys, apartment layouts, and their employers' schedules.[39]

After this dramatic escape, Williams's legend magnified. An aura of invincibility, previously associated only with North Americans, surrounded him. Many West Indians became convinced that he was an obeah man with occult powers. Wanted posters of Williams lined the streets of the Zone-Panama borderland. His family and friends collected his press clippings, as did many West Indians who followed his exploits in the paper every day along with the standings of their favorite baseball and cricket teams.[40]

Exaggerations from the West Indian grapevine flourished around Williams. Only five-foot-four and 140 pounds, his reputation far exceeded his actual stature. Zonians, West Indians, and the police on both sides of the line credited him with numerous crimes he never committed. For instance, though no evidence exists for the event, older West Indians swear that Williams robbed the Zone governor's mansion while Governor Harding and his wife slept. Before leaving with a sack full of jewelry, Williams allegedly left a note on the governor's pillow—"Your wife is ugly but she makes good chicken"—testifying to Williams's picaresque wit.[41]

After his first escape from the Zone Police, Williams remained at large for fifteen months, frustrating U.S. authorities to such an extent that they hired a Pinkerton agent, Ronald H. George, from the United States to help apprehend him. George set up several police stings involving prostitutes in Colón to entrap Williams, but the outlaw had an instinct for avoiding ambushes. It was during this fifteen-month string of burglaries that Williams achieved the status of Canal Zone Public Enemy Number One, for "terrorizing hundreds of homes all over the Isthmus."[42]

At four in the morning of December 9, 1920, a Zone resident spotted Williams vacating a window at the home of M. L. Dodson in Ancon. The informant called the police, who quickly converged on the scene with nearby U.S. military units. Williams fired on Police Sergeant Paul Kallay, who wounded Williams in the arm with return fire and forced him to drop "a purloined watch and Christmas plum pudding." A second Zone policeman wounded the burglar in the thigh. Still, in the darkness and confusion Williams slipped through the police cordon and briefly visited his parents in Calidonia. Exhausted and bleeding, he heeded his mother's tearful pleas and turned himself in at the Ancon Police Station. Newspaper accounts of the shootout and Williams's surrender give a sense of the fascination that Americans had for him: "Twice wounded and exhausted from two hours' profuse bleeding, Peter Williams yesterday morning voluntarily delivered himself to the Ancon police station and collapsed into a chair, after being hunted by almost every member of the Canal Zone police and successfully evading capture. . . . Peter Williams now lies in the Balboa police station with one arm practically shot off and a bullet in his left thigh. He is not expected to live."[43]

In the custody of his enemies, Williams told a clerk, "I'm tired of bucking the Canal Zone Police." But his resignation proved temporary. The U.S. District Court convicted him on sixteen counts of burglary and sentenced him to fifty years hard labor at Gamboa Penitentiary, the same sentence Lester Greaves received in 1946. Panama waived extradition, preferring to let the gringos handle the dangerous folk hero. The court also sentenced Williams's sister to five years for aiding his crimes. His father died the next day, allegedly from a "broken heart."[44]

Williams worked the infamous Gamboa road gang, wearing a striped convict's uniform and a heavy ball and chain. Still, he vowed to fellow inmates that no prison could hold him. Cleverly he played the part of a model prisoner in an effort to lower guard vigilance. In September 1921, when an inmate attacked one of the guards, Williams intervened and wrestled the convict into submission. He drew praise from the U.S. warden for saving the police sergeant's life. "Please note the conduct of our former notorious burglar," the warden wrote in the margins of his report.[45]

But on February 13, 1922, five months to the day after rescuing his guard, Williams made another break for freedom. While working the quarry detail near Gaillard Highway, he pickpocketed the key to his shackles and slipped into the bush. Once again Williams eluded an extensive Zone Police–U.S. military dragnet, probably by clinging to a Panama railcar undercarriage.[46] During his first night of freedom he committed three burglaries to gain civilian clothes, cash, and burglary tools. For his last break-in, he robbed Police Captain E. P. Jessop's home in Ancon, a fatal misstep. Jessop awoke during the burglary and called out his men. Alerted to Williams's location by a barking dog, Sergeant Carl Wanke discovered the convict hiding under a house, waiting to make a dash for the border. When Williams emerged and sprinted toward the Fourth of July Avenue boundary, Wanke shouted for him to halt. "Damn you!" Williams cried out, his last words before Wanke shot him fatally in the head.[47]

Williams's last words were a fitting epitaph for his short but exciting life. They no doubt summed up his attitude toward the U.S.-administered Zone, its police, and probably Panama as well. For Williams remained an outlaw on both sides of the line, suffering the fate of many West Indians from his era: discriminated against in the Zone, resented and unwanted in Panama. A novice observer might think that Williams holds a revered place in the pantheon of Panamanian heroes. As a militant fighter who gave his life in the struggle against the Zone, perhaps he should stand beside Ascanio Arosemena, the student leader slain by the Zone Police in 1964; the nationalist firebrand Arnulfo Arias; or Omar Torrijos, hero of the 1977 treaty. But the average Latin Panamanian today has never even heard of John Peter Williams.[48]

This is curious because Williams was a *Panamanian* born in Panama City, not the West Indies. But in the early twentieth century the idea that someone of West Indian heritage could be a Panamanian hero rang false to most of the republic's citizens. Panama's white elite, its majority mestizo population, and even costeños and negros nativos considered West Indians outsiders, lackeys of the Americans, aliens to any authentic patriotism. Ultimately, to most Panamanians, Williams was just a crazy chombo. The official history of his life, compiled by U.S. and Panamanian authorities, branded him a habitual criminal with no political agenda. The fact that Williams was black, a burglar, and from the lower classes further invalidated his standing for most middle-class and elite Panamanians, *respectable* nationalists who wrote the history of Panama. Official publications referred to Williams as a "bandit," the term authorities applied to denigrate a broad range of popular rebels, from Mohammed to Ho Chi Minh to Ché Guevara.[49]

Critics of Panamanian nationalism sometimes referred to Panama as "a country without heroes," a simplistic and false stereotype. During the postwar era even some Latin American radicals chided Panamanians for their perceived complacency toward U.S. power.[50] After Panamanians purportedly welcomed (at least in heavily edited American media coverage) the U.S. invasion in 1989, this critique resurfaced with a vengeance.[51] In this militant view of struggle, Panama lacked sufficient numbers of rebels willing to lay down their lives in a war against the gringos. While his motives may have been pecuniary, John Peter Williams *did* lay down his life in the struggle against the gringos, and thousands of West Indians celebrated his efforts in secret, though they dared not speak this truth in front of Zonians or Latin Panamanians.

While most Panamanians denied Williams's hero status, Zonian officials incredibly tried to bestow a certain "whiteness" upon him. Following Williams's autopsy, the Zone pathologist Herbert Clark concluded that he must have been some kind of white mutation or super-negro to have won so many victories over them. Clark stated that "Williams' skull was more like that of a white man than the most elevated type of the negro race, being exceedingly thin rather than thick like most negro skulls."[52] Clark's eugenics drew angry protests from West Indians: "This statement coming as it does from a scientist carries much weight and ought to be correct. . . . His statement is not only startling but insulting to the negro race. . . . Dr. Clark must be quite aware that the negro race has subscribed its quota of great intellects to the world's record and therefore should not be surprised that we challenge him to substantiate the accuracy of his statement."[53]

Even in death Williams was a lightning rod for borderland racial tensions. White authorities cremated his body and buried the remains in a numbered grave, the standard procedure for impoverished criminals. But Williams's anonymous entombment also conveniently eliminated any gravestone that might serve as a shrine for future West Indian or Panamanian resistance. His pauper's interment was, in part, an attempt to erase his legend. As such, it failed. Despite an official autopsy that showed Williams died from a standard .45 caliber bullet to the head, West Indians still maintain, ninety years after the event, that the Zone Police killed him with a *silver bullet*. Only such a supernatural instrument could take the charmed life of the Zone werewolf. "They couldn't kill him except with a silver bullet, mon," an older West Indian testified. "He was an Obeah Mon like dem from the islands. He had the spirit on him and in him." "You can only kill a mon what's got magic with magic, too."[54]

Like Billy the Kid, John Peter Williams died a violent death in his early twenties and ascended to the realm of legend. Years after his death, when pies left to cool on windowsills disappeared, West Indian bakers claimed Peter Williams took them. The example of "Old Pete," as he was called, could be used as both an admonition and a compliment. "You'll end up just like Peter Williams!" postwar West Indian mothers scolded their unruly sons. But when a young boy demonstrated toughness in the schoolyard or showed a knack for escaping the law unscathed, proud fathers told male friends, "Look at him, mon, a regular Pete Williams!" If one could steal from "de whyte mon" and walk away with a smile, one carried the spirit of the Canal Zone Robin Hood. It was this spirit, along with considerable cultural strengths, that sustained West Indians throughout their long struggle against both yanquis and panameños in a highly racialized borderland.[55]

The West Indian Dilemma

When pressed like John Peter Williams, many ordinary West Indians of the post–World War II era also stood up for their dignity, though typically in less overt ways. Angus Brown recalled how in the 1950s his Zone boss Mr. Peterson used to call together all the silver workers for a group photo at Gatun. "Get a picture of me and my niggers," he told the company photographer. Angus corrected Peterson with a smile: "I ain't your nigger, Mr. Peterson." "Okay," Peterson admitted. "Take a picture of me, Mr. Brown, and my niggers." While such corrections did not change race relations at Gatun, Angus still remembers his small victory.[56]

West Indians often felt compromised in this manner during the postwar era. While they abhorred the discrimination in the Zone, they still considered their white American bosses necessary evils to endure in order to feed their families. Even the substandard housing for West Indians in Silver City, Paraiso, and Rainbow City in the Zone proved superior to the slums of Colón and Panama City that successive Panamanian governments appeared to have ignored. West Indians found themselves living on the horns of a dilemma: they wanted to protest more for their personal dignity, yet they feared going too far lest they lose the benefits and protection of the U.S. borderland. "We was always halfway to bein' rebels, but we could never go all de way."[57]

In 1949 this West Indian insecurity in confronting Zone discrimination paved the way for the demise of Local 713 of the United Public Workers of America. The U.S. and Zone governments effectively destroyed Local 713, an aggressive new CIO union that emerged on the isthmus in the postwar years with Jewish American as well as Panamanian and West Indian leadership, unified toward the goal to end racial discrimination in the Zone. U.S. authorities, including the Federal Bureau of Investigation, demonized the organization as communist-influenced and a cold war threat to the Canal's security. The local's actual threat lay in its efforts to recruit all non-U.S. Canal workers, regardless of race, nationality, or ethnicity, into a powerful and combative union led by a charismatic West Indian, Ed Gaskin. More moderate, security-conscious activists and workers, George Westerman among them, acquiesced in Local 713's demise. They rejected its confrontational style and formed a more accommodative, breakaway union, Local 900. That local chose arbitration over militant agitation against the white power structure, especially when such protest might be linked to dangerous, "communist" ideology at the height of the cold war.[58]

Cognizant of changing attitudes on race, decolonization, and Panamanian nationalism, postwar West Indians on both sides of the line exerted themselves more forcefully in the 1950s and the 1960s. In the 1950s a West Indian Panamanian writing under the pen name "Africanus" castigated Zonians for barring him from membership in an all-white church in the enclave. "They are out to encourage only the entry of white people into heaven," Africanus wrote, "and thus try to keep the place as select as their churches here apparently are." A Zonian responded, "Why must he try and push himself into places. . . . I have too much pride to push myself into places where I am not wanted," an argument simply to accept racism that West Indians increasingly rejected. On the Panamanian side of the line, second-generation West Indians entered adulthood with a greater sense of confidence in the changing schema of identity politics and global decolonization. Panamanians called this isthmus-born generation of Antilleans criollos, which many resented. "We are not criollos, we are Panamanians just like all the rest," one Panama-born Antillean who lived in the republic complained in a letter to the editor of La Hora, a popular Latin Panamanian daily. The newspaper's editors published his letter under a separate main-page headline that bespoke growing sympathy for the West Indian plight and a desire for political alliance among all non-Americans on the isthmus.[59]

In 1952 Zonian hotel managers refused a Jamaican doctor and his wife admittance to the government-run Washington Hotel in Colón, which provoked a wildcat strike by West Indian waiters and bellhops and a protest from Antillean leaders in Panama and the Zone. The doctor, Gervaise W. Harry, was on the isthmus to attend a medical conference at the invitation of the American College of Surgeons. He had made his reservation over the phone from Jamaica and hotel officials just assumed he was white. The story produced angry headlines on the isthmus and outrage from West Indian labor, religious, and professional leaders. Dr. Harry and union officers of Local 900 wrote a pointed letter to the Canal Zone government and to President Truman demanding an apology and a change in segregationist policies of the enclave, which they deemed "particularly stupid during this period of world unrest," that is, when the United States was fighting a war in Korea to protect the "free world" from communism.[60]

The Granville Brown traffic case in 1956 provoked another racial protest and small triumph for the West Indian community. U.S. military police refused a West Indian taxi driver, Granville Brown, entrance to military bases even after the U.S. District Court found him innocent of speeding at Fort Clayton. West Indians agitated and picketed on Brown's behalf for months. Eventually the military police acquiesced and allowed him to work on the bases again.[61] From the mid-1950s onward, select West Indians also protested Lester Leon Greaves's fifty-year prison sentence with greater alacrity, joining Latin Panamanians in their calls for his pardon and early release.

Greaves Resurfaces as a Symbol of Apartheid Injustice

When in the 1950s Lester Greaves fought with U.S. guards who consigned him to the "hole" at Gamboa Penitentiary, activists accused authorities of racial and political harassment. Radical Panamanian writers even suggested that Zone officials had framed Greaves for his 1946 rape conviction. They claimed that the woman Greaves "supposedly raped" was actually his girlfriend, that no violence had occurred, and that the Zone Police had railroaded Greaves for violating the borderland's chief sexual taboo: intimate relations between black men and white American women. In interviews decades later Greaves maintained his innocence and hinted at previous relations with his victim even though he clearly admitted his guilt at his trial and in two written documents while serving his sentence.[62]

The actor, singer, and activist Paul Robeson condemned Greaves's sentence indirectly during a trip to Panama in 1947 to protest racial discrimination in the Zone. In 1958, when Zone governor William Potter pardoned Gustave Smith and Gerald Thomas, two GIs serving twenty-five-year sentences for the murder of a West Indian night watchman, Panamanian protests over Greaves's sentence intensified. Potter released Smith and Thomas after they had served only eight years each for a particularly vicious murder; by that time Greaves had already spent twelve years in Gamboa. West Indian civic, religious, and labor leaders visited Greaves in prison, casting the young man as a victim of "Canal Zone Justice" and "a political prisoner" of the Zone apartheid system. Eventually U.S. Congressman Adam Clayton Powell and the NAACP joined the campaign for Greaves's early release.[63]

With his novel *Los Forzados de Gamboa* or *Gamboa Road Gang* (1960), the Panamanian author Joaquín Beleño put the racial plight of West Indian borderlanders front and center in the growing cultural protest against the Zone. He cast his protagonist, Atá, a young mulatto Panamanian unjustly sentenced to fifty years at Gamboa for rape, along the lines of the Greaves case. Atá falls in love with Anabelle, the daughter of a powerful Zone official. His mother is a black West Indian who works as a maid in Anabelle's home, but the youth's father is a white GI. Due to his childhood friendship with Anabelle and her family, Atá increasingly views himself more as a white American than as a Panamanian mulatto. When the Zone Police discover him making love to Anabelle, Atá nobly but naïvely admits to sexual assault to spare Anabelle the scandal of their forbidden love.[64]

While enduring the racist cruelties of Gamboa Prison and the taunts of his fellow inmates of color, who consider him a fool, Atá takes solace in the letters he receives from Anabelle. He believes that she will wait for him and that they will one day marry. But Atá is shattered by the news that Anabelle has returned to the States to study and has fallen in love with a young white American whom she will soon wed. With this crushing revelation, Atá at last casts off his "false colonial consciousness," his absurd dream of being a white American who will one day marry a Zonian girl. In the novel's conclusion, Zone prison guards kill Atá when he tries to escape, completing his tragedy of racial injustice and colonial subjugation.[65]

The story of Beleño's Atá explores the racial complexities of the Zone-Panama borderland with its varied interactions among different races and ethnicities. Beleño based the character of Atá partly on his own conflicted experience as a mixed-race child, the son of an Afro-Panamanian woman and a mestizo Colombian father. In one aspect the doomed protagonist Atá represents "the tragic mulatto," a familiar archetype in Caribbean literature, torn between two worlds and never wholly accepted by either.[66]

But Atá's character bears key differences from the real-life Greaves. Greaves was not a fair-skinned mulatto and in fact had two West Indian parents. Greaves entertained no illusions of being either white or American. No proof exists in his penal records of his ever receiving letters in prison from the woman he raped (though he would later claim that U.S. prison officials burned them). He had a previous record in Panama of assaulting a woman and a conviction for fighting with a West Indian in the Zone. He first denied his guilt only in a controversial interview in 1956 granted to a West Indian daily, the *Nation*, after the protest campaign on his behalf had started. In 1962 Canal Zone governor William Carter, under the direction of President John F. Kennedy, pardoned and released Greaves after sixteen years' servitude. Washington granted the pardon as a goodwill gesture and as part of Kennedy's hopes for a new, more equitable relationship with Panama.[67]

Still, Beleño's popular novel held enormous mythic power. His portrayal of Atá and Anabelle became the stuff of legend in the borderland. "Yes, I remember that Greaves case. It was like Romeo and Juliet. They were very much in love but from two different worlds. Naturally, they took it out on the black one. What do you expect? They were all Southerners, you know," a Panamanian remarked. "She was in love with him. Maybe he was a little rough with her, but you know de womens, some of dem, dey like it that way. She waited for him, mon. Dat was why she took the night train so late right when he was gettin' offa work," another West Indian recalled. "He was set up by de whyte mon." Perhaps the most telling comment on Greaves's guilt came from John Hampel, a veteran policeman of the 1940s–1960s: "The particular rape case that I refer to is still questionable by many as to whether it did or did not occur, as the complainant alleged. Perhaps if it was a white Panamanian rather than a black who did the deed, and if the girl's father was not the Director of a Division, the person might have been found innocent. But the Court's decision was 'guilty'; the criminal to be incarcerated for fifty years. Any sane person who had intent to commit a similar crime in the Canal Zone would think many times before committing such an offense."[68]

The collective memory surrounding the Greaves case reveals volumes about differing gender and racial perceptions among West Indians, Latin Panamanians, and North Americans. Such recollections also demonstrate the stark sense of injustice and distrust that many West Indians felt toward the Zone administration. In the 1950s, for example, when Zone doctors first began giving spinal taps to older West Indians to detect meningitis and encephalitis and several died afterward, rumors spread throughout their community that white authorities were deliberately killing off West Indians near retirement age to avoid paying them their pensions. "Don't go for 'de back ponch,' mon!" West Indians told one another repeatedly. "Dey whyte mon, he kill you with 'de back ponch,' so he don't have to pay you your money!"[69]

Education and Language in the West Indian Borderland

The U.S. decision in 1955 to grant Panama more influence over the Zone's West Indian workforce further politicized Antilleans already enduring a difficult transcultural evolution. As part of the Eisenhower-Remón Treaty of 1955, Zone officials replaced local-rate schools in the enclave with "Latin American" schools. This proved a neat euphemism since none of the system's pupils were Latin Americans but rather English-speaking descendants of African slaves who came to the isthmus from British-ruled islands at the behest of the United States. The new treaty called for a strictly Panamanian curriculum in Spanish in all West Indian classrooms. Almost overnight West Indian children had to learn a new language, history, and literature. Gradually this pulled more West Indians toward a Panamanian national identity. In effect, both Latin Panamanians and West Indians began the process of taking back the borderland, at least where the education and political indoctrination of non-U.S. citizens were concerned.

Much confusion reigned during the first few years, when even West Indian teachers could not speak Spanish fluently and crammed Spanish courses at night before teaching their Antillean pupils by day. "Our teachers and we students both learned Spanish together," a West Indian reminisced. "And very badly most of the time!"[70] But once students stepped out of the classroom and into their silver, Zone-based community, they again confronted the dominant English-speaking culture. After 1955 U.S. Zone officials evicted more and more West Indians from the Zone and into Panamanian housing to eliminate this duality and to evade federal discrimination charges for maintaining racially separate housing and school systems. For Zone authorities, once West Indians resettled on the other side of the line, even if they still worked for the Canal, they ceased to be a U.S. problem, at least regarding the recent *Brown v. Board of Education* decision. Such policies unintentionally strengthened the bond between younger West Indians' struggles for justice in the Zone and the Panamanian nationalist crusade against the enclave. What the curriculum reforms said to West Indians via the Panamanian government was "You are no longer foreigners; we want you to become one of us."[71]

While this policy left many West Indians conflicted over their identities, it also held portentous ramifications. After 1956 Panama gained the right to tax the incomes of West Indians living in the Zone. This measure imposed financial hardship on previously untaxed West Indians, but it also brought unexpected benefits to them. If the dictum "No taxation without representation" holds validity, the reverse is also true. For the first two generations after construction, Panamanians had largely ignored the plight of the Zone-ruled West Indian and never considered him a reliable ally. After 1956, and especially following the 1964 uprising, Panama's government began to agitate more aggressively for the rights of its "imprisoned citizens" living under "the jackboot of U.S. racism and imperialism." This stance became a useful wedge issue for attacking the U.S.-ruled enclave. Furthermore within the republic, West Indians now constituted an important voting block that Panamanian politicians could no longer ignore and in fact openly courted for victories in tight elections.[72]

Still, many Antilleans, especially those who lived in the Zone, moved hesitantly toward this new *West Indian–Panamanian* identity after many generations of association with Great Britain and then with the U.S.-dominated Zone. While resenting their treatment by both "protectors," large numbers of West Indians refused to place full confidence in Latin Panamanians, particularly Arnulfistas, the supporters of Arnulfo Arias whose 1941 Constitution had so wounded and insulted them as a people. Several Latin Panamanian leaders still condemned the historical role of West Indians as collaborators with the Zonians. One writer even referred to the West Indians as the "forced Panamanians."[73] An embittered Antillean revealed the complexity of this racial and ethnic divide: "There is a prejudice against us because we speak English. But rich Panamanians send their kids to U.S. schools in the Zone *to learn English*. We are discriminated against not because they think we are inferior but because they resent blacks being here. Panamanians are strange. They speak bad about you, but then they treat you like friends."[74]

This process exasperated many Antilleans. Grace Maynard Clark, a West Indian who was a schoolgirl in the 1950s, remembered all her report cards from the Panamanian school that she attended in Río Abajo, a West Indian neighborhood near the Zone, listing her as "Grisela" Clark. This Hispanicizing of West Indian names was common during the postwar nationalist revival, when Panamanian schoolteachers saw it as their duty to "convert" or "assimilate" West Indians to Panama and away from the United States. Some West Indians chose to Hispanicize their names voluntarily to make the transition to living in the republic easier when dealing with Panamanian neighbors and authorities. Clark especially recalled her communion with fellow West Indians at the Church of God on Sixteenth Street as a source of cultural

3.3. U.S. Canal Zone publications emphasized the brawn and loyalty of the segregated West Indian workforce, as shown in this photo of a West Indian laborer receiving an Employee of the Month award from a U.S. white official. Such images of fealty toward the Zonians angered many Panamanian nationalists. Courtesy of the *Panama Canal Spillway* in the Panama Canal Museum Collection, George Smathers Library, University of Florida, http://ufdc.ufl.edu/pcm.

and ethnic unity among her many friends and relatives in Río Abajo. Gloria Branch remembered the constant prejudice that she and other West Indian youths faced in Panamanian schools and barrios in the 1940s and early 1950s. Joheta Clark recalled the cultural confusion West Indian borderers confronted every day, speaking Spanish in school and on the street but facing reprimands from family if they attempted to do the same at home. Home was still the sacred refuge for bajan English, Caribbean cuisine, and West Indian folkways. Melva Lowe de Goodin saw herself as racially African and proud of her Caribbean roots, but nationality-wise she increasingly recognized herself as a Panamanian citizen as she matured into adulthood. West Indians' deep Protestant faith, be it Methodist, Baptist, or Presbyterian, linked to a strong adherence to daily readings of the Bible, also marked one of their core cultural foundations. As Earl Newland stated, "I am Panamanian, I accept that, but above all else, I am a human being. I am a child of God, and as such I must live and share my life with everyone regardless of who dey are." Newland was an activist in the Zone local-rate defense workers union, Local 907. There he fought for better wages, work conditions, and benefits during many hard years in a transitional borderland.[75]

After 1956 West Indians evicted from the Zone and even some of those still living there experienced further complications to their "dual" identities. From the mid-1950s on, they found themselves not just compelled to speak Spanish in the republic but also to celebrate Panamanian holidays, folkways, and festivals, not just American or Antillean ones. Throughout such confusing identity transformations, they also strove to maintain their own way of life. West Indians had to wear, in effect, three faces: a happy English-speaking Canal Zone face, a happy Spanish-speaking Panamanian face, and a somber English-speaking West Indian face that they could share only with fellow sufferers. In *White Masks, Black Faces*, Frantz Fanon elucidates the tragedy of "false consciousness" that colonized peoples endured through generations of European rule. But Fanon's Algerians struggled with only one "imposed consciousness," that of a coerced French colonial identity. West Indians in Panama had two, and in the case of the older ditch-diggers, three.[76] One retiree in his early nineties recalled, "As a boy I was a British subject when my family came to Panama. Then I was a ward of the Americans when I worked for dem for tirdy years. Then after the '55 treaty, I became a Panamanian when the Americans made me leave the Zone. But deep down, I was always West Indian. They could never wash dat pain offa me."[77] Many of these Panamized Barbadians and Jamaicans also resented the more common use of the Spanish term *antillano* for them. They preferred to be called West Indian. "*Antillano* was a word pushed by the sellouts, the butches, dem dat sold out to the Panamanians to lift up their own fat arses on a playte uh silver. I don't buy dat. I'm no *antillano*, I'm a West Indian!" one complained.[78] But another remarked, "*Antillano* is still better than *chombo*."[79]

Radical Expressions of West Indian Identity

Just as Marcus Garvey and Paul Robeson inspired earlier generations of borderland West Indians to struggle for dignity and liberation, U.S. civil rights currents in the 1960s–1970s influenced a new generation. Both Martin Luther King and the more radical Malcolm X had their adherents among West Indian baby boomers. While older West Indians and white officials labeled them "rebels," "boat-rockers," and "trouble-makers," these younger West Indians sported afros on the job, gave one another Black Panther salutes and high-fives, and refused to defer automatically to whites in the manner of their fathers. In early 1964 the military's Maintenance Division sent a young West Indian, George Barnabas, the first black licensed plumber to work for the U.S. Army in Panama, to Corozal to fix the "white toilet." Corozal was the same military base where Lester Greaves had worked prior to his arrest in 1946. Barnabas had gained his job through the apprentice program, approved in the 1955 Eisenhower-Remón Treaty that for the first time promoted advancement to better-paying gold jobs for Panamanian employees of the Canal. Barnabas, a muscular youth, began his repairs immediately by using a sledgehammer to smash down the large metal partition that separated the "white" from the "colored" toilets. "Ain't no white toilet now!" he shouted to the astonished army contractor. "Ain't no black toilet either! Just the same toilets for everybody!" To Barnabas's surprise, U.S. authorities refrained from punishing him and integrated all the latrines at Corozal later that year. "I broke the color bar at Corozal—with a sledgehammer!" he still boasts to this day. Barnabas also speaks proudly of his many fistfight victories in Parque Lefevre during his youth, when he tangled with any Latin Panamanians who dared to insult him racially.[80]

In the late 1960s at the Canal Administration Building on Balboa Heights, a handful of young West Indian workers began drinking from the gold water fountain in defiance of Zone etiquette. Zone bosses repeatedly reprimanded them and wrote them up for misconduct. But in 1970, despite white complaints, all water fountains and bathrooms at the Building were integrated, due in part to resistance from young politicized West Indians. Similar direct action by West Indian youths in Gamboa ended segregation at Dredging Divisions bathrooms in the mid-1970s. In 1972 a group of black U.S. servicemen who called themselves "the Concerned Brothers" joined the fight against discrimination by picketing the local Elks clubs until the organization agreed to accept black members. In several demonstrations in front of the Balboa club, young West Indian activists joined the black GIs. Protests against segregation in education also erupted at West Indian "Latin American" high schools in 1972, such as in Paraiso, that convinced authorities of the growing threat of racial unrest.[81]

West Indian agitation against Jim Crow also gained a key ally in Panama's new military government. Coming to power in a coup in 1968, General Omar Torrijos sought support as a populist caudillo with sympathies for Cuba and later Nicaragua's Sandinistas. The mestizo general put the weight of his government's rhetoric behind condemnations of U.S. discrimination and colonialism in the Zone. Unlike past white oligarchic leaders, Torrijos openly solicited West Indians as allies in his efforts to gain full sovereignty over the borderland. The general supported the publication of a serialized biography of John Peter Williams in the government-backed magazine *Más Para Todos* that briefly lionized Williams as a Panamanian patriot. Torrijos promised equality to West Indians in his vision of a new, gringo-free Panama. While betrayed by past Panamanian promises, West Indian leaders moved grudgingly toward partnership with the racially liberal Torrijos. Known in the countryside as "Cholo Omar" for his darker complexion and informal bearing, the general burnished his progressive credentials when he criticized Jim Crow in the Zone and pressured white U.S. officials to implement reforms. The Canal Zone Junior College had admitted black students as early as 1961, but the Zone's white grammar and high schools held out the longest against West Indian and Panamanian pressure. The schools did not integrate until the final Carter administration's negotiations with Torrijos, at which point the West Indian victory proved moot since all U.S. pupils moved to the DOD school system and most West Indians from the enclave enrolled in Panama's public schools.[82]

In the late 1960s the U.S. military in Panama experienced numerous racial brawls and fistfights between black, white, and Puerto Rican troops. Assertive, insubordinate West Indian workers only added to what the Zone administration viewed as a growing "racial tinderbox" within the borderland. U.S. officials attempted to assuage West Indian pride with symbolic gestures. In 1966 they dedicated a park and a plaque in Pedro Miguel to Samuel H. Whyte, who founded the West Indian Employees Association in 1924; it was the first major memorial to one of the Antillean labor force's heroes.[83] The Zone administration also negotiated with Local 900 and Local 907, the non-U.S. unions in the enclave with majority West Indian memberships, to upgrade working conditions and wages for local rate workers. But on the repressive front, the Zone's Internal Security Office moved to evict rebellious West Indian youths from their parents' housing once they turned eighteen if they did not have a job on the U.S. side of the border. U.S. officials also tried to remove them from company payrolls, though this proved more difficult due to union protections. The more assertive West Indian identity of the 1970s complicated the Zone's white supremacist policies. In linking their efforts to the civil rights crusade in the United States and to the larger Third World decolonization movement in Vietnam, Angola, Namibia, Mozambique, and South Africa, West Indians gained new leverage and legitimacy, to the annoyance of U.S. officials.[84]

3.4. West Indian and Latin Panamanian teachers receive scholarship checks for their outstanding students from the Canal Zone superintendent of schools. This marked progress as such aid allowed students of color to attend the formerly all-white Canal Zone Junior College, though the K–12 system of the Zone remained segregated throughout the borderland's history. Courtesy of the *Panama Canal Spillway* in the Panama Canal Museum Collection, George Smathers Library, University of Florida, http://ufdc.ufl.edu/pcm.

And yet ironically, with the Zone's demise in 1979, long promoted as the crucial day of liberation, many West Indians lost their privileged position in Panamanian labor. Long accustomed to earning three times Panamanian wages, West Indians faced hard times and a difficult adjustment when the U.S. presence wound down. Many West Indians still managed to find jobs with the Panama Canal Commission (1979–99) or on the U.S. military bases in the new Panama Canal Area. But several West Indians alleged Latin Panamanian discrimination against them and a "get even" attitude, as U.S. influence within the Commission waned.[85] Lots of older West Indians refused to believe that the United States, the most powerful nation on earth, would ever transfer the Canal Zone to "dat poodle dog, Panama." A few even taunted

Latin Panamanians on the streets during the run-up to treaty ratification in 1978. Their shock at the passage of the treaties surpassed that of even some Zonians. Fortunately for the local-raters, stipulations in the enabling legislation attached to the treaties granted many senior West Indian workers U.S. green cards and a fast track to U.S. citizenship that they eagerly snatched. Holding two passports, these "exiled" canal laborers split their time between working in the United States (mostly in New York) and visiting and vacationing in Panama. With the demise of the Zone under the 1977 treaties, Jim Crow humiliation of West Indians ended. But the accords also dismantled a powerful refuge for West Indian culture in Panama. The centuries-old transculturation process of immigrants to the isthmus obtained as the yanqui employers departed. That process had actually begun in the mid-1950s with the Eisenhower-Remón Treaty.

The new Afro Antillano Museum in Panama City belatedly recognizes the contributions of West Indians to Panama's history and culture and speaks to a greater Panamanian acceptance of West Indians in isthmian society. West Indian organizations also gather every August 14 near the Pedro Miguel Locks to celebrate the completion of the Canal and to affirm their community's mass participation in that great transformative event in U.S., Panamanian, West Indian, and global history. Tellingly Latin Panamanians do not celebrate the Canal's opening due to its painful associations with U.S. colonialism. But fewer and fewer young people of West Indian ancestry speak English or practice wholly West Indian customs. Older West Indians lament the loss of the once vibrant Antillean social life as memberships in voluntary associations and clubs have declined and there are fewer colorful Sunday gatherings at churches and baseball fields. They also resent the growing poverty in and government neglect of the city that had once served as the West Indian cultural capital, Colón. Sadly, in many cases West Indians watched their children become Hispanicized, or more correctly Panamized, seemingly neglecting the heritage of their hero-worker forebears.[86]

Yet a competing viewpoint holds that the U.S.-run Canal Zone and its adjacent borderland only retarded and warped this normal assimilation process, engendering unnecessary racial and cultural discord between Antillean and Latin Panamanians for generations. Such critics condemned the U.S. use of a "divide and conquer," third-nation labor strategy. Both the beneficiaries and victims of this policy, older West Indians remain conflicted over the process and over their trifurcated identities as West Indians, Panamanians, and in some cases U.S. citizens as well. The borders of the Zone, at once guarded, open, porous, and concrete, forced all parties to wrestle with such identities.

"We played a big part in buildin' dis country and dis Canal. Dey won't tell you dat, neither de whyte mon nor de Panamanian mon. But we dun it! Wit bodies and wit blood while dem other two was watchin' on." And so the long and complicated struggle over the West Indians' rightful place in the larger narrative of Panama and Central America continues. Their enduring contribution and determination to carve out a place on the isthmus left an indelible mark on the borderland that they helped define.[87]

DESIRE, SEXUALITY, AND GENDER

IN THE ZONE-PANAMA BORDERLAND

On Friday night, April 16, 1955, two enlisted men from the U.S. Army, Sergeant William J. Mitchell, twenty-five, and Corporal Vernon O. Helton, twenty-four, met two Panamanian sisters, twenty-one and twenty-four, at a USO-sponsored dance at the Fort Amador NCO Club on the Pacific side of the Canal. After the dance the two soldiers drove the women to a bar in the Panamanian border town of Arraijan for drinks, although the older sister insisted on only having Coca-Cola. They left the bar separately, but the soldiers encountered the women again at a nearby bus stop and offered them a ride home. Since it was near midnight and the buses had stopped running, the two women accepted. But instead of taking them home as promised, Sergeant Mitchell pulled off onto the jungle K-10 military road just inside the Canal Zone and parked in a clearing. According to the older sister's court testimony, Corporal Helton, seated in the back, grabbed her and attempted to rape her. She cried out that she was "a maiden," but he forced himself upon her, pulling her by the hair. Her younger sister, sitting in the front seat with Mitchell, hit Helton over the head with her shoe when he pounced on her sister. Helton then seized the older sister and dragged her out of the car, where he tore her dress but failed in his efforts at penetration during a violent struggle on the ground. Meanwhile Mitchell raped the younger sister in the front seat. She later ran into the jungle looking for her older sister, who had fled the scene. The men followed.[1]

After a heated argument, the two soldiers managed to convince the terrified women to get back in their car for a ride home. The soldiers' attorney later used this acquiescence against the women, suggesting that no sexual assault but consensual relations had occurred. After only a few miles Mitchell stopped the car, as a Canal Zone Police car was blocking the intersection while adjudicating an accident. Screaming and weeping, the two Panamanian women leaped from Mitchell's car and ran toward the police, crying out that they had been raped. The police noted the women's torn dresses and disheveled appearance as well as the soldiers' disorderly countenance and scratches on their faces and arms. They arrested Helton and Mitchell and took them and the sisters back to the Balboa Police Station for questioning. The next afternoon Panamanian newspapers carried the story of the assaults as front-page news, warning readers of the perils of dating unknown *gringo soldados*.[2]

The Helton-Mitchell rape case marked one of the worst incidents of U.S.-Panamanian sexual relations, but it was one of many that went beyond physical and emotional intimacy into violence. Indeed sexual and gender relations among the populations of the borderland formed an integral part of the imperial structure that Washington fashioned there. Panama became the locus of U.S. desire on many levels from the mid-nineteenth century through the U.S. exit on December 31, 1999: the U.S. desire to possess Panama and its transit zone, the obsession with penetrating the isthmus completely and successfully with a canal, and the desire to hold onto its "prize possession" long after it made geostrategic sense. And just as powerful as the U.S. hunger for a feminized Panama was the Panamanian attraction to the masculine power, modernity, and glamour of the American presence. For the most part, and with reason, scholars have focused their analyses on the republic's nationalist rejection of the United States, but Americans also served as powerful objects of Panamanian desire. American women too responded to the allure of the sexual "other," that is, Panamanian males.[3] One of the most shocking murders in twentieth-century Panamanian history occurred on Bastille Day, July 14, 1939, when a married U.S. woman, Eileen Watson, gunned down her young panagringo lover, Madison Love, at the Union Club following an elite gala. The subject of a Zonian novella, *Death Came Dancing*, this slaying occurred on the eve of World War II, when the isthmian brothel trade and U.S.-Panamanian sexual interaction reached their apogee.[4]

Throughout these borderland encounters different concepts of gender, race, and sexual mores infused relations among U.S. citizens from the First World, West Indians, and Panamanians and other Latinos from Third World Hispanic cultures. Differing gender constructions, customs, and behaviors functioned in and around the Zone that contrasted with those in the Panamanian interior or the continental United States. Still, cooperation as well as conflict shaped these encounters. For instance, both Zone and Panamanian officials regarded a tightly regulated sex industry as necessary to bolster U.S. soldiers' morale, limit the spread of sexually transmitted diseases, and reassure Panama's upper and middle class that the U.S. military presence would not upset the local moral order. The U.S. military strove to limit GIs' sexual relations to foreign prostitutes and to working-class and lower-class isthmian women. Sexual relations with these groups helped foster binational accommodation among the popular classes while avoiding offending the increasingly nationalist Panamanian bourgeoisie. But U.S. and Panamanian strategies of sexual containment often backfired in unexpected ways when sexual violence ignited widespread, nationalist outrage. The Helton-Mitchell rape case marked one of these public relations disasters.[5]

Although they belonged to Panama's working class, the sisters assaulted by Helton and Mitchell rejected the degradation that U.S. soldiers and institutions meted out to them. The U.S. military community in Panama of around twenty thousand (ten thousand troops and ten thousand dependents in 1955) traditionally maintained better relations with the Panamanian population than did the U.S. civilian employees, the Zonians. Working-class GIs on the isthmus interacted more frequently with ordinary Panamanians than did most middle-class Zonians. Thus class divisions and military and civilian cultures both played roles in the Helton-Mitchell case and in other sexual scandals.[6]

Defining Sexual Mores and Gendered Archetypes at the Borders

Definitions are important in assessing the intimate relations among the various peoples of the Zone-Panama borderland. Scholars accept that there is nothing innately biological or essentialist about gender roles; they are culturally constructed and vary across time and place. Similarly human sexuality, once viewed as a strictly physiological impulse involving desire, orientation, and action, has been reexamined; anthropologists and sociologists have discovered that a variety obtains concerning what is "proper" and "natural' sexual desire, activity, and preference for partners. Few universal concepts of what is fitting and acceptable exist, although admittedly dominant notions of appropriate relations between the genders hold sway (e.g., that rape is wrong) in various settings, social environments, and time periods. These evolving ideas and behaviors regarding intimacy between men and women from a variety of racial and national backgrounds influenced larger relations within the Zone-Panama borderland.[7]

U.S. efforts at enforcing sexual controls at the borders "provided a key site for the production and reproduction of sexual categories, identities, and norms" among the typically unequal relations that abounded along an imperial frontier.[8] For example, Canal Zone Police and MPs frequently arrested sexual "transgressors" along the enclave's borders and categorized, classified, and ascribed behaviors and identities to them that were often untrue, mistaken, or self-serving for the U.S. border-control mission. Thus Panamanian lovers became prostitutes; effeminate Colombian males, homosexuals; and Panamanian Carnaval revelers, cross-dressers. This is because, in a majority of cases, those authorities on the more powerful side of an imperial borderland get to make the rules and determine the categories for those on the less powerful side. In a similar fashion, a tendency emerges in most borderlands to view sexual infiltration across the frontier from a less powerful state into a hegemonic one as the entry of "foreign bodies" from unclean regions into a sanitary and morally superior land.[9]

Ultimately attempts at controlling sexuality along the Zone-Panama corridor failed due to the lack of fear and powerful legal proscriptions. The fear factors in place regarding sexual relations with the "other" along a highly militarized frontier, such as Europe's Iron Curtain, or between fiercely divided religious communities, such as in the Ulster borderland, never existed along the more open and porous isthmian frontier.[10] Those convicted of illegal street prostitution in Panama or in the Zone paid a small fine or suffered brief incarceration. And these penalties applied only to the prostitute, not to his or her customer. The Canal Zone code that strictly segregated public facilities along racial lines said nothing about who one could or could not marry or who one could or could not have sexual relations with—as long as sex was not performed in a "lewd or public" manner, such as in a park or on the street. Panama maintained a long tradition of tolerance toward miscegenation and prostitution; while intermarriage among Americans and Panamanians faced some social stigma and bureaucratic hurdles, such practices encountered no restrictions within either Panamanian or Canal Zone law. U.S. commanders tried to keep their soldiers' sexual activity confined to Panama City and Colón's "red zones," but as long as GIs broke no laws, they had the right to go anywhere in Panama. And Zonians, as nonmilitary U.S. citizens, faced no restrictions on who they interacted with sexually in the republic (with the exception of Panamanian minors, age fifteen and younger).[11]

The Helton-Mitchell Debacle

On April 18, 1955, Zone court officials held an initial hearing on the charges against Helton and Mitchell in Balboa Municipal Court. Gawking spectators, most of them U.S. citizens, since the trial was held in the Zone, packed the small courthouse. A number of Zonian teenagers laughed during the Panamanian women's emotional testimony describing the servicemen's attacks. U.S. Judge Edward Altman admonished the spectators for making fun of the women, but the trial quickly became a magnet for cross-national tensions. Meanwhile in Panama, Spanish-language media dramatized the details and barbarity of yanqui lust.[12]

On June 8 Corporal Helton's attempted rape case came to trial in the U.S. District Court in Balboa, with Judge Guthrie Crowe presiding. The court empanelled a twelve-member jury of all-white U.S. citizens, ten men and two women. English-language newspapers described the prosecution's key witnesses, the two Panamanian women, as light-skinned mestizas or women of mixed Spanish and Indian ancestry. The prosecutor instructed the jury that it had two choices: to convict Helton of attempted rape, which carried a maximum sentence of fourteen years imprisonment, or to convict him of simple battery, which called for a thirty-day sentence and a $100 fine.[13]

Panamanian accounts of the trial depicted Helton's assault in symbolic terms as a U.S. attack upon the nation. Panamanian journalists made much of Helton's hulking, overweight physique. One Panamanian reporter referred to him as "a sadistic ape." During his opening remarks even the U.S. prosecutor William Sheridan called Helton "a 268-pound blubber bag of lechery." In comparison, reporters for Panamanian dailies such as La Hora and El Dia described Helton's Panamanian victim as "slight, innocent, and sweet-faced." For Panamanian nationalists, the striking contrast between Helton and the young rape victim personified the entire U.S.-Panamanian relationship as that of a 268-pound gorilla and a small, slender innocent, the Panamanian nation, hoodwinked and exploited since 1903.[14]

In these accounts Panamanian observers feminized their country as virtuous and dignified in the face of predatory U.S. masculinity. This approach contrasted with more masculine images of Panamanian resistance during the 1964 anti-American riots. In that celebrated uprising, hundreds of young male protesters invaded the enclave to plant the staff of the republic's flag in the "sacred soil" of the Canal Zone. They fired weapons at gringo troops, overturned cars, and torched U.S. symbols of power. But in this earlier appeal to justice, Panamanian writers preferred the notion of dignified victim-hood as their chief stratagem to shame the yanquis.[15]

In the Balboa courtroom Helton's Panamanian defense lawyer, Woodrow Castro, immediately cast the young Panamanian women in an unflattering light. "They went onto the base unescorted. . . . They went to pick up some-one. They weren't prostitutes but they were out to seek contacts perhaps to get married eventually." Castro spoke of women's "traditional attraction" to the military "in art and story, as well as in life. But the attraction is no lon-ger epaulettes, it is allotments," referring to the generous stipends U.S. mili-tary men and their Panamanian wives received for rent when living off-base. Speaking for the soldiers and the U.S. community in Panama, Castro placed the two sisters within the hierarchy of sexual opportunism that Americans felt had long operated along the borderland. Within this hierarchy street-walkers occupied the lowest rung, followed by *artistas* who worked the legal brothels in Panama City and Colón. Higher up in the order were the so-called gate girls, who presumably included the two sisters.[16]

The Complexities of Borderland Gendered Relations

"Gate girls," named for their gathering outside U.S. military base gates, were poor, working-class, and even some lower-middle-class Panamanian women who entered the Zone every Friday and Saturday night to attend mili-tary dances in the hopes of establishing a relationship with a GI. The Pana-manian novelist Joaquín Beleño referred to these women, with their darker complexions and lower social status, as *rabicolorados* (colored-tails), in con-trast to the upper-class *rabiblancos* (white-tails) who had long ruled the roost in Panama.[17] On the Pacific side of the Zone most of these women came from Arraiján, Chorrera, and Capira as well as the blighted barrios in the capital. Middle-class Panamanians attached a certain stigma to gate girls, whom many saw as little more than prostitutes. Nonetheless gate girls comprised a broad range of Panamanian and Colombian women, some certainly pros-titutes, whom the military attempted to screen; some with previous relation-ships with and children by U.S. servicemen; and many novices, like the two sisters, curious to cross borders and meet Americans.[18]

This last group had its own moral code and generally would not sleep with a GI on the first date; rather they sought long-term relationships or marriages with servicemen. They were aware that giving in too quickly to soldiers' advances might mark them as "cheap" or "easy," in GI parlance, thereby damaging their chances for serious courtship. At the same time, opportunities to spark a relationship with a U.S. soldier were rare, and some Panamanian women felt pressure to give in to a serviceman's desire rather than lose the chance to develop a deeper connection. Such stark choices left many Panamanian women in a quandary. Sexual codes of conduct were never as strict in Panama, with its Caribbean culture, as, for example, in the Andean countries, yet despite North American stereotypes that branded all Panamanian women as naturally promiscuous, many isthmian women came from religious backgrounds and were quite strict in their personal deportment. Panamanian women from the lower middle class, such as the two sisters, knew the dangers of bringing dishonor to their families with an unwed pregnancy or the gossip that cavorting with gringo soldados could bring.[19]

That said, having a GI as a steady boyfriend or husband provided one of the few escapes available for borderland women with little education or economic opportunity. A senior U.S. sergeant in Panama in the mid-1950s earned more money than many Panamanian lawyers or professors. Such economic distortion, typical of colonialism, shaped sexual and gender relations between the two nationalities. To have an American beau meant that a Panamanian woman could spend every weekend in the nightclubs and resorts of Panama and the Zone, living a lifestyle most Panamanians could only live vicariously through telenovelas (soap operas). But it is important to note that the power differential between privileged U.S. soldiers and economically deprived isthmian women almost always placed GIs in the superior power position, with all its attendant dangers for abuse.[20]

Another problem with U.S.-Panamanian gender relations concerns the crossed signals the two parties often sent one another. Social space in Panama was customarily closer than in the United States, and Panamanian women had long been acculturated to be more tactile and physically expressive of their emotions than U.S. women. Panamanian women typically embraced and kissed male strangers on the cheek when first meeting them and fed their dates using their own forks, conduct that in 1950s America might be construed as provocative. Panamanian women danced very closely with U.S. soldiers, held their hands, and often stared into their eyes upon first meeting them. Rhythmic salsa dances intensified this feeling of easy intimacy between the sexes. U.S. soldiers new to the isthmus frequently assumed that Panamanian women "were coming on to them" when this was not necessarily the case.[21]

At the same time, Panamanian women viewed ardor on the part of a North American suitor as similar to that of a Panamanian male. Such public passion was a key component in the theater of courtship and attraction so prevalent in stylized Panamanian dances and art. While cultural misunderstandings can never excuse sexual assault, they do help explain how U.S. men and Panamanian women frequently misread one another's intentions, often leading to embarrassing or tragic consequences. Language barriers added to the difficulties. While upper-class Panamanians spoke English, poor and working-class Panamanians were rarely bilingual, and GI fluency in Spanish was generally abysmal and limited to a few phrases and obscenities.[22]

During the first trial for Helton, U.S. women in the courtroom again tittered, drawing rebukes from Judge Crowe. Crowe would later say that he could not help it that "some people find sex funny," an odd comment since rape was the charge at hand. From their behavior we can surmise that at least some middle-class U.S. women in the courtroom regarded the Panamanian women with contempt as little more than trollops who got what they deserved. They may have also despised these women as possible sexual competitors for U.S. males in the Zone, for while Zonians prided themselves on maintaining a clean-living, family lifestyle, American bachelors, disgruntled husbands, and womanizers often drove into Panama for liaisons with local women. Zonian women were acutely aware that the other side of the line always presented this alternative sexual playground for U.S. males.[23]

Adopting an alternately paternalistic and hostile attitude toward the women, the soldiers' attorney denigrated the two sisters either as naïve or as knowing seductresses. He questioned their veracity, implying that they either knew or should have known the rules of the game when it came to Panamanian women courting GIs. Castro played upon the U.S. jury's negative stereotypes about isthmian women: loose, promiscuous creatures willing to "throw themselves" at GIs if it might lead them to the altar and eventually to U.S. citizenship. In this manner he appealed to the jury's acculturated expectations of borderland sexual relations: that they were always consensual and inevitably aligned servicemen's desire for a good time with Latinas' goals of U.S. wealth and passports.[24]

That Castro was of Latin American descent boosted the credibility of his argument and lent a powerful authenticity to the jury's prejudices. Simultaneously he reminded the Zonians that whatever their ethical failings during the assault, both Helton and Mitchell had strong service records, the latter having served with distinction in the Korean War. Here Castro appealed to the jury's chauvinism and to the tendency of U.S. borderlanders to close ranks and support fellow citizens when threatened by the cultural "other," in this case "devious and unchaste" Panama.[25]

Castro's condescending portrait struck a chord. Despite strong corroborating testimony from the Canal Zone Police, torn dresses, undergarments, and photographed contusions on the women's bodies, the jury found Helton guilty of only the lesser charge of battery and sentenced him to thirty days and a $100 fine. The Panamanian journalist Joaquín Beleño expressed his outrage over the verdict in *La Hora*, contrasting the jury's finding with the infamous rape case in 1946 of the Panamanian West Indian Lester Greaves, who had received a fifty-year sentence in the same court for raping a white Zonian girl.[26] It was no accident that Greaves's case gained renewed interest as a cause célèbre following the Helton-Mitchell trials.[27]

In a dramatic turn of events Judge Crowe canceled the trial of Helton's codefendant, William Mitchell, on the more serious charge of first-degree rape when the two Panamanian sisters refused to return to the courtroom. The mother of the women told Panamanian and U.S. reporters that she would not permit her daughters "to face ridicule, laughter, and injustice." Indeed GIS had faced numerous rape charges against Panamanian women during World War II and afterward, and like Helton and Mitchell, they generally drew light or suspended sentences or had their cases dismissed. As a result Panamanian women had little faith in "Canal Zone justice." Crowe called upon Panamanian detectives to bring the sisters in as reluctant witnesses, but the detectives could not persuade them. The court enlisted the commandant of the Panamanian National Guard, General Bolívar Vallarino, to intercede, but Vallarino pointedly refused. In the discourse of the Panamanian media, these women defended the nation's dignity in their refusal to cooperate with the gringo tribunal. For a nation long humiliated by U.S. dominance, the concept of dignity held special cultural import. Little wonder that in the 1980s the Panamanian strongman Manuel Noriega named his street gang supporters "dignity battalions."[28]

The Helton-Mitchell rape case of 1955 had far-reaching consequences in Panamanian cultural politics. Panamanian nationalists saw the event as one more example of the moral corruption that the United States and its cultural products (movies, television) and troops had brought to the borderland. Panamanian journalists referred to the U.S. military dances as *mercados de carne* (meat markets). On the heels of the trial the government launched a crackdown on street and child prostitution, pornography, and the narcotics trade. Finally, Archbishop Francis Beckman of Panama banned the wearing of bathing suits at Panamanian beauty contests. He threatened women who did so with excommunication. On June 15, 1955, days after the Helton trial, the Hotel Panamá canceled the Miss Panamá Contest for that year and withdrew its participation in the Miss Universe Contest in Long Beach, California.[29]

U.S. Gendered Images of Panama

From early construction days U.S. citizens, soldiers, and officials feminized Panama in the negative sense, fostering an image of the republic and its people as emotional and duplicitous, given to carnality and seduction. The virtuous American Adam arrived in the isthmian Garden of Eden to confront a wily Panamanian Eve holding forth her tempting fruit and seductive geography. As even one of Noriega's colonels later proclaimed, "We're like a narrow-waisted woman; everyone wants us."[30] As late as 1960 the U.S. ambassador to Panama continued this tendency to view the republic as a troublesome woman. "We are married to Panama," he lamented, "and we can't divorce her."[31]

As well as feminizing Panama, the U.S. government and the Zonians had a habit of infantilizing the republic. They viewed the locals as wayward, mischievous children in need of parental instruction.[32] U.S. military personnel and Zonians often referred to the Panamanians as "the little guys." Occasionally even Panamanians accepted these assignations when trying to explain their borderland relations. A leading publisher said, "The love part of our relationship has to do with the advantages our unique association brings: the Canal, our trade situation, and so on. The hate part is like what a teenager feels about his overprotective father: he knows he should love him but he wishes that his father would just leave him alone for while."[33]

Forbidding feminine images of the Panamanian jungle also figured prominently in long-held U.S. notions of male conquest and sexual danger. Even medical reports on the challenge of yellow fever emphasized that it was "the Panamanian female mosquito's need for blood meals" that spread the disease that claimed so many workers' lives. Following Dr. William C. Gorgas's victory over these fiends and his establishment of proper sewage and garbage removal, the diseased Panamanian prostitute emerged as the new major health threat to the Canal borderland.[34]

Prostitution in U.S.-Panamanian Relations

On Ash Wednesday morning, March 4, 1965, a time when U.S.-Panamanian relations had reached a nadir following the 1964 riots, a maid working in an L Street apartment building in Panama City recoiled in horror from a third-story flat she had just entered. The maid had discovered the naked, butchered body of a twenty-two-year-old Chilean artista lying in blood-soaked sheets on her disordered bed. The victim's name was Roxana Hermosillo, and her murder became front-page news in all local papers for the next three weeks. Photos of the statuesque and beautiful Hermosillo dancing at the famed Ancon Inn nightclub filled both tabloids and the more respectable dailies, along with pictures of her savagely mutilated body. The mystery over her murder threw the capital into a panic, especially the community of artistas who worked so many of the borderland clubs and brothels.[35]

The Panamanian police investigation quickly pointed toward the U.S. military, the chief client base for the borderland sex industry. U.S. military and Canal Zone Police joined their Panamanian colleagues in the manhunt for the artista's killer. The vicious nature of the crime shocked both the public and investigators. Hermosillo had been raped and then stabbed over a dozen times in the chest, arms, neck, and face. "Gringo Asesino!" the newspaper headlines cried when the joint investigation finally apprehended a GI for the atrocity. In the process Roxana Hermosilla, a Chilean-born prostitute, incongruously became a heroine and sainted representative of the brutalized Panamanian nation. The revelation that her killer was an African American soldier complicated the racial, national, and gendered responses to her brutal rape and murder.[36]

The Origins of Panama's Borderland Prostitution

Prostitution had long existed in Panama, predating the U.S. presence by three and a half centuries. As in most port cities, prostitution flourished in Panama City as well as the Caribbean ports of Portobello and Nombre de Dios from the years of the Spanish Conquest through Colombia's war for independence in the early nineteenth century. Later all-male railroad and banana workers from the Caribbean brought a new tide of customers for isthmian brothels.[37] As in most Latin American and Caribbean nations, prostitution was legal in Panama, though an important distinction existed between official government-sanctioned brothels and the illegal streetwalker trade.[38] Besides servicing foreigners, the prostitutes of Panama had a domestic client base among Panamanian males of all classes in the region's urban centers.[39]

The next two population surges on the isthmus resulted from the French and U.S. Canal projects, both of which imported tens of thousands of overwhelmingly male workers. Prostitutes from France (officially known in company documents as "lobsters" to avoid public exposure) accompanied the

French foremen and engineers, although the majority of sex workers were women from nearby Colombia and the Caribbean islands.[40]

From 1904 to 1914 scores of prostitutes emigrated from the United States during the U.S. construction era.[41] So prominent were these U.S. working girls in the republic, especially in the role of madams, such as Mamie Lee Kelly of the Navajo Club, that the term *American woman* or *mujer americana* came to signify "prostitute."[42] Throughout the construction years Panama was noteworthy for a shortage of women, while nearly sixty thousand male laborers toiled on the big ditch and the U.S. garrison took shape. This scarcity led to the shipping of U.S. mail-order brides to the isthmus, as well as prostitutes from all over the Americas. The international composition of this group testified to the globalized nature of the Zone-Panama borderland even in its formative years.[43]

Following the Canal's completion, however, the influence of the World War I "purity crusade" in the United States briefly reoriented American attitudes toward the brothels. In 1918 General Richard Blatchford, commander of the U.S. garrison, temporarily banned prostitution and gambling in the capital and in Colón, cities that he referred to as "Sodom and Gomorrah." His efforts aroused enormous anger among U.S. enlisted men and Panamanians alike, especially those who worked the border vice trades. At the war's end, when Washington recalled Blatchford, the cantinas and cathouses of Panama reopened "in a Saturnalian celebration."[44]

The largest expansion of the prostitution industry in Panama occurred during World War II, when the combination of an enlarged U.S. garrison, Third Locks workforce, and thousands of daily transiting troops created a tremendous demand for sexual services. By the 1940s the Panamanian government had established a policy of employing mostly foreign prostitutes from Central America and the Caribbean Basin in its state-sanctioned industry. Government officials believed that such a practice would dampen nationalist resentment that might have arisen over U.S. exploitation of solely Panamanian women.[45]

Despite this policy, large numbers of Panamanian women operated as legal and illegal prostitutes, streetwalkers, and bar girls without government assent. The whole question of who was a prostitute and who was a girlfriend or lover who constantly asked her U.S. beau for money arose in this period, as large numbers of Panamanian women operated in the gray area between prostitution, concubinage, and dating. Referred to locally as *chulas* (the word also signifies "procuress"), these women often arranged their encounters with their GI *novios* in cheap hotels, lean-tos, automobiles, army barracks, alleyways, and even their own homes while their Panamanian boyfriends or husbands were away.[46] The World War II financial boom fueled by fat military payrolls created myriad opportunities for creative sexual-economic relations along the border.

Prostitution and the Marinadas

World War II Panama became celebrated for its famous *marinadas* when thousands of U.S. sailors, marines, and soldiers flooded the streets of the capital and Colón. Isolated for months on warships and troop carriers, these men alighted from their vessels with up to six months' pay determined to spend it all in two or three days on women, alcohol, and gambling. While deriving enormous profits from the marinadas, many middle-class Panamanians came to view the servicemen's arrivals as foreign invasions. Drunken GIs routinely attacked taxi drivers, policemen, bartenders, waitresses, and even ordinary Panamanian shoppers. The general attitude of these sailors and soldiers was that "anything local in a skirt was a whore." This presumption led to fights with the Panamanian brothers, fathers, and boyfriends of assaulted women. Gangs of sailors from the same ship stuck together and generally got the better of their opponents before U.S. shore patrols intervened.[47]

On leave, the U.S. military transformed the borderland seaports into more exotic locales than they actually were. Aware of U.S. servicemen's association of Panama with jungle exotica, Hindu and Chinese merchants sold the swaggering arrivals parakeets, monkeys, parrots, iguanas, and snakes, which adorned the sailors as they staggered between cantinas. These tropical animals, imported from Colombia and Costa Rica, frightened many Panamanian city-dwellers; they especially feared the monkeys, who scampered across bars and onto the heads of Panamanian women to the raucous laughter of the GIs who egged the simians on. Thus the U.S. military in conjunction with local merchants created a "jungled Panama" that existed only during their stays. Since naval regulations forbade sailors and soldiers from taking these pets on board their ships, the men resold or simply abandoned them in bars. The recaptured parrots frequently enunciated newly taught phrases that Panamanians were unfortunately familiar with, such as "Fuck you, spic!" and "Drop dead, nigger!"[48]

In addition to these animals, flush sailors hired Jamaican musicians from their street-corner stations to accompany them on their jaunts, banging on pots and drums and blowing trumpets as they sauntered down alleyways. Whooping gangs of GIs scaled national monuments to pose for photos that ignited riots. Some Panamanians gathered open-mouthed at the Plaza de Cinco de Mayo to watch these revelries that inverted the initial binational encounters during construction, when Americans viewed Panamanians as strange and primitive beings.[49]

Among the Panamanians who gathered to watch the marinadas were professional pickpockets and thieves, who robbed drunken sailors when they strayed too far from their mates. Panamanian bartenders routinely maintained the "two-bottle system" in their cantinas: they poured full-strength liquor for sober servicemen's initial drinks, then switched to watered-down cocktails once they became inebriated. Local hucksters also pulled in huge profits from GIs with rigged three-card Monte games and "loaded" dice.[50]

The gross domestic product of Panama tripled between 1939 and 1945, bestowing at least some benefits on the Panamanian population. Jack Bell, a Chicago *Daily News* reporter, ignited a controversy in 1945 when he wrote, "Just now with both the Army and the Navy pouring so much money into the place, every inhabitant should be filthy rich. . . . In reality, our presence there has resulted in wealth for a very few and vice and continuing poverty for most of the populace." Bell went on to paint an unflattering portrait of borderland casinos and bordellos that provoked angry Panamanian responses: "The monies spent by soldiers, sailors, and civilians from the Canal Zone in the cities and towns of Panama are not largesse. . . . If it is spent in our saloons, cabarets, roadhouses, and other dens of vice, the spenders undoubtedly get satisfaction for their money. If in these dens of iniquity they are 'rolled' or 'gypped,' they can find comfort in the fact that it would be just as easy to get 'rolled' or 'gypped' in the vice-mills of the great cities of their Great Country."[51]

The Structure of Borderland Prostitution

During World War II lines up to a hundred yards formed in front of the brothels in Colón on Cash Street and in Río Abajo's red zone in Panama City. The most efficient bordellos maintained "bullring" operations, in which three small cubicles were attached to a central trick room where the prostitute serviced her customers. In the attached rooms sailors and soldiers undressed, washed their privates in an antiseptic bowl, donned condoms, and redressed before leaving. A conveyer system kept all three rooms occupied by "johns" either getting ready to enter the trick room, having sex, or preparing to leave. This proved the most efficient way to get the maximum number of customers per prostitute and resembled modern medical facilities in which a number of patients wait in separate dressing rooms to be attended by a single doctor, whom they may see for only five minutes.[52] As dehumanizing as this system was, John Hampel, a Zone policeman during the war, noted that even the most squalid stalls had "a picture of the Child Jesus or Mother Mary on the wall. I don't believe, however, that any of the sailors, soldiers, or civilian men ever took notice of these paintings. Other than a plain chair, a rumpled bed, and an empty pail, the room was bare."[53]

The traditional Panamanian brothel maintained a more relaxed, accommodative atmosphere for its clients. Typically seminude dancers gyrated on stages to music, while other women worked the bar and tables where servicemen drank. Prostitutes encouraged their customers to buy them watered-down Blue Moon cocktails, hence the term "Blue Moon girls," given to Panama's B-girls for generations. The servicemen chose an artista and proceeded upstairs to a maze of bedrooms. Guards stood at the entrance to this section of the brothel, and the customer paid up front at a caged booth, where he received a token before entering a small bedroom stall with his chosen woman. Sand hourglasses measured the john's fifteen minutes. As an alternative to escape the state fee for a brothel license, some nightclubs operated downscale bars and dance shows, where the male customers would accompany a B-girl across the street to a small pensión, where the john would pay her for a specific sex act. The woman then had to kick back a fee to her employer for each man she took "across the street." Many of the dancers at these nightclubs maintained the fiction that they were not prostitutes but "entertainers," since they did not technically work in a brothel. Zonians called the small pensiones that accommodated such trade "San Blas hotels," rudimentary wooden structures on J and K Streets with common sinks and latrines, cleaned and guarded by Kuna Indians, hence the name assigned to these primitive "shack-ups."[54]

U.S. entertainers and prostitutes also set up shop in Panama during World War II, drawn by the lure of plentiful money and the wide-open atmosphere of the borderland. While the majority of bordello owners were Panamanian, U.S. madams and crime figures also established brothels, as did minorities such as Chinese, Hindus, Arabs, and Jews. Legitimate entertainers from all over Latin America and the United States staged elaborate shows at the Happyland, Kelly's Ritz, the Club Montecarlo, the Realto, the Lido, the Roxy, and the Montmartre, among them Dale Hall and "her primitive Indian rhythms"; Fifi Alonzo, "White Goddess of the Negro Rhumba"; Olga Negueruela; the "cute Cuban bombshell" Gloria Grant ("Watch This Shapely Dame Tangle with Her Giant Snake"); and the most infamous act, Jade Rhodora's "The

Rape of the Ape," in which she undressed and contorted as half-woman, half-gorilla.[55]

Panamanian Prostitution in Popular Culture

A number of Hollywood movies dealt with the theme of expatriate, good-time American gals in World War II Panama: *Panama Lady* (1939), Cole Porter's *Panama Hattie* (1942), and *Panama Sal* (1957). All these works featured female protagonists who worked the borderland as dancehall girls, night-club singers, or hoteliers: covers for prostitutes under the Hays censorship code. A common theme involved an all-American savior, typically a GI, who rescues one of these fallen angels and returns her to bourgeois respectability in the States. The stranded heroines in these movies were white Americans of Irish descent (Lucille Ball as Lucy McTeague, Ann Sothern as Hattie Maloney, and Elena Verdugo as Sal Regan). The only nightclub entertainer of color in any of these films who approximated the looks of the majority Caribbean women working the trade was Lena Horne, who made her film debut in 1942's *Panama Hattie*.[56]

While these films stressed the merriment of Panamanian nightclub life, darker themes emerged. Lucy in 1939's *Panama Lady* appeared as a world-weary chanteuse struggling on the fringes of prostitution. She connives in the robbery of an elderly oil prospector whose younger partner, Mack, drags her away to the jungle to work off her debt as his live-in maid. Similarly Hattie Maloney in *Panama Hattie* plays a sassy saloon-keeper in Panama who latches onto a handsome U.S. naval officer to escape a low-life existence ameliorated by catchy Cole Porter tunes, such as "Did I Get Stinkin' at the Savoy" (a famous Colón bordello), "Good Neighbors," a salute to FDR's Latin American policy, and "I've Still Got My Health!," a major concern for many gonorrhea- and cirrhosis-ridden GIs in the borderland red zones.

Authentic isthmian bargirls and their flophouses proved sterner material. Most of the women came from abusive rural Central American families mired in poverty. According to one study, 65 percent of these women regularly abused drugs and alcohol, and 53 percent claimed to have been sexually molested as children or adolescents.[57] On February 21, 1941, a Panamanian prostitute and dancer at the Happyland nightclub enticed a U.S. sailor, Edward Cabot Pearse, to the Hotel Estación, where her madam and lover, Ana Luis Palma, stabbed him to death during an argument over prices. In August 1942 in Colón, Enrique García shot and slashed to death his ex-lover, Rosita Palau Lane, an artista who had recently married a North American engineer, Walter Lane. In June 1943 Esteban González Marique, the young Panamanian boyfriend of a twenty-five-year-old artista, Adriana Rodríquez, shot and killed a retired sixty-six-year-old Zonian, Joseph Brown, who had proposed to Adriana. In June 1948 perhaps the most famous artista of World War II Panama, Carmen Sánchez Salazar, a onetime country girl from Chiriquí known as "La China" for her enticing Asian looks, died, poisoned by her young lover Alberto in revenge for La China's ongoing affairs with a former Zonian paramour and with her current Panamanian pimp. Local tabloids covered all these atrocities in detail, while mainstream papers decried the moral cesspool that the capital had become during the raucous war years.[58]

These tabloid scandals and their more sanitized film versions fed into the popular U.S. notion of 1940s–1950s Panama (similar to Bangkok in the present day) as a site of sexual license, endless fiesta, and whoredom. As Charlie Fears, a retired Canal Zone Police chief, stated, "We used to say that if you could put a roof over all of Panama, it would be the biggest whorehouse in the world." Such freely expressed contempt drew resentment from the majority of Panamanians who worked outside the vice trades and viewed the problem as arising not from any local immorality but from the U.S. military's presence and its global network of vice.[59]

These transnational links had a transportation and communication system all their own. In 1943 top military brass summoned Zone policeman John Hampel to a meeting in Colón regarding the high-security transit of the aircraft carrier USS *Franklin*, headed for combat in the Pacific. Authorities advised Hampel on the need for absolute secrecy and that the *Franklin*'s arrival time must be held in strictest confidence. Hampel therefore expressed dismay when he gathered his men at Cristobal Harbor at the appointed hour only to find a large throng of prostitutes holding up signs that read, "Welcome USS *Franklin*! We Love You!"[60]

U.S.-Panamanian Regulation of the Borderland "Trade"

As part of the original 1903 Hay–Bunau-Varilla Treaty, the United States supervised all sanitation in the borderland cities of Panama and Colón that included sewage and garbage removal, pest control, and the regulation of brothels. A U.S. military doctor, typically a colonel, held the title of Panama's health officer from 1904 to 1953.[61] Even afterward the U.S. military monitored houses of ill repute and servicemen expenditures at bordellos. In a 1945 report gathered from elaborate questionnaires, the U.S. military estimated that its men spent $6,010,000 on prostitution and vice in Panama that year, exceeding U.S. foreign aid to Panama by $4 million. As part of its oversight of the brothels, U.S. military doctors received notification of which clubs and women had been licensed and inspected. At the famous "Limits" border entry into Panama City, U.S. medics handed out condoms to GIs entering Panama and set up prophylaxis stations for those returning. The top U.S. brass put pressure on unit commanders for low venereal disease rates by showing health films, encouraging prophylactic use, and holding unit seminars. This strong tradition of U.S. disease control in Panama apparently worked, as the Zone's garrison reported the lowest VD scores of all U.S. overseas commands.[62]

Off-Limits

U.S. medical officers and adjutants-general declared various Panamanian bordellos, bars, nightclubs, hotels, restaurants, and even individual houses in the borderland to be "Off Limits–Out of Bounds" for U.S. servicemen. The reason for barring soldiers from these facilities was due to their "adverse effect upon the health, welfare, morals, and soldierly conduct of military personnel."[63] Proscriptions ranged from a high incidence of venereal disease, unlicensed or underage prostitutes, watered-down liquor, and drug use to robberies, shootings, knifings, rigged gambling, subversive propaganda, pornography, and transvestite activity, or as one U.S. veteran put it, "all the things that make a joint interesting."[64]

The U.S. military maintained a long list of off-limits establishments during World War II and the postwar era. These sanctions included entire towns that bordered the Zone, such as Chilibre, Camaron, El Coco, Capira, and Cativa, most of Chorrera, and whole sections of Colón. The off-limits list even included towns within the Canal Zone where "local-raters" (i.e., West Indians) lived. The Zone military pronounced virtually all of the legendary brothels of Panama off-limits at one time or another: the Gruta Azul, the Villa Amor, the Ancon Inn, the Golden Key, the Café Tropical, the Café Fenix, La Gloria, and the China Doll on the Pacific side, and the Victoría, the Samba, the Savoy, the Copacabana, the Aurora, the Black Cat, and the Ebony on the Atlantic side. One serviceman remembered enduring the monthly reading of off-limits establishments while standing at attention with a hangover in the hot sun: "I kept thinking to myself how much easier it would be to just list the places you *could* go to; it was a helluva shorter list." When first posted to Panama in the late 1950s, Private Wayne Bryant sat on a special bus detailed for new arrivals: "They drove us around to all the 'off-limits' joints in Río Abajo. 'You can't go there, you can't go there,' they told us. We wrote down the addresses on pads they gave us and went down to them *that night*, whooping it up and having a grand old time."[65]

Military police and shore patrols monitored these off-limits establishments in search of U.S. service personnel, but before entering, they would thump their nightsticks on the front door several times, stand in the door frame, and shout, "U.S. Provost Marshal entering for inspection!" They then waited about thirty seconds, giving those GIs who were not hopelessly drunk time to rush out the side or back doors or hide under beds. "Otherwise they would have to arrest half the army! We'd have more guys in jail than on duty."[66] Civilian Zonian customers, including teenage boys, felt no need to flee, as the military police held no jurisdiction over them. They viewed MP entrances and GI flights as part of the floor show.

Panama operated more perverse after-hours shows in off-limits establishments in the more dangerous parts of the city frequented by the drug and transvestite trade. These shows included bestiality, "live sex" performances that featured Latin American women performing sexual acts with dogs and donkeys to the cheers and guffaws of intoxicated servicemen. These "specialty shows" were favorites of those GIs who favored "a walk on the wild side," to experience the most depraved spectacles of the borderland. Such displays clearly delineated the differences between "barbarous Panama" and the neat and well-ordered U.S. base complex, with its chapels, libraries, and golf courses, that is, the perceived line between Third World debauchery and First World civilization. For many Zonians, GI attendance at such revues reinforced their belief that U.S. enlisted men were but one step up from the gutter, and in many cases were "even worse than the Panamanians."[67]

Borderland Crackdowns and Working Girls' Blues

Periodically during election years or after a particularly vicious brothel murder, the Panamanian police cracked down on street prostitution and "abhorrent acts" in the off-limits clubs. Cynical Panamanians viewed these redzone sweeps as the actions of one group of vice lords trying to snuff out their competition. Indeed the rising Panamanian strongman of the postwar era, José Antonio Remón, head of the National Guard and Police (1947–52) and president of the republic (1952–55), proved a chief beneficiary of such "blue raids," as he increased his stake in the cabaret and drug business. (Speculation still flourishes that Remón's drug trafficking led to the contract hit on him by a machine-gun assassin at the Juan Franco Racetrack on New Year's Day 1955.) In the late 1940s–1970s Panamanian police routinely rounded up unlicensed and underage prostitutes, transvestites, streetwalkers, drug peddlers, and pornographers, all private competitors to the government-sanctioned vice industries. Such morality crusades began in the postwar years as a reaction to the nationalist revulsion over wartime excesses.[68]

With the drastic reduction in the U.S. garrison from a wartime high of sixty-seven thousand to a postwar average of ten thousand to fourteen thousand troops, Panama's sex industry suffered severe cutbacks. During the cold war the United States also increasingly stationed its overseas forces on permanent European and Asian bases. As a result fewer troop transports and personnel transited the Canal, which led to further reductions in the trade. Still, as late as 1951 Panama City alone boasted 250 authorized brothels.[69]

In the wake of the World War II bonanza, many Latin American prostitutes returned to their native countries; the government even deported these "undesirables." In 1945 a popular Nicaraguan artista, Rosa Guerrero, attempted suicide when the republic forced her to board a ship for her homeland and abandon her bartender boyfriend in Colón.[70] Remaining artistas struggled in an environment of high unemployment and shifting political attitudes. Many of these women shouldered the added burden of supporting illegitimate children from GIs. One complained in a letter to an English-language newspaper under the pseudonym of Bula: "May I ask a few questions? What are we the Latin American women going to do now for a living? This constant nightly raiding is getting bad. Just think some of us have kids to take care of without fathers and we can't afford to have someone take care of our children while we are out of work. Instead of picking up women on the streets why doesn't the Executive Power see to it that we the Latin American women get some decent jobs."[71] The Panamanian wife of a U.S. serviceman expressed sympathy for the plight of these sex workers: "It's about time something was done about these women of the Canal Zone with their 'holier than thou' attitude who give the good women of Panama a black reputation. . . . It's about time we gave the cabaret girls a break. There are many fine women in show biz and as to the help they gave our boys in the last war, they get my thanks."[72]

In the postwar era, however, Canal Zone and military authorities applauded the Panamanian government's efforts to "clean up" if not eliminate vice. Above all else, officials feared "disorderly prostitution." Health officers preferred a controlled and contained trade in designated red zones where all of Panama's sex workers were medically inspected, quarantined, and kept in line with the fear of deportment if they strayed too far from the rules—or too close to the Zone border. Other overseas empires, such as the British, employed a similar strategy.[73]

Prostitution in the Canal Zone

In 1904, shortly after its establishment, the Zone outlawed prostitution within its own borders. But throughout the history of the enclave, prostitutes from Panama continually entered the Zone, giving little thought to what many regarded as an artificial boundary. Early on and continuing into the 1970s, despite efforts by the Canal Zone and U.S. military police, prostitutes found their way onto military barracks and into the bachelor quarters of canal workers, the homes of divorced U.S. civilians, and even their lodges and clubhouses. In December 1945 one Zonian complained of a late-night nude swimming party in the Balboa Clubhouse pool: "From whom do nightclub girls from Panama City get authority to swim in the Balboa pool? I'll admit the three of them did put on quite a show the other night. What next?" Sergeant Lee Amberths described a scene in the late 1950s: "[There were] naked girls in the washrooms at the Balboa YMCA where I was staying before I got my housing assignment. Imagine, in the YMCA!"[74] One of the reasons exclusion proved so difficult was that in the prosecution of solicitation cases, authorities brought a relatively mild penalty against the female or male prostitute—and none against his or her U.S. customer.[75]

Among the all-male Canal Police, a "boys will be boys" tolerance for male sexual high jinks flourished, especially in the case of servicemen, civilian bachelors, and divorced U.S. males, many of whom were the policemen's drinking buddies. While the police arrested prostitutes in the Zone, they also picked up many and simply deposited them on the other side of the border with warnings not to return.[76] Only women who operated brazenly and repeatedly within the enclave faced prosecution. Doris Rud, a diminutive West Indian woman, became something of a legend on the Zone during the 1950s–1960s, where she was continually arrested and imprisoned. Rud displayed good humor in the Zone court, expressed a world-weary affection toward Judge Crowe, and became one of the regulars at the women's prison in Pedro Miguel.[77]

A typical Zone Police report of the 1950s described the police entering a bachelor's quarters with a maintenance crew, all of whom were "surprised" when a naked Panamanian girl leaped out of a closet and ran from the building, clutching a towel and some clothes. The male occupant said "he didn't know who she was, maybe a burglar." But from the bachelor's damp and half-naked state it was evident that he had just shared a shower with the "burglar." Prostitutes even attended to GIs while they were on guard duty. The Zone court and the U.S. military did prosecute the pimps who brought these women into the enclave. Most panderers were Panamanian, although a few were U.S. expatriates living on the other side of the line. Many pimps had connections with the brothels, as did a variety of Panamanian taxi drivers. "Whores here were like fast food," one Zonian recalled. "You could order take-out over the phone." But the majority of Zonian married men and bachelors avoided the embarrassment of being spotted in the enclave with "dark, scantily-dressed women." One recalled, "This place was a giant Peyton Place where everybody found out about everything. So if you wanted to act up you were better off going downtown [to Panama City or Colón]."[78]

Race and Prostitution: The Slaying of Roxana Hermosillo

The slaying of the Chilean artista Roxana Hermosillo in 1965 exposed many of the racial tensions implicit in the borderland sex trade. Following a long investigation and days of interrogation, an African American soldier, Private Eliahu Bey, broke down and confessed to the murder. At first Bey tried to blame the crime on his Colombian wife. He claimed that she had stabbed Hermosillo after she discovered the two of them in bed. A recently converted Muslim, Bey and his wife lived in the same apartment building as the victim.[79] Over time Bey had developed an obsession for the beautiful artista, arising, at least in part, from the sexual taboo of black men having sexual relations with white women. In the weeks preceding the murder Hermosillo repeatedly turned down Bey's attempts to solicit sexual services, telling him that she did not "date" black men. This practice was common among lighter-skinned isthmian prostitutes, who found that their price and desirability among their white and mestizo customers fell if they developed a reputation for servicing black men.[80]

The proscription against borderland prostitutes sleeping with black men related, in part, to the popular stereotypes about black men's large penises and that if a woman had repeated intercourse with such men, her vagina would become stretched and less pleasurable for her white and mestizo customers. These racist beliefs, as Lara Putnam has shown, were also common among prostitutes and their clients on banana enclaves in Panama, Costa Rica, and Colombia.[81] Bey finally convinced an exhausted Hermosillo on Ash Wednesday morning, after she returned from a long night shift, to have sex

— El Soldado Eliahu Bey —

Porque le Escupió la Cara y lo Llamó Negro Mató a Roxana

4.1. A Panamanian cartoon rendition of the murder of the Chilean *artista* Roxana Hermosillo by a GI in March 1965 that so shook the borderland and upset U.S.-Panamanian sexual relations. Courtesy of *La Hora*.

with him. But she insisted that Bey pay her $20, twice her normal rate, since he was black.[82]

After intercourse, according to Bey, Hermosillo complained about his roughness and the foul smell of his body. Bey responded with obscenities. He tossed her a $10 bill and shouted, "That's all you're worth!" She punched him repeatedly, demanding another $10. Bey testified that she then pulled out his commando knife from a paper bag that he kept by the bed and threatened him with it. Though the jury failed to believe him, Bey insisted that he wrestled the knife from Hermosillo's hands only to defend himself. Finally, in frustration, he stabbed her repeatedly. Fearful of being caught, Bey sopped up the pools of blood around her body with towels and put them and the murder weapon in a plastic bag that he tossed into the brush near Albrook Air Base.[83]

Bey's capture and confession ended the Holy Week panic throughout the borderland brothel district, although for several weeks afterward some prostitutes refused to service black GIs. A Panamanian court sentenced Bey to twelve years in prison for second-degree murder. Bey's menacing, dark photo adorned the front pages of several Panamanian tabloids. Since the 1950s Panamanian nationalists had constructed a demonology of the gringo presence along the border, with the U.S. soldier as a principal villain, the despoiler of Panamanian virtue. To Panamanian radicals, the great apologist for yanqui imperialism in Panama and an equal villain was the disloyal West Indian, servile to the Americans and obsessed with sex and violence due to his base African nature. A third malefactor lurked among those business minorities in Panama: Chinese, Jews, Hindus, and Arabs, whom many Panamanians condemned as alien parasites sucking the lifeblood from the mestizo majority. As a Muslim African American soldier, Bey combined all three perils to a sovereign Panama.[84]

Conversely, the slain *chilena* came to embody a national heroine for the republic's citizens. Roxana Hermosillo's murder occurred a little over a year after the January 1964 riots that claimed twenty-one Panamanian lives, many of them killed by U.S. soldiers. Monsignor Ignacio Martínez recalled his parishioners purchasing masses for Hermosillo's soul: "Imagine that, they had masses said for her. My parishioners were middle class, *gente decente*. In their everyday life, they would never have anything to do with a woman like Roxana. But she became like a saint during those weeks after her murder. . . . That tells you how strong the anti-American feeling was. I think the people were fed up with them [the Americans] and all that prostitution and indignity to the nation. It had been going on for over twenty years since the Second World War."[85]

In keeping with the cult of Roxana, her fellow *artistas* claimed that she still had the Holy Wednesday ashes on her forehead from Mass on the morning that Bey butchered her. For Holy Week 1965, anyway, Hermosilla reigned supreme as the virgin-whore of Panama sacrificed on the altar of U.S. imperialism.[86]

U.S.-Panamanian Military Marriages

Besides the violence and racism so prominent in the Hermosillo case, several persistent problems plagued relations between U.S. servicemen and Panamanian women and Latinas in the Zone borderland. These included the desire of some U.S. servicemen to marry isthmian prostitutes, bigamy, the frequent abandonment of official and common-law wives and children, and the problems U.S.-Panamanian couples encountered with the color line back in the United States. Despite officer opposition, some GIs married Dominican, Colombian, and Panamanian women who worked the trade. A military document from the 1950s decried, "So many of our servicemen continually want to marry prostitutes from Panama." This desire, among other things, upended the national and racial hierarchy of the borderland, at least legally if not socially and culturally, because once married, these allegedly morally and racially "inferior" Latinas became bona fide U.S. citizens.[87]

In the postwar era military officers and counselors tried to dissuade U.S. servicemen from entering into such unions. "That was my job," recalled Lee Amberths, who worked for the U.S. Army in Panama in the 1950s–1960s as a detective in the Criminal Investigations Division (CID): "I had to try and talk these kids out of marrying these women. I remember one kid, nineteen, who wanted to marry this black Dominican woman who worked as a hooker downtown. She was thirty-four. She had four kids. But this GI insisted on marrying her. 'I love her,' he would tell us with tears in his eyes. She sat in the office next to him holding his hand with two of her kids on her lap. . . . Some of these GIs, eighteen, nineteen, were having sex for the first time in their lives, and they lost it completely. 'Oh, I can't live without her!' We had to do background checks on the girls. That was the main way to stop them."[88]

Before Amberths did his investigations, unit commanders would sit soldiers down and "read them the riot act. But if they were really persistent and they had the right paperwork; they were hard to stop." Amberths would check on the women applicants' criminal records with the Panamanian detective bureau, the DENI. "Generally it took a felony to kill the application." In a case in 1954 the CID report found, "Irrespective of the eligibility of the intended spouse, to obtain an immigration visa for permanent residency in the United States, it is recommended that the proposed marriage be disapproved in view of her repeated history of venereal disease and her two previous convictions in Panama."[89]

Still, from the 1950s to the 1970s an average of fifty marriages per month occurred on the isthmus between U.S. soldiers and Panamanian, Colombian, Dominican, and other Latin American women. The great majority of these women were not prostitutes, but in a few scandalous cases artista wives continued to practice their trade after they married their husbands, some of whom apparently acquiesced in their wives' return to work. In 1946 the Canal Zone Police arrested Mariña Clothilde de Smitt, the wife of Private Henry A. Smitt, for trespassing into the Canal Zone "for the purpose of prostitution." Private Smitt acknowledged that he was aware of her activities and, according to the police investigation, "willingly profited from his wife's return to her former trade and served as her panderer on occasion."[90]

While skeptical at times, Amberths prided himself on helping many former prostitutes. His mother was Puerto Rican and he spoke fluent Spanish, which made him a prized officer in the CID. After retiring from the army, Amberths went to work for the U.S. consulate in Panama City, where he processed visas. He recalled, "If you liked the kid and if the girl seemed like a decent person, sometimes you could fix the paperwork so it went through. I was supposed to stop these marriages, but sometimes I helped them. . . . And a lot of them worked out. They would write me later from the States to thank me."[91]

Contestations of Power within U.S.-Panamanian Sexual Relations

As noted, the overwhelming proportion of Panamanian women and Latinas who married GIs were not prostitutes. They often came to an arrangement with their military husbands, many of whom were Puerto Rican. The women agreed to live with them in the United States or in Europe and Asia at military posts throughout their careers, provided that, upon retirement, the couple would return to Panama. With the couple's children now grown and living in the States, the Panamanian wife would get a job in the republic. With that income and her husband's military pension, they settled into a comfortable life in the old borderland or in Boquete in the western highlands.[92]

"I always thought it was ironic that during the fifties and sixties, when I served down here, the big dream of all the Panamanian women was to get the hell out of here, to get to the States," Amberths recalled. "They used to call it 'the Land of the Big PX.' But after twenty years up there, they all wanted to come home. . . . I had a Panamanian friend who used to tell me, 'You damned gringos are stealing all the beautiful women in Panama and taking them back to the States. But now I tell him, 'Don't worry they're all coming back!'"[93]

While many U.S.-Panamanian military marriages flourished in an atmosphere of contented, if acquired, compatibility, others suffered from domestic abuse, bigamy, abandonment, and the color bar in the United States. The U.S. military police frequently arrested soldiers for domestic violence against their Panamanian wives and children on base housing. In the republic Panamanian police detained abusers when neighbors reported fights and shouting matches. The sense of racial, national, and gendered superiority that many U.S. enlisted men felt toward Panamanians probably contributed to these behaviors. Local maids, seamstresses, and cooks faced similar disrespect on numerous occasions. Analogous attitudes often obtained among working-class Panamanians. In 1955 a Panamanian wrote to a U.S. sergeant whose wife had voiced a complaint in the *Panama American*, urging the GI to "take a leather strap to his wife" for her temerity. Another example of isthmian machismo emerged in the statement of Enrique García in 1942 after he slashed the throat of his ex-lover, Rosita Palau Lane, who had married an American "behind his back." García told the Panamanian police "that she was his property, that he had brought her here from Spain, that he had killed her, and that he would do it again and again."[94] In 1954 Corporal Raul Calderon-Ramos hurled his Panamanian lover-prostitute Gladys Vasquez from her third-floor apartment balcony in Panama City; she died of a fractured skull. These were extreme cases that in no way reflected the majority of U.S.-Panamanian sexual relations, but they evinced disturbing patterns that mirrored the hegemonic power that Americans had constructed along the borderland.[95]

U.S. imperialism often operated within sexual relations on a very personal basis. Margarita Aldama, who once lived in impoverished Chorrillo, recalled her relationship with her GI fiancé, Billy, in the mid-1960s: "Billy was a nice boy. But when he drank he became very violent. One day after he had beaten me, I went to my father and told him, 'I want to break up with Billy.' But my father told me, 'You are not breaking up with Billy. Every Saturday, Billy brings us a turkey, a ham, and a case of Budweiser from the PX. He siphons the gasoline from his jeep into your uncle's car. If you date a Panamanian boy, he will beat you too, but he will bring nothing to our table.'"[96]

Bigamy, Abandonment, and the Stateside Color Line

During World War II and the postwar era, bigamy plagued many U.S.-Panamanian relationships; GIs with wives in the States married Panamanian and Colombian women at local churches to avoid a marriage on base that required prior investigations into their civil status. They then lived with these women in apartments in Panama to evade official notice. There were numerous such cases among Puerto Rican soldiers, some of whom had as many as four wives: one in the United States, one in Puerto Rico, one in Panama, and one in the Canal Zone. The U.S. District Court untangled these arrangements and fined and imprisoned the male perpetrators. In 1942 Zone Judge Bunk Gardner complained about "the large numbers of American soldiers and sailors with wives at home, committing bigamy down here on the isthmus": "I see these cases all the time and I intend to put a stop to them. People seem to think that the solemn vows of matrimony spoken by them in the United States are without meaning in the Canal Zone and Panama."[97]

Bigamy in the borderland did not run one-way; on occasion Panamanian women married more than one GI. In 1951 Melva Esther Isaza caused a stir when authorities discovered that she had married two servicemen, Private Robert Clayton Bassinger and Corporal Nathan Kotch. Mrs. Bassinger/Kotch drew separate apartment allotments, PX privileges, and pay from both of her husbands. Her ingenuity proved one of the many creative ways in which borderland women upended U.S. hegemony to their own advantage.[98]

While many U.S.-Panamanian military marriages flourished on the isthmus, Americans' abandonment of Panamanian wives, girlfriends and binational children also proved common. GIs fled to the States or to another overseas posting without informing their Panamanian or Latina wives (common law or official), leaving them insolvent and stranded. Until the 1970s when U.S. authorities instituted reforms in the all-volunteer military, Panamanian wives of absent U.S. husbands struggled to obtain financial support from their partners. Helen Escobar of Chorrera spoke of the heartbreak and privation her mother endured after he left her with Helen as an infant: "It took my mother years and years to get over this, and so many letters and phone calls to my American father, most that were never answered. I just remember her being so sad all the time. And some of our neighbors treated her like a criminal because she had a child by a GI. I didn't miss him so much myself because I was just a baby when he left. I have no memory of him except my mother's pain."[99]

After many decades of these injustices, the U.S. military finally began attaching soldiers' pay, no matter where their posting, and sending the money back to their abandoned partners and children once parentage was proved through blood tests. Indeed more cynical Panamanians and Zonians often commented on the practice from the 1970s on of Panamanian women with three children from three different GIs drawing a stipend of $200 per month per child: "Some of these women lived very well on that in Panama, getting $600 a month for eighteen years until the children came of age." With such strategies at least a few Panamanian women found ways to survive the emotional and economic shock of desertion and prosper from their liaisons with U.S. borderlanders.[100]

Panamanian-GI couples from the 1940s–1960s often confronted strong racial discrimination when the husband's posting ended and the newlyweds were transferred to the States, especially to Southern bases. John MacTaggart, who married a Panamanian and served several years on the isthmus before returning to work for the Canal, recalled, "The longer you were in Panama, the lighter the girls seemed. And of course the reverse was also true. When GIs took them back to the States, they suddenly became a lot darker." Racial taboos regarding miscegenation in North America held little force for most U.S. males in Panama's multiracial society, but the return to the States of a "racially mixed" couple could prove harrowing. "I remember one corporal in the late fifties posted to Biloxi, Mississippi, with his Panamanian wife who called back to the Zone, 'Sarge, you've got to get me outa' here. They're burning crosses on our lawn. Nobody will talk to my wife or me at the PX, the cafeteria, or in town. We're like lepers. I don't care what kind of paperwork you have to rig, just get us back to Panama!'"[101]

Class and Culture in Borderland Relations

The class and racial perceptions within U.S. military marriages between poorer isthmian women and GIs were less of an issue in upper-class unions between Panamanians and North Americans. As noted, Archbishop Marco MacGrath, the borderland's foremost panagringo, was the product of just such a marriage. But differing cultural perceptions toward gender and matrimony affected upper-class unions as well. Marriages between middle- to upper-class American men and middle- to upper-class Panamanian women appear to have higher success rates. But when the husband was Panamanian and the wife was American, these elite marriages suffered more problems. "I think it was more difficult to assimilate to a society that one considers inferior to one's own than it is the other way around," opined the veteran diplomat Miguel J. Moreno, having witnessed the failure of several marriages between his upper-crust male friends and middle-class Zonian women. U.S. wives of Panamanian males also found it difficult to conform to the formality, patriarchy, and cultural differences of their elite Panamanian husbands. Panamanian families could be closed to a gringa and protective of their own in the presence of an outsider, especially one who came from a group that already lorded over their country. William Jorden, a chief negotiator on the 1977 Carter-Torrijos Treaty and later U.S. ambassador to Panama, wrote of the hurt that a Zonian woman married to Panamanian ambassador José Antonio de la Ossa suffered over her husband's many affairs.[102]

Another difficult adjustment lay in what some Americans perceived as the "suffocating" Panamanian extended family. Zone-born Mary Coffey who came from a famous "ditch-digger" family stated, "I was never that attracted to the idea of marriage to a Panamanian man for the simple reason that when you marry a Panamanian, you marry his entire family." In the postwar era Americans increasingly saw marriage as a union between individuals rather than clans, as was, and still is, the practice among many Panamanians.[103] Some U.S. males with Panamanian spouses expressed similar consternation over the practice of Panamanian families' constantly congregating in large numbers. Doug Philips, a Canal Zone lockmaster married to a Panamanian, lamented, "It's tough when you come home and there's a dozen of them over the house watching TV and jabbering away in Spanish. Then she [his wife] used to wonder why I was out drinking half the time. . . . 'The more the merrier,' that's the motto in Panama. . . . On any given day half the country's out of work; so you've got to take that into account."[104] Such chauvinism marked many American attitudes throughout the borderland. But Panamanian women also complained about the coldness of Zonian society, from which they often felt alienated: "When you were a Panamanian, even if your U.S. husband was well-liked, you had the face of the enemy to many of them. You felt awkward in situations, like when your husband's friends were saying bad things about Panama. It was difficult to watch the American police who were so mean to your own people. But you kept it to yourself because you did not want to hurt your husband's career. Were you an American or a Panamanian? I don't think one should have to choose, but in the Zone, you felt like you had to."[105]

Despite this discrimination and problems of conflicted identity, middle- and working-class Panamanian women sometimes expressed a preference for North American husbands who they judged as less machista, more devoted to family, more active in the raising of children, and more financially responsible: "I saw my American husband as a companion more than a boss like my first Panamanian husband was. But he always says, 'I was a boss that you never listened to!'"[106] Lots of exceptions existed within these stereotypes, as significant numbers of Panamanian women had little interest in and even fear of North American men: "They were always so loud and drunk, especially the soldiers, we would never have anything to do with them! We ran from them when we saw them coming as girls. Our men were so much more handsome, polite, better dressed, and they understood our culture, our society. No, I never wanted to go out with a gringo!"[107]

Income disparities, typical in the borderland, also led to troubles in binational relationships. Few middle-class Panamanian males made sufficient money to keep Zonian women in the lifestyle to which they were accustomed. In 1956 the Canal Zone Police arrested Hickson A. Belizaire, a forty-seven-year-old married Panamanian, for embezzling $800 from his job at the U.S.-run Tivoli Hotel in the Zone. Belizaire had been conducting an affair with a thirty-six-year-old American woman, Linda Doyle. He claimed he stole the money to court Doyle "in the style she was used to." He also gave his American girlfriend money to replace funds that she had defrauded from her clerk's job in the Zone so they could both live "an American lifestyle" in the borderland. Belizaire lost his job of thirty-one years, agreed to pay restitution, and served six months in Gamboa Penitentiary. Zone authorities shipped Doyle back to the States for her collusion in the embezzlement and, perhaps more important, for her violation of the sexual and racial hierarchies of the borderland.[108]

Homosexuality in the Borderland

Throughout the postwar era U.S. authorities regarded the "aberrant behavior" of homosexuality as a special problem, in part because the Canal Zone represented a U.S. showcase in Latin America, as well as an instrument of what scholars call "hegemonic masculinity," that is, the cultural domination of certain types of male comportment. Therefore if the Pentagon deployed what officers regarded as "sissified" or "unmanly" troops in Panama, soldiers who were willing to engage in passive sexual relations with Panamanian men, that mission faced derision. Similarly the presence of lesbian women within the enclave exposed what officials viewed as "degenerate" behavior by individuals who should serve as models of wholesome American womanhood.[109]

Most prosecuted homosexual acts within the U.S. military occurred on bases, in the bachelor barracks, where single or divorced recruits slept and congregated. Officers of the guard would catch men in bed together or performing fellatio or sodomy in the barracks latrine. On occasion purportedly heterosexual soldiers would initiate these arrests by complaining that they had been molested or fondled while sleeping in their quarters. When confronted with the evidence of their homosexual acts, accused servicemen typically admitted to the perceived "immorality" of their actions. But whether these soldiers did so under the pressure of legal penalties during harsh interrogations or peer pressure from heterosexual comrades is open to question. Military authorities vigorously prosecuted these offenses, discharging men from the service, shipping some to Stateside military prisons, and condemning these behaviors as degenerate, unnatural, and, most tellingly, "unsoldierly." The uniformed comrades of the accused typically shunned them in an institution where hypermasculinity, camaraderie, and unitwide social acceptance were supreme values.[110]

In a few cases U.S. soldiers reported that they had been raped in the republic by Panamanian males. Army CID officers expressed doubts over whether these soldiers had actually been assaulted or had engaged in consensual homosexual acts with local men, after which they concocted rape charges to explain visits to infirmaries for anal bleeding or venereal disease.

For some officers, the idea that Panamanian men possessed the capacity to overpower and force themselves on U.S. soldiers apparently challenged their hegemonic masculinity as guardians of the borderland.[111]

During the postwar era military police in the Zone arrested U.S. Army nurses and a few WACs and WAVEs for practicing lesbianism. Army CID officials typically branded sexual liaisons among women as psychiatric disorders, diagnosing such women as "frigid," "cold," "mannish," "lacking feminine qualities," and "hostile toward men." Because lesbians in the ranks did not pose a grave challenge to the imperial masculine identity of the armed forces, officers typically spared them imprisonment. Authorities simply dismissed them from the service and shipped them home with diagnoses such as "homosexuality, overt, with repeated manifestations of unnatural activity under the influence of alcohol, but with evidence of other secondary manifestations."[112]

During World War II male military officials expressed more concern over the heterosexual activity of WACs and WAVEs in Panama, especially with local "brown" and "black" Panamanian men. Due to a shortage of gender-separate housing on Zone bases in 1942–43, military officers put up newly arrived WACs and WAVEs in temporary tent cities within base fences. Lester Greaves recalled the sexual aggressiveness of U.S. military women frustrated over the nonfraternization regulation that forbade them from openly dating locals: "They would grab me right by the arm sometimes when they were out there drinking in those tents. I worked at Clayton then, and they would say, 'Come here, you black boy! Come here!' and pull me right into the tent and we would have a party sometimes with more than one. I was only seventeen and those WACs, they really loved me good and pretty, mon."[113]

Regardless of the veracity of Greaves's boasts, many WACs, WAVEs, and military nurses in Panama found themselves for the first time serving overseas, far from home in an alien culture with little family, church, or community supervision. During World War II heavy drinking and promiscuity reigned supreme along the Zone borderland, deemed a cushy posting and rear-echelon party area. Like their male counterparts, white U.S. servicewomen found abundant opportunities in Panama to act on their formerly repressed desires for intimacy with people of color.[114]

Many tragedies arose from the prosecution of gays in the borderland. In 1946 thirty-two-year-old Martha Loewer, a former WAC and Zone secretary, committed suicide in Balboa rather than face a pending investigation into her affair with a Zonian woman.[115] Several male homosexual servicemen also committed suicide in Panama due to the shame and depression they experienced from official prosecution and shunning by fellow GIs. Sexual "deviance" carried a heavy price for whites in a borderland setting like Panama, where they were expected to measure up to an often unrealizable imperial ideal.[116]

Gender Roles on the Zone Side of the Border

While American men's purported virtues and financial status may have attracted some Latinas, American women in the postwar borderland, especially new arrivals, expressed little enthusiasm for them. In 1948 a single secretary wrote, "I never have seen such a place where the percentage of men are so sloppy, uncouth, disrespectful, and of a lower caliber as here on the Zone. Where down here do you find a gentleman who is well-groomed, suave, sophisticated, pleasant, and who has something else to talk about besides the Panama Canal? . . . Men dress worse than the natives. . . . They're starting to look like Kuna or Panamanians."[117]

The frustrations of living mostly on the U.S. side of the borderland grated on single American women. Possibilities were limited in the small U.S. dating pool, evidently devoid of Cary Grants. One woman described the evening social scene as one of "constant catcalls, whistling, and ogling. Clubhouse romeos offer to take a girl out and began leering and pawing at her before they get to the beer gardens [located on the Panamanian side of the border]. . . . Someone should teach these louts some manners."[118] Frustrated U.S. bachelors and married women, suspicious of single-girls-on-the-make, defamed them: "There *are* gentlemen in the Canal Zone but single women shouldn't go out at night to clubhouses *without an escort*. . . . Do you believe that a coat and a tie make a gentlemen? Why do you only go out with *married men*? If you can't handle men any better, you will be locked up in your room forever."[119] Conservative officers' wives disapproved of how far some U.S. women went to attract both American and Panamanian males. In 1956 an air force wife wrote, "I've had enough of these loose women of the Zone in their v-neck, backless dresses, and thin blouses with no slip. . . . To Panamanians, please do not think that all women in the States act and behave like most of the women here."[120] A constant conflict between "decent-minded" and more daring women emerged as one of the key gender themes of the borderland, especially in the postwar era, when the region experienced more influences from the rapidly changing metropole. Zone matrons in particular tended to associate vivacious and sexy American women with their century-old nemesis, the Panamanian cabaret girl.[121]

Due to their presence in an enclave clustered with military installations and their jobs operating the strategic Canal, many Zonian males subscribed to a martial persona. "Real men" on the isthmus hunted, fished, owned and fired guns, navigated boats, drank, and fornicated in Panama and mostly ignored complaints from the women in their lives. With Panamanian servants at home, none had to endure the "indignity" of doing "women's work," washing dishes or changing diapers, as some of their counterparts in the States did. Exceptions existed: college-educated professionals who worked as doctors, teachers, and lawyers and had interests in history, literature, theater, and art. Many blue-collar Zonians viewed these "eggheads" with suspicion, which they returned in kind. In 1956 a dissident male Zonian wrote a sarcastic letter ridiculing those "honest-to-goodness jungle men" hunting near his home with their noisy dogs. His mockery received a pointed reply: "We're sorry we disturbed you. Were you 1.) out orchid hunting? Because one of your caliber is too afraid to go out in the bush and have one little itsy-bitsy hunting dog bark at you. 2.) Are you the type who is afraid to do what you want to, afraid of your wife? 3.) Are you the type who always finds fault at what a group of men want to do: hunting, golfing, fishing, and water-skiing? Maybe you should play canasta with the girls?" The letter summed up notions of hegemonic versus subordinated masculinity, as well as the divisions between blue- and white-collar Zonians, though such judgments are a simplification: lawyers, teachers, and doctors in the Zone also liked to hunt, and presumably some Zone tradesmen enjoyed novels and the Theatre Guild.[122]

The warrior ethos of many Zonian males intensified during World War II, the Korean War, and the Vietnam War, when increased military traffic accentuated the strategic raison d'être of the waterway. Regional cold war crises, such as the CIA coup in Guatemala in 1954, the Bay of Pigs invasion in 1961, the Cuban Missile Crisis in 1962, and the U.S. invasion of the Dominican Republic in 1965 also raised U.S. testosterone levels in the Zone, whose bases supported all these missions. During the blockade of Cuba in 1962 military commanders shunted aside all commercial shipping, directing U.S. warships to the head of the line and rushing them through the locks. For the first time since World War II, excited Zonians and the military garrison had a real sense of importance again. Zonian children gathered along the Canal banks to watch the parade of U.S. naval might.[123]

During the flag riots in 1964 Zonian warrior sentiment reached its apogee, especially among those U.S. inhabitants of Ancon and Curundu near the Panamanian border. In the days following the riots Zonian males sat out in their yards near the border fence, hunting rifles in hand, guarding their homes from possible attack. They tossed Molotov cocktails flung at them from the Panamanian side back over the fence and imbibed rum cocktails of their own. These male Zonians embodied a type of "New Frontiersmen" that the Kennedy and Johnson administrations had not counted on. Among them, toting firearms, were Zonian women.[124]

The Changing Role of U.S. Women on the Zone

In the postwar era the role of U.S. women in the Canal Zone went through key changes, similar to those in the United States though at an admittedly slower pace. During World War II, when the U.S. defense establishment in Panama suffered labor shortages, authorities recruited local Zonian women as typists, drivers, and office personnel. Resentment surfaced against this practice, since in the 1940s two-income families threatened the equalitarian mind-set of white Zonians whose families all had around the same income and lifestyle. Working women also challenged the prime gender role for women since construction, that of wife, mother, and homemaker, not competitors with U.S. males who built an empire in the tropics. Some men also worried about military-employed wives having affairs with their servicemen rivals, "whispered love between officers and married stenographers all at $5 per hour," one complained.[125]

The ideal postwar Zonian woman celebrated in company publications was a helpmate to her man and a doting mother to her children. Such women partook in social and charitable activities as nurturers and caretakers. But women's clubs in the Zone exposed class divisions in a purportedly classless enclave. "The women's clubs were for the snobs," Nina Kosik remembered. "They were for the older Zonian families and the wives of the bosses who thought they were better than everyone." Though resented by some, these women provided social and philanthropic leadership. They published daily sections in the Zone's English-language newspaper, the *Panama American*, entitled "Women's World," "Atlantic," and "Pacific Society News," and "Cocina Corner," a recipe column that included North American and traditional Panamanian dishes. (Some recipes were not entirely apolitical, such as "Lazy Maid's Tartar Sauce.") In local magazines, such as the *Panama Canal Review*, the *Spillway*, and *This Month in Panama*, domestic images of Zonian women dominated, helping their children with their homework, playing in the yard with toddlers and local jungle animals, teaching West Indian women home economics, and volunteering at hospitals and Panamanian orphanages.[126]

4.2. Besides the fearless jungle tomboy, young Zonian women also clung to the more traditional 1950s role of cotillion queens. Here a group of Zonian high school girls partake in a Christmas gala. These roles would be challenged by a new generation of U.S. and Panamanian working women. Courtesy of the *Panama Canal Review* in the Panama Canal Museum Collection, George Smathers Library, University of Florida, http://ufdc.ufl.edu/pcm.

But following World War II more Zonian women discovered that they enjoyed earning paychecks of their own. Hundreds of women nurses, teachers, and secretaries had done so since construction days.[127] When women lost their war jobs in lay-offs in 1945, they sought employment with the Canal Company, the Canal Zone government, or the DOD. Several Zonian women worked as secretaries for Panamanian, U.S., and foreign businesses on the Panamanian side of the border. Higher divorce rates in the Zone during and after World War II created a small pool of divorced Zonian women who needed to work to keep their Zone housing, commissary, health, and mail privileges, as only employees and their dependents had the right to live in the enclave. And married U.S. working women were denied the tropical differential if their employed husbands already earned one.[128] Despite this gendered discrimination, as early as the 1950s working women from all the borderland angles became an economic force to reckon with: "Panamanian wives of U.S. citizens claim U.S. citizenship for privileges in the Zone and Panamanian citizenship for jobs in Panama. We have married U.S. women working in Panama, married U.S. women working in the Canal Zone, and married women from Panama working in the Canal Zone. Nothing short of a hydrogen bomb will stop these girls. Long live the working married women!"[129]

These "new postwar women" challenged older Zone matriarchs for a greater say in the enclave's public and social life. After 1968 the administration granted them paid maternity leave for the first time.[130] These women also broke ground in subverting many upper-class, "lady-like" stereotypes. In 1948 "vivacious, dark-haired Mrs. Mabel Kimmel" became the first woman in isthmian history to transit the Canal paddling alone in a cayuco: "A former Chicagoan, born and raised in New York City, Mabel came to the Zone in 1941 when her husband took a job as a pharmacist. With her typical zest for doing things, Mabel quickly became a civic counciler and then a camp director. . . . She frankly admits that she finds so many things more worthwhile than housework and is happy to leave the 'picking up' to her maid while . . . working at the Army Signal Corps. She is also Deputy Commissioner for the Canal Zone Girls Scouts, ham radio operator, and . . . loves to trek the Cruces trail following the march of Morgan's pirates."[131] Such women became the prototypes for the postwar Ama-Zonian, women and girls who reveled in outdoor physical life, who fished, hunted, hiked, and rode horses with their husbands, fathers, and brothers.

Bette Ford, a female bullfighter, provided another startling postwar example of changes in borderland gender models. In the 1950s she became a favorite of both Panamanians and Zonians at La Macarena Stadium in the capital, where she fought and killed several bulls to the cheers of a mixed pan-American crowd. Ford, who lived in the Zone during her travels to the isthmus, toured Latin America in the 1950s as a matador, opening up possibilities for the postwar woman by excelling in the most macho of Hispanic professions.[132]

In neighboring Panama a burgeoning postwar women's movement also took shape. In his 1941 Constitution, the populist president Arnulfo Arias granted Panamanian women the right to vote and hold office for the first time, as well as the right to divorce. These actions, combined with the war boom, proved a turning point in opening up public life and jobs to isthmian women on the other side of the line. In 1950 Maria S. De Miranda emerged as the republic's first woman cabinet member, serving as minister for labor and social welfare. In an interview De Miranda expressed her philosophy of feminism: a combination of traditional *marianismo* (devotion to family and God modeled after the mother of Christ) with an assertiveness that mirrored postwar Zonian women's attitudes: "She brushes aside the suggestion of a conflict between the life of a wife and mother and that of a successful 'career woman.' 'My family and I have always been partners. They help me with my problems and are my greatest source of relaxation. . . . We should be collaborators with men. But it should all be done,' she stressed, 'with our femininity.'" Despite her measured deference, De Miranda was something of a revolutionary. She spent a year in jail for her activities in the unsuccessful Arnulfista uprising in July 1948.

Throughout the 1960s Thelma King, a Panamanian deputy and woman of color, provided a radical critique of the Zone that bespoke the new nationalist, anti-American voice of politically minded Panamanian women. On her program, *Radio Tribuna*, in her newspaper columns, and in her many speeches, King was a relentless opponent of the U.S. enclave. Her patriotic rhetoric unnerved a U.S. community that increasingly sensed itself under siege and viewed King as an especially vitriolic enemy whose gender and mixed-race background lent a powerful credibility to her critique.[133]

Declension of Gendered Colonial Values in the Borderland?

In the late 1960s and the 1970s what at least some Zonians regarded as pernicious influences from the United States entered the enclave and neighboring Panama that threatened cherished gender roles. The U.S. civil rights and women's movements certainly played a part in weakening the idealization of the white, European-descent male as king of the borderland. The arrival of the sexual revolution, drugs, and rock and roll among younger Zonians also raised concerns. A slight rise in teenage pregnancies in Balboa and Cristobal high schools and greater use of marijuana and cocaine among the Zone's youth increased fears that "malignant" influences from the metropole might destroy the enclave from within, and not the Panamanian "barbarians" at the gates.

Inordinate drinking and experimentation with soft drugs among adult Zonians also signaled what many Zonians viewed as a decline in the "moral imperatives" of the enclave. Card-playing Zonian wives of the postwar era had long held a reputation for heavy drinking that continued through the 1960s–1970s with greater alacrity. Zonian men even began to wear their hair a little longer and sported bell-bottoms and multicolored striped shirts, a startling change from the crew-cut, buttoned-down Zonian of the 1940s through the late 1960s. The cross-gender themes of the counterculture—peace, free love, environmentalism, and individualism—undercut strict male-female dichotomies that had long dominated the borderland. The antiestablishment bent of the period especially confounded older Zonians, for whom the Canal Zone was the ultimate establishment.[134]

After the anti-U.S. uprising in Panama in 1964, fewer Zonians ventured into Panama. This relative withdrawal from cross-border social and sexual contacts combined with more "liberated" U.S. sexual attitudes in the enclave led to the establishment of a few wife-swapping clubs among a small minority of Zonians. Wife-swapping actually held a certain rationale in a borderland setting among white men and women who sought sexual adventure yet rejected intimate relations with people of color from the other side. Indeed the 1978 Carter-Torrijos Treaty that put the final nail in the Zone's coffin left numerous Zonians and Panamanians "sexually adrift," unsure of how their relationships would continue once the borderland shut down.[135]

Summary

From World War II to 1979 sexual identities, gender roles, and codes of behavior along the Zone borderland provided cornerstones to the U.S. presence that reinforced the racial, economic, and strategic imperatives of this imperial frontier. Culturally assigned categories for men and women in both the Canal Zone and neighboring Panama buttressed one another, especially those that subordinated Panamanian women of color to heterosexual white males on both sides of the line. The sexual playground of the isthmus for white men proved a hard school for impoverished Panamanian women and Latinas, who struggled to survive in an environment where the hierarchies were typically stacked against them. Unequal power equations between white U.S. men and Panamanian women and Latinas fueled abuses and tragedies that undermined the aura of U.S. moral superiority so vital to borderland dominance.

The Zone's security forces, often in conjunction with Panamanian authorities, attempted to channel and control the flows of sexual desire across the frontiers, but for the most part their efforts to impede, to categorize, and to contain failed because the border remained fairly open—except during political crises—and the penalties and fear factor of engaging in cross-border relations was never a strong enough deterrent. The resulting incidents of miscegenation, concubinage, troubled marriages, assault, rape, bigamy, abandonment, and murder exposed the ugly side of unequal gender and national relations. Combined with the U.S. attempt to feminize and infantilize Panama, these scandals and tragedies turned increasing numbers in the republic against the U.S. imperial project. This metamorphosis proved damaging as Washington had long strived to maintain a level of local consent on the isthmus that relied, in part, on the allure of U.S. cultural norms and gender hierarchies for the republic's citizens.

THE U.S. MILITARY

Armed Guardians of the Borderland

On the afternoon of November 22, 1956, U.S. Army Private Harold Rose, age nineteen, hurled the twenty-month-old son of his Panamanian girlfriend, Blanca Maria Castillo, against the cement wall of their apartment in Panama City, killing the child. His trial later revealed that he did so out of anger over the boy's repeated crying after soiling his diapers. Called by neighbors, Panamanian police arrived on the scene. After listening to Rose and Castillo's contrived claim that the child had accidentally fallen from the kitchen table while being changed, the police arrested the couple. Within days the death of "little Eduardo" Castillo became front-page news in all of Panama's newspapers, with pictures of the small, handsome boy and his frightened mother featured on page 1. Poignant photos of Eduardo's tiny corpse in the morgue highlighted these tabloid editions, along with photos of a smirking Private Rose in his U.S. Army uniform.[1]

The Rose child murder case marked a low point in postwar relations between the U.S. military and the Panamanian people. But other conflicts before and after Eduardo's death strained relations among these two border communities as well. Virtually every night during the 1940s–1960s Panamanians and U.S. service personnel on furlough fought one another in the streets of Panama City and Colón. U.S. military vehicles frequently injured and even killed Panamanian citizens in localities all along the line. Panamanian women suffered sexual and domestic abuse from GIs. Panamanians were not just the victims of violence, however, as the local populations fought, robbed, killed, and on occasion raped U.S. servicemen, punctuating a stark resistance to U.S. military hegemony along the border.

The U.S. military, especially the army, were the armed guardians of this landed, imperial frontier—and its ultimate arbiters of power. Panama was not an island like Puerto Rico, Guam, or the Philippines, where U.S. naval dominance assured security. The U.S. presence in Panama created two fifty-mile-long landed boundaries east and west and two smaller, urban frontiers north and south that required ground force capability "to hold the lines" against any hostile incursions. In periods of crisis, along with the civilian Zone Police the U.S. Army provided the last resort to force, much like the Roman legions along the ancient Rhine borderland or Hadrian's Wall. The U.S. military also encompassed a unique culture and identity in Panama that placed GIs in conflict and accommodation with all the major groups that vied for ascendancy along the Zone-Panama corridor.[2]

For Panamanian nationalists, the timing of the Rose case proved propitious. The same month that Rose committed his heinous act, Anglo-French forces stormed Port Said, attempting to reassert control over another imperial borderland: the recently nationalized Suez Canal Zone. The Suez Crisis in 1956 electrified Panamanian patriots and ignited a new round of protests against the U.S. occupation of the Zone. Indeed numerous GI crimes against Panamanian citizens during the 1950s–1960s reinforced this intensified critique against the U.S. presence. Many Panamanians interpreted these acts as further evidence that the yanqui soldados formed the dark heart of a degrading occupation.[3]

The Panama riots of January 1964, in which U.S. soldiers killed at least seven Panamanians and wounded nearly two hundred, signaled the nadir of U.S. military–Panamanian relations. Photographs and cartoon images of the uprising in Panamanian newspapers featured GIs as principal villains. Since these disturbances lacked any personal pathology on the soldiers' part, as in the Rose case, many Panamanian activists regarded their actions as outright political murder. Ironically, however, in light of the fact that U.S. soldiers killed and wounded over two hundred Panamanians, most citizens of the republic blamed the deaths and casualties on the extreme jingoism of the Zonians at Balboa High School and their three generations of condescension. They held these beliefs despite the fact that, with the exception of their police force gunning down an estimated six students and wounding several dozen others, the Zonians did not kill any other Panamanians.[4]

Part of this reasoning stemmed from locals' blaming the Canal Zone governor, Robert Fleming, for ordering the U.S. military into action, unaware that the authority of Southern Command's chief, General Andrew O'Meara, superseded Fleming's during this emergency and that the general, not the governor, literally "called the shots."[5] Once the emotional explosion of riots had abated, Panamanians also recognized that the U.S. military had exercised considerable restraint while being fired upon by local snipers, as was borne out in the International Jurists Report published after the uprising. U.S. soldiers fired teargas, buckshot, and rubber bullets at surging Panamanian crowds and used special antisniper squads that targeted only those who fired upon U.S. forces. Had the fourteen thousand soldiers in the U.S. garrison used the full force of their firepower against the local population they would have killed thousands, not seven.[6]

Another reason why postwar Panamanians held less animosity toward GIs than Zonians lay in the many personal interactions between soldiers and ordinary Panamanians, including marriages, sexual relations, civic action, health campaigns, and base and service employment. These activities contrasted with Zonian indifference, even hostility toward so many Panamanians' plights. Cynthia Enloe and other feminist scholars of international relations have explored the dependencies and abuses that arise from the class and sexualized dimension of U.S. imperialism around overseas bases. Such a presence inevitably enforces a gendered and economic hegemony on the local environment where extreme poverty draws people of color into the financial orbit of U.S. forts and facilities. The prevalent female service occupations of maids, cooks, laundresses, cocktail waitresses, and prostitutes among the bases' direct and indirect labor force testify to the hierarchies in play. These same processes of exploitation and co-optation clearly operated along the Zone borderland, with its large male garrison juxtaposed beside the poorest barrios and towns of the transisthmian corridor.[7]

For all the ugliness and violence that marked borderland interactions between Panamanians and U.S. soldiers, friendships, love affairs, and economic accommodation also shaped their associations. As the Panamanian Osvaldo Jordan Romeros explained, "Better to beat me, to fight with me, to make love to me rather than to have nothing to do with me, to keep oneself separate and apart from me—like most of the Zonians did. The military at least had human relations with the people."[8] Exceptions to this social distancing existed, but the perception of the aloof Zonian who coveted his own special piece of borderland rankled local sensibilities more than the U.S. military presence, for all its garish belligerency.

Class clearly played a role in this dynamic. Unlike the middle-class Zonians, most U.S. enlisted men came from working- or lower-class backgrounds; hence they blended in more easily with the majority Panamanian population and its working-class and campesino ethos. Puerto Ricans and other Hispanics in U.S. uniform composed a large percentage of the garrison. These Spanish-speaking Latinos acculturated readily to the salsa, fiestas, and Caribbean ambience of the isthmus. The limited duration of military tours in Panama also influenced both GI and Panamanian perceptions. "They were only here for two or three years and then they were gone, off to Germany, Korea, or Japan," recalled former Foreign Minister Miguel J. Moreno. "They didn't act like they owned the place like many of the Zonians did."[9]

In the postwar era the U.S. military's relations with Panamanians proved complex, contradictory, and ambivalent. Nowhere did the love-hate syndrome of U.S.-Panamanian interactions find fuller expression than in the encounters, for better or worse, between GIs and ordinary Panamanian borderers. Their exchanges marked the "everyday forms" of resistance and accommodation that so frequently occur astride imperial frontiers. A simultaneous attraction and repulsion toward these young men in uniform spending their yanqui dollars freely became a fixture of Panamanian urban life. To further complicate matters, postwar racial conflicts within the U.S. military and animosities between GIs and the civilian Zonians provided Panamanians with powerful wedge issues that ultimately strengthened their nationalist mission against the enclave.[10]

The U.S. military in Panama never constituted a monolithic institution; internal divisions among Anglo, Latino, and African American recruits wracked the armed forces. The unique alliance between the U.S. military and the Kuna exposed racial tensions and colonial attitudes, as did the large numbers of Puerto Ricans serving under white officers and NCOs. Binational class perceptions also played a role in Panamanian upper- and middle-class perceptions of U.S. enlisted men compared to their smartly uniformed, more diplomatic officers. Ultimately U.S. paternalism and racism within the armed forces fostered resentments that turned increasing numbers of Panamanians against the U.S. presence, mapped out so brazenly with its bases and personnel that thronged the streets of the borderland. Yet the military's economic contribution to Panama's lower classes remained so strong that as late as the 1990s, opinion polls revealed that some 60 to 70 percent of the Panamanian people favored retention of the U.S. bases.[11] These results proved an embarrassment to nationalists, both in the Arnulfista party and the Partido Revolucionario Democratico, who viewed such dependency as a betrayal of the long Panamanian struggle for independence. During the postwar era the ambivalence of that struggle intensified along the borders that demarcated Panamanian streets from the sanctuary of the Zone.

The Rose Debacle

In late 1956 the diplomatic fallout over the Rose child murder case escalated. Neighbors' testimony from the apartment building where Rose and Blanca Castillo lived revealed that Rose had systematically tortured the infant Eduardo for months before his death, beating him with a wet towel, whipping him with an electrical cord, leaving him hanging from a clothesline in the apartment while he screamed for help. Initially Private Rose tried to blame the child's death on his mother, but she refused to go along with his story. Further investigation exposed the source of Rose's hatred toward the boy. Eduardo was a mulatto; his father had been a black GI, Blanca's lover before Rose began living with her. According to witnesses, Rose repeatedly called out to Eduardo with racial insults such as "Come here, you little nigger!" and "I'll get you now, you black bastard!" before he beat him. Panamanian accounts erroneously claimed that Rose was an Alabaman; he had actually been born in Maine, but in the anti-American attitude of the day, all racist Americans in Panama were seen as perverted Southerners. As part of their criticism of the Canal Zone and its segregated gold and silver system, Panamanian dailies gave broad coverage to the ongoing Montgomery bus boycott in 1955–56, in addition to the Suez Crisis. Panamanian nationalists writing in La Hora and La Nación thus presented "little Eduardo" as a victim of the two principal U.S. vices in the borderland: racism and imperialism.[12]

Since Rose killed Eduardo in Panama when he was out of uniform and not on duty, the Panamanian courts held jurisdiction in the case. Fearing prejudicial treatment of Rose in a lynch mob atmosphere, the U.S. Army attempted to extradite him to the Canal Zone for court-martial. But Panamanian officials, responding to popular emotion, refused. Indeed angry protesters gathered outside the Panamanian Second District Court at Rose's arraignment. The Panamanian police struggled to hold back the crowds that demanded vigilante justice. Rose did not help matters by grinning nonchalantly for photographers in the courtroom. These photos of a callow, unconcerned Rose in his U.S. Army dress uniform infuriated ordinary Panamanians. The revelation that Rose had a seven-month-old daughter, Raquel, with Blanca and that Blanca was five months pregnant with another of Rose's babies further incensed locals.[13]

Eduardo's mother came under criticism from Panamanians as well. She eventually faced charges as an unfit mother for her part in Eduardo's death. Panamanian accounts described Blanca as a *cholita interiorana*, an Indian from the countryside. Cholitas frequently worked as maids in the Zone and in Panama. These women proved the racial and social type most preferred by U.S. servicemen as sexual partners; allegedly docile and easy conquests, these racially mixed women had an exotic appeal to many white U.S. soldiers. Their coffee-colored skin, long black hair, and "Asiatic" features intrigued them. To Panamanian nationalists, life in the countryside, particularly in Azueros peninsula and Chiriquí, exemplified the true Panamanian identity before the creation of the urbanized, U.S.-dominated borderland engendered by the Canal. A strong moral lesson pushed in local accounts of the Rose case stressed the corruption of country girls like Blanca by city life, with its pernicious U.S. influences. According to these accounts, yanqui soldiers and their degrading culture were destroying the innocent cholita, once the repository of the Panamanian soul.[14]

In July 1955 the Panamanian daily *La Hora* ran a series of melodramatic articles about the plight of Dora García, another young cholita caught up in a web of U.S. sins. Twenty-three years old, García created a sensation by leaving her two-and-a-half-year-old daughter, Carmen, with a girlfriend and abandoning her eighteen-month-old son, Juan, in a dirty, rundown room for three days while she cavorted with GIs in the aptly named Harem and El Mambo cantinas where she worked as a bargirl. Authorities rescued the nearly starving Juan, who, thanks to the Children's Hospital, survived. Panamanian journalists portrayed Juan, like "little Eduardo," as another casualty of U.S. cultural malevolence.[15]

A series of front-page articles first denounced García, then chronicled her and her children's state-sponsored rehabilitation. Cameramen photographed her mother, Norberta, arriving in the capital by bus from Chiriquí. "A virtuous country woman," Norberta bailed her daughter out of jail. She then began teaching her the errors of her way by instructing her in the preparation of traditional Panamanian dishes. Norberta packed up García's and her children's belongings, and in the final installment of the serial took her daughter and grandchildren back to the healthy countryside. The fallen cholita returned to Chiriquí, where she, little Carmen, and Juan, reconciled with their family, could live a decent life far from the wicked *barrios de tolerancia* (red zones) and their perverted yanquis. According to this discourse, urbanization and the U.S. military presence threatened the nation's virtue. As an ironic sidelight, the serial's final installment featured the happy family posing beneath a photo of the recently assassinated Panamanian president José Remón. In reality Remón had been the owner of numerous brothels similar to those where García had worked.[16]

The Rose Murder Case Resolved

The Panamanian government delayed Rose's trial, hoping to calm emotions in response to U.S. concerns for a fair hearing. His parents hired a veteran Panamanian attorney, José M. Faundes, to defend their son. On January 3, 1958, in an anticlimactic trial, a Panamanian judge found Rose guilty of only accidental manslaughter and not the initial second-degree murder charge. Faundes did a good job convincing the judge that Eduardo's death had been a tragic mistake that a remorseful Rose regretted. He introduced evidence of Rose's earlier attempts to adopt Eduardo and of his now legal marriage to Blanca, who resided on base housing in the Zone with their remaining children. Rose served less than fourteen months imprisonment in Panama before his quiet release in January 1958.[17]

In their year-end editions Panamanian dailies listed the Rose case as one of the ten most important events of 1956, along with the Suez Crisis, the Soviet invasion of Hungary, and the election of Ernesto de la Guardia as president of the republic. The Rose case generated a flood of antigringo sentiment, just as the Suez Crisis reignited nationalist fervor. Eduardo Castillo came to symbolize small, multiracial Panama trampled by a racist U.S. brute. According to Panamanian journalists, the U.S. military indoctrinated its troops, many from disadvantaged backgrounds, into a culture of aggressive masculinity, violence, and racism. The GI hero of World War II had degenerated into a monster.[18]

Indeed in the 1940s–1950s the typical U.S. soldier of European descent did view himself as superior to most Panamanians. Such a soldier or airman regarded himself as a member of an elite, the most powerful military on earth, serving the strongest nation on the planet. When a U.S. soldier or airman crossed the border into Panama, he encountered a small Latin American republic that deployed "a glorified police force," the Panamanian National Guard. As compared to the United States, the republic had 1 percent of the population, 0.25 percent of the land space, and 0.33 percent of the GDP.[19] "If we were number one, they were number one hundred and fifty," one U.S. soldier remarked. "It was kind of hard to take them seriously. I mean . . . they were *Panamanians*."[20]

To their credit, U.S. officers offered pamphlets, area handbooks, and orientation seminars aimed at dissuading recruits from such condescension. But these efforts often failed. The presence of so many Panamanian street vendors, shoe-shiners, prostitutes, and beggars near the "Limits," the gateway to the borderland, unfortunately confirmed many soldiers' degrading stereotypes regarding Panama. The fact that many of these street denizens were the victims of endemic poverty and lack of opportunity apparently escaped the viewpoint of numerous GIs.[21]

Even more educated U.S. officers sometimes revealed prejudices. The official brochure of the Caribbean Command's Strategic Seminar, held in Panama in 1954 and attended by Army Chief of Staff General Matthew B. Ridgway, featured a drawing entitled "Panama Street Scene." The sketch showed an ancient, apparently syphilitic black lottery vendor selling her tickets in a Panamanian slum. Given all the possible representations of Panama's natural beauty available to the illustrators, the pamphlet's choice evinced U.S. insensitivity to Panamanian dignity. But despite these negative attitudes, many U.S. soldiers gradually formed friendships and romantic liaisons in the republic that afforded them a more complex and sympathetic understanding of Panamanian society. Indeed profound exceptions existed to the stereotypical drunk and disdainful GI staggering about the borderland.[22]

The U.S. military held no monopoly on racism and superiority complexes either. Dominated by *rabiblanco* ("white-tail") elites prior to the National Guard coup in 1968, the Panamanian government forbade the stationing of African American troops on the isthmus until the U.S. government insisted on their deployment in the mid-1950s. Lighter-skinned Panamanians complained that the United States had brought "enough blacks" to Panama through its importation of West Indians for canal construction. Except for a few wartime exceptions, Washington generally acceded to these Panamanian prejudices, just as the Pentagon refrained for decades from stationing Jewish American personnel on Saudi bases. For their part, many Panamanians from the upper classes regarded U.S. enlisted personnel, whether of Puerto Rican or white working-class descent, with derision. Educated Panamanians saw them as *brutos* and *groseros*, people of low caliber, given to base instincts. The weekend carousing of many GIs did little to dissuade such appraisals. But to understand the complicated relationship between the U.S. military and the Panamanian people, it is necessary to explore the roots of a complex, border-framed association.[23]

The Origins of the U.S. Military in the Borderland

The first Americans to arrive on the isthmus in 1903 to establish a century of dominance were the U.S. military. Even earlier, from the completion of the Panama Railroad in 1855 to the Panamanian Revolution in November 1903, the U.S. military had intervened thirteen times on the isthmus "to restore order" and "to protect American lives and property." Prior to 1903 most U.S. incursions aimed to *prevent* Panamanian secession from Colombia, with whom Washington hoped to negotiate canal rights. But in November 1903 U.S. naval and marine intervention assured the success of the U.S.-approved secessionist revolution.[24]

Once the treaty of November 17, 1903, ceded the Zone to Washington as a virtual "state within a state," the U.S. military's role in guarding this new imperial frontier mushroomed. In 1904 a marine battalion established the first permanent U.S. base at Camp Elliot. From there the U.S. isthmian base complex grew in leaps and bounds. Canal security concerns during both world wars justified further expansions. By 1948 fourteen permanent bases remained within the Zone: Fort Amador, Fort Clayton, Fort Kobbe, Quarry Heights Headquarters, Rodman Naval Station, Corozal Army Reservation, and Howard and Albrook Airbases on the Pacific side; on the Atlantic side, the Pentagon operated Fort Davis, Fort Sherman, Fort Gulick, Fort Randolph, Coco Solo, and Galeta Island. Despite the popular perception of the Canal as a naval base, the U.S. Army dominated the military presence there, constituting over 70 percent of uniformed personnel.[25]

During World War II and the cold war, the significance of the bases' missions grew. In 1943 the Pentagon founded the Inter-American Air Force Academy (IAFA) at Albrook to train Latin American airmen. In 1946 the military established the U.S. Army Caribbean School at Fort Amador, which moved three years later to Fort Gulick on the Atlantic side. In 1963 the Kennedy administration expanded this facility and renamed it the School of the Americas. The Fort Gulick installation (1949–84) trained nearly sixty thousand Latin American officers and NCOs in counterinsurgency, civic action, interrogation techniques, and psychological warfare in support of Washington's cold war crusade in the hemisphere.[26] The IAFA trained another twenty thousand. In 1957 the Pentagon opened the Jungle Operations Center at Fort Sherman, the premier U.S. jungle training facility. The Pentagon rotated many of its elite units through Sherman, such as Marine Recon, Airborne Rangers, Special Forces, and Navy SEALs. The Kennedy administration also deployed the 8th Special Forces Group to Panama to instruct at both the School of the Americas and the Jungle Center.[27]

U.S. Caribbean Command, renamed Southern Command in 1963, housed all the major telecommunications, satellite-radar, and intelligence-gathering assets for monitoring Central America, South America, and the Caribbean. Ironically, as the strategic importance of the Canal declined in the postwar age of a two-ocean U.S. Navy, the importance of the Canal's base complex grew. Though modest in troop numbers, comprising between ten thousand and fourteen thousand U.S. personnel from 1946 to 1979, the Zone's military facilities represented the chief listening post, training center, and staging area for the Pentagon in Latin America as well as the armed guardians of the Zone's borders.[28]

In the postwar era Panamanian nationalists protested this expanded U.S. military role. In the 1960s and 1970s increasingly radical Panamanians condemned Washington's use of facilities, such as the School of the Americas, for violating the 1903 treaty that granted Washington military rights for Canal defense only. These new training sites emerged as an extralegal instrument of hemispheric repression, operating on Panamanian soil without popular consent or legal justification.[29]

Social Life in the Military Borderland

For most U.S. soldiers in the postwar era, the Canal Zone bases represented an easy posting, a virtual rest and relaxation assignment, particularly for officers and support personnel.[30] Unlike their comrades stationed in Vietnam, on the East-West German border, or along the 38th parallel in Korea, the officers of Southern Command enjoyed plentiful leisure time playing golf, swimming, imbibing cocktails, sunbathing, and fishing. They also participated in Panama's favorite masculine sport: romancing the isthmus's alluring young women. A sex industry that catered to U.S. servicemen plus the presence of thousands of Panamanian women eager to date GIs and officers made the isthmus a sexual playground for many servicemen. So relaxed was the officer corps in Panama that it nicknamed Southern Command "Southern Comfort." Senior officers about to retire drew assignment to Panama as a golden parachute. "What better way to end a career than on Quarry Heights?," Admiral Gene La Rocque remarked. "A tour in the Southern Command is most aptly described as a two-year vacation."[31]

Cocktail parties, unit balls, dances, coming-out parties for officers' daughters, and welcoming and farewell dinners filled the military social calendar. Officers' wives organized charity events. At one point up to six different military yachts hosted parties as well as fishing tournaments and coastal excursions. "There's nothing like it in the world, a party every night and never a wait on the golf course," one colonel quipped. The top-heavy officer corps also played tennis, bridge, and shuffleboard; they shot skeet and held target competitions with rival officers stationed in Puerto Rico and Guantánamo. The Zone made available to the U.S. garrison seven golf courses, six riding clubs, five beaches, fourteen swimming pools, fourteen movie theaters, four yacht clubs, five bowling alleys, two roller-skating rinks, six gymnasiums, and sixty-eight tennis courts. U.S. rank-and-file troopers also participated in baseball, basketball, boxing, swimming, and fishing leagues to promote morale and keep GIs out of trouble. Occasionally these teams competed with Panamanian teams, though fights sometimes marred the proceedings.[32]

The relaxed atmosphere on Panama bases drew sharp criticism from some authorities. A surprise readiness drill at Fort Kobbe in 1958 revealed to the inspector that "approximately one-fifth of the soldiers were absent without leave. . . . They had gone into Panama the previous night or had not yet returned. Troops who were present reported to their duty posts in various states of dress. Many appeared to be suffering the effects of overindulgence in alcohol from the previous evening. They did not respond well to emergency orders. . . . We discovered several bottles of *Carta Vieja* rum in the soldiers' quarters. . . . Four Panamanian women—dates or acquaintances of service personnel—emerged from the barracks and ran for the fence when the air raid signal sounded. I have ordered them to be detained and interrogated to ascertain how they got onto a secure military facility."[33]

In contrast to such breakdowns in discipline, GIs in combat units trained hard in tropical heat and downpours, and they lived in more spartan quarters than officer housing. But such men constituted a minority of personnel. Officers, NCOs, and even ordinary "dogfaces" typically found a way to secure weekend passes or three-day furloughs. They then simply walked or taxied into the red-light districts of the capital and Colón. "We weren't really under threat—except from the women," Corporal Juan Jiménez-Ramírez explained. "We had tense times, like the 1964 riots and when Torrijos was pushing all those demonstrations, but most of the time it was pretty light duty. Except when you got one of these hard-ass officers who wanted to march twenty miles through the jungle with all your goddamn equipment."[34]

In the postwar era, besides Special Forces, the U.S. Army deployed three combat battalions, each numbering around seven hundred men, in Panama. Two battalions, one mechanized infantry and one airborne, guarded the Canal's Pacific entrance near the capital. Southern Command stationed a single infantry battalion on the Atlantic side near Colón. The other roughly eight thousand to twelve thousand U.S. troops formed support units: engineers, artillery, anti-aircraft, military police, signals, supply, motor pool, and so on. "This place was a paradise compared to Korea or Japan—or even the States. You had a tropical climate, great night life, and the women. . . . The

Panamanians were basically easygoing people. In the barracks, we had Kuna Indians who made our beds and shined all our buckles and boots. I mean, what more could you ask for?" For the Kuna, duties often comprised hard work for low pay as well as enduring racism and mistreatment from at least some GIs.[35]

The concept of the Zone as an "easy posting" faced challenges as early as the 1930s. During that time the *Panama American*'s U.S. editor, Nelson Rounsevell, wrote a series of scathing articles that renamed Fort Clayton "Fort Suicide." Criticizing the harsh training of combat troops there, Rounsevell blamed the recent commander for the suicides of several enlisted men and junior officers. Suicides plagued the Panama garrison throughout its existence. According to army psychiatrists, the reasons for them ranged from depression to marital unhappiness, gambling debts, alcoholism, spousal infidelity, homosexual guilt, and drug addiction. In several cases from the 1950s–1960s psychiatrists also mentioned the sense of cultural alienation and isolation that some U.S. troops experienced. While the majority of enlisted men and officers adapted well to Panama's allegedly exotic ambience, to others the host nation remained a strange and forbidding place that challenged their moral and societal beliefs. These individuals stayed on base during off-duty hours and drank inordinately out of boredom and homesickness. Their deaths in isolation also marked the price of empire in the U.S.-dominated borderland.[36]

Borderland Conflicts between the U.S. Military and Panamanians

During World War II U.S. Army Air Corps planes accidentally dropped bombs and landing gear through the roofs of Panamanian houses, including the home of the legal counsel in Los Santos while his young daughter was home. Unexploded U.S. ordnance killed some fifteen Panamanian children during and after the war. In Colón an American pilot crashed his plane into a busy intersection, killing two Panamanians and burning down a number of houses. During training exercises, U.S. airmen strafed pigs and draft animals. In the capital and in the interior GIs gang-raped young girls and made unwanted advances on Panamanian women. They broke into homes and assaulted, robbed, and terrified locals on the streets. While only a small fraction of U.S. forces participated in these crimes, their impact on a nation as small as Panama was profound. Deliberate offenders (not those involved in accidents) were tried by military courts and sentenced to stockades in Panama or at Fort Leavenworth for longer terms. The Panamanian Foreign

Ministry sent reams of protests, condemning U.S. behavior and demanding reparations that Washington usually paid, quieting complaints with cash settlements and apologies. *Mea culpas* even came from President Franklin Delano Roosevelt. The avalanche of dollars during the war years helped salve Panamanians' wounded feelings, but it was no accident that the strongest anti-American riots of the decade occurred in 1947, when memories of wartime abuses still abounded.[37]

U.S. soldiers robbed Panamanian establishments during the war and afterward. In 1950 three debt-ridden soldiers robbed a Panamanian bar in Colón.[38] In 1952 four GIs robbed Las Palmitas cabaret in the capital while a National Guardsman lunched at the counter.[39] Soldiers tipped Panamanian waitresses generously, then filched back their tips.[40] They stole automobiles, buses, bottles of liquor, donkeys, pigs, monkeys, tropical birds, and cayucos from the countryside, and on one occasion a maid who dozed in the backseat of her mistress's Ford, when a drunken GI absconded with the car.[41]

In more serious incidents, service personnel killed or crippled Panamanian civilians with their military vehicles. Such accidents, often perpetrated by reckless GIs, infuriated the local population. A Panamanian woman recalled her terror in the 1970s when a convoy of heavy army transport trucks roared by her and her children in their small Toyota along the road to Piña: "They forced us off the road. They were so foolhardy and arrogant. Stupid nineteen-year-old boys with no sense of responsibility. We could see them all laughing at us as they drove by, like it was all a joke! But people died over these jokes!"[42]

Traffic injuries and deaths became a fact of life with so large a military presence frequently conducting exercises in Panama. The Department of Defense paid out tens of thousands of dollars in settlements that ranged from $50 to $1,000 per claim. Another factor in these injuries centered on inebriated GIs speeding through the border streets of Panama on furlough with their local girlfriends, who often became victims of crashes. Zonians long ridiculed Panamanians for their reckless, devil-may-care driving, but GIs often outdid them in what some called the "Panama Grand Prix" on the Transistmica and the Pan-American Highway every Friday and Saturday night.[43]

U.S. Disrespect toward the National Guard

The third favorite pastime of U.S. troops in Panama, when not drinking or visiting brothels, was mixing it up with the Panamanian police (after 1953 called the National Guard). "Disrespect toward the National Guard" was the most prevalent GI crime in the borderland. In Panama (and several other Latin American nations) disrespect toward the government or its officials constituted a crime even when the offense embodied only critical language. The U.S. Constitution protects such free, if insulting, speech, though Panamanians saw the issue differently, as an attack upon the dignity of their state. U.S. disrespect toward the local constabulary included not only words but physical assault: knocking off guardsmen's hats, throwing drinks in their faces, breaking rum bottles over their heads, and kicking them down stairwells. Typically, however, where GIs were concerned the charge addressed simple curse words and brawling. In the postwar era such conflicts assumed a new significance as the National Guard's power rose as a direct consequence of U.S. cold war policy to strengthen it as a deterrent to "leftist subversion."[44]

U.S. service personnel came out on both the winning and losing ends of these encounters, often winding up in Panamanian courts, where they added insult to injury by cursing Panamanian night judges. One soldier sang the "Star-Spangled Banner" while a Panamanian judge harangued him in Spanish. Another told the magistrate to "shut the hell up" and yelled, "This whole country is a dump!" "I don't even know what you're talking about you goddamned idiot!" shouted a third. A U.S. military lawyer attended the proceedings as an observer. He normally put up the $50 fine before taking the soldier or sailor into custody and returning him to his base, where he faced additional disciplinary action and deductions from his pay for the fine.[45]

Still, to many U.S. enlisted men, getting into a tussle with the *guardia* signified a badge of honor and a right of passage. Since U.S. troops in Panama had no specific enemy to focus on, the local police served as a handy substitute. The despised racial identity of the Panamanian mestizo, mulatto, or black police increased the contempt that many white GIs displayed toward them. Puerto Rican troops provided exceptions to this rule, although they too expressed a fierce antipathy toward the guardia. A typical report described a recruit from San Juan: "Pvt. Romero has a reputation for being a good duty soldier but he is a confirmed pay-day drunk and brawler."[46] Military police and shore patrols made frequent arrests of unruly GIs to dampen cross-national conflict. But Panamanian guardsmen patrolled these same "red zones." While detained by MPs, GIs often lunged out at accompanying guardia, who had little to do with their arrests.[47]

In August 1950 the most notorious incident of postwar GI-Panamanian violence occurred when two U.S. soldiers murdered sixty-four-year-old Sewell Codrington, a West Indian night watchman, during their robbery of the Cristobal YMCA. The two soldiers, Privates Gerald Thomas and Gustave Smith, each received twenty-five-year sentences in the Canal Zone court for their beating death of Codrington. While causing quite a stir in the Zone, the case initially elicited less protest from Panama, perhaps because the crime's adjudication took place within the enclave and the murder victim was a West Indian.[48]

Battles with Panamanian officials frequently garnered more attention. In June 1947 a Panamanian national deputy attacked a GI after enduring his insulting remarks about the republic in the men's room of the cabaret El Bohio. The legislator, Anthony DeReuter, a former Dutch national and U.S. soldier, had renounced his U.S. citizenship, become a Panamanian, and won election to the Assembly as an Arnulfista, a generally anti-American party in the postwar republic. The career of DeReuter personified the cosmopolitan nature of the Zone borderland, where self-invention was an art form. DeReuter slugged Sergeant Adam Melber, of whom the U.S. incident report read, "Although not bitterly disliking Panama or its people, he has been known to make derogatory remarks about them not unusual among enlisted ranks." The local police immediately arrested Melber, but not the Panamanian deputy, who due to his office held immunity from prosecution.[49]

In 1952 an equally incendiary assault occurred when a U.S. soldier tore down and trampled on a Panamanian flag at a bar. Hauled off by the Panamanian police and arraigned in night court, the soldier called the judge "an idiot," for which he received ninety days. In other cases of disrespect to the National Guard, the Panamanian flag, and Panamanian judges in the 1950s, U.S. soldiers laughed uproariously during judicial proceedings, urinated in the courtroom, called the judge "a moron," his court a "pigsty," and its procedures "a joke." U.S. soldiers set off firecrackers at the feet of National Guardsmen. One drunken soldier wiped his excrement-laden shoes on the uniformed pants of a guardia, while another blew marijuana smoke in a guardsman's face. Insults ranged from "dirty spic," "goddamned niggers," "piece of shit Panamanians," and "pananiggers," to the more generic "sons of whores, bitches," "asshole greasers," "goddamned queers," "spic faggot motherfuckers," "fucking bitos," or the always popular suggestion "They should take this whole shit hole country and flush it down a goddamn toilet!" Many times the Panamanian officials being insulted did not understand exactly what the GIs were saying, although, as one U.S. veteran remarked, "they got the general drift." Denigrating the masculinity of the guard proved a focal point of these insults as GIs frequently saw themselves as the only "true men" in the borderland (this proscription also included civilian Zonians), serving in a real (read: powerful) army. Thus GIs projected a form of "hegemonic masculinity" against the presumed "subordinated" or "marginalized" masculinity of Panamanians.[50]

The wartime high of over two hundred cases of disrespect dropped by the early 1950s, after the U.S. provost marshal held regular meetings to stem the tide of arrests. When in 1968 the National Guard seized political power in Panama, the number of disrespect and assault charges fell considerably as the ascendant Panamanian military enforced stricter penalties for a crime that General Torrijos saw as a direct assault upon his revolutionary state.[51]

The civilian Zonians rarely got into fights with the National Guard, though they expressed their hostility toward the organization among themselves and in angry letters to the English-language dailies. Zonians particularly disliked the guardia ticketing their parked cars in Panama. (Their Zone license plates gave them away.) Later, in the 1970s, guardsmen seized long-haired Zonian youths and gave them forced crew cuts in local barbershops. In 1972 guardsmen ordered a lounging Zonian teenager and his father to stand at attention and salute the Panamanian flag as they lowered it at sunset on Taboga Island. After the 1968 coup the National Guard flexed its muscle more frequently to intimidate and retaliate against Americans, both civilian and military, something it had done infrequently during the oligarchic era. Rex Raspberry, who worked as a nurse in the 1970s at Gorgas Hospital, remembered U.S. soldiers with split skulls, broken noses, jaws, and cheekbones being transported to the emergency room nightly, "especially on those payday weekends when they decided to mix it up with the guardia."[52]

U.S.-Panamanian Military Cooperation

Accommodation and not just conflict shaped U.S.-Panamanian military relations. The U.S. military helped create the National Guard and trained most of its officers and NCOs at the School of the Americas. They maintained a strong liaison and frequently cooperated at command and staff levels.[53] Both militaries often worked together in pursuit of suspects on their respective sides of the border, until the Panamanian military government (1968–89), first under General Torrijos and later General Noriega, took a more independent, at times hostile stance toward the U.S. military.[54]

The greatest borderland cooperation between the U.S. military and the Panamanian people occurred in the area of civic action and philanthropy. Southern Command and all its units regularly donated to Panamanian charities. U.S. battalions sent Santa Claus detachments with gifts to Panamanian

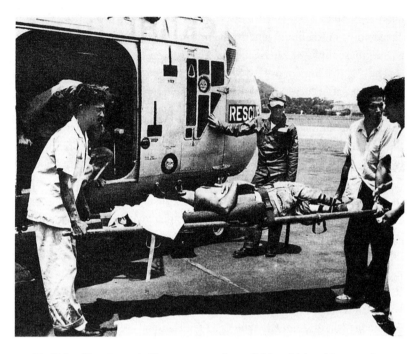

5.1. The U.S. military's goodwill rescue evacuations of sick and injured Panamanians helped improve relations between the borderland communities and increased Panamanians' more positive appraisal of the U.S. military, as distinct from the civilian Zonians. Courtesy of the *Panama Canal Spillway* in the Panama Canal Museum Collection, George Smathers Library, University of Florida, http://ufdc.ufl.edu/pcm.

schools and orphanages; they distributed toys and candy at Halloween and Easter. The military routinely inoculated, treated, and medivaced sick Panamanians from the countryside.[55] U.S. engineer and construction units built schools, clinics, and roads in isolated regions of Panama. During environmental disasters such as floods, mudslides, and fires, the U.S. military's rescue units typically arrived first on the scene since their transport and equipment were so superior to those of the Panamanian government. During the horrific Chorrillo fire in 1950, the U.S. military and various Zone organizations drew kudos for their aid to the victims and their help in rebuilding the barrio. The U.S. military repeated these Good Samaritan efforts in the equally tragic San Miguel fire in 1958.[56]

The highpoint of such philanthropy occurred from 1960 to 1963, right before the explosive anti-American riots. The U.S. Army commander in Panama, General Theodore Bogart, launched Operation Friendship to in-

tensify U.S. aid and promote more positive contacts with the local populace. As part of the Alliance for Progress in Panama and a companion piece
to the "winning of hearts and minds" in Southeast Asia, Operation Friendship drew praise from moderate Panamanians. Unfortunately for U.S.-Pan-
amanian relations, these efforts did not include much Zonian participation.
An illegal flag-raising by Zonian teenagers, and not some GI antic, touched
off the disaster in January 1964.[57] Panamanians later expressed shock when
General Bogart, quite popular on the isthmus for his goodwill efforts, sent
a congratulatory telegram to Southern Command's General O'Meara during the 1964 riots when U.S. soldiers' actions claimed at least seven of the
twenty-one lost Panamanian lives.[58]

Taxi Wars

Another group that often came into conflict with the U.S. military was Panama's colorful *taxistas* (taxi drivers). Known for their aggressive driving,
sharp language, and street smarts, taxistas derived a good living transporting inebriated soldiers to borderland nightclubs and *casas de citas* (brothels).
For those servicemen and Zonians who journeyed to the republic strictly for
such activities, local taxis became the medium by which they experienced
Panama, for them a series of bleary urban scenes viewed through their taxi's
typically smudged windshield. "I went to Panama a lot," one serviceman remembered, "but only to the bars and cathouses. So I really couldn't tell you
much about the country, you know, the politics, the history."[59] Taxistas became the facilitators or filters for these Americans' constructions of Panama.

When driving soldiers to bordellos, taxistas received commissions from
the owners for delivering a paying customer. Panamanian taxi drivers also
endured considerable abuse from U.S. soldiers, including insults, assaults,
and refusals to pay when they jumped out at red lights or bars and ran for it.
Angered at what they regarded as fare gouging, many drunken GIs felt justified in refusing to pay. "Failure to Pay a Taxi Fare" emerged as the second
most common Panamanian charge against U.S. troops, after "Disrespect
to the National Guard." In 1954 one taxista, José Bethancourt, complained
to the U.S. military police: after driving a soldier "to his post at Miraflores
Bridge the enlisted man refused to pay his fare and forced Bethancourt to
leave at the point of a gun."[60]

One might ask why Panamanian drivers took the risk of picking up such
aggressive GIs. The answer is that they paid two to five times the standard
Panamanian rate, depending on their drunkenness or generosity. Liberal

American tipping became legendary among taxistas. To this day older drivers tell stories of a colonel who had forgotten his wife's birthday and needed a rapid ride to Avenida Central to purchase a gift, handing a taxista a $20 propina (tip), a week's salary. In the postwar era the U.S. military provided the bread-and-butter clientele for hundreds of these well-paid drivers.[61]

An experienced taxista constituted a guide or mediator to Panamanian culture for many GIs, negotiating conflicts and preventing arrests of personnel who could barely speak Spanish. Following the 1964 riots, taxistas drove frightened GIs who lived in Panama across the border to safety in the Zone. They navigated gingerly through crowds of angry countrymen with a GI under a blanket in the backseat or even in the trunk. "He's a good man, he's with me: he just wants to get back to his base," they told hostile protesters. In light of twenty-one Panamanian deaths in the riots, such rescues required courage and testified to the apolitical nature of many borderland relations— or rather to their socioeconomic primacy.[62]

A Divided Military: Puerto Rican GIs in the Borderland

The U.S. military community on the isthmus was divided by race, class, gender, and national identity, and the constant crossing of borders brought these divisions into sharp relief. Puerto Ricans made up the largest minority group within the Panama garrison.[63] At one point in the 1920s Puerto Ricans constituted over 50 percent of personnel, forming a classic colonial army of white officers and NCOs directing "colored" (i.e., Puerto Rican) conscripts. This arrangement was similar to the British-led Indian Army that garrisoned much of the Victorian Empire in Africa and Asia.[64]

Up until the 1950s Pentagon officials believed that Puerto Rican troops were unsuited for combat in colder climes such as Korea, Germany, and Alaska and should be deployed only to tropical regions: "It is definitely established that Puerto Ricans will not be given general assignment. The War Department plans for the use of Puerto Ricans in the Caribbean Area only. However because of the present world situation [the Korean War], individual Puerto Ricans in established units will be used in areas other than the Caribbean. They will not be used in the continental Zone of the Interior (United States). The reason for the latter is because of the 'color line.'" Caribbean Command issued this memorandum two years after President Truman's executive order in 1948 to desegregate the military. Such orders moved slowly through the borderland, where the U.S. military, like the Canal Zone government, proved adept at circumventing progressive decrees from the metropole. One way the Pentagon got around the order to desegregate such units was to classify all–Puerto Rican regiments as "locally-raised," "insular," or "Spanish-speaking troops" rather than ascribe them a racial designation.[65]

The term *Anglo–Puerto Rican conflict* presents an incomplete description of intraservice hostilities within the garrison. While Puerto Rican troops considered all white enlisted men to be Anglos, many were of Irish, Italian, or Eastern European descent who disliked their Anglo officers almost as much as the Puerto Ricans did. One group that could legitimately be termed Anglos, namely white Southerners, did compose a significant slice of the military's NCO corps. These soldiers frequently derided Puerto Ricans with racist terms such as "greasers" and "Spanish niggers" (shortened to spiggers, spigs, and ultimately spics). U.S. officers organized boxing and baseball competitions between these rival units to channel their animosity along positive lines, but Puerto Ricans and whites in the stands often fought during and after the contests.[66]

In January 1943 the all–Puerto Rican 65th Infantry Regiment joined the all–Puerto Rican 42nd Infantry Regiment in the Canal Zone to replace continental U.S. forces headed for North Africa and the Pacific. Two more Puerto Rican National Guard regiments, the 295th and the 296th Infantry, followed, increasing the "Latinization" of the Panama garrison. These substitute deployments followed a consistent racist pattern that would continue until the Korean War of replacing continental units in Panama with Puerto Ricans deemed unworthy of facing "first-class" (i.e., German or Japanese) opponents.[67] A notable change in this policy occurred in 1950, when the manpower-strapped Pentagon sent the 65th Infantry Regiment into combat in Korea as part of the 3rd U.S. Infantry Division. Thereafter the practice of raising separate all–Puerto Rican units ended (with the exception of the Puerto Rican National Guard). But the Pentagon continued to assign most Puerto Ricans to Caribbean duty.[68]

As a result even as late as the 1950s–1960s, Puerto Ricans made up around a third of all GIs in Panama. These Latin American recruits spoke Spanish, danced salsa, and appreciated the Caribbean culture that suffused the Panamanian side of the borderland. Puerto Rican recruits often served as mediators or translators for white U.S. troops. "A Puerto Rican soldier was the best friend you could have in Panama," one veteran remembered. "He spoke the lingo, could show you the ropes, introduce you to the girls, teach you the dances, the whole nine yards." Caribbean Command saw other advantages to employing insular troops. Their Spanish fluency and ability to blend in with the locals provided a valuable intelligence asset. The CIA and G-2 maintained Puerto Rican agents and informants in the Panama borderland on a routine basis.[69]

In the chatty cantinas and bordellos of Panama, *bochinche* constantly swirled about. As an international transport hub, Panama City maintained its reputation as "the Casablanca of the Caribbean," a magnet for criminals, foreign nationals, exile plotters, tax dodgers, spies, and ne'er-do-wells. Puerto Rican soldiers had a sharp sense of what went on beneath the surface of Panamanian society. Pillow talk added to their acumen. For many Panamanian women, Puerto Ricans seemed ideal lovers, Spanish-speaking Latinos who earned U.S.-scale wages. They immediately had an entrée into elements of borderland society denied to most continentals.[70]

But in the 1940s–1960s the majority of U.S. Latinos remained enlisted men, not officers, due to racial discrimination in Caribbean (later Southern) Command. More were promoted after the affirmative action of the 1970s–1980s. During the U.S. invasion of Panama in 1989, General Marc Cisneros, a Mexican American, commanded U.S. Army South. Many soldiers regarded Cisneros as the best army chief Southern Command ever had since he was so culturally and linguistically attuned to the isthmus. A member of General Noriega's dignity battalions and a prisoner of war following the U.S. invasion, Rolando Sterling Arango, recalled confronting Cisneros shortly after his capture: "I remember seeing this big gringo general with his staff walk by me when they had me handcuffed so I called out to him: 'So you are the head of this racist, imperialist army!' I was surprised when he stopped and spoke back to me in *perfect* Spanish. He really told me off." Sterling laughed. "I did not know he was Mexican!"[71]

Puerto Rican–Panamanian–North American Conflicts

Pentagon officials also believed that maintaining large numbers of Spanish-speaking troops in Panama promoted better relations with the local populace. While this maxim generally held true, some Panamanians disliked Puerto Rican troops as much as continentals, viewing them as haughty and boisterous *bulleros*. This stereotype derived from groups of inebriated Puerto Ricans shouting and singing in the streets on furlough. "You could always hear them from far away," one Panamanian recalled.[72]

Horrific acts of violence carried out by Puerto Rican GIs against individual Panamanians also exacerbated tensions. In July 1953 a Puerto Rican corporal enraged at a Panamanian woman's refusal to marry him and the hostility of her younger sister slashed the throats of both sisters on a street corner in Panama City, then ended his own life by swallowing rat poison. This gruesome double homicide-suicide shocked residents in the capital and heightened hostility toward U.S. troops in general. The traditional machismo of some Puerto Rican soldiers may have contributed to aspects of these episodes, but this is difficult to gauge and unfair to assume since mainland soldiers, such as Harold Rose, carried out equally atrocious acts against the local population.[73]

Indeed Puerto Rican GIs found themselves in a unique pressure cooker in the borderland. They faced discrimination from their continental comrades and nationalist hostility from Panamanians. Their own U.S. commanders frequently denigrated their abilities. In 1946 a U.S. general noted "their low intelligence quotients" and "tendency toward emotional instability," typical racist statements that unfortunately matched prevailing stereotypes.[74] In an article about the 65th Regiment after its combat in Korea, war correspondents wrote of "the guitar-plucking, happy-go-lucky Puerto Ricans of the 65th Regiment." An accompanying photo showed two Puerto Rican soldiers in straw hats swinging on hammocks as they strummed their guitars. Puerto Rican veterans of the 65th resented the charges of cowardice in the field that thirty-seven of their number faced following the disastrous retreat from the Yalu River in December 1950 after the massive Chinese counterattack on UN forces in Korea. Other black and white units from within the 2nd and the 24th Infantry Divisions also "bugged out," but Puerto Ricans from the 65th felt that the Pentagon had unfairly singled them out for disgrace.[75]

Besides disputes over race, Puerto Rican and continental troops battled constantly over language. U.S. Army sergeants and officers repeatedly reprimanded Puerto Rican troops for conversing among themselves in Spanish. Many white NCOs suspected, perhaps correctly, that Puerto Ricans were disparaging them in their native tongue. During the 1940s–1950s, despite the establishment of a twelve-week English-language course for insular recruits, many Puerto Rican soldiers spoke little English and only felt comfortable conversing in Spanish.[76]

In early 1951 four Puerto Rican recruits beat and stabbed their platoon sergeant, Herbert Crosby, at Fort Clayton after a series of incidents in which the sergeant abused them over their refusal to speak English in the barracks.[77] In May 1951, while shooting at the Empire firing range, Private José Medina aimed his M-1 rifle at his firing instructor, Corporal Albert Davis, with whom he "had bad blood" from several incidents of Davis badgering Medina for his failure to speak English. A nearby trooper wrestled the rifle from Medina before he could squeeze off a round. The army later charged Medina with attempted murder, although they eventually reduced the charge to assault.[78]

Another telling incident over language occurred in the early 1970s, when a U.S. captain who constantly berated his Puerto Rican sergeant to "stop speaking Spanish, damn you!" called him into his office. "Sergeant Torres-Rivera," the captain began in a conciliatory tone, "the guardia have arrested my son for possession of marijuana. You speak Spanish, right? I want you to go down to the jail in Chorrillo and see if you can get this straightened out. Here's twenty dollars. Buy a case of beer and a ham at the PX for the local *comandante* to smooth things over." Torres-Rivera remembered thinking to himself, "Oh, so my Spanish is okay now."[79]

On the issue of race, another controversy arose concerning the treatment accorded "white" Puerto Ricans in contrast to "colored" Puerto Ricans in Panama. Until the early 1950s the U.S. Army classified insular troops into these two categories. Bowing to Panamanian wishes, the U.S. military abstained from stationing "colored" troops in Panama, be they African American or Afro–Puerto Rican. As a result the military kept darker-complexioned Puerto Ricans on its bases in Puerto Rico and refrained from deploying them to Panama. The populist Puerto Rican governor Luis Muñoz Marín protested this discrimination; indeed under Article 23 of the 1941 Panamanian Constitution that forbade the immigration to Panama of "any blacks whose original language is not Spanish," "colored" Puerto Ricans should have been granted an exemption. But as one Panamanian official stated, "Colored Puerto Ricans don't speak Spanish; they're Americans." The presence of African American and darker Puerto Rican GIs in the borderland also discomfited Zonians when these recruits tried to enter their segregated commissaries, swimming pools, and beaches.[80]

Discrimination against Puerto Rican troops sometimes erupted in extreme violence. In August 1953 Private Angel Ramos, a Korean War veteran, took over a sand-bagged position near the Miraflores Bridge and began firing his .50 caliber machine gun at all the white soldiers and officers in the vicinity. Over a hundred U.S. Army police laid siege to Ramos's position while he unleashed thousands of rounds, cursing and calling out for the MPs to try to take him alive. Ramos initiated the crisis by tackling and disarming a white sentry who questioned him about his tardiness in reporting to his post. After a six-hour stand-off, he surrendered to the MPs. Confined to a hospital for psychological observation, he "complained about his experiences in Korea and about the way he was treated in the Canal Zone as a Puerto Rican soldier."[81]

During the riots in January 1964, Panamanian students made direct appeals to Puerto Rican troops to join them in their anticolonial struggle. "Come fight with us; you have no flag either!" they shouted to Puerto Rican troops arrayed against them. Yet no Puerto Rican deserted during the crisis. While many harbored resentments toward continental NCOs and officers, Puerto Rican GIs remained institutionally, if not ideologically, committed to the army. Many were "lifers" who made a career of their profession. Insular troops were also aware of the privileges and benefits that U.S. citizenship afforded them that elevated their status in the borderland above most Panamanians.[82]

Predictably given their prevalence in the ranks, the second U.S. serviceman killed during the 1964 riots was a Puerto Rican, Sergeant Luis Jiménez-Cruz, shot in Colón on the first night of the uprising. Panamanian radicals claimed that U.S. troops had killed Jiménez-Cruz, that they had deliberately shot him in the back. The next night protestors cajoled and taunted Puerto Rican troops along the skirmish line by waving a Puerto Rican flag. A few days later, when Jiménez-Cruz's widow and two small children arrived at Arlington, Virginia, prior to his funeral, no U.S. officials showed up to accompany them and the sergeant's body to the morgue. The U.S. Army claimed a scheduling snafu and apologized to her in writing. When Jiménez-Cruz's wife later insisted that her husband's casket be opened so she could see where he had been shot, the army complied. The sergeant had died from a frontal head shot. Apparently annoyed at the widow's suspicions, the army sent her a $25 bill for opening the casket. Zonians in Panama took up a collection for the widow and her children. The fact that Jiménez-Cruz died fighting Panamanians may have prompted this fleeting Zonian identification with the Puerto Rican sergeant.[83]

Stung by their failure to attract Puerto Ricans to their decolonization cause, a few radicals even castigated them on the streets after the riots as *tío toms*. Majority criticism remained more subdued. As one Panamanian expressed it, "The Puerto Ricans' situation seems very confused. Who are they? What do they want to be—an independent nation, a state of the U.S., or continue as a dependency? Even they are not sure."[84]

African American Troops in the Borderland

Due to decades-old Panamanian hostility toward their deployment, African Americans were among the last continental minority groups to serve in significant numbers in the Zone. By the early 1950s, however, in response to pressure from President Truman's desegregation order in 1948, the U.S. military finally began assigning them to the isthmus in small numbers, despite local objections.[85] A judge advocate asking for instructions on the changing policy expressed both hope and confusion:

1. We have never been confronted with the problem of enlisted negroes here, a statement of policy is required. . . .
2. The latest written information from the Department of the Army is that only individual negroes may be stationed in Panama not entire colored units.
3. This man is an American citizen. Why he is in Panama has not been determined, and is not particularly relevant, except for the possibility that he may be down here as a test case on this matter.
4. It is recommended that American negroes applying for enlistment in this area be processed and enlisted as any other individual without fanfare or comment. It is recommended that we make it a policy to assign them to units containing both Puerto Rican and Continental personnel, where possible. Such a policy would minimize the effect of color and at the same time protect us from any charges of discrimination which might result if we only assigned such personnel to an all–Puerto Rican unit.[86]

The deployment of larger numbers of black troops to the Canal Zone in the 1960s coincided with the growing civil rights movement in the United States and protests against the Vietnam War. The same morale problems that afflicted the U.S. military in Southeast Asia, Europe, and the States intruded on the borderland garrison. These maladies included a rise in disciplinary offenses: drug charges, AWOLs, desertions, and interracial violence. The turn toward black nationalism among some African American draftees led to black power salutes and rhetoric, as well as the sporting of afros and Fu Manchu beards in violation of military grooming regulations. In army barracks and at the Snake Pit, a popular servicemen's nightclub in the Zone-Panama borderland, interracial brawls between African American, white, and Puerto Rican soldiers erupted.[87]

Radical Black Protest in the Borderland

African American soldiers frequently segregated themselves voluntarily during this era for their own security and a sense of solidarity. In 1971 African American soldiers formed a group called Concerned Brothers that joined the demonstrations and a lawsuit against the Elks Club's color bar. In the early 1970s the Brothers participated in the small, anti–Vietnam War protest in the Zone organized by the Quakers, drawing the attention of the brass.[88]

In the spring of 1971 a particularly embarrassing set of racial incidents unfolded for the U.S. military in Panama. In March Vernard Pryer and Tobey Wagner, along with fifteen other black GIs at Fort Davis, had brawled with white MPs when they tried to arrest one in their group for fighting. The MPs incarcerated the two black soldiers, and a dozen other participants, at the Fort Clayton stockade. On the night of April 27 the two escaped from the pen and fled across the border to Panama. A few days later, in cooperation with the U.S. military, the Panamanian National Guard arrested Pryer and Wagner in Calidonia.[89]

Incarcerated at a Panamanian police station, Pryer and Wagner surprised the local officials when they asked for political asylum. Their request shocked the U.S. liaison officer present, but he was even more surprised at the Panamanian willingness to honor their petition. This incident proved a godsend to Torrijos's military regime, which had started a drumbeat of protest against the U.S. racial policies in the Zone. By coincidence, another U.S. soldier, Esteban Llaña, had recently deserted and sought refuge in Panama as well. Born in Panama of Chilean parents, Llaña had joined the U.S. Army, as many Latinos from the borderland did, for the pay and the fast track to U.S. citizenship. But like Pryer and Wagner, Llaña grew disillusioned with military life. He had originally returned to Panama on a two-day pass to attend the funeral of his father and then went AWOL to support his widowed mother and younger siblings.[90]

In May 1971 Foreign Minister Juan Antonio Tack of Panama held a news conference at which he introduced Pryer, Wagner, and Llaña to the Panamanian and international press. Pryer and Wagner stated that they had both sought refuge in Panama "because of the racial discrimination in the Canal Zone and in the U.S. military." In their petition to Panama they stated, "We the undersigned have formally requested from the Panamanian government political refugee status. . . . We do not believe we can keep faith with a non-practicing democracy. We served faithfully in Vietnam but we believe we have not been faithfully served by the government of the United States, as long as there is oppression for Black Americans, such as we and other Black soldiers, and our families and friends back in the United States."[91] Pryer and Wagner then told reporters that whites had all the best jobs in the Zone, while blacks were mistreated and punished for the tiniest offenses. They "regretted their past service in Vietnam. That war was a problem for the

Vietnamese and the United States had no business there. . . . They preferred now to live and work in Panama, a place where freedom for all opinions and races existed, rather than in the United States." As if this bombshell were not enough, Llaña stated that Latin Americans faced discrimination in the Zone as well, and that he too wanted sanctuary in Panama. At a time when Washington celebrated Soviet, Eastern bloc, and Cuban asylum seekers, the defection of its own personnel to a free world ally proved deeply embarrassing.[92]

The U.S. public relations disaster only worsened. On May 10, as a treat for the defectors, the guardia took them to dinner at the Kentucky Fried Chicken on the Via España. When the guardsmen and their charges started to enter the restaurant, a red jaguar with Canal Zone plates pulled up abruptly. Both its occupants got out and rushed the three GI deserters, attempting to arrest them. When the guardsmen intervened, the mystery men fled, but alerted Panamanian police quickly arrested them at a nearby gas station. The two detainees, Specialist Carlos Wattino, a Puerto Rican from New York, and Specialist Jésus Rosales, a Mexican American, were both members of the U.S. Army's Criminal Investigations Division.[93]

Panamanian police charged the two with attempted kidnapping, a crime punishable by up to twenty years. Foreign Minister Tack issued a formal protest to Washington and condemned this violation of Panamanian sovereignty. U.S. officials embarrassed themselves further with that awkwardness peculiar to large bureaucracies by first denying that the men were U.S. agents, then admitting that they were but that they had acted on their own and exceeded their authority. This public relations disaster stemmed in part from U.S. intelligence agents becoming so used to operating with immunity in Panama that they just assumed they could do whatever they pleased on the other side of the line.[94]

But by the early 1970s the political milieu of the Zone-Panama borderland was changing. The Torrijos regime rejected the acquiescence of earlier oligarchic governments toward Washington. As one local columnist proclaimed, "The passive attitude of the Panamanian government and the Panamanian people has ended. . . . We have undertaken the road to dignity and there we will stay." With the botched kidnapping case, Torrijos achieved a media coup against the gringos.[95]

The case ended anticlimactically two months later, when Pryer, dissatisfied with life in Panama and wishing to see his relatives in the States, surrendered to the U.S. military. Representatives Ronald V. Dellums and Shirley Chisholm of the Congressional Black Caucus helped arrange Pryer's transfer through a Panamanian attorney.[96] Like several of the borderland's cultural chameleons, Pryer discovered that while Panama was a fascinating place to visit, he really did not want to live there. Three months later, MPs arrested Wagner when he crossed the border into the Canal Zone for an apparent drug buy. The U.S. military sentenced both soldiers to fifteen months' hard labor at Fort Leavenworth. Officials showed less alacrity in seeking Llaña's arrest and left him unmolested in Panama. As a quid pro quo the Panamanian government quietly released agents Wattino and Rosales and dropped the charges against them.[97]

U.S. Military–Zonian Conflicts in the Borderland

The U.S. military also came into repeated conflict with the civilian Zonians. At times the two groups despised one another; at other times they tolerated each other's presence. Sent to Panama during the transitional phase that ended the old Zone and its clubhouse and commissary system, Colonel Larry Liberty remembered talking to an older Zonian one morning and mentioning that he had served two tours in Vietnam. "Well, we're a lot alike then," the old-timer said. "How's that?" Liberty asked. "Well, you guys held the fort in Vietnam, and we held the fort down here in Panama." Liberty remembered exploding with rage. "I really let this guy have it and read him the riot act. The idea of suggesting there was any equivalency between fighting in Vietnam and living in the Canal Zone with all its perks and privileges made my blood boil! But that was the way it was with a lot of them down here. They had this incredible . . . I can only call it a colonial mentality . . . like the Raj in British India."[98]

Social tension between military personnel and civilian townies had long existed in every U.S. base town, so it was not surprising that the same frictions operated on the Zone. Class disparities deepened tensions between the bourgeois Zonians and working-class enlisted men. That Zonians had better housing and superior benefits, made more money, and enjoyed draft exemptions also incensed conscripts. For their part, Zonians resented the policy that granted use of all their civilian facilities to service personnel but limited many military venues and all PXs to GIs only. Except during the emergency years of 1941–43, when the Canal faced the real possibility of Axis attack, Zonians did not express much love for the garrison. As one Zonian wag wrote in 1945, "Boys, the war is over and also I might add so is your honeymoon. . . . . Your war in the Officers Club will be pretty damned hard to explain to the families in the States who are paying for your honeymoon and had sons die in the mud of Okinawa and Germany."[99] When a soldier complained about the inordinate salary and privileges of the Zonians, he received a stinging rebuke:

> Open your rum bleary eyes and face up to it. If we make more money, it's because we have been down here for 10, 20, 30 more years than you.
>
> 1. You are in the service because you don't really have any choice.
> 2. You are in the service because you are afraid to return to civilian life and go back to work (look up that word; it's in the dictionary).[100]

In turn, service personnel in Panama often referred to Zonians, who had to work thirty years before they could receive a pension, as "dead at thirty, retired at sixty." But the roots of this hostility went back to construction days and centered on who was the most important group: the Canal builders or the armed guardians of this new imperial frontier.

After the victory celebration in September 1945, the Canal administration shifted the focus from heroic GIs to a new sanitary plan, Fight Germs Not Germans. One veteran wrote, "I was a soldier here in 1939, 40, 41 and I can truthfully say that a soldier was thought of less of than a dog. So I decided to get out of the Army and see why the Canal Workers disliked the soldiers. Well I found out that if you weren't in the clique of the Zonians, you didn't get very far down here either. I didn't think much of their way of life anyway getting drunk every night. In fact they were the biggest bunch of hypocrites I'd ever laid eyes on."[101]

Soldiers' wives took the snubs of canal workers even more personally since such biases excluded them from much of the borderland's social life that Zonian women dominated.[102] In the postwar era military animosity toward the Zonians resurged with a vengeance due to the confluence of two events: Zonian protest over the end of their income tax exemption and the outbreak of the Korean War.[103] In letters to the editor, Zonians enumerated their sacrifices living under "tropical hardship" that merited their tax-exempt status. The GIs did not buy it: "The average man in the States doesn't have much choice 'buying goods' just as in the CZ, either. . . . All the nice long shiny cars, rattan furniture, and collector's items from Panama, all those beautiful boats out in the bay are items that the average American dreams about but could never own. Since when does living in the tropics age someone badly, it must be from dissipation? The snow and ice of Minnesota is no fountain of youth either. Expected lifespan of a combat infantryman in Korea isn't so hot either."[104]

U.S. servicemen dating Zonians' daughters was another source of borderland social conflict, though Zonians objected less to their daughters dating middle-class officers than consorting with enlisted men. Puerto Rican troops represented an especial taboo.[105] In 1956 one of the worst donnybrooks between Zonians and military personnel erupted when male Zonian high school students attacked two U.S. airmen who tried to date girls from their families after a football game. Neighbors called the Canal Police, who arrested all five students for starting the fight. The Zonian youths, in this case, adhered to their community's long tradition of monitoring Zonian women. This guarding of respectable white women's sexuality fit in with the racial and gendered paternalism of the enclave. Zone kids denounced any girl who went out with a serviceman as "Rappy bait," in reference to regular army personnel (RAP); her peers considered her "cheap" and "easy." But there were advantages to dating servicemen rather than Zonian boys: they had more money, many owned cars, and they had access to all the amenities of the military bases. Servicemen also sported uniforms and weaponry and embodied a certain heroism that Zonians lacked.[106]

To the Zonians, the prime negative aspect of servicemen's sexuality rested in their connection to "unclean Panama" as GIs formed a large customer base for borderland brothels. Thus for a Zonian girl, a liaison with a soldier risked disease and contamination, the enemies of the enclave since construction days. A Zonian girl who dated a common soldier repudiated her moral standing within the civilian community for the "debauched" lifestyle of a GI. While not strictly the "other" to the Zonians (that role was reserved for Panamanians), U.S. servicemen remained racially "compromised" due to their relations with Latinas or their own Hispanic heritage.[107]

With their fathers denigrated as draft dodgers by service personnel, some Zonian teenage boys felt the need to fight GIs to prove their manhood. Kurt Buttelmann, who grew up in the 1960s–1970s near Colón, remembered brawling with soldiers: "We used to fight with them all the time. They'd usually start it by calling us Zone brats and spoiled punks, telling us to fuck off when we'd go into the whorehouses or bars where they'd be drinking. That didn't impress me; I'd go right at it with them. I won more than I lost, and I *never* backed down."[108] Despite his and his friends' many altercations with servicemen, Buttelmann also profited financially from them. "We used to go down to the perimeter of the Fort Sherman when the Special Forces had their thirty-day survival training. The Rangers would parachute in to live off the land for a month: eat snakes, plants, monkeys. We used to sell them

Snickers bars, peanut butter–and-jelly sandwiches, and ice-cold Cokes from our coolers for $3 a piece. You want to see these guys wolf that stuff down."[109]

The rivalry between the military and the Zonians extended to the enclave's schools. Cliques made up of Zonian youths and military kids competed in the middle schools and high schools of the Zone. Tom Carey, a student in Balboa High School in the 1960s, remembered the competition and cultural distinctions: "At first we were stand-offish with the military kids. We'd have some fights. They just arrived from the States or Germany, Japan. They didn't know the lay of the land. We were a lot 'cooler' than them. We knew all the hangouts in Panama and in the Zone, which girls were easy, what families were bosses. But the military kids were hipper in other ways. They just came from the States so they knew the latest clothes, music, expressions. We used to run them ragged, though, because the Zone was our home turf. . . . A lot of the military kids were *afraid* to go into Panama! We'd all been in the whorehouses and bars there since we were fourteen."[110]

The U.S. Military and the Supreme Crisis of the Borderland

The deepest rift between the military and civilian communities in the Canal Zone occurred during the borderland's gravest crisis, the uprising of January 1964. Because many military lived in Panama rather than in the Zone, their wives and children got caught up in the cataclysm. Panamanian neighbors sheltered them from angry crowds and protected their cars from vandalism by removing their Zone plates and replacing them with their own. Those in the U.S. business community and their families endured a similar nightmare as virtually all of them lived in the republic. Because a majority of the military blamed Zonian high school kids and their chauvinistic parents for fomenting the uprising, the rift between the two communities widened. Military wives saw their husbands called to combat and their frightened children locked down on bases. As the casualties mounted into the second day of fighting, authorities evacuated the civilian dependents back to the States.[111]

Tearful and angry scenes unfolded at U.S. airports during these emergency evacuations, with wives clutching children and venting their frustrations to reporters. Speaking of the civilian Zonians, wives complained, "They conduct themselves like colonists" and "They think they own the Canal." "They provoked the whole thing," one officer's wife declared. "Some of these Zonians lived there for 20 years and never set foot in Panama or learned one word of Spanish. They treated the Panamanians like 'scum.'" Another army wife told journalists that they were "treated like riff-raff by the aristocratic Zonians." On the issue of the infamous flag-raising at Balboa High, Diane Zorn, the wife of Sergeant James Zorn, said, "The parents of the U.S. students incited their actions. This sounded organized to me." Zorn's words contrasted sharply with those of the Zonians, who held that Panamanian communists, and not their own community, had been the chief organizers of the riots.[112]

The military evacuees complained that many of them had lived in Panama, but the privileged Zonians all lived "in their precious enclave." U.S. military families claimed they had made friends with and appreciated Panamanians. These same "Panamanians shielded or hid them from the angry crowds": "[They] offered us milk, coffee, and bread from their own kitchens." The military wives resented the Zonians for "their 25% tropical differential" that service personnel did not enjoy and "for their $70 per month rented homes." "The Zonians have lived outside the United States for too long," one wife said. "There was a mistake in the evacuation," another army wife concluded. "The Zonians should have been the ones removed from Panama!"[113]

The Panamanian journalist Hector Trujillo, who wrote follow-up pieces to these interviews, ranked borderland relations with Americans in three categories:

1. Americans in general—good relations
2. U.S. Service personnel who come and go every two to three years—generally good relations
3. Zonians—three generations of bad relations. Their existence symbolizes prejudice and privilege. They have purposely frustrated all attempts at reconciliation with the United States.[114]

Panamanians, according to Trujillo, agreed with the military evacuees. But while the anger of the military families was understandable, they were also caught up in the emotion of the day. The majority of military families lived on post, not in Panama. Most of these base families ventured intermittently into Panama and spoke limited Spanish. They might cross the Fourth of July Avenue to drink in the Atlas Beer Gardens or shop at the nearby Avenida Central, but most military dependents relaxed on the Zone, where Southern Command maintained abundant facilities for just that purpose. Single GIs, rather than military families, interacted more significantly with Panamanians as they spent the bulk of their off-duty time there in the bars and brothels or with their Panamanian girlfriends at the fiestas, *ferias*, and nightclubs of the isthmus. The U.S. business colony that lived almost entirely on the Panamanian side of the borderland also had much closer ties with Panamanians (in the Lions Club, the American Society, and other associations) than did most military families.[115]

Zonian–U.S. Military Cooperation

The crisis atmosphere of January 1964 also masked an important reality: for all their jealousies and resentments, Zonians and military personnel often got along fairly well throughout most of the borderland's history. They closed ranks at commemorations (the Fourth of July, Flag Day, Armed Forces Day, and Veterans Day); ROTC programs in Zonian schools garnered recruits from military, civilian, and even Panamanian families; and the Zone held annual General-for-the-Day and Admiral-for-the-Day events in which both Zone and military kids vied for the role of top commanders for a few hours. Ultimately the Zone constituted an imperial frontier manned by soldiers and civilians alike, despite Colonel Liberty's understandable aversion to the old-timer's exaggerations. When the crisis of January 1964 struck, U.S. troops did not throw the Zonians to the Panamanian mob; on the contrary, they defended them. After decades of talk about Axis, Soviet, and Cuban threats, the borderland garrison finally had a mission: to repel invaders and not just make rum Cokes. Despite marked differences, both groups shared the same privileged portion of the borderland for sixty years and remained linked by a common history and ideology: that of white and U.S. supremacy.

During the 1964 uprising Nina Kosik, who worked for the Defense Department, remembered speaking to her colonel about concerns over the military's use of force at the border. "I'm not worried about the soldiers, Nina," her boss replied. "I'm more worried about the 'Canal Zone militia.'" The colonel was referring to Zonian patrols that manned the fences near the boundary, several of whom fired shots at the Panamanian crowds. Their stance resembled that of white home and business owners during the race riots in Los Angeles and Detroit in the 1960s. In the crunch of 1964, in spite of soldiers' annoyance at the civilians for stirring up this hornets' nest, the two groups united to defend a common frontier.[116]

Coda for the U.S. Military in the Borderland

During the saddest days for the Zonians, the Carter-Torrijos Treaty negotiations in 1977–78, divisions between the two U.S. borderland identities sharpened. According to the draft treaties, which all Americans knew about through "the company grapevine," the Canal Zone would end after a two-year transition period, but the military presence would continue for twenty more years, until December 31, 1999. At the witching hour of the treaty's passage, Zonians received their comeuppance from GIs. When they recall this period, some U.S. servicemen remember with glee the spectacle of the "crybaby Zonians": "They were finally going to lose their paradise and they couldn't stand it. Boo hoo!" Civilian defense workers could stand aloof from this communal mourning also as their base structure, schools, and PXs continued for twenty more years. Bob Taht, a civilian DOD worker, recalled, "The Zonians always treated us like crap down here. So when the Senate ratified the treaty, I didn't give a damn. My job was safe. But the Zonians really got it in the neck. I didn't want to . . . but I did feel a little sorry for them. They lost everything. And they couldn't believe it. Some of them even tried to transfer to defense jobs; that's how bad it was. But most ran like rabbits back to the States when they should have stuck around and found something."[117]

The U.S. military presence in Panama continued until the close of the century. During those years the military strove to improve its image through enlarged civic action, emergency responses, and philanthropy. In addition to these official efforts, hundreds of intermarriages by U.S. servicemen to Panamanian and Colombian women strengthened local ties. But the violent U.S. invasion in 1989 killed hundreds of Panamanian civilians in Chorrillo and embittered thousands of poorer Panamanians against the gringo soldados. The U.S. military strove to rebuild its popularity throughout the 1990s with its gradual shutdown of bases, handing over each facility in emotional ceremonies to cheering Panamanian crowds. As a Panamanian woman recalled regarding the legacy of U.S. troops, "We never had such strong feelings against the soldiers one way or another. It was the Zonians who we saw as our enemies. They were the ones who thought this was their country. They were the ones we had to drive out."[118] Thus the attitude in the 1980s and 1990s proved consistent with that of the postwar decades of U.S. military–Panamanian cohabitation, and the emotional, sexual, and, above all, economic ties between the two groups persisted. On some level, Panamanians even perceived at least some U.S. troops as part of their borderland community, those GIs who intermarried with them, lived and retired in the republic, and spoke some Spanish. This was a compliment that they extended to few Zonians.[119]

And yet the stark divisions of race, class, gender, and identity within the U.S. military on the isthmus were fertile ground for exposing the contradictions of a colonial project that claimed to "protect" Panama as a "free world" choke-point—an apt term, as many Panamanians faced considerable brutality, racism, and hostility in their encounters with the borderland garrison. And periodically the cry for vengeance against the yanqui soldados appealed to nationalist Panamanian hearts. Such feelings of victimization and denigration helped sustain the independence cause all the way to the Torrijos era, when Panamanians finally wrested a long-sought sovereignty from the world's greatest power. The conflicts among Panamanians, Zonians, and the "guardians of the frontier" formed a key crucible to this process.

"INJURING THE POWER SYSTEM"

Crime and Resistance in the Borderland

"I'm so broke, I'm eating a cable!" ("Estoy tan limpio que estoy comiendo un cable!") Panama's poor and unemployed frequently exclaim, a remark that puzzles visitors to the isthmus. To add emphasis, black and mestizo Pana- manians hold up an imaginary piece of cable with both hands, bare their teeth, and chomp down on it. No other Central American people use this expression. And just how, one wonders, can anybody eat a cable? For genera- tions along the borders of the U.S. Canal Zone, impoverished Panamanians did "eat" cable, stealing thousands of feet of U.S. copper and aluminum wire and selling the material to scrap dealers in the republic. In the postwar era cable theft from the Canal Zone reached such proportions that U.S. officials created a special charge against it in their criminal code: Statute 1592, Injur- ing or Obstructing the Power System.[1]

For scholars of borderlands, crime in all its manifestations has always constituted a key category of conflict. Issues of security, smuggling, theft, illegal immigration, and illicit drug and sex trafficking emerge powerfully where borderers on the weaker, more impoverished side of the line can ac- crue an advantage by operating in the more advanced or prosperous side. But dangers await such trespassers as jurisdictional differences at the borders often translate into harsher punishments on the more powerful side. Hence colonized borderlanders often encourage privileged groups from the other side to engage in illicit acts in the poorer, more "wide-open" polity. There such citizens typically enjoy virtual immunity from prosecution or easy ac- cess to cross-national networks of contraband and vice. Another fundamental dimension to felonious activity along imperial borders is how and to what degree such activity expresses political resistance.

The power system of the U.S. Canal Zone—the Zone government, racial hierarchy, military, court, and police—faced its gravest threats during overt insurrections, such as the anti-U.S. base riots in 1947 and the flag riots in 1959 and 1964. But resistance to the power system at the borders often assumed less spectacular forms. In *Weapons of the Weak* and *Domination and the Arts of Resistance*, James Scott has demonstrated the myriad modes of defiance that subordinated groups marshal against their perceived oppressors. According to studies by Scott, Ranajit Guha, Eric Wolf, Eugene Genovese, and others, serfs, slaves, and colonized peoples challenge their subordination with a variety of strategies along imperial borderlands other than outright revolt or violence.[2]

Mass uprisings are typically the last resort of enslaved or colonized populations. Such groups well appreciate the dangers and harsh punishments such actions provoke and choose them only when the state is weakest, oppression is most unbearable, or the opportunity for revolt has some chance to succeed. Until such conditions gel, the weak dissemble, subvert, malinger, *and steal.* Public accommodation goes hand in hand with such covert resistance. West Indians who worked in the Zone during the postwar era would smile and doff their hats at their white U.S. foremen, then shuffle out of the warehouse with a stolen screwdriver tucked away in a sock. This kind of petty theft occurred constantly in the Zone, supplementing the income of West Indian borderers and providing a means of survival for indigent Panamanians. West Indians even had an expression for such deceptive, respectful comportment toward whites: "Alligator walk, alligator talk—but alligator eat with knife and fork."[3]

Scholars of power have written of "the mask of command," the impenetrable show of fortitude that colonial elites felt compelled to demonstrate when confronting "the lower orders" along imperial frontiers. Of equal importance in the power equation was "the mask of servility," which the enslaved, the colonized, and the subordinated showed daily to their "social betters." Behind this mask, people of color hide their true feelings about whites, subordinates repress their hatred of bosses, women restrain their disgust toward men. Free to express his feelings twenty years after the demise of the borderland, Albert Brown, a West Indian, admitted, "These Zonians, they'll all tell you about what a paradise it was down here. But remember, it was a paradise for *them,* not for *us.* It was no paradise for *my people!*"[4]

The question of when crime is simply crime and when it is a political act has long confounded sociologists, philosophers, and legal scholars. Marxist theorists claim that what the capitalist system calls "crime" is merely a self-serving bourgeois invention for social control. When the disenfranchised and impoverished seize a small portion of the moneyed classes' property, these folks are simply exercising their legitimate right of redress. What this theory fails to explain is the millionaire stock swindler who cons his upper-class friends or the lower-class thief who preys upon his fellow ghetto dwellers. Marxist ideology relegates such "aberrant" behavior to the psychiatric wards.[5]

Webster's Dictionary defines crime as "an action or an instance of negligence that is deemed injurious to the public welfare or morals or to the interests of the state and that is legally prohibited."[6] If one judges crime as an act contrary to the public welfare, the first question that arises is: Whose welfare? Eugene Genovese has shown that slaves in the antebellum South did not regard pilfering food from their master's larder as immoral.[7] In a less extreme vein, beginning in the 1960s nationalist textbooks taught young Panamanians that the United States had expropriated their geography unfairly and denied their nation prosperity by siphoning off canal profits for Washington's gain. Earlier, during a speech in 1911, former president Theodore Roosevelt substantiated this charge of U.S. piracy when he boasted, "I took the Canal Zone and let Congress debate!"[8]

For three and a half centuries before the arrival in 1850 of the United States on the isthmus to build the Panama Railroad, local people of color lived under an oppressive colonial state. That imperial Spanish state (1509–1821) was superseded by an elite-dominated Colombian state in 1821, followed in 1903 by a Panamanian colonial structure that exists in many aspects to this day. The chief characteristic of this order remains a socioeconomic hierarchy in which a minority of wealthy whites of European descent dominate a majority of poorer blacks, browns, and indigenous. Panamanians suffered from this internal colonialism long before they confronted any external U.S. presence. Hence in 1904 the U.S. project in Panama superimposed an external imperial structure upon an already existing colonial society.[9]

This distinction is important because to those Panamanians living at the bottom of this system, stealing from either the North American borderers or well-to-do Panamanians seemed equally appropriate. Popular uprisings by the underclass often expressed as much hostility toward the Panamanian oligarchy as toward the Canal Zone's U.S. residents. Aware of this, Panama's merchant elite frequently fanned nationalist hostility against the Zone as a means of deflecting criticism from their own indifference toward the suffering masses of the republic.[10]

But for Panama's embittered underclass, the colonial whites of the U.S.-run Canal Zone offered more accessible targets than their own oligarchy. Panama's elite lived in heavily policed neighborhoods some distance from the worst slums. The oligarchs surrounded their ornate homes and apartments in Bella Vista, Cangrejo, El Carmen, and Punta Paitilla with gates, walls, and window bars. In the 1960s security increased with fences, barbed wire, burglar alarms, German shepherds, and shotgun-toting guards. Later in the postwar era elites built their country estates in El Valle and Coronado Beach, far from Panama's poor. In comparison, the Canal Zone bordered the republic's worst slums. Despite the efforts of its efficient police, the enclave provided a more open locale for theft, robbery, and poaching, particularly at night. The Zone's long rural borders remained unmarked and unguarded. Before the completion of the boundary fence in November 1959, entry across the Zone's urban border in the capital was largely unimpeded. And even after 1959 thousands of Panamanians routinely entered the Zone to work, ensuring the enclave's vulnerability to crime.[11]

Criminals also faced harsher incarceration in Panama than on the U.S. side of the border. Panamanian judges sent law-breakers to the notorious Carcel Modelo, where families had to bring food for prisoners who suffered under a severe regime. Serious felons labored on the infamous Coiba Island penal colony, a Panamanian Devil's Island in the Pacific. During the postwar era, in comparison, the U.S. Penitentiary at Gamboa provided a clean, safe environment, adequate food, and vocational training. White Zonians obeyed the law, and their well-trained police force usually demonstrated restraint during arrests. In contrast, Panamanian criminals often faced vigilante justice from their fellow citizens. Brutal beatings, pickpocketing, sexual coercion, and a number of abuses marked the behavior of the Panamanian police that only worsened under the military regime (1968–89).[12]

Novice thieves quickly learned that the safer, more lucrative pickings lay in the Canal Zone rather than the borderland streets of Colón or Panama City. The Zonian consumer lifestyle, wedded to the cornucopia of military goods, provided a veritable shopping mall of bicycles, toys, clothing, food, tools, and building materials for enterprising robbers. By day the security apparatus and racial order of the Zone appeared firm, but, as the popular West Indian adage went, "At night, all cats are gray."

The Origins of the U.S. Justice System in Panama

The official Canal Zone Police history states that "the Isthmus of Panama was a land of lawlessness and disease when the United States and . . . Panama entered into the Hay–Bunau-Varilla Treaty of 1903," a fairly breathtaking statement of U.S. chauvinism. While Dr. Gorgas and his staff battled the second half of this predicament, yellow fever, the Canal Zone justice system presumably moved against the first, crime and disorder. The close juxtaposition of these twin threats in Zone publications remains telling since many Americans equated crime with Panamanian *disease* and *contamination* as if they were intrinsic or natural to Panama and its citizens. An article published in 1951 in the *Panama American* was actually entitled "Diogenes Can Stop Looking: The CZ Police Have Found an Honest Man in Panama." Fifty years after the establishment of the enclave, a Zonian praised a Canal Police drive against street crime in New Cristobal for having "driven the rats back into their holes."[13]

On February 29, 1904, shortly after the Panamanian legislature ratified the Hay–Bunau-Varilla Treaty, President Roosevelt appointed the first Isthmian Canal Commission to organize a U.S. government in the borderland. Roosevelt proclaimed, "The laws of the land with which the inhabitants are familiar and which were in force on February 26, 1904 will continue in force in the Canal Zone and other places on the Isthmus over which the United States has jurisdiction, *but there are certain principles of government which have been made the basis of our existence as a nation which we deem essential to the rule of law and the maintenance of order and which shall have force in said zone.*"[14] Acting on these instructions, in 1904 U.S. officials drew up a criminal code based largely on the code used by the state of California. It incorporated Spanish civil law in existing Panamanian statutes, and not simply U.S. jurisprudence (i.e., English common law and the Bill of Rights). Gradually the principles and procedures of U.S. law in revised code books came to prevail on the Zone side of the border. In 1904 the Canal Commission also established five municipal courts, three circuit courts, and a supreme court for the Zone.[15]

In a final judicial reorganization in 1914, the Zone reduced its four district courts to one with two divisions, Balboa and Cristobal, and abolished the Canal Zone supreme court. Appeals to the district court's decisions henceforth went to the Fifth Federal Circuit in New Orleans. Significantly the few Canal Zone cases sent to the U.S. Supreme Court were dismissed "for lack of jurisdiction." Thus the Canal Zone justice system, while partially connected to the U.S. continental system, remained separate and unique in many regards until its demise in 1982. (Aspects of the U.S. police and court continued for two and a half years after the Zone officially ended.)[16]

On June 2, 1904, the United States established the Canal Zone Police Force to maintain order among the "unruly natives and foreigners" of the new borderland. The official police history failed to recognize that North Americans were *foreigners* on the isthmus and often quite unruly themselves. The new Panamanian frontier teemed with tens of thousands of "overseas workers, ne'er-do-wells, prostitutes, and assorted criminals." But it was the U.S. Canal project, unmentioned in such accounts, that drew and even imported such groups to the borderland.[17]

Initially commissioners envisioned a West Indian constabulary with U.S. white officers in the Zone, but problems arose with this scheme when U.S. and European whites refused to submit to black policemen's authority. Thereafter the force recruited two types of officers, "first-class policemen" who were white U.S. citizens and an auxiliary group called "regular policemen" who were black and from the West Indies. Regular policemen monitored silver workers since "in dealing with these people, Americans were apt to be too aggressive and overbearing."[18] Thus from the first day, U.S. authorities designed a police apparatus that reinforced the white supremacist order of the enclave.[19]

In 1914, with the Canal completed, the police closed its temporary prisons at Ancon, Cristobal, and Culebra and established a single Zone Penitentiary at Gamboa. Over 90 percent of those initially arrested were imported workers or "foreign adventurers." Only a small percentage of Americans committed serious crimes on the Zone, a phenomenon that continued into the post–World War II era, facilitated by full U.S. employment, good wages, and a policy of shipping troublemakers back to the States.[20]

Extraterritoriality in the Borderland

The establishment of a U.S. justice system with courts, laws, police, and a prison on foreign soil immediately raised the issue of extraterritoriality, a controversial subject among both colonizers and colonized in the early twentieth century. An explicit U.S. right to maintain a separate justice system in Panama does not exist in the 1903 treaty. Washington based its establishment on a broad interpretation of Articles II and III: U.S. citizens who committed crimes in the Canal Zone, as well as any Panamanian or foreign national who did so, were subject to the U.S. court there, but if an American committed a crime in Panama, he or she came under the jurisdiction of Panamanian, not U.S. justice. This procedure proved less hegemonic than the near total immunity from Chinese law that many Americans enjoyed for decades in China.[21]

In practice, however, during the protectorate era in Panama (1903–39), Panamanian police often displayed a reluctance to arrest U.S. civilians for minor offenses, such was the power of the United States on the isthmus. As Panama's president Belisario Porras lamented in 1912, "I meet with difficulties even in arming my police properly and they are frequently victims of mysterious outrages. Persons from the Canal Zone assault my police agents and return with impunity to North American territory after committing breaches of the law and municipal ordinances."[22] Indeed American authorities removed the right of Panamanian police to carry high-powered rifles in 1916 following a number of binational brawls in the Coco Grove red-light district that cost the lives of several U.S. servicemen. This aura of U.S. omnipotence began to erode by the 1930s, however, with the creation of Panamanian national institutions that arose from the Acción Comunal movement. Simultaneously the Panameñismo program of the 1930s–40s assumed an increasingly pro-Panamanian, antiyanqui stance.[23]

In May 1943 two Americans, Robert Scales and Carl Johnson, committed the most egregious crime in the borderland's history when they beat to death two Panamanian night watchmen while robbing the Lux Theater. The local court sentenced them to the maximum penalty for such an offense under Panamanian law, twenty years imprisonment.[24] Had they committed their crimes in the Canal Zone, Scales and Johnson might have received the death penalty or life imprisonment due to the harsher Canal Code. The Zone hanged its murderers, though those executed were typically West Indians. On November 20, 1908, Canal Zone authorities executed their first murderer, Hubert Stout, a black Barbadian, for first-degree murder.[25] In 1920 the Zone hanged three West Indians for murdering two West Indian security guards during the robbery of an explosives shed in 1916. These were the last executions that U.S. officials carried out in the Zone.[26]

Conflicting Law Codes on a Conflicted Border

Capital punishment demonstrated but one example of the tougher stance North Americans applied, at least in the area of proscribed penalties, within their jurisdiction. Such divisions highlighted the sense of the Zone-Panama frontier as a borderland where one could confront a different legal world simply by stepping across an arbitrary line. Just as in movie westerns where desperados splashed across the Rio Grande to escape either U.S. or Mexican jurisdiction, Panamanian criminals sprinted, crawled, or raced in getaway cars across the border to flee one form of justice in favor of a perceived advantageous form. Depending on the circumstances, these fugitives could either head out of the Zone and into Panama or out of Panama and into the Zone.[27]

Codified penalties varied significantly. Those convicted of second-degree murder in the Zone could receive sentences of ten years to life, compared to four to twelve years in Panama. Rape in the Canal Zone drew from four to fifty years imprisonment; in Panama the sentence ranged from three to six years, and in the case of a child victim, four to eight years. Panamanian judges sentenced burglars to between six and twenty months; Canal Zone judges sentenced first-degree burglars for up to fifteen years and second-degree burglars for up to five years, reflecting the enclave's concern for the protection of U.S. property and citizenry.[28]

But the differences in maximum sentences could be deceiving. The Canal Zone Code gave U.S. judges more latitude than Panamanian judges in lowering sentences. Because of the space limitations of around two hundred inmates at Gamboa and another two hundred in U.S. jails, Zone judges typically meted out probated sentences for first-time misdemeanors and even nonviolent felonies. Those convicted simply walked out of court under probation. U.S. judges also exercised the option to "deport" Panamanians convicted of more than one offense from the Canal Zone to Panama for periods of three to five years rather than incarcerate them. Panamanian officials protested such deportations as illegal.[29]

In cases of petty theft and burglary (by far the most common crimes), U.S. judges generally showed leniency toward first offenders, although these same judges could be quite strict with repeat criminals. A parole and good behavior program at Gamboa Prison reduced U.S. sentences from one-half to one-third.[30] In Panama, however, convicts generally served their full sentences. Thus the sharp differences in code book punishments between the two systems often lessened in actual practice, depending on the U.S. judge's stance. In 1957 Judge Guthrie F. Crowe commented on this rough equivalency in blunt ethnic terms while sentencing a burglar: "Now, we here in the Canal Zone do not give the severe penalties that they do in the other courts under the American Flag because we live alongside the Republic of Panama where penalties are less because of the thinking of the Latin people."[31]

More substantive differences between the two societies emerged in the definitions of what constituted crime. The Canal Zone Code considered adultery, begging, gambling, selling lottery tickets, cockfighting, prize fighting, hunting without a license, prostitution, obscene exhibitions, making and selling bottled alcohol, operating bawdy houses, vagrancy, and cruelty to animals as criminal activities. Panama had no laws against such behavior. In part this reflected a Latin Catholic acceptance of sin, a more tolerant understanding of human frailty in social relations. In contrast, the Protestant approach to law in the Zone strove toward the perfectibility of man and his society through the inclusion of strict moral codes within the law. Since the Zone constituted a government reservation, any allowance of unethical behavior within its territory might signal a U.S. sanction of "immorality."[32]

To some degree the Zone achieved its goal of a crime-free white citizenry by banishing to the States any North American convicted of a serious crime. The Zone held the threat of dismissal and deportation over the heads of juvenile delinquents' parents as well. "If a kid kept screwing up down here, they'd send him back to the States. And sometimes they'd send his parents back too," a former Zone teacher recalled.[33]

The threat of termination from the Canal Company deterred most West Indian workers from committing serious crimes. Cashiered laborers would lose their privileges and face eviction to Panama, where unemployment approached 20 percent and laborers earned one-third of what silver wages paid. In an illustrative case in 1949, a West Indian, Winston Piggot, faced just such a Zone "excommunication" when the court convicted him of stealing a case of chickens from the Cold Storage Plant in Cristobal. Confronting certain termination and beggary, Piggot pleaded for mercy. But Judge Joseph J. Hancock told him, "Piggot, it is very unfortunate that you have destroyed a record that you have been able to build up—twenty-five years at one concern. . . . Now it means this . . . that you are placed on a black list and that from that time on you will never get any more work here; and it strikes me that people working and depending on their labor as a basis of living should think twice before they undertake to do something wrong. . . . Of course, we cannot let this go unpunished."[34] Hancock sentenced Piggot to six months at Gamboa. The Zone immediately fired him, took away his family's commissary privileges, evicted them from their Zone quarters, and stripped Piggot of his pension. Piggot swore he stole the chickens to feed his family. That may have been true, but pilferage abounded at the Cold Storage Plant and fed into a network of contraband that flowed into Panama every day. Piggot may well have been an honest man who yielded once to temptation, or he may have been a successful thief who finally got caught. In either case, his crime embodied the small, everyday malfeasance against the white man in the Zone and the price of such defiance.

Despite the U.S. effort to separate the problem of crime in the Zone from U.S.-Panamanian relations, the issue of extraterritoriality persisted. Washington repeatedly rejected Panamanian overtures from the 1950s to the 1970s to replace the U.S. justice system with binational, jointly administered courts since it viewed any diminution of its de facto "sovereignty" as a threat to U.S. supremacy. Few Zonians appeared to comprehend the bewilderment and injustice that Panamanians faced under such a system. But locals did: "'It's not right,' exclaimed a local newspaper editor, as he drove along the Fourth of July. 'One minute I am in Panama. The next I can be picked up by a foreign policeman, tried in a foreign court, and sent to a foreign jail—all in my own country!'"[35]

"Our Greatest Trouble Here Is Burglary"

As early as 1911, when a young U.S. recruit, Harry Franck, enlisted in the Canal Zone Police, the inspector of the force informed him, "Our greatest trouble here is burglary." Franck later referred to "Culebra with its prison where burglarizing negroes go." Demographics and unemployment after World War II heightened the practice of Panamanian burglary in the Zone. Four options existed for the local burgeoning poor of this era: get a manual job in Panama that paid very low wages; obtain a Zone job (almost impossible to finagle for a Latin Panamanian and difficult even for a West Indian after the reorganization cutbacks in 1951); work indirectly for the Zone in the borderland service economy; or steal from the enclave. Experience of past discrimination in the Zone, dislike of Americans, and the failure to garner employment in the first three options pushed many Panamanians into the fourth. Official unemployment rates of between 15 and 25 percent in the terminal cities throughout the postwar era also drove many desperate borderlanders toward this decision. The heightened postwar nationalism even supplied some political cover for malfeasance against the U.S. enclave.[36]

To rob from the gringo could be construed, in part, as a patriotic act by at least some embittered Panamanians, although in court cases surveyed only 8 percent of Panamanian defendants in the 1950s–1970s who spoke up in court made overt political statements regarding their crimes. A majority of defendants said nothing at trial, relying upon their court-appointed lawyers. Yet the *perception* of such crime as being justified gained greater credence among indigent Panamanian borderlanders as the anticolonial protests against the Zone mounted.[37]

The nexus of Panamanian poverty and Zone crime emerged more power-fully in the court testimony of Panamanian defendants than in direct state-ments of political resistance. "You can appreciate how conditions are in Panama," one burglary defendant in the late 1950s told Judge Crowe. "It's true that I have a record but after I left prison I was working. I worked for three different places for short hitches. . . . Each time the job was terminated because the work was finished. . . . But I have proof I have been working. You can see by the conditions of my hands."[38] Two years later Roberto Bayl-iss, a burglar, told Crowe with more defiance, "My father just died and I have to help my mother. How do you expect I am going to make a living?"[39] In 1959 a Panamanian trespasser made a similar appeal: "I have been out of work for years. Nobody gave me anything to eat. Nobody clothed me. I was barefoot and in tatters. That's why I had to do what I did."[40] In an analogous case in 1961, Crowe listened but showed little sympathy: "Yes, I will be merci-ful and compassionate, but I also want to protect our community from people like you who do wrong things, who steal the property of others. . . . You can say, 'I am poor; I do not have work,' things like that—but we can't and don't accept that as an excuse because this is a world in which people can make a living if they try."[41]

The percentage of Panamanians living in poverty on the day Judge Crowe spoke was officially 46 percent. In the Canal Zone, where Judge Crowe worked, the unemployment rate was 0 percent: everyone had a well-paid gov-ernment job. For this reason the poverty rate in the enclave was also 0 per-cent, making the Zone one of the few places on earth with such remarkable quality-of-life statistics. In contrast, a pre-sentence report in 1964 described the life of a Panamanian petty thief: "The defendant has been sleeping on park benches and in alleyways in Colon for the past five months. He has no relatives or friends in Colon to help him. He claims he was desperately hun-gry and so he decided to go into the Zone to look for something to steal."[42] The burglar in question was a black Panamanian with a fifth-grade educa-tion. In 1964 the unemployment rate in predominantly black Colón was 28 percent.[43]

Even U.S. officials recognized some connection between political resis-tance and crime in the Zone. In August 1960, several months after the flag riots of 1959, Crowe told an unrepentant burglar, Carlos Antonio Franklin Stewart, "A lot of Panamanian people apparently have the idea that this is Panamanian territory and Panama has sovereignty and the laws of the United States cannot be enforced here. Well, they are going to find out that they are gravely mistaken. . . . If you or any of your companions have such an idea, you should get it out of your minds right now."[44] In a case in 1959, Crowe spelled out even more clearly to Virgilio Rodríquez how the crime of burglary represented an attack upon the United States: "You have been convicted by your own admission of the crime of entering a room wherein a person was sleeping at night and robbing that person . . . one of the most dangerous type of crimes to the person or property of the citizens of the Canal Zone or anyone under the United States Flag."[45] Yet Crowe failed to mention one unusual aspect of burglary in the Zone that always gave it a political dimension when committed by a Panamanian: since all buildings and residences within the Zone and even many personal items, such as furniture, appliances, automobiles, and tools, were government property, stealing from the Zone meant stealing from the U.S. government. This did not hold true in the cases of all personal items, such as televisions, radios, jewelry, and clothing, but the specific act of breaking into a U.S. installation or dwelling in the Zone, since they were all U.S.-owned, constituted a crime against Washington, whatever the motive.

In a similar vein, the U.S. government employed every worker in the Canal Zone, with the exception of a few private contractors and shipping agents. So whenever a Panamanian assaulted, robbed, or defrauded an individual, he or she committed a crime against an employee of the U.S. government, not merely a private citizen. These unique conditions added a political component to much of the crime committed on the Zone side of the border, particularly in the context of Panama's strong nationalist opposition to the enclave from the 1950s onward.

Rising Postwar Crime in the Borderland

Arrests in the Canal Zone more than doubled between 1939 and 1946, reflecting in part the wartime bonanza and population increases in the terminal cities. U.S. military personnel committed a considerable percentage of offenses. The 1942 wartime high of 10,143 arrests for 11,293 charges in the Zone fell only slightly to 8,722 arrests for 9,387 charges in 1946, when the wartime boom had ended and the U.S. military garrison declined to prewar norms. Of these charges in the Zone in 1942, 5,291 were of Panamanian residents, 4,956 were of Zone residents, and 1,046 were of transients, mostly transiting U.S. troops. Arrests, of course, are not an entirely accurate gauge of crimes and convictions; this is especially true given the Canal Zone Police's frequent bias against Panamanian "trespassers." Although the conviction rate in the Zone remained as high as 81 percent in one year (Zone statistics do not provide the number of convictions every year, as they do arrests), detentions are always higher in number than convictions. The fact that Zone residents were 49 percent of those arrested also reflects the U.S. garrison's size at the height of the war, as well as the thousands of imported Third Locks workers living in the borderland. By 1946, with the lowering of U.S. military strength and the end of wartime construction, Zone residents composed only 30 percent of detainees.[46]

The term *Zone resident* must also be analyzed carefully. By far, U.S. military personnel and the Canal's West Indian and Panamanian employees encompassed the highest percentage of Zone residents detained for offenses, some 96 percent; U.S. civilian employees made up less than 4 percent. These straightforward statistics can also be misleading. Of the 8,722 arrests in 1946, 4,820 or 55 percent were for traffic violations. This occurred in an era when the Zone contained few private cars, albeit many military vehicles. In subsequent years, when private automobile ownership exploded on both sides of the border, traffic offenses constituted 85 percent of all Zone arrests. Of the nontraffic charges, most were petty crimes and misdemeanors, so-called Class II offenses; among the most prevalent were petty larceny, battery, loitering for prostitution, vagrancy (being in the Zone without a reason), trespassing, public intoxication, disturbing the peace, and being a fugitive from justice (fleeing from Panama into the Zone to escape arrest). Class I offenses, however, comprised murder, manslaughter, robbery, fraud, aggravated assault, burglary, and grand larceny.[47]

The largest crime increases (measured by the admittedly flawed rubric of arrests and conviction statistics) occurred during the fiercest nationalist protests against the Zone: the late 1940s, early 1960s, and the mid- to late 1960s. These were also periods of the greatest population stresses in the terminal cities. In the 1960s Panama experienced a demographic surge similar to that in other developing nations when its youth population increased markedly. A higher percentage of young people resulted in higher overall crime rates, since most criminal activity occurs among teenage and young males. Periods of nationalist protest and a skewed youth population also corresponded with high unemployment and economic crisis. In the late 1940s, like most of the world, Panama experienced a postwar recession, although more pronounced due to its strong dependence on U.S. military and canal spending. In the early 1960s Panama's economy, like many in Latin America, suffered from insufficient investment and growth to satisfy an emergent yet frustrated middle class. This stagnation spurred, in part, President John F. Kennedy's decision to launch the Alliance for Progress.[48]

The reorganization of the Zone in 1951 further cut the enclave's workforce, providing less stimulation to the overall Panamanian economy. The silver or local-rate workforce fell from 23,347 in 1945 to 10,444 twenty years later. In the mid-1940s economic benefits from the Zone was 40 percent of Panama's GDP; by the mid-1960s this figure had dropped to 25 percent. In the late 1960s Panamanian economic growth did improve, but rising population and falling export prices robbed Panama of its long-hoped-for postwar prosperity. Unequal distribution of national wealth also exacerbated social tensions. The top 5 percent of Panama's population controlled some 60 percent of the nation's wealth.[49]

Panamanian Theft in the Zone Borderland

During the postwar era many of Chorrillo's and Colón's poor simply walked into the Zone to steal things, mostly small items that some thieves felt they needed to survive. Clothesline theft especially abounded. Zonian backyards billowed with shirts, dresses, and pants, as well as towels, bed sheets, bathing suits, and sneakers. The average resident of Colón, San Miguel, and Chorrillo owned a few articles of clothing and some decrepit sandals. If left unattended for too long, Zone laundry inevitably disappeared. Timid thieves removed a few articles, but professionals would clean out entire clotheslines and jam the apparel into sacks to be hidden in underbrush and retrieved later that night.[50] "Sometimes, it was incredible," one Zonian remembered. "Our maid came out of the backyard for two or three minutes to drink a cup of coffee, [and] when she stepped back out, all our clothes were gone!"[51]

Such theft often led to comical scenes. Panamanians robbed Zonians of their clothes while they skinny-dipped, forcing Americans to walk naked to the U.S. authorities to report the crime. In 1956 three U.S. embassy employees, two young men and one young woman, were robbed of their clothing and valuables while swimming nude. U.S. soldier Danny Cooper remembered drinking in a bar on J Street in Panama City one Saturday night in the mid-1970s; after downing several rums, he looked across the smoky bar and saw a Panamanian youth "wearing [his] favorite shirt." Cooper, whose family had recently suffered a clothesline theft, lit after the youth, chasing him from the bar. After pursuing him for two blocks, Cooper burst into laughter, caught his breath, and walked back to the bar for another rum. "What the hell, I thought, let the kid have the shirt." Not so forgiving, Zone authorities frequently incarcerated large-scale clothing thieves.[52]

Panamanian thieves even stole U.S. military uniforms from clotheslines and Canal Police caps from unattended squad cars. In the 1960s–1970s several Panamanian thieves and burglars penetrated the Zone dressed in U.S. military uniforms, facilitating their entry and free movement. Since so many Puerto Ricans served in the Zone's military units, racial differences escaped notice. Zone Police caps, on the other hand, proved wonderful "souvenirs" for Panamanian youths to display to one another. Few thrills could match the excitement of robbing the hated policía zonieta.[53]

The Things They Took

Petty larceny in the Zone extended beyond clothing to just about anything Americans owned. Panamanians stole tools, lawn mowers, cars, bicycles, tricycles, basketballs, basketball hoops, bats, gloves, bases (not just during games but at night, when no one was playing), coolers, fishing rods, garden hoses, plants, screens, purses, wallets, grills, lawn furniture, hammocks, pillows, mattresses, watches, radios, liquor, and more.[54] A Panamanian who lived in Chorrillo observed, "They [the Zonians] just had so much, and they would leave it lying around like they didn't even care about it. And we had so little. So of course people took things. Can you blame them?"[55] Struggling Panamanians anywhere near a cafeteria or commissary in the Zone, including several employees, walked off with chickens, hams, pork chops, steaks, hotdogs, ketchup, cooking oil, dishwashing powder, and a variety of canned goods. Female Panamanian and West Indian shoplifters played a prominent role in these "commissary capers."[56]

But petty stealing from the powerful provoked retaliation. A Panamanian remembered the theft in 1960 of a bicycle belonging to a U.S. general's daughter: "Military police and CID agents, there must have been about fifteen of them, poured across Fourth of July Avenue into Panama and entered this apartment building. They kicked in doors and threatened people and broke things, and finally they found the bicycle. They carried it back into the Zone with these two kids in handcuffs. I remember how frightened we all were. It was like an invasion. The Americans thought they could do anything—and they could! The guardia just stood there." Critics of U.S. policy in Panama condemned the 1989 U.S. invasion with reason, but scores of mini-invasions like this one occurred along the Zone-Panama border.[57]

Panamanians also absconded with "unusual items." In 1976 one group of creative thieves stole an entire military bridge, dismantling it and carrying it back to Panama in pieces over the course of two nights. Panamanian trappers captured tropical birds from the Zone's rain forest. Panamanians in cayucos paddled into the Pacific, the Caribbean, and Lake Gatun to "borrow" Zonian yachts. In 1955 Panamanian youths stole three guinea pigs diseased with tuberculosis from the Zone's Board of Health laboratory, touching off a health panic. Another group removed dozens of toilets from abandoned jungle latrines. Toilet seat theft was popular in the Zone as well; Panamanian thieves entered bathrooms in Zone buildings with a screwdriver, unscrewed the seat, wrapped their jacket around it, and carried it home. Occasionally an absent-minded Zonian entered the bathroom afterward and "fell into the drink."[58] Panamanians also stole trees that they cut down as lumber or Christmas trees as the U.S. custom grew popular even on the Panamanian side of the border during the postwar era.[59]

Zone crime reached other comic or tragic heights (depending on one's perspective), such as when Zone Police arrested Panamanian dogs for trespassing into the Zone. Veterinary officials gave the mongrels their rabies shots and held them for thirty days' observation before the dogs were "extradited to Panama for good behavior." If officials determined a Panamanian dog had "no substantial value, four days after its incarceration, it would be destroyed." Likewise headlines read "RP Youth Fined $10 for Coconut Theft" and "Young Panamanian Mango Thief Treed in the Zone." On one occasion Zone Police even arrested a Panamanian parrot "for loitering." The police "informed him of his right to remain silent" before the case was adjudicated. Some of these articles had a deliberate human interest slant; others were quite serious. All of them expressed the Zone's obsession with controlling social behavior as well as the pervasive fear of Panamanian infiltration from across the border.[60]

Crafty Panamanians invented another form of resistance against the Zone, "bill splitting," by using the common currency of the two nations. While more sophisticated bunko artists counterfeited U.S. bills, ordinary folk simply cut a $5 bill and a $1 bill into halves. They then taped the halves together, creating two hybrid bills that were half $5 and half $1. Folded so that the $5 portion was always face up, the bills usually passed as legitimate $5s, yielding $10 worth of goods for $6. After the 1964 riots Panamanian students employed a new currency sabotage by stamping the back of all U.S. bills they got their hands on with seals that read "Panama is Sovereign in the Canal Zone!" When these "desecrated" bills circulated along the borderland,

North Americans complained and the U.S. ambassador denounced the students' actions as "illegal and inflammatory."[61]

U.S. Collusion in Zone Robbery

In the 1950s Panamanians officially stole between $43,000 and $112,000 worth of Zone items each year. By the end of the 1970s the average yearly losses reached some $200,000. And these numbers included only reported theft; significant amounts of larceny occurred outside the accounting system, such as when Zonians sold or donated redundant or excess tools and materials to Panamanians. For this reason the true financial effects of crime in the Zone are difficult to gauge.[62]

Panamanian theft was not the only kind that occurred in the Zone. The U.S. court adjudicated numerous cases of pilferage, embezzlement, fraud, and larceny committed by both U.S. soldiers and civilians. Working in conjunction with Panamanians, GIs established networks of stolen goods and contraband. Soldiers driving trucks out of the Zone would drop off "liberated" construction materials, tires, auto parts, tool sets, even entire vehicles to the families of their Panamanian girlfriends, wives, or favorite prostitutes. Panamanians erected many of the hovels that bordered the Zone from just such "surplus" U.S. materials.[63] The fact that so many "lost" items were government property that Zonians and soldiers could easily reorder from Uncle Sam facilitated tolerance for larceny. Thus a system developed in which the U.S. government effectively subsidized theft in the borderland.[64]

U.S. soldiers supplemented their incomes by selling weapons, ammunition, beer, cigarettes, and siphoned gasoline to Panamanians. Accommodation constituted the flip side of resistance in these alliances of illegal exchange. In return for PX scotch, nylons, dresses, stereos, records, and television sets, Panamanians traded marijuana, cocaine, Carta Vieja rum, and sexual favors to eager GIs. Civilian Zonians and military officers practiced such shenanigans as well in a more subtle manner, often building and furnishing their weekend houses in the interior with materials that disappeared from military storage yards or from the Section I warehouse for surplus goods. "You might as well say they stole whole houses!" one Zonian detective recalled, though this process occurred over a series of months or even years, and much of it (surplus materials removed from Section I where U.S. residents could take discarded supplies) was legal.[65]

More brazenly, entire containers of appliances, food, and clothing vanished from Zone piers. Thieves drove trucks from warehouses loaded with cement, cinderblocks, and cigarettes to sell in the interior. Panamanians hawked U.S.-stamped, duty-free meat from their pickups on borderland street corners, shouting, "Comisariato! Comisariato!" as a boast of its quality. One gang liberated a railroad crane from the Panama Railroad in the mid-1960s; U.S. detectives never recovered it, and rumors abounded that it ended up in Costa Rica, working for a mining company.[66]

Although only a small minority of Zonians and GIs participated in such crimes that were limited in number, larceny on this scale required significant cooperation, whether from individual military or civilian managers, foremen, police, or security guards. As one American recalled, "The level of graft and theft from the Zone was higher than most people realize because a lot of it that involved Zonians [i.e., whites] was never prosecuted. The whole setup was an 'old boys club.'"[67] "Livin' la vida Zona" could be sweet indeed for some Zonians and their Panamanian friends. This collaboration became so intimate at times it was difficult to tell whether a particular theft was a U.S. or a Panamanian enterprise. Within this expanse of crime, resistance, and accommodation, the colonizer and the colonized melded into one, the great *fear* of the originators of the system—Theodore Roosevelt, George Washington Goethals, and Charles Edward Magoon—who desired clearly delineated boundaries between "upstanding" U.S. citizens and their view of the republic's mixed-race, Catholic degeneracy.

Servant Theft in the Borderland

Panamanian servant theft also remained a constant worry in the Zone. This fear of thieving servants permeated all colonial societies; indeed middle- and upper-class Panamanians referred to untrustworthy domestics as *las ratas de la casa* or "house rats."[68] West Indians and Panamanian servants in the Zone constituted a potential fifth column in this respect, as did the servants of color in colonial Kenya, Algeria, and India. Most Zonians employed West Indian women as cooks, laundresses, or maids; some Zonians hired them through references, others right off the street in Colón where local women gathered near the border each morning in search of work. A minority of Zonian women preferred indigenous girls from the countryside, so-called cholitas, whom Zonians judged uncorrupted by urban life.[69]

Zonian wives considered West Indian maids and cooks as more loyal and trustworthy than Panamanian women. "Most of them were thieves," Peggy Roberts, a Zone wife throughout the 1960s and 1970s, recalled of her negative experiences with them. Roberts finally found a Panamanian girl from the interior whom she trained properly and praised for her honesty and work ethic.[70] Still, petty theft, the taking of an occasional item of clothing or left-over food, remained a common practice even among cholitas and other-wise faithful West Indian maids.[71] Many U.S. women chose to overlook such pilferage; others discouraged theft by insisting their maids take home left-over food and by donating old clothing, appliances, and furniture to their maids' families. Such customs were one of the great benefits of working for Americans. Panamanian employers proved less generous and frequently decried Americans for spoiling servants: overpaying them, giving them too much food, and imbuing them with insolence. Panamanian domestics, be they West Indians or Latin Panamanians, often expressed a preference for American employers over well-to-do Panamanians, who frequently forced them to wear uniforms and to live in their homes in dingy maid's rooms on twenty-four-hour call for late-night parties. In contrast, many Zonian fami-lies formed strong bonds with their maids; some helped with their children's education, and the purchase of Christmas hams and gifts for a maid's family became customary. But maids in the Zone also suffered abuse and conde-scending attitudes from numerous white U.S. employers both on military bases and in civilian communities.[72]

Despite U.S. efforts to discourage theft, the dishonest maid remained the bugbear of the Zone. English-language newspapers devoted consider-able space to exposés of these women. An article published in 1952 entitled "Housewife, Cop Find Stolen Garments at Jungle Hideout" was typical. Al-though this incident involved the theft of a U.S. household in Panama, and not in the Zone, its discourse fits many Zone larceny cases:

An American housewife living in Panama City feels that her property is more secure today after the cooperation she received from the [Panama-nian] Secret Police. . . . A quick trip to the Police . . . revealed that the missing servant had an older sister who was promptly questioned. The housewife, older sister, and policemen drove out to the suburb of Rio Abajo. . . . Finally the older sister pointed out the shack where the family lived. When the door was pushed open the missing maid peeked out from under the bed and the American housewife's finery was openly displayed on a rack. Far from being repentant the haughty domestic is in jail today until she can remember where she put the remainder of the clothes. And meanwhile, the new maid who applied for the job was given a front row seat at the proceedings by her mistress. The American housewife some-how feels the new employee won't steal.[73]

The article is so didactic that it reads like an eighteenth-century poaching case in Ireland. The arresting and prosecuting officials in this incident were all Panamanians, confirming the alliance of the Panamanian elite in enforcing the borderland's imperial order. This incident is very much a product of the early 1950s. Such consensus in support of the system eroded markedly after the anti-American riots in 1964.

Theft and the Culture of Panamanian Poverty

The majority of postwar Panamanian theft in the Zone was not so well organized or planned. Poor Panamanians, many of them illiterate, hungry, or even suffering from mental illnesses, simply wandered into the Zone and took small things, such as marbles, candles, and facecloths. This kind of random crime particularly annoyed U.S. officials, who seemed to prefer premeditated to irrational malfeasance. In the early 1960s Judge Crowe expressed his consternation at the petty theft of one Panamanian defendant. "What does he actually steal?" Crowe asked. "Junk. Just junk," the U.S. prosecutor replied. "All petty senseless larcenies," the judge fumed.[74] Getting by day to day, one meal at a time, as many indigent Panamanians did, appeared incomprehensible to middle-class Zonians, with their secure, goal-oriented view of life. Hungry Panamanians sometimes committed small crimes, for instance, in the hope of getting caught and sent to Gamboa Penitentiary for regular food and shelter. For these reasons, much borderland crime represented a cultural conundrum that Americans found difficult to grasp.[75]

The boundaries between work and crime remained fuzzy for semi-employed Panamanians. After pleading guilty to theft in 1961, a defendant tried to explain his actions. Judge Crowe responded, "What bearing does this have on the case? You admitted you stole the roofing and declared yourself guilty." "But a man appeared there and he told me to get two sheets which was required for the chicken coop," the defendant responded. "Who is this man that you are referring to?" "I don't know," the defendant admitted. "He is a watchman in the Canal Zone, and he had a black overcoat. . . . Maybe I did steal those things but when I did, I did not think it was stealing."[76]

Falsely denying guilt in court is a universal proclivity, but for impoverished Panamanians eking out a living at the margins of borderland society, evasion and fabrication encompassed a survival mode ingrained since youth. Sometimes Panamanians and West Indians were lying when they claimed that mysterious white men ordered them to steal, but sometimes they spoke the truth. Smuggling rings at Zone piers and warehouses frequently involved

Panamanian theft at the behest of Zone foremen who craved discounts lower than duty-free commissary prices.[77]

An Epidemic of Cable Theft in the Borderland

Panamanians also routinely cut and removed communication and power cable from the Zone. Miles of copper and aluminum wire for power, radar, telephone, and military communications crisscrossed the enclave. Electrical feeder lines from the Madden and Gatun Dams flowed through the Zone, providing power for the enclave and for much of nearby Panama. The U.S. military and the Canal Company frequently replaced this valuable cable, leaving the old lines stored on giant wooden spools near unguarded work sheds. Since Uncle Sam, or Tio Azucar (Uncle Sugar), as he was called in Panama, provided an endless supply of cable, authorities were lax in guarding it.[78]

At night Panamanians carrying axes and cable-cutters crossed the border to steal this wire; some treated it almost as a job, much like the legitimate laborers and domestics who crossed the Zone border every day to work. Their wives and girlfriends would even pack them lunches. Old disconnected cable proved the easiest to steal; cutting live cable was more dangerous. Poachers would wrap pieces of rubber around their axe handles to avoid shocks and conduction. Nonetheless occasionally cable thieves electrocuted themselves and died. But because scrap dealers in Panama paid good money for copper many unemployed Panamanians tried their luck in "the cable game." After liberating a large and unwieldy length of wire, thieves cut it up into two-foot sections and put it in sacks to carry back to scrap dealers. They often worked in pairs or teams.[79]

This profligate theft created endless headaches for the U.S. military. Officers would pick up secure phones to contact units, only to discover the line had gone dead. Soldiers had trouble calling their Panamanian girlfriends. During the visit of Queen Elizabeth II to the Canal Zone in 1953, two key lines went dead in the middle of security arrangements. Somewhere out in the jungle, a lone Panamanian wielding an axe amid a shower of sparks had disrupted the Zone world.[80]

The District Court of the Canal Zone tried to put a stop to this activity. In 1951 Judge Hancock told the prosecutor in the case of Joseph Nathaniel Rawlins, "The difficulty, Mr. Sheridan, is this. Here in the last sixty days we have had quite a few cable felonies committed right along. This cable stealing is costing the Army thousands of dollars. And just for the purpose of permitting these people to gain maybe two or three dollars. We are going to have to put a stop to it someway and somehow."[81] What Hancock failed to disclose was that three dollars, while a trifling sum to most U.S. workers, provided sufficient funds for a poor Panamanian family to survive a week on rice, beans, and plantains. For this reason cable theft continued. In a case prosecuted in 1955, Judge Crowe took a similar stand against cable theft when he confronted Tirill Haynes for stealing a length of "abandoned wire." Haynes dissembled brilliantly and tried to defend himself on the grounds that the cable was redundant. "Sir, I didn't think it had any use. I wasn't trying to hide what I was doing. . . . I was in plain view." Finally, Judge Crowe silenced Haynes: "Don't you know all the trouble we are having with these cable thefts? There has been a great deal of publicity in the papers. . . . The Canal Zone is literally threaded with cable that defense organizations have for communication. You people who touch them after all the publicity are putting your heads in the noose."[82]

Despite the efforts of the Zone police and courts, cable theft continued to plague the borderland until its demise in 1979 and continued with the Panama Canal Area (1979–99) and Panama Canal Authority (2000–). This "eating of cable" entered the popular vernacular and symbolized the way that struggling Panamanians chipped away at U.S. supremacy little by little, day after day.[83]

Frontier Judges in the Borderland

U.S. judges proved key mediators and enforcers of border justice. They also represented symbols of U.S. injustice to many locals. In 1957 a Panamanian burglar ransacked the official residence of Judge Crowe while he vacationed at his beach house in Santa Clara. At the trial of the suspect, Federico Zapata, Crowe recused himself. In a response that typified the rising Panamanian nationalism of the late 1950s, the accused challenged the U.S. court's authority: "I want to say the truth. You people have a great discrimination against Panamanians. I have been given one year for deportation in the past. But in Panama, they never deport any American who enters Panama. Panama is a free country like Ecuador or Chile." Judge Edward Tatelman rebuked such insolence from a career criminal who had deliberately attacked the U.S. court in the most personal way. Tatelman even stooped to ridiculing Zapata for his illegitimate birth: "Despite the fact that your father died in 1914 and you were born in 1925, you are not responsible for that! It is the judgment of the Court that you be confined to the Penitentiary at hard labor for three years. Take him away."[84]

Canal Zone judges maintained the habits of frontier magistrates long after the Zone matured from its wilder construction days. In 1951 Cristobal Division Judge Joseph J. Hancock shot and wounded twelve-year-old Peter Adams, the son of an army colonel, when the boy attempted to retrieve his wind-blown cap from the shrubbery near Hancock's quarters. The boy's parents declined to press the matter. This incident also touched on the U.S. paranoia over trespassers. In a case a year before he shot Adams, Hancock condemned the recent rash of burglaries: "It's come to the point where people's property has got to be given some protection down here!"[85] In 1954 Hancock took particular umbrage at purse-snatchings: "I am determined to put an end to this plague no matter what it takes!"[86]

Though nowhere near as volatile as Hancock, Judge Crowe, who served from 1955 to 1977, cut something of a legendary figure as well. During the 1964 riots Panamanian protesters targeted his home and hurled Molotov cocktails onto his porch. Displaying the coolness of Judge Roy Bean, Crowe strode out to confront the mob with a pistol and kicked the incendiaries off his porch. He threw pans of water on the areas that caught fire and then calmly faced down the crowd until Zone Police and U.S. military arrived. With his actions Crowe demonstrated "the mask of command" that borderland elites typically strove to maintain in the face of "unruly natives."[87]

Crowe also displayed a sense of humor in his courtroom and earned respect even from Panamanians for his no-nonsense manner. In the mid-1950s a West Indian burglar gang known as the Sparrows committed a series of break-ins in the Atlantic-side towns. Crowe queried one of the gang members from Paraiso, but the West Indian refused to divulge his accomplices, stating proudly, "Sparrows don't talk!" "Well, this crow does!" the judge shot back, banging his gavel to laughter in the courtroom. "Five years hard labor at Gamboa!" Crowe could also be sardonic at times. In 1957 he admonished Jose Felix Fuella, "Every year you and your wife have another baby while you are out stealing and you now come in here and ask me to be sympathetic towards you because you have a big family. That's like saying be sympathetic to a man who kills his father because he is an orphan."[88] In the Fuella case Crowe represented a patriarchal American father lecturing his Panamanian charges. Indeed the early hopes of the enclave's founders, and even some Panamanian elites, were that the Zone might serve as an instrument of uplift for the entire Panamanian nation, like the Puritans' "City upon a Hill." Much to officials' frustration, ordinary Panamanians never did adapt to such paternalist notions, as people being talked down to rarely accept their duly-appointed lessons.[89]

Gauging "Zone Justice"

Although U.S. District Court judges frequently lectured Panamanians, they rarely displayed egregious bias in their sentencing and procedures; defendants generally received the same sentences for the same crimes, be they U.S., Panamanian, or foreign litigants. But important exceptions obtained involving Panamanian and West Indian physical attacks on U.S. citizens. Such crimes made up a minority of offenses but remained crucial for what they revealed about a system that privileged U.S. citizens and their property above Panamanians. The most infamous of these exceptions, previously noted, was the sentencing of Lester Greaves for rape in 1946. In the same vein Panamanian-on-Panamanian or West Indian–on–West Indian violence garnered lighter sentencing. Judicial reactions to homicide prove difficult to measure as the borderland rarely experienced the Panamanian homicide of a Zonian. The only documented case occurred in 1967, when a Panamanian burglar, Vernal Watson, killed a Zonian, Frank Burling, during a break-in. In addition Zone docket books recorded very few Panamanian assaults or armed robberies of U.S. citizens.[90]

Another problem in comparing the sentencing of Panamanians and U.S. citizens is that practically all U.S. felons were first-time offenders since the Zone shipped North Americans convicted of serious crimes back to the States. A larger proportion of Panamanians were repeat offenders who received higher sentences for violating their probation. A letter to the *Panama American* complained, "Recently a 16-year-old privileged American with little or nothing wanting planned and committed a robbery; he got 10 days in jail. A few days later, a Panamanian boy of the same age was sent to jail for 60 days for unlawfully entering.—Please, Justice."[91] The U.S. editor of the English-language version of the paper replied, "The Panamanian boy in question is a chronic offender. . . . The American boy's crime is his first offence." Even some Zonians complained about judicial bias: "The court's sentencing is a disgrace to the American people. . . . A man steals $1200 from a church and walks away scot free. . . . If the embezzler had been a local-rater [West Indian] or a Panamanian he would have spent life in Gamboa. A U.S. citizen killed a woman with his car and received a $100 fine. Another pushes a woman from his car, leaves the scene, and receives a small fine—after the woman died!"[92] The church embezzler, Reverend Charles Delaney, had stolen $1,236.72 from his collections. As a man of the cloth with no previous record, Delaney received a five-year suspended sentence with the understanding that he would make restitution. Like most U.S. courts, the Zone's showed greater lenience toward white-collar crimes than toward the street crimes that poorer Panamanians were more likely to commit.[93]

The second case alluded to *was* a shocker. Driving while intoxicated, a Zonian, John L. Dougan, forty-eight, ran over and killed Mrs. Delta Forrest, sixty-one, on Bolivar Avenue in Cristobal. The court ruled that Mrs. Forrest "caused her own death through carelessness" by darting out into traffic and jaywalking and fined Dougan $100 for drunk driving.[94] The last case criticized by the letter writer dealt with the death of a Panamanian prostitute, who, according to the U.S. lock guard Richard Kresby, twenty-six, leaped from his car while he was driving her back to his apartment. The Panamanian woman, Muriel Scott, twenty-five, of Colón, split her skull on the pavement and died. Kresby left the scene without notifying authorities. The next day, after police discovered the body, Kresby turned himself in and was charged with manslaughter. After a short hearing, Kresby received a thirty-day suspended sentence and a $100 fine "for not reporting an accident." Many West Indians and Zonians remained convinced that at the very least Kresby had committed involuntary manslaughter. Gender, race, and criminal record probably all influenced this outcome, as the word and worth of a white male Zonian no doubt carried more weight in the borderland than that of a dead black Panamanian prostitute.[95]

The Zone court also showed surprising fairness on occasion, in contrast to its popular Panamanian image. In a case in 1955 that outraged many Zonians, Magistrate Judge Edward Altman threw out a resisting arrest and assault charge against a Panamanian on the grounds that while struggling with the Canal Zone Police, the suspect had exercised "a reasonable right to defend himself against false arrest."[96] In 1945 Balboa Magistrate Judge Robert Schmorleitz dismissed a loitering charge against a Panamanian girl who worked at Fort Kobbe. "This whole case is ridiculous," he told the prosecutor. "First these servicemen proposition this girl who was working her legitimate job, and then the police step in and arrest her for prostitution? This is disgraceful."[97] For this reason a few Panamanian defendants acknowledged the fairness of the court in their testimony, although one should read such declarations with caution, as possible attempts to flatter and influence judges' decisions.

While Panamanian activists often decried the U.S. Court's bias, Zone Police assailed it for coddling criminals. In a letter to Judge Crowe, a Panamanian wrote in 1956 of a police officer in court muttering, "What's the use of hauling in all these damned niggers and Latins if they don't get sent to the pen. I might just as well close my eyes and earn my eight hours pay and not give a damn what happens on my beat." The author decried the "high tension racial lines that run through the Canal Zone Police and the Canal Zone Courts." He applauded Crowe's attempts to favor "probation, restitution, and reparation over incarceration" and his "policy of regeneration over degeneration."[98]

But not all Zonians approved of such a "liberal" approach: "I am tired and mad of reading articles in the Mail Box by aliens who get their bread and butter from my tax money running down my country. . . . Just for your information, of the last 50 cases in the Zone courts—other than for traffic offences—49 were *colored people* of your country. Of these there were 23 thieves, 13 prostitutes, 12 queers, and 1 miscellaneous."[99] This Zonian invective drew an impassioned Panamanian response: "You emphasize that aliens are running down your country. Let me emphasize that *you* are the aliens *here*. . . . The court convictions you mentioned are small, petty offences compared to the murders and outrageous sex killings in your country. Leave us here with our prostitutes, queers, and thieves. We can still walk our streets at night."[100] The intensity of this exchange reflected the conflict at the heart of U.S. borderland justice. What neither author mentioned was that a high percentage of Panamanian prostitutes and "queers" arrested in the Zone crossed the border to service U.S. military and Canal Company personnel.

Zone Justice and the Resources of Panama's Poor

The inability of Panamanian defendants to afford counsel also doubtless played a role in their high incarceration rates. Wounded by a lifetime of poverty, confused by U.S. procedures, and unsure of the court translator's veracity, Spanish-speaking defendants typically took their chances with the judge, often appealing directly to him for mercy and waiving a jury trial. Both male and female Panamanians frequently addressed Judge Crowe in very personal terms as a *patrón* who would take pity on them.[101]

Besides their inability to secure counsel, poorer Panamanians lacked the resources to post bail. As such, they languished for sixty days in jail before Crowe or Hancock could throw out a case against them for lack of evidence or improper procedure. Panamanian defendants had difficulty procuring Panamanian witnesses, as many indigent Panamanians with minor records feared entering the Zone and the dreaded U.S. courthouse. Therefore, while the court strove for fairness, the imperial nature of the system stacked the deck against Panamanian borderlanders. West Indian Panamanians had an expression for the unfair nature of the system: "Canal Zone justice." According to one West Indian in his eighties, "De whyte mon don't steal, he borrow. De whyte mon don't kill, he execute. De whyte mon don't rape, he make love. De Panamanian mon, de West Indian mon, he do all dem evil things. De whyte mon, he only do de good thing. He build de Canal. But my people dug it. He don't tell you dat. . . . And then dey put dem in jail for drinkin', for fightin', for takin' home some girl or some contraband. But it weren't right. It weren't God's law. It was *de whyte mon's law.*"[102]

A fundamental problem with examining Canal Zone justice solely through U.S. court and police records is that such an approach fails to capture the totality of the colonial system at work. Herman Wilkinson, a Zone Protective Services detective, explained the problem this way: "You have to understand that the general rule down here was: If he's white, don't bother him. Kunas, West Indians, or Panamanians who stole stuff from the commissaries or the docks where I worked, we arrested them; they went to jail. But the white bosses and managers took what they wanted and nobody bothered them; unless they got too greedy or did something outrageous. They'd tell a Kuna or a West Indian, 'Take one of those TVs out of that container and put it in my car.' 'You got it, boss!' You give the guy five bucks and you get a color TV. If anything goes wrong, *the black guy* goes to jail. You can look at all the court records you want, but that won't tell you much about what happened down here because Zonians didn't just run the Canal Zone; they *owned* the place."[103]

Resistance at Gamboa?

The reality of Gamboa Penitentiary, the U.S. federal prison in the borderland, differed in many respects from its black legend. Founded in 1914, the penitentiary served as the main holding center for felons for sixty-six years. By the 1970s the inmate population averaged around 150 prisoners, 96 percent Panamanians and 4 percent U.S. citizens or other nationals, up from fewer than one hundred inmates during the 1940s and 1950s. This 40 percent increase of inmates at Gamboa reflected the rise in crime and population along the borderland during the 1950s–1970s and, for at least a few inmates, the increased nationalist crusade against the U.S. enclave.[104]

Gamboa was, in effect, a U.S. prison for Panamanians, and mostly Panamanians of color. The few U.S. prisoners consisted of a handful of Zonians and GIs convicted of felonies and awaiting transportation to U.S. prisons. Gamboa also held a few third-country nationals for maritime and drug trafficking offenses. Although a federal penitentiary, Gamboa functioned independently of the U.S. Bureau of Prisons, another example of the strange way in which the Zone, while connected to the federal government, operated almost like a separate state.[105]

The infamy of Gamboa Penitentiary gained credence with Joaquín Beleño's novel *Los forzados de Gamboa* (*Gamboa Road Gang*), published in 1960. But the prison's tough image had historical roots. U.S. penal authorities at Gamboa operated a harsh regime from its establishment all the way through the 1950s. Inmates at Gamboa, the majority of them black and brown, worked in chain gangs along the roads or in the quarries of the Zone, manacled together with shackles and wearing striped uniforms. White, shotgun-toting U.S. police monitored these convicts, along with West Indian guards. The Zone maintained a segregated prison at Gamboa. White prisoners, lighter-skinned inmates, and trusties stayed in A Block; B Block housed black and mixed-race prisoners. Homosexual prisoners were relegated to C Block, and D Block contained the punishment cells.[106]

Rebellious inmates or those who attempted escape wore additional balls and chains. Up until the early 1950s guards chained problem prisoners to the walls of their cells at night. Convicts also worked under a strict caste system. Inmates with privileges and good behavior points wore the letter A sewed on the right side of their trousers just below the waistline. All new arrivals who had not yet earned sufficient conduct points, as well as "troublemakers," wore the letter B. Prison regulations required a convict to touch his cap before he could address a white guard, who had to be addressed as "Officer." In the infamous "hole" at Gamboa, in D Block, attempted escapees and rebellious prisoners languished in extreme heat on a diet of bread and water.[107]

When Lester Greaves first arrived at the prison in 1946 to serve fifty years for rape, most components of this harsh regime still functioned, but during the late 1940s Zone officials began initiating some reforms designed to create a model prison.[108] By the late 1950s the practice of chain gangs had ended; prison gangs still worked the transportation arteries of the Zone, mowing grass and removing litter, but not in chains. In 1968 authorities eliminated road work altogether. Beginning in the late 1940s wardens placed more emphasis on rehabilitation, expanding the penitentiary's workshop, library, and paint shop and establishing tailor, shoe, barber, and carpentry shops for vocational training. The prison eventually boasted poultry, pig, and trout farms, extensive vegetable gardens, and fruit orchards to encourage other work activities.[109]

The prison also fed itself through its farming enterprises, and the food improved after the war years. Veteran West Indian prisoners serving as cooks provided some of the best food on the Zone, according to many former prisoners and guards. Zone Police officers would vie for the opportunity to transport a prisoner to Gamboa so that they could enjoy a hearty lunch there. Authorities also formed baseball teams among the inmates. Motion pictures played two nights a week at a makeshift outdoor theater.[110]

Zone officials enacted these reforms as part of a new policy that promoted education and training to mold repeat offenders into productive citizens. This effort included input from probation, medical, and psychiatric professionals. But the program largely failed. By the 1970s recidivism rates at Gamboa ranged between 60 and 65 percent, which, while lower than recidivism rates at U.S. prisons and an improvement from the 83 percent recidivism of the 1950s, was not a ringing success. A major problem with Gamboa's reform program was that it prepared prisoners to return to a U.S.- or Zone-style economy, and not to Panama, which suffered high unemployment and meager wages for semiskilled laborers.[111]

Another contradiction at Gamboa in its last decade and a half rested in the enormous alienation many Panamanian prisoners felt toward the U.S. administrators, guards, and instructors. Particularly during the 1960s–1970s increasing numbers of inmates at Gamboa viewed themselves as political prisoners, although their U.S. guards disagreed. Just as Irish Republican Army inmates at the Maze Facility in Northern Ireland or Palestinians in Israeli prisons held their British and Israeli guards in contempt, so growing numbers of Panamanian convicts saw the U.S. guards as agents of an unjust occupation, as revealed in the new political discourse of protest and treaty negotiations that dominated the borderland in this period.[112]

But a majority of Panamanian inmates never expressed such strong political beliefs. Many were institutionalized recidivists who appreciated the safety and good conditions at Gamboa. Like most strict penitentiaries, Gamboa maintained a relatively secure environment, a benefit not lost on veterans of Panama's jails, where random violence, miserable food, and poor sanitary conditions abounded.[113] Inmates invariably left Gamboa with higher weight, no sores, and good teeth thanks to the prison dentist. During the 1940s–1950s released prisoners exited Gamboa with $20 "gate money," a sufficient sum to live for a month in Panama. By the 1970s prisoners could earn and accumulate up to $80. "Gamboa wasn't that bad a place," one ex-prisoner recalled. "I used to consider it a refuge when I was really broke and hungry."[114]

Not all Panamanians adjusted so well to penitentiary life. Resistance as well as accommodation marked servitude "at the pen." Inmates stole food and produce; they assaulted prison guards, usually local-rate Panamanians or trusties, deemed traitors by hardened convicts. Occasionally U.S. guards endured assaults as well. In 1945 a Panamanian visitor to Gamboa pulled a knife and threw it at a U.S. guard before he was shot and tackled. Prior to 1945 thirty-four prisoners escaped from Gamboa, although the guards captured all but one, who had fled to Colombia.[115]

Tool sabotage and feigning sickness to avoid work assignments were more common forms of resistance, as was pretended stupidity in response to work orders. The secret production of alcohol from shaving lotion, mouthwash, rubbing alcohol, and sugar, as well as drug smuggling into Gamboa, persisted despite guard vigilance. Some inmates employed other, more creative types of resistance. In 1944 a former tailor and West Indian prisoner working in the penitentiary's tailor shop embarrassed officials by outfitting several prisoners in Zoot suit–style uniforms, presumably to facilitate escape. A prisoner cook once made several guards sick by serving them tainted meat. Another convict who fled five miles from the prison before recapture insisted that he had not escaped; he was only "chasing a rabbit for dinner."[116]

Increased vocational training, the rewarding of privileges for "good behavior," and a parole system that released many prisoners after serving half of their terms kept the peace at Gamboa throughout the postwar era. Officials constructed a small chapel for the prisoners, expanded the vegetable gardens, and permitted postage of three rather than one letter per week. They even sanctioned prisoners' painting of religious murals in the penitentiary dining room.[117]

But Gamboa was still a strict institution in which hundreds of Panamanians seethed over their separation from family and loved ones. In February 1974, despite the reforms and new privileges, Panamanian prisoners rioted and briefly took over D Block. Forty Canal policemen arrived from Balboa and Cristobal to recapture the cells, using teargas and batons, without the loss of life or serious injury. Although local newspapers described the riot as "a disturbance," one veteran officer, Frank Dupree, remembered it as "a real mutiny" that lasted two days and took a strong force with gas masks and riot gear to suppress: "Don't forget, some of them thought they were revolutionaries with all the crap Torrijos was stirring up in Panama."[118]

Borderland Conflicts with the Canal Zone Police

The mostly white Canal Zone Police Force provided the key friction point along the borderland between the U.S. enclave and the Panamanian people. A majority of U.S. citizens remembered the Zone's finest with affection: "They were like family"; "They always watched out for us and protected the

6.1. This photo captures an idealized image of Zonian life that many former and current U.S. inhabitants of Panama still embrace. A happy white U.S. family is guarded by the friendly and efficient Canal Zone Police. (Panamanians and West Indians held more negative views of the enclave's constabulary.) The snapshot also shows the Zonian obsession with order and regulation, as a police officer is assigned the job of crossing guard that students might hold in the States. Courtesy of the *Panama Canal Review* in the Panama Canal Museum Collection, George Smathers Library, University of Florida, http://ufdc.ufl.edu/pcm.

community"; "If any of our kids got into trouble, they'd straighten them out or come to talk to us about it first." Panamanians held a different view of the Zone constabulary. "They were sons of bitches. Real Nazis," one Panamanian observed. Even a veteran of the force admitted to the fearsome image that the U.S. police projected: "The Canal Zone police officer wearing a belt of bullets, leather shoulder strap, a .38 police positive loaded with snub nose ammunition, hand cuffs, and a foot-long club made out of lignum vitae wood, as well as a hard leather puttees, looked like a Nazi Storm Trooper."[119]

While many Panamanians shuddered at the sight of the U.S. police in their dark sunglasses and imposing Smokey hats, others swore at them, spat at them, wrestled with them, and even tried to run them over. As the nationalist struggle intensified along the border from the late 1950s on, resistance against the police grew. As early as the late 1940s Panamanians complained about the hostile behavior of Zone Police who shoved them aside when, as students, they paraded in nationalist demonstrations too close to Zone sidewalks.[120] In 1950 Panamanians protested "rude Canal Zone police" who strong-armed them when they tried to board the commercial launch for Taboga Island so that Zonians could board first.[121]

One of the most common conflicts between Panamanians and the Zone Police occurred over traffic enforcement. In the 1950s, paying a $10 ticket for driving 35 miles per hour in a 25-mile-per-hour zone represented a week's pay for a working-class Panamanian. Zone Police would tag Panamanian cars for parking more than twelve inches from the curb after measuring the distance with a ruler. The police strictly enforced fifteen-minute parking in front of Zone banks and post offices, chalking Panamanian tires and brandishing watches. Unlike in Panama, Zone tickets could not be "fixed" by friends or politicians. Because of the different license plates, Zone Police easily identified Panamanian cars for profiling. A Panamanian who failed to pay his fines could find himself in jail the next time he transited the border.[122]

The Zone Police would issue traffic tickets for failure to make a hand or directional signal or come to a complete stop at a stop sign or for driving too close to another vehicle, practices common in Panama. In 1961 a Canal Zone officer wrote up a Panamanian *chiva* (small bus) driver, Felecio Benedí, because one of his license plates had "rust on the bottom of it that interfered with its visibility."[123] Canal Police conducted this petty harassment principally to keep Panamanians, whom they regarded as interlopers, out of the Zone. According to Richard Koster, they also did so out of boredom: "You have to remember, they weren't really cops. What I mean is, not like cops in New York or Detroit that had real crime to deal with: murders, armed robberies, stick-ups. . . . Down here it was all penny ante stuff: property theft, small-style burglary, traffic tickets. There'd be a murder once every five years in the Canal Zone; in New York you'd have fifteen murders a week."[124]

The Zone police could also be tough on fellow Zonians. "They gave out tickets to everyone, not just the Panamanians," one Zonian emphasized. In the mid-1970s, Rex Raspberry remembered, he received a ticket for jaywalking when he crossed an empty street on foot one Sunday morning.[125]

More than a few Zonians resented the U.S. cops as "overpaid, underworked, and superior": "Big drinkers, every one of them, but they'd pull you over for drunk driving"; "Real tough guys when it came to beating up Panamanian kids. That takes a lot of guts, huh?" In a letter of complaint in 1950, a Zonian wrote, "Best job on the Canal Zone today is that of policeman. Overtime pay, night pay, holiday pay. As a matter of fact I wouldn't be surprised to see them get paid for attending all the parties they throw for their retiring members. . . . And 20 years retirement due to the 'dangerous' nature of their job? Tch. Tch. What danger exists? Flat feet? Dive bombing via mosquitoes while selling insurance in front of the Administration Building? Riding around in brand new cars?"[126]

But if the Canal Police evoked resentment and jealousy from some Zonians, they inspired pure hatred from working-class Panamanians. "A lot of the police here had a real redneck attitude," recalled Edgardo Tirado, who came on the force in the early 1970s. "They really pissed off the Panamanian community and made it hard for cops who were trying to do a good job. There was no need for the way they treated the locals. 'Shut up, spic,' 'Listen, nigger,' that kind of stuff. But they had that ingrained in them from living down here so long." "Red?!" Pablo Prieto remembered. "Some of these guys were so red you'd think they just walked in from Alabama." The fact that the vast majority of suspects whom the U.S. police arrested for burglary and theft were Panamanian only validated the policemen's prejudices.[127]

The Price of Borderland Police Abuse

But Zone Police harassment extended not just to Panama's poor. Lorena Riba, a fair-skinned Panamanian from a middle-class family, remembered staying late bowling one night in Balboa in the mid-1970s with her U.S. school friends. When she walked toward the bus stop in the dark, the U.S. police apprehended her and took her to the police station. Fourteen years old at the time, she can still recall her terror as she wept on the phone while calling her mother to pick her up.[128] Initially the Zone Police treated her like a prostitute and expressed disbelief at her truthful explanations. Riba had violated a key borderland rule: that Panamanians "get out of the Zone by sundown." "They [the Zone Police] really enjoyed humiliating us," another Panamanian woman recalled with deep anger. "Most of them were very ignorant people with a high school education at best. But they liked to denigrate us, especially educated, well-to-do Panamanians. I guess it made them feel important."[129]

Still, poorer Panamanians of color were the most common victims of abuse. In 1961 a Zone Police officer pulled a bus over when he spotted a Panamanian woman drop a gum wrapper from her window. The young officer dragged the middle-aged Panamanian domestic off the vehicle. He made her get down on her hands and knees in the dirt and sift through leaves until she retrieved the gum wrapper. He then gave her a $10 summons that, for a maid in 1961, amounted to a week's pay. All the while, the Panamanian woman kept her head down and wept in shame. A U.S. serviceman's wife on board witnessed the event and later wrote a letter of complaint.[130]

For poorer Panamanians, such treatment encompassed the chauvinism and petty cruelty of the U.S. borderland. These humiliations had little to do with treaties or diplomats but constituted the reality of everyday life for Panamanian and West Indian workers. In 1964 Zonians expressed shock at the thousands of Panamanian rioters who charged the Zone in collective fury. Arguments abounded over the immediate cause of the eruption: a flag incident, leftist politics in Panamanian schools and universities, Fidel Castro's allegedly malevolent influence. But it was sixty years of Panamanians enduring such small degradations, dodging police to gather mangoes, acceding to demands for identification, listening to the words *spic* and *nigger* that planted the seeds of 1964. Zonians rarely understood the pain of such debasements because they had been nurtured since childhood in an atmosphere that ensured U.S. comfort and superiority over the local community. Exceptions certainly obtained for a minority of favored Panamanians with U.S.-rate jobs, but in general the enclave, especially through its police force, reminded West Indians and Panamanians every day of the distinctly second-class nature of their status.

Violent Resistance against the U.S. Borderland Police

While the more common forms of Panamanian resistance to the Zone Police involved verbal insults and chicanery, defiance sometimes turned violent. When Canal Zone officer William Long attempted to break up a disturbance at the Gatun silver clubhouse in 1946, several West Indians attacked him and beat him unconscious before reinforcements arrived to quell the riot. In 1950 a chiva driver, Rafael Bonilla, tried to run over a Canal policeman, Walter Alves, when Alves blocked his path to give him a speeding ticket. The following year another chiva driver, Vincente Guerra, deliberately rammed Canal Zone officer William Hoelzle, knocking him off his motorcycle during a wild chase to avoid a nuisance citation.[131]

As Panamanian nationalism surged in the 1950s, resistance grew bolder. In June 1955 alone, three different Panamanians assaulted three different Canal Zone Police officers, shocking the Zone community. Constant victims of racism in the Zone, West Indian Panamanians perpetrated all three assaults.[132] The Zone's silver commissaries became prime sites of altercations between Panamanians, Zone Police, and contraband inspectors whose job was to prevent the overbuying of items for sale or as gifts for relatives in Panama. In Panamanians' eyes, the inspectors were in the second-most-despised profession in the borderland. With hungry mouths to feed, West Indian mothers saw these battles over their right to buy duty-free groceries as matters of life and death. "Every inspector has been assaulted more than once, had clothes torn, his face scratched by irate female violators who resented being questioned," a journalist wrote of these "commissary cat fights."[133]

In December 1955 John Blanchard, a West Indian, wrestled Officer Jessie Martie's gun from his holster during an arrest for vagrancy in La Boca, pinned the officer to the ground, and held the gun to Martie's head before other police rescued him.[134] In 1967 a bus driver, Charles Anthony Reid, refused to sign a $10 speeding ticket handed him by Zone officer William Steele. Steele tried to arrest Reid, hitting him on the head several times with his blackjack, until an enraged Reid flung the patrolman off his bus. Reid then sped into Panama, followed by a bloody yet determined Steele and several other Zone troopers. Reid's stunned Panamanian passengers, all of them domestic servants working for Americans, cheered as Reid drove away triumphantly to the disgust of police, who could not follow him across the border.[135]

Without doubt, Pedlecador Caparossa earned the title of the fiercest criminal resister of the postwar Zone. In 1967 he wrestled with five Canal Zone policemen during his arrest on burglary charges. While incarcerated at the Balboa Jail, he organized a riot that led to dozens of police and prisoner injuries, extensive property damage, and the teargassing of the jail. U.S. officials considered Caparossa so dangerous that they shipped him across the isthmus under special guard. In an effort to make an example of him and discourage future rebellion, Judge Crowe sentenced him to fifteen years at Gamboa, an unusually harsh sentence for an unusually defiant Panamanian. When vacating the court, Caparossa shouted to the Canal Zone policemen who took him away in hand and leg irons that "he would see them all in hell!"[136]

As early as 1961 Canal Zone governor William Carter warned of the growing local contempt toward Zone law. He spoke of excessive loitering, vandalism, theft, and "disrespect toward the police," a coded term for Panamanians openly insulting Zone constables. Arrests in fact increased 19 percent from 1960 to 1961, rising from 4,269 to 5,077.[137] The flag riots in November 1959 may have sanctioned assaults against the yanqui police as a means of opposing the "U.S. occupation."[138] After the uprising in 1964 a popular consensus formed in Panama that the Zone must either radically change or end—and soon. In such a charged atmosphere, crime against the gringos took on the convenient mantle of patriotism for at least some Panamanians.

Canal Zone Police Reforms

The Canal Zone Police did change between 1945 and 1982, their last year of existence. U.S. officials instituted a number of "reforms," some useful, some pernicious, to deal with growing Panamanian defiance. In 1952, at the height of the Red Scare, the Zone established the Internal Security Branch. This agency fired hundreds of local-rate Panamanian and West Indian workers due to past associations with leftist parties and unions, especially the communist Partido del Pueblo. The Internal Security Branch brought a heightened sense of surveillance and paranoia to the Zone, worsening animosities during the 1950s.[139]

In the late 1950s the Canal Zone Police introduced courses in the use of submachine guns, teargas, and riot shotguns as part of its new "crowd control training." In prior years the Canal Police had relied on its erstwhile ally, the National Guard, to handle "unruly mobs" from Panama, but in the growing nationalist atmosphere the police decided to take no chances. In 1958 the force designated several U.S. customs agents, postal workers, and lock guards "as auxiliary policemen to supplement the regular force in the event of a severe emergency" (i.e., invasion from Panama).[140]

In late 1959, following large-scale anti-American riots, officials came up with the novel idea of giving Spanish-language courses to one-fifth of the force so that its members "might better communicate with Panamanians," or as one Chorrillo resident put it, "After 1959 some of the cops learned how to swear at us in Spanish."[141] In August 1964, in response to the shocking riots, the Canal Zone Police purchased armored cars and water cannons. The U.S. government also hired Panamanian citizens for the first time as first-class police officers, some forty of them, or one-eighth of the force. While most U.S. police and Zonians opposed this initiative, designed to promote better community relations, the hiring of Panamanians gradually had the effect of reducing conflict with local citizens. Panamanians who served on the force understood the native culture and proved adept at resolving petty disputes verbally.[142]

Finally, in 1975 both the Panamanian and Canal Zone governments initiated a pilot program of joint police patrols. Individual Canal Zone policemen teamed up with Panamanian National Guardsmen to walk the Zone borders.

While the Canal Zone Police rank and file initially opposed it, this cooperative policy resulted in a drop in misdemeanor offenses and petty thefts during the mid- to late 1970s. A Panamanian policeman who participated in these joint patrols recalled his surprise at how well he got along with Zone Police after an initial coolness during his first couple of walks with them. U.S. authorities appointed Spanish-speaking officers, most of them Panamanians, to work with the guardia, which no doubt facilitated cooperation. Felony arrests, however, continued to rise throughout the experiment, from 338 in 1972 to 577 six years later. But drug charges skewed these figures, as they accounted for a higher percentage of detentions for serious crime than in the past.[143]

The joint patrols' greatest accomplishment consisted in lessening overall tension between the U.S. police and the Panamanian citizenry. While arrests diminished, charges continued to rise, from 7,439 in 1970 to 12,454 in 1979, but these statistics proved misleading since traffic violations accounted for 85 percent of the charges in 1979. Dramatic growth in Panamanian car ownership also helped to explain the near doubling of traffic offenses in the 1970s.[144] (See table 6.1.)

Summary

After the coup in 1968 the Panamanian military increasingly sought a monopoly on resistance against the Zone with its own carefully organized demonstrations. Torrijos cracked down on University of Panama students, previously the foremost proponents of anti-*yanquismo*.[145] But every night freelancers crept into the enclave to conduct their own private wars against the gringos. By their very crossing of borders whose legitimacy they defied, these outlanders rejected the political status quo. Thus Panamanian crime in the enclave weakened the whole colonial enterprise, exposing a web of contradictions and inequities that made it difficult to tell who was stealing, sharing, or wasting the Zone's resources more: Zonians, Panamanians, or the U.S. military.

For sixty-six years Gamboa Penitentiary stood as a hated symbol of U.S. injustice for many Panamanians. On December 31, 1980, U.S. officials handed the facility over to Panama as part of the Carter-Torrijos treaties of 1977. Former convict Lester Greaves, the prison's most famous inmate, attended the ceremony as a kind of guest of honor (his presence as a convicted rapist angered many Zonians). President Aristedes Royo announced a pardon for forty-seven of Gamboa's prisoners "serving lighter terms, who had demonstrated good conduct." But the Panamanian government transferred

Table 6.1 Crime Arrest Statistics for the Canal Zone, 1939–1979

Year	Total arrests	CZ residents	Residents of Panama	Transients
1939	3059	916	1841	302
1940	3977	1155	2316	506
1941	7647	2798	4249	600
1942	11293	4956	5291	1046
1943	9858	4295	4898	665
1944	8525	3188	4935	402
1945	7735	2308	4878	549
1946	8722	2634	5344	744
1947	8885	2803	5701	381
1948	8079	2367	5342	370
1949	7985	2739	4838	408
1950	8553	2910	5294	349
1951	5798	1948	3629	221
1952	5745	1857	3573	315
1953	6310	2132	3855	323
1954	5868	1788	3832	248
1955	5304	1365	3799	140
1956	4943	1240	3541	162
1957	5009	1417	3390	202
1958	4566	1215	3116	235
1959	4164	946	3046	172
1960	4269	1106	3027	136
1961	5077	1524	3399	154
1962	4684	1435	3072	177

Male	Female	Total charges	Felonies	Misdemeanor and traffic offenses
2888	171	3315	93	3222
3776	201	4324	108	4216
7348	299	8199	159	8040
10925	368	12066	297	11769
9488	370	10481	406	10075
7879	646	9214	403	8811
7314	421	8289	280	8009
8192	530	9387	312	9075
8232	653	9417	361	9056
7622	457	8446	320	8126
7366	619	8438	280	8158
7854	609	9144	235	8909
5267	531	6107	216	5891
5219	526	6060	239	5821
5696	614	6704	265	6439
5146	722	6180	203	5977
4636	668	6299	892*	5399
4194	749	6302	1383*	4909
4480	529	5364	267	5097
4238	328	4921	298	4623
3836	328	4455	281	4174
3919	350	4532	209	4323
4642	435	5300	181	5119
4284	400	4898	224	4674

continued

Table 6.1 Crime Arrest Statistics for the Canal Zone, 1939–1979, *continued*

Year	Total arrests	CZ residents	Residents of Panama	Transients
1963	4741	1474	3113	154
1964	4887	1661	3046	180
1965	6063	2207	3728	128
1966	7398	2895	4352	151
1967	8229	3061	4971	197
1968	7969	3130	4656	183
1969	7262	2874	4152	236
1970	5944	2567	3185	192
1971	3544	1569	1974	—**
1972	3448	1471	1977	—
1973	3451	1560	2195	—
1974	3468	1454	2315	—
1975	3562	1206	2356	—
1976	3497	1311	2186	—
1977	2842	998	1844	—
1978	3082	1110	1972	—
1979	2923	1037	1886	—

* In 1955–56 the Felony category was replaced with Class I offenses (Major Crimes).
** After 1971 transients were included in the CZ residents' figures.
Sources: *Annual Reports of the Governor of the Panama Canal 1939–1951; Annual Report of the Panama Canal Company and the Canal Zone Government, 1952–1979.*

Male	Female	Total charges	Felonies	Misdemeanor and traffic offenses
4431	310	4962	201	4761
4484	403	5104	145	4959
5492	571	6269	130	6139
6759	639	7649	206	7443
7562	667	8516	174	8432
7324	645	8300	188	8112
6718	544	7531	147	7384
5510	434	7439	174	7265
3307	237	10751	197	10554
3278	170	9024	338	8686
3451	304	10115	384	9731
3468	301	10687	434	10253
3292	270	10506	531	9975
3205	292	13277	446	12831
2581	261	12143	523	11620
2785	297	13334	577	12757
2634	289	12452	461	11991

the remaining inmates (recidivist convicts, violent offenders, and drug traffickers) to other jails in the republic. Contrary to their rhetoric of the past years, Panamanian authorities did not regard all of Gamboa's inmates as political prisoners after all.[146]

Panamanians did not just "eat" cable; they ate away at the Canal Zone, little by little, piece by piece, one bicycle and screwdriver at a time. An older West Indian explained it best: "You look at dat termite, he's not dat smart, he's not dat strong. He's smaller dan your big toenail. He dohn't even mahke a noise. But him and his friends, dey just keep eaten' an' eaten' an' eaten'. And pretty soon, dey bring de whole mohn-sion dawhn!"[147]

International pressure and high-status diplomacy between the Torrijos government and the Carter administration shut the Zone mansion down, not low-level crime that many Panamanians viewed as resistance. But these daily infractions exposed the enclave's fundamental characteristics: economic inequality, racism, and national chauvinism. "They only came here to steal," one Canal Zone policeman remembered about the local population. But a Panamanian protester writing in the Zonians' favorite newspaper made a similar accusation: "And what did you Americans come here for—except to take what you wanted with your power—and leave us with little or nothing? Well then, we will take what we can get too!" Thus crime along the frontier followed a familiar trajectory of imperial borderlands in which theft, contraband, and even prostitution assumed different meanings, depending on which side of the border one lived, what class or race one belonged to, and whose identity one embraced or was ascribed.[148]

Epilogue

THE ZONE-PANAMA BORDERLAND

AND THE COMPLEXITY OF U.S. EMPIRE

Historians of U.S. foreign relations still debate whether the United States constitutes an empire in the classic sense, such as that of the Roman or British Empire. Even those scholars who accept the concept of the United States as an empire continue to argue about what kind of empire Washington has maintained since the late nineteenth century. Historians of U.S. western expansion and Manifest Destiny contend that long before 1898, the United States consciously forged a *contiguous* imperium. Since the birth of the republic, and even before, Americans have conquered the lands of Amerindians, Spaniards, Frenchmen, and Mexicans on the North American continent.[1] Foreign relations scholars have put forth different notions of the twentieth-century overseas U.S. empire, all of them notable by their qualifiers: democratic empire, empire by invitation, enlightened empire, empire by integration, defensive empire, protective empire, empire by default, and even accidental empire.[2]

Among large sectors of the American public, reluctance still persists to admitting that the United States has, now or ever, constituted an empire in the British, French, or Spanish manner. The whole notion cuts against the central ideology of the American Revolution: popular sovereignty and self-determination forged in an anticolonial war for independence. The pejorative use of the term *American imperialism* by the Soviets, Latin Americans, and other critics throughout the twentieth century has further discredited such a concept in the minds of many U.S. citizens. To such dogged skeptics of empire, this study can only state, paraphrasing President John F. Kennedy at the Brandenburg Gate, "Let them come to Panama."

In Panama imperial doubters would have discovered another "Berlin Wall," as locals called the eight-foot-high barbed-wire cyclone fence that ran the length of the Canal Zone's urban borderland. Behind that protective barrier, the United States ran a state within a state, with a classic imperial hierarchy of race, national identity, and gender. Four generations of U.S. civilians, the Zonians, enjoyed the perks and privileges of this unique colonial lifestyle. Throughout the century Zone authorities operated their own government, police force, court system, schools, hospitals, and the only U.S. federal penitentiary outside American soil. The Zonians ate U.S. food, drank U.S. liquor, and played U.S. games on the athletic fields of U.S. high schools in the Zone. They imposed racial and national segregation in housing, education, shopping, and social life within the borders of their enclave. And both they and their sponsor, the United States, influenced much of the culture and economy of the neighboring Panamanian territory that ran along this overseas imperial frontier.[3]

In 1963 a white U.S. traveler to the Zone could sit at the long mahogany Roosevelt Bar in the Empire Lounge of the Tivoli, the Zone's famous hotel reminiscent of, but more downscale than, Raffles in Singapore or Shepherds in Cairo. Comfortably ensconced in a Windsor chair, he or she could sip Aged Wood, a Kentucky-style bourbon, distilled on the isthmus for American tastes, served by West Indian waiters in white tunics. He or she could stare out through the broad plate-glass window at the U.S. imperium just beyond the tropical ferns, the nation of Panama. The same traveler could taxi up to the nearby summit of Ancon Hill, the highest point in the capital and the location of Spanish fortifications from another imperial era. There, beside a billowing U.S. flag and military communication towers, the visitor could look down upon Panama and the Pacific spread out like "a feast upon a red, white, and blue tablecloth." Gazing north, east, or west, the observer would note myriad U.S. flags flying from bases and installations as far as the eye could see.[4]

Our traveler could then board a Panama Railroad coach and proceed along the line of the Canal to dine at the Cristobal Yacht Club in the Caribbean port of the Zone. Along the way the traveler would note the golf and tennis courts of the Zone, its carefully contoured landscapes, its all-white and all-American suburban communities. What such a tourist might miss, however, were the segregated local-rate towns peopled by West Indian laborers, the Kuna Indians working in the mess halls and barracks of the U.S. base complex, the Chinese gardeners growing fruits and vegetables, and the mixed U.S.–Latin American neighborhoods in Ancon and Curundu. The train also conveniently avoided, except at its terminals, the urban slums of the Zone-Panama borderland juxtaposed along the more populated regions of Colón and the capital. Hiding in the brush on either side of the railroad track were Panamanian timber poachers, burglars, and cable thieves from those very regions, who waited for night to fall. And in the bachelor quarters and guard posts of the Zone, Latina prostitutes plied their trade.

Nationality marked a key indicator of status along this borderland, as on most colonial frontiers. U.S. citizens enjoyed the benefits of subsidized housing, utilities, recreational facilities, shopping, health care, vacations, and promotions that far exceeded those of the local-rate workforce or those of the impoverished Panamanians who dwelled in the blighted barrios on the other side of the line. Their status as whites also elevated most Americans' standing within the larger borderland society. The Zone-Panama corridor, especially after the anti-American riots in 1959, was noteworthy for its gates, fences, checkpoints, guard posts, and barriers that channeled and privileged human traffic according to U.S. priorities. White Americans alone held the legal and social status to cross virtually all these boundaries, whether they were interior or exterior. (The elite Panamanian Club Unión and some U.S. military facilities for U.S. civilians provided the only exceptions to this rule.) They alone could enter practically all of the commissaries, towns, beaches, bars, and stores on either side of the line. Their lighter skin even provided them admittance to the exclusive clubs, casinos, discotheques, and neighborhoods of the capital and Colón, sites barred to many Latin, Chinese, Hindu, and West Indian Panamanians.[5]

Gender also established key boundaries within the borderland. All-male clubs, lodges, and associations kept even white women from enjoying the privileges that U.S. males reserved for themselves. Women of color, West Indians and Latinas, worked as the maids, cooks, and laundresses of the enclave, while most white women raised children with the help of these colored servants and submitted to their husbands' authority as junior partners within their marriages. White U.S. males held all the top administrative and military positions in the Zone, reifying their masculine, imperial identities. Along the enclave's borders, Panamanian and other Latina women worked as barmaids, waitresses, salesgirls, seamstresses, entertainers, and prostitutes. A gendered order that relegated women to secretarial, nursing, and service positions within the Zone held sway until the late 1960s, when the Canal administration finally promoted some U.S. women to midlevel management.[6]

Class also proved a key determinant to status within borderland society. Enlisted service personnel and DOD workers often felt shunned by the middle-class employees of the Panama Canal Company and Canal Zone government. Contractor and shipping agent families had more material wealth and clout, as did upper-echelon administrators and managers. West Indian chauffeurs drove Panama Canal pilots, the aristocracy of the borderland, back and forth to work, to the bars and clubs of the Zone, and to the brothels and casinos of the republic. In contrast, poorer Panamanians of color often found themselves subject to Canal Police harassment, surveillance, and demands for IDs when they tried to cross some of these same frontiers. Even in the Panamanian regions of the borderland, locals frequently found themselves ignored by shopkeepers and clerks, who favored yanqui and GI customers over their own countrymen. "They had plenty of power even on our side of the line, I can tell you that for sure!" one remembered.[7]

As a strategic and not a settler colony, the Zone operated very much like a military base with a significant civilian component and transportation function. In this respect, much of the Canal Zone's structure pointed toward the empire of bases that the United States now operates around the world: gated communities, enclaves of U.S. power and culture with PXs, clubs, shops, pools, gyms, and even fast-food franchises that dot the globe. Like the old Canal Zone, these facilities exert U.S. power and cultural influence, hire locals for cheap service labor, yet remain exclusive to the majority of the surrounding populations, alienating their national pride and challenging their traditional ways of life. Empire as borderland emerged, in fact, as an early model of U.S. intervention in the Caribbean and Latin America that started with railroad enclaves, such as the Panama Railroad in the 1850s, and continued with numerous banana, sugar, mining, and rubber enclaves, as well as military cantonments in Cuba, Nicaragua, Haiti, Mexico, and the Dominican Republic.[8]

In the Canal Zone this concept had already expanded by construction's end into a large and powerful instrument of hegemony—a super enclave of sorts—that far surpassed all others in breadth, size, purpose, and influence. There were two reasons the Zone exerted such force: because the U.S. presence there and its links to the metropole proved so much stronger than that of the small, relatively weak, host nation, and because the sheer size and specialized location of this borderland cut the republic in two, blocked normal east-west traffic across an entire nation, and controlled the highly profitable transport routes, north and south, across the isthmus. These factors, combined with the global explosion of U.S. cultural power after World War I, made the Zone-Panama borderland a unique colony; while it did not control all of Panama, it exerted sufficient power to reduce the republic to a near annex of the Zone. This was especially true in the decades before Panamanian state formation coalesced.[9]

The selective populating of the Zone and its environs further established a number of oppositional borderland societies within and along the enclave's frontiers that virtually crowded out the supposed "macro-society" of Panama in these years. As a result, a number of ethnicities shared in the economic largesse of this borderland, except for the majority Latin Panamanian population. Quite the contrary, these darker-skinned and mestizo isthmians were frequently shunted aside, affronted and overwhelmed by this giant, fenced, and guarded imposition to their daily lives, especially from World War II through the 1970s, when U.S. security concerns predominated official thinking.[10]

People of color quickly learned to exit by sundown if they did not have a documented reason for being on the U.S. side of the line. One Panamanian diplomat compared the borderland "as a ten-mile-wide, foreign-controlled territory along the Mississippi from the Great Lakes to the Gulf," would have divided and polarized the United States. "Can you imagine traveling through your own country and having to cross the borders of another state to do so? Being stopped and questioned by foreign police who spoke another language? But this is what Panamanians from the interior experienced for eighty years!"[11] This wound of exclusion proved a universal experience for people of color living along a white man's empire. The multitudinous encounters between these various groups often fostered accommodation, illicit trade, and sexual interaction. But in the end these contacts derived from such an unequal power dynamic that they inevitably provoked hostility and resentment from growing numbers of locals who congregated in such large numbers along the Zone's urban frontiers after World War II.

It is also important to note that social, cultural, and even psychological factors all played a role in the lengthy U.S. presence. While powerful state actors, such as the executive branch, the Congress, the Pentagon, and the State Department, created the enclave and sustained it through numerous postwar crises, the day-to-day encounters among ordinary Zonians, GIs, Panamanians, and West Indians clearly revealed its chauvinism, its racism, and its paternalism, as well as its accommodations, appeal, and contradictions. Empires endure not only by domination but also by their ability to co-opt and bedazzle the colonized. Up to eighty marriages a month between U.S. citizens and Panamanians at the height of the postwar era testified to the degree of accommodation at work along the border. Networks of sex, gambling, contraband, drugs, and larceny brought ordinary Panamanians,

Kuna, West Indians, and U.S. citizens together in cooperative interactions every day, not to mention the more legitimate avenues of employment and commerce that included canal jobs, service work, Chinese restaurateurs, Panamanian shopkeepers, and Hindustani peddlers.

The Zone operated as the supreme diffuser of U.S. popular culture on the isthmus. Its television shows, radio programs, movies, plays, food products, books, customs, and sports fascinated many Panamanians. Just as rum became a favorite drink in the enclave and Zonians danced and swayed to música típica, thanks to the Zone, Panamanians fell in love with jazz, Hollywood, rock and roll, Motown, blue jeans, Coca-Cola, and football long before globalization struck their Latin American brothers farther south. U.S. clothing styles, mannerisms, and ways of walking, talking, and gawking all found their imitators in Panamanian youth culture, especially in the transisthmian corridor, where U.S. influence and glamour waxed powerful. Christmas trees, Thanksgiving turkeys, and storefront Santa Clauses flourished in some of the borderland's West Indian and Panamanian regions, along with Mustang coupes, pizza, hot dogs, cheeseburgers, and Marlboros.[12]

To some degree borderland imperialism proved less onerous to locals than a full-scale U.S. occupation might have entailed. Attractions, appealing cultural models, and the cachet of U.S. association mitigated some of the worst aspects of colonialism while drawing local adherents toward support or at least acceptance of the status quo. But by the 1960s U.S. indignities, paternalism, and chauvinism proved too much for the majority of Panamanians to bear. The Zone could not provide enough jobs for them, challenged their rising nationalism, and in fact favored "privileged" minorities, such as West Indians and Kuna, over the bulk of the local population.

The Canal Zone embodied a unique imperial borderland in other respects. A government reservation and strategic colony, it contained no plantations, indentured workforce, or even private property. While judged affluent by impoverished Panamanians and the ultimate in Western imperialism by critics, the enclave was actually structured as a socialist polity with a functional aesthetic for its two dominant groups, the Zonians and the U.S. military—with the important exception that it stood as a U.S. overseas showcase on occupied, foreign soil beside a republic where de jure segregation did not exist, in contrast to the enclave's oppressive racial order.

Stresses on this borderland mounted steadily, first with the advent of World War II. Panama's demographic surge brought increasing numbers of the republic's citizenry into close proximity with the Zone at its urban borders, where they grew more politicized through participation in political parties, unions, and demonstrations. The ideals of the Atlantic and United Nations charters for self-determination combined with the postwar assault on empire and segregation challenged the Zone's very raison d'être. Darwinist notions of white supremacy crumbled before the revealed horrors of Auschwitz and Emmett Till. In the U.S. metropole, segregation in the military, in Major League Baseball, in the South, and even in the new suburban developments of the North faced increasing challenges. By the late 1950s a committed civil rights movement dominated headlines. Malcolm X and Fidel Castro, among others, stressed the connection between racial colonialism at home and U.S. imperialism abroad, and to many on the ascendant left, the Vietnam War appeared to prove them right. The Canal Zone suddenly looked like a colonial white elephant, a shameful relic, caught in a time warp yet fast running out of time.[13]

A resurgent nationalist movement in Panama added to U.S. borderlanders' distress. Once confident of their role as progressive technocrats embarked on a holy mission, the Zonians now found themselves portrayed as Afrikaners, colons, or Englishmen of the Raj. Much of their lifestyle and social structure, the drinking, the clubhouses, the servants of color, and the local sex industry, all painted U.S. citizens in Panama as distinctly un-American in their colonial pride and sometimes decadent culture. But most Zonians were government workers, Mom and Pop bureaucrats and mechanics, not jungle bwanas or big game hunters. As many admitted, life on the Zone was fairly boring, and the majority of U.S. workers followed mundane pursuits. Hannah Arendt wrote of the "banality of evil" regarding the bureaucratic conformity of ordinary, unquestioning men who helped fuel the Holocaust. On many levels, especially in quieter times, the Zone spoke to the banality of empire. Its institutions of control and co-optation, run by bureaucrats, police, and functionaries "just following orders" and tradition, ground on daily, regardless of their psychic and economic cost to Panamanians. Most Zonians rarely interacted with the local populace except as employers directing servants. Few of them, growing up in this comfortable colonial ambience, recognized that this hierarchical dynamic *was the problem*.[14]

As Emily Rosenberg has noted, "borders are messy places."[15] Record Group 185, the Records of the Panama Canal, is one of the larger series in the U.S. National Archives. Like its counterparts in Panama, the volume of its postwar files grew exponentially with exasperating bureaucratic conflicts, complaints, and controversies among all the borderland's inhabitants. These included local-rate workers, irate Zonians, frustrated Panamanians, angry black GIs, marginalized U.S. Latino citizens, demanding public employee unions, and West Indian interest groups. Court cases, discrimination complaints, lawsuits, strikes, protests, and crimes fill these records' bulging folders.[16] All this greatly complicated and confused the Zone administration and its former sense of mission, while lending Panamanian state actors and local activists useful wedge issues. The job of governor of the Canal Zone, once considered a perk and a golden parachute after a lifetime's service in the Army Corps of Engineers, became an increasingly thankless and stressful job. By the 1960s the holder of that office faced constant ridicule and opposition in Panama, ceaseless complaints from Panamanian and U.S. employees, and growing pressure from Washington to enact reforms.[17]

In the larger strategic sense, the Canal gradually lost its military significance, starting at the end of World War II. Wielding a two-ocean cold war navy (and massive deployments on European and Asian land bases), the Pentagon no longer needed the isthmian waterway to funnel vital resources to either ocean. In an age of nuclear missiles following the launch of Sputnik in 1957, the Canal's locks were a sitting duck. And they remained too narrow to handle the latest aircraft carriers and supertankers. With the U.S. military moving from sealift to airlift, the Canal appeared strategically obsolescent. Yet despite this reality, as late as the 1970s the waterway remained a sufficient source of U.S. historic pride for the Zonians and thousands of their domestic supporters to mount an impressive, last-ditch stand to hang onto it.[18]

Borders, which played such a huge role in the Zone-Panama nexus, force individuals to confront, and in many cases to reconfigure, their notions of identity, their relations with the state, even the extent of their loyalty or hostility toward an opposing polity. In their daily engagements along the Zone-Panama borders, inhabitants of various backgrounds faced some of the most defining and confounding experiences of their lives. These encounters refined what it meant to be a Zonian, a Latin Panamanian, a West Indian, an American businessman on the isthmus, a Puerto Rican GI in Panama, a Kuna borderer, an elite Panamanian student at Balboa High, a panagringo, a black GI on the isthmus, a Chinese diasporic shopkeeper, and myriad other identities that dwelled along this complex cultural frontier.[19]

The Canal Zone that evolved into such a barrier to sovereignty for majority Panamanians also served paradoxically as a protective barricade for numerous West Indians, Chinese, Kuna, and even some Panamanian political exiles. "Which side are you on?" was a U.S. civil rights song and catchphrase that encapsulated the quandary of so many isthmian borderers of the postwar Zone. Many among them had a foot in both camps. "I had a wife and kids in the Zone—and a girlfriend and kids in Panama!" American electrician Rick Broggi recalled. The Tirado brothers, Edgardo and Carlos, both members of the Canal Zone Police who gained their U.S. citizenship after service in Vietnam, expressed shock when sent to block a nationalist march on the Bridge of the Americas in 1975 when they discovered in the front row of the demonstrators, their Panamanian mother. "Mom, what are you doing here?!" Edgardo exclaimed. Rolando Sterling Arango, a member of the Panamanian Communist Party and fervent opponent of the Zone in numerous riots and marches, admitted how embarrassed he was when he had to tell his comrades that "my Dad was a U.S. army sergeant who adopted me as a boy after he married my Panamanian mom in Colón. Imagine, I grew up in the Zone with all its privileges, the very place I spent the rest of my life protesting!" And Thelma King, the nationalist firebrand who so enraged the Zonians with her columns and radio broadcasts against them, quietly requested a special travel visa in 1962 to visit her eldest son whom she had enrolled in an American military academy in upstate New York. While a committed anti-imperialist, King wanted her son to have the discipline and English-language education that so many members of Panama's upper classes sought when they sent their sons to such schools in the States.[20]

Individuals, such as those described above, were forced to choose each day the extent to which they would collaborate with, resist, ingratiate themselves with, or defy the strictures of U.S. colonialism or Panamanian nationalism, because besides encompassing a larger strategic construct, empire is a face-to-face, day-to-day, lived experience for those subjected to its whims or trying to reshape its impacts to their own advantage. Zonians and GIs, for instance, often ignored mandates from Washington, Balboa Heights, the Pentagon, and their local unit headquarters. Similarly individual Panamanians took little notice of their own government's dictates regarding the Zone when their own "flexible" approach better served their interests.[21]

In the postwar era such choices and possibilities widened or narrowed, reflecting larger changes in U.S., Canal Zone, and Panamanian policies. These included changes in government administrations, new treaties, and exacerbations or resolutions of binational tensions. But individual agency, from all the players, frequently trumped the orders from on high. "Sometimes you got to choose what you're going to do. If there was a Zone cop there, I drive slow and I don't talk to no one. But if there's no cop, I drive fast and I get two hams from the commissary from my friend, Luis, and then I get the hell out of there—and fast!" a Panamanian recalled with a laugh.[22] How people on both sides of the line adjusted to and manipulated such forces illuminates our understanding of the creative ways in which locals, often in cooperation with U.S. citizens, influenced the operation of empire at the borders. These same processes unfold every day at U.S. military bases, embassies, and cultural and economic enclaves around the globe. But the Zone's frontiers proved such an enduring and dominating reality on the isthmus and in the circum-Caribbean region that these choices took on even greater salience for a variety of borderlanders locked in postwar conflict.

Such struggles extended to the metropole's supreme corridors of power. The Vietnam War and economic decline in the 1970s revealed the limits of U.S. power to citizens and policymakers alike. Another jungle counterinsurgency, this time in Central America, was the last contingency that Washington desired by the mid-1970s. And such a prospect was easily avoidable since the Carter White House and State Department had a generally cooperative ally in Panama with whom to negotiate a reasonable and gradual retreat. (Resolving the U.S.-Cuban borderland at Guantánamo would have presented a much greater challenge at this juncture, given the intense cold war animosities and political consequences in play there.) And so negotiation, always a key activity in borderlands, extended from the personal and the cultural to the realm of statecraft at both centers of power. In the fall of 1977 high-status actors finally hammered out an agreement to end the borderland. Daily pressures, conflicts, entanglements, and troubles, as revealed in this study, all played a role in gradually wearing down U.S. resolve, strengthening Panamanian fortitude, and helping to push the process of imperial retreat toward its successful, if compromised, conclusion.[23]

Notes

Introduction

1. Arosemena G., *Historia Documental*, 173–89; Beluche Mora, *Acción Comunal*; Escobar, *Arnulfo Arias o el credo Panameñista*.

2. Chamberlain, *Decolonization*; Shipway, *Decolonization and Its Impact*; Kruse and Tuck, *The Fog of War*; Winant, *The World Is a Ghetto*; Griswold del Castillo, *World War II and Mexican Civil Rights*; Borstelmann, *The Cold War and the Color Line*; Dudziak, *Cold War Civil Rights*.

3. Donnan and Wilson, *Borders*; Truett, *Fugitive Landscapes*.

4. Adelman and Aron, "From Borderlands to Borders"; Taylor, *The Divided Ground*; Bannon, *The Spanish Borderlands Frontier*.

5. Seegel, *Mapping Europe's Borderlands*; Okun, *The Early Roman Frontier on the Upper Rhine Area*.

6. Moffat, *The Wall*; Gold, *Stone in Spain's Shoe*; Thornhill, *The Road to Suez*; Baker, *Crossroads*; Lipman, *Guantánamo*. The Spanish outposts at Ceuta and Melilla in North Africa form another example of noncontiguous borderlands; see Carabaza and de Santos, *Melilla y Ceuta*.

7. Diener and Hagan, *Borderlines and Borderlands*.

8. LaFeber, *The Panama Canal*; Conniff, *Panama and the United States*; Major, *Prize Possession*.

9. *Census of the Panama Canal Zone, 1960*; *Annual Report of the Panama Canal Company and the Canal Zone Government 1960*.

10. Shaw, *Colonial Inscriptions*, 1.

11. Geertz, "Thick Description," in *The Interpretation of Cultures*, 3–29.

12. For the role of memory in historical constructions, see Burke, "History as Social Memory"; Hutton, *History as the Art of Memory*; Irwin-Zarecka, *Frames of Remembrance*.

Chapter 1: Borderland on the Isthmus

1. For sex through the fence, James Reid, U.S. businessman in Panama, interview with author, Balboa, Republic of Panamá (RP), April 30, 2001; Enrique Cantera, retired laborer, interview with author, April 16, 2001; William Thrush, retired U.S. Army sergeant, interview with author, Balboa, RP, November 21, 2001; Memorandum: "Prostitutes Near Zone Borders," Jeffries to Randolph, February 10, 1964, File 250.1 (Unusual Incidents); Office of the Provost Marshal (OPM), Record Group (RG) 349, National Archives and Records Administration (NARA), College Park, Maryland.

2. For Puerto Rican presence in the Panama garrison, see Memorandum: Puerto Rican Recruitment in U.S. Army Caribbean," July 1, 1960, Headquarters U.S. Caribbean Command

(HUSCC), RG 349, NARA. For national breakdown of Panamanian prostitution, see Hyman, *Particularidades de la Prostitución en Panama*, 19–24.

3. Enrique Cantera, interview with author, Panama City, April 6, 2001; Rigoberto Cardenas, Panamanian professor, interview with author, Amador, RP, March 10, 2001.

4. For concept of "docile bodies," see Foucault, *Discipline and Punish*, 135–69.

5. For view of Canal Zone (CZ) as a monstrous imposition on Panama, see Torrijos Herrera, *La Batalla de Panamá*; Marthoz, *Panama*; Darío Souza, *Panamá*; Yau, *El Canal de Panamá*.

6. "14,600 Panamanians at Work for PanCanal and U.S. Military," *Spillway*, May 1, 1964, 5.

7. For information on CZ contribution to Panama's GDP from the 1930s to 1979, see *Panamá en Cifras, Años 1936–1979*; "Canal Purchases of Supplies in Panama Increased $250,000 in Six Month Period," *Panama Canal Review*, March 7, 1952, 1; "Millions Flow from Zone into Panama's Economy," *Spillway*, January 20, 1964, 4; "Canal Zone Benefits to Panama," *Spillway*, February 10, 1964, 3–4. For marriage statistics, see *Censos Nacionales, 1940–1980*. For financial contribution of U.S. military bases to Panama, see Moreno, *Las Bases Militares y el Desarrollo Nacional*, 2: 39–41, 171–88; Harding II, *The History of Panama*, 121; Panama Canal Treaty Implementation Plan Briefing, U.S. Southern Command, December 1003, cited in Barry et al., *Inside Panama*, 159. For the social impact of U.S. military spending in the 1990s, see Michael Winfrey, "U.S.-Panama Divorce Gathers Pace as Army Leaves," *Reuters*, July 29, 1999.

8. For U.S. road, hospital, and school construction, see McCain, *The United States and the Republic of Panama*, 97–106; Conniff, *Panama and the United States*, 93–94; Conn and Fairchild, *The United States Army in World War II: The Framework of Hemisphere Defense*, 316–19; Sanitation in the Canal Zone, Annual Report 1955, 9–14.

9. McCullough, *Path between the Seas*, 119–32; Conniff, *Panama and the United States*, 73–74; "External Aid to the Republic," *Spillway*, February 17, 1964; "Two New Mains Will Increase Supply of Canal Zone Water to Panama, Colon," *Spillway*, February 10, 1964. For U.S. military interventions, see Lindsay-Poland, *Emperors in the Jungle*, 16–17. For income disparities in Panama, see Morley, *Income Distribution Problem in Latin America and the Caribbean*, 149–56.

10. Memo, Visit of President Chiari: President's Talking Paper, June 7, 1962, National Security Files (NSF) Countries, Panama, John F. Kennedy Library; *Living and Working in the Canal Zone*, 9.

11. Anderson, *Frontiers*, 1–4; Donnan and Wilson, *Borders*, 1–7, 12–17, 45–47.

12. Prescott, *Political Frontiers and Boundaries*, 12–14, 36–63.

13. Donnan and Wilson, *Borders*, 107–27; Muldoon, *Identity on the Medieval Irish Frontier*, 1–26.

14. Kemble, *The Panama Route*; Schott, *Rails across Panama*; McGuinness, *Path of Empire*.

15. Arosemena G., *Historia Documental del Canal de Panama*, 162–73; LaFeber, *The Panama Canal*, 16–31.

16. Charles D. Ameringer, "The Panama Canal Lobby of Philippe Bunau-Varilla and William Nelson Cromwell," *American Historical Review* 8 (Fall 1963): 346–63; John Major, "Who Wrote the Hay–Bunau-Varilla Treaty?," DH 8 (Spring 1984): 115–23; LaFeber, *The Panama Canal*, 28–36.

17. Conniff, *Panama and the United States*, 75–80; Lindsay-Poland, *Emperors in the Jungle*, 16–17; Pizzurno Gelós and Araúz, *Estudios sobre el Panamá republicano*, 79–112.

18. LaFeber, *The Panama Canal*, 65–70; Mora, *Acción Comunal*; Pérez and de León, *El Movimienta de Acción Comunal en Panamá*; LaFeber, *The Panama Canal*, 63–65.

19. For program and philosophy of Panameñismo, see Escobar, *Arnulfo Arias o el credo Panameñisto*; Robinson, "Panama for the Panamanians," 157–71. The most comprehensive biography of Arnulfo is Conte-Porras, *Arnulfo Arias Madrid*.

20. For U.S. military figures, see Conn and Fairchild, *The U.S. Army in World War II: Guarding the United States and Its Outposts*, 300–315. For worker statistics in Panama during World

War II, see Darío Carles, *La evolución de la policía de empleo y salarios en la zona del canal y el desarrollo económico de Panamá*.

21. For the wild night life of World War II Panama, see Hampel, *Viva Panama*, 53–55, 73–75, 190–96; Rolando Linares, retired PanCanal worker, interview with author, Balboa, RP, January 11, 2002. On use of special ankle bracelets by prostitutes, Cristina Ramos, interview with author, Curundu, RP, December 30, 2001; Albert Brown, retired Autoridad del Canal de Panamá (ACP) archivist, interview with author, Balboa Heights, RP, November 22, 2001. For rapes, assaults, and manslaughter by U.S. military during World War II, see *Departamento de Relaciones con la Zona del Canal*, vols. 10–22: *Expedientes de la Serie*: "Zona del Canal, Incidentes entre soldados del Ejercito de los Estados Unidos y ciudanos panameños," Archivo del Ministerio de Relaciones Exteriores (AMRE).

22. For Panamanian opposition to "little Canal Zones," see Pearcy, *We Answer Only to God*, 109–32; Hull to Wilson, June 29, 1943, *Foreign Relations of the United States* (FRUS), 1943, vol. 6: *American Republics*, 644–45; Fábrega to Brett, Military Intelligence Division, File 1941–1945, "Reports on Incidents of July 3, 1943 and November 22, 1943," RG 165, NARA; Miguel J. Moreno, former minister of foreign relations, interview with author, Panamá, RP, April 12, 2001; Major, "The Panama Canal Zone," 268–69.

23. "Zonia," from Pal Joey, "New Directions," Mailbox, *Panama American*, July 12, 1950.

24. For analysis of Panama's World War II economic boom, see Biesanz, "The Economy of Panama"; Major, "The Panama Canal Zone," 239–41. For development of the Panamanian middle class, see Biesanz et al., *Materials para el estudio de la clase media en la America Latina*, vol. 4.

25. For Panamanian officials' collusion in vice trades, see Major, "The Panama Canal Zone," 269. For demographic patterns of Panamanian prostitution, see Hyman, *Particularidades*. For Happyland, see Linares, interview with author, Balboa, RP, January 11, 2002; "Storied Nightclub Closes: Happyland's Final Night," *Star and Herald*, January 2, 1959.

26. Arosemena G., *Historia Documental del Canal de Panama*, 191–99.

27. Pearcy, *We Answer Only to God*, 109–37; Acosta, *La influencia de la opinión publica en el rechazo del convenio Filos-Hines de 1947*.

28. Virgilio Sánchez, retired taxi driver, interview with author, San Miguelito, RP, February 3, 2001.

29. For 1951 reorganization, see *Annual Reports of the Governor of the Panama Canal*, 1951, 1–12; "Canal Company to Go on Break Even Basis with Fundamental Changes in Fiscal Status," *Panama Canal Review*, February 1, 1952, 1.

30. Pippin, *The Remón Era*. For U.S. perceptions of Remón's approach to negotiations, see Dulles, Memorandum for the President, Subject: State Visit of President Remon of Panama, September 25, 1953, Folder Panama (2), Ann Whitman File, Dwight D. Eisenhower Library.

31. See 1955 Treaty of Mutual Understanding in Arosemena G., *Historia Documental del Canal de Panama*, 310–28.

32. For an account of the 1955 treaty's impact on U.S.-Panamanian–West Indian matrix, see Conniff, *Black Labor*, 145–53. On changes to the Spanish curriculum in "colored schools," see "The Canal Zone Colored Schools, 1905–1955" and "Canal Zone Latin American Schools, 1955–1974," in Phi Delta Kappa, *Schooling in the Panama Canal Zone*, 101–34.

33. For Dulles's views on Suez and Panama, see Dulles to Eisenhower, September 28, 1956, Folder Panama (3), Ann Whitman File, Dwight D. Eisenhower Library. For Panamanian view of Operation Sovereignty, see Castillero Reyes, *Raices de las independencía de Panamá*, 116–19.

34. For U.S. Caribbean Command's account of riots, see Headquarters, Department of the Army, Office of Deputy Chief of Staff for Military Operations, Situation Report, November 4, 1959, White House Office, Dwight D. Eisenhower Library.

35. Headquarters, Department of the Army, Office of Deputy Chief of Staff for Military Operations, Situation Report, November 4, 1959, White House Office, Dwight D. Eisenhower Library. For placement of barbed-wire barricades, see Caribbean Command, Subject: Background Information concerning Recent Incidents in Panama, November 13, 1959, White House Office, Dwight D. Eisenhower Library.

36. For history of the fence, see "Fact Sheet: Fences between the Canal Zone and the Republic of Panama," in Memorandum from Leber to Whitman, March 13, 1962, Panama Canal Company, Washington Office Subject Files, RG 185, NARA; Memorandum: Canal Zone Boundary Fence, February 7, 1962, Folder Panama, 1/62–6/62, White House Congressional Staff Files, Folder: CO232 Panama, John F. Kennedy Library. For popular reaction to the fence, see Jules DuBois, "Panama Bears Tension Signs," *Chicago Sunday Tribune*, December 20, 1959.

37. For crisis of U.S.–Latin American relations in the late 1950s and early 1960s provoked by Cuban Revolution, see Rabe, *Eisenhower and Latin America*; Rabe, *The Most Dangerous Area in the World*. For insensitivity of Zone officials during the crisis, see Memorandum: Summary of Number of Reports Pertaining to the Causes of Dissatisfaction with United States in Panama and Suggestion for Improving Relations with Panama, Folder Panama Canal, White House Office, Dwight D. Eisenhower Library.

38. For CZ government's praise of U.S. actions during 1964 riots, see Fleming to Newcomer, January 29, 1964, Records Relating to the January 1964 Disturbances, Folder REP 6–4–I SEC-A2, RG 185, NARA.

39. Porter to Corrigan, Subject: Use of "Avenue of the Martyrs" in ads in *La Estrella de Panamá* and the *Star and Herald*, June 30, 1965, Folder REP6, Panama Canal Company, Internal Security Office, RG 185, NARA. For a similar process in the French and British empires, see Robert Aldrich, "Putting the Colonies on the Map," in Chafer and Sackur, *Promoting the Colonial Idea*, 211–23; Brenda S. A. Yeoh, "Street Names in Colonial Singapore," *Geographical Review* 82.3 (1992): 313–22.

40. For the Panamanian financial crisis after the riots, see Jorden, *Panama Odyssey*, 63–66. For Panamanian economic dependency on the Canal Zone and the United States, see LaFeber, *The Panama Canal*, 101–2.

41. Martínez, *Border Peoples*, 3–10.

42. "Southern Command: Off-Limits Order: Social Consequences," O'Meara to Fleming, January 16, 1964, Records Relating to the January 1964 Disturbances, Folder Military Personnel Directives, RG 185, NARA; William Edwards, retired U.S. sergeant, interview with author, Tampa, Florida, August 14, 2001; Rolando Sterling Arango, Panamanian professor, interview with author, Albrook, RP, May 12, 2001; Virgili, *Shorn Women*.

43. "Storm over Panama," *Time*, January 15, 1964, 55. For analysis of the "Lost Treaties of 1967," see LaFeber, *The Panama Canal*, 113–16.

44. No smoking gun exists for the U.S. role in the October 1968 coup, though it is hard to imagine any important Guard actions without Southern Command's knowledge or approval. Former U.S. ambassador to Panama Jack Hood Vaughn, interview with author, May 18, 1999, Austin, Texas; "Political Refugee Problem in Canal Zone," Leber to Porter, December 12, 1968, Internal Security Office, RG 185, NARA. For examples of Panamanian political refugees in CZ during 1945 and 1951 crises, see "Problems Presented by the Political Opponents of the Government of Panama Taking Up Residence within the Canal Zone," January 1, 1945, Butler to Stettinius, FRUS, 1945, 9: 1239–45; "New Administration in Panama," May 10, 1951, Bennett to Milller, FRUS, 1951, 2: 1549–54; Scranton, *The Noriega Years*, 117–29.

45. "Panamanian Political Refugees in Canal Zone," Parker to Snyder, April 15, 1971,

Folder C/REP4–1, Internal Security Office, RG 185, NARA; Rangel M., "Ceremonia a Rio Hato," in Comentarios Vespertinos, El Panamá America, August 24, 1970.

46. For critiques of the Torrijos regime, see Koster and Sánchez, In the Time of the Tyrants; Guevara Mann, Panamanian Militarism. For a more sympathetic take on Torrijos, see Priestley, Military Government and Popular Participation in Panama; Harding, Military Foundations of Panamanian Politics; Subject: Fence along Fourth of July Avenue, Parker to Rogers, August 1, 1972, Folder C/REP/6B Panama-U.S. Relations, Internal Security Office, RG 185, NARA.

47. Subject: Meeting with General Torrijos over Removal of Fence along CZ/RP Border, August 6, 1972, Folder C/REP/6B Panama-U.S. Relations, Internal Security Office, RG 185, NARA.

48. For the Ford administration's objectives and frustrations in negotiations, see National Security Council Meeting, December 2, 1975, Folder Meetings and Memorandums, 10/1/75–12/31/75, NSF Files, Gerald R. Ford Library. For the importance of the Canal in the 1976 presidential campaign, see Hogan, The Panama Canal in American Politics, 114–31.

49. Fox and Huguet, Population and Urban Trends in Central America and Panama, 176, 190. For winding down of CZ, see Major, "The Panama Canal Zone," 329–57.

50. Fox and Huguet, Population and Urban Trends in Central America and Panama, 174–78. For historical background to demographic shifts, see Jaen Juarez, La poblacion del istmo de Panama, 9–15, 20–48, 474–88.

51. For rising crime rates in terminal cities in postwar era, see Pearcy, We Answer Only to God, 59–161.

52. Fernando Manfredo Jr., "Panama y el Canal Interoceano: La difícil a tarea de desmatelar el enclave colonial de la Zona del Canal con un minimo de costo social y sin afectar la efeciencia de la seguridad de la via interoceanica," Revista Lotería 430 (May–June 2000): 17–31; Jaen Juarez, La población del istmo de Panama, 474–88.

53. For problems in the red zones during World War II, see U.S. Army, Caribbean Defense Command, Historical Section, Control of Venereal Disease and Prostitution 1945.

54. For U.S acknowledgment of the "gate girl" problem, see "Community Relations—U.S. Army Caribbean (USAC): Incidents Leading to Unfavorable Reaction in Panamanian Press," December 1, 1956, RG 338, NARA, addressing Panamanian view of USO dances as barely disguised prostitution operations. For figures on intermarriage of Panamanians and U.S. service personnel, see Estadistica Panameñas: Mujeres y Hogares, vols. 5–39. For cultural dimensions of intermarriage, see Krauss, Inside Central America, 247–48.

55. "Home from the States: Zonians Return from Summer Sojourn," Spillway, August 25, 1958: John Carlson, president of the Isthmian Historical Society, interview with author, La Boca, RP, May 30, 2001.

56. "El Valle—Eden-Like, Unspoiled," Panama Canal Review, August 12, 1966: "Santa Clara: Pacific Paradise," Panama Today, March 1968; "Boquete—Retirement Refuge and Land of Eternal Spring," Star and Herald, January 17, 1975.

57. Among the literature most critical of the Zonians are Ernie Pyle, "Americans on the Isthmus," Chicago Tribune, October 3, 1943: Roland Evans and Robert Novak, "Trouble in Panama," Washington Post, January 16, 1960; Trevor Ambrister, "Panama: Why They Hate Us," Saturday Evening Post, March 7, 1964, 68–82; Jan Morris, "A Terminal Case of American Perpetuity," Rolling Stone, June 1, 1976; Theroux, The Old Patagonian Express, 201–30.

58. For this pattern in another colonial environment, see Kennedy, Islands of White.

59. "Cunas Visit Zonians, Zonians Visit Cunas as Isthmian Good Neighbors Swap Calls," Panama Canal Review, October 2, 1953; "Play Ball! The Morti Hydros, the First Cuna Baseball Team in Darien Pose before a Workout," Spillway, March 3, 1967; Howe, A People Who Would Not Kneel, 297–99.

60. Conniff, *Black Labor*; Lewis, *The West Indian in Panama*; Biesanz, "Race Relations in the Canal Zone"; Biesanz and Smith, "Race Relations in Panama and the Canal Zone," *American Journal of Sociology* 57 (March 1952): 7–24; Newton, *The Silver Men*; Westerman, *The West Indian Worker on the Panama Canal*.

61. Conniff, *Black Labor*, 79–121.

62. Price, "White Settlement in the Canal Zone." For the fiftieth anniversary of the CZ, *Panama Canal Review* published a series of articles on the gold and silver towns: "Your Town: Ancon, Canal Zone," October 1, 1954; "Your Town: Diablo Heights, Canal Zone," March 5, 1954; "Your Town: La Boca, Canal Zone," June 5, 1954. See Carew and Berkow, *Carew*, 11–28.

63. Earl Barber, Autoridad del Canal de Panamá archivist, interview with author, Balboa Heights, RP, January 4, 2002.

64. "La Boca, Once Largest C.Z. Town, Will Soon Become Just Another Memory," *Panama Canal Review*, September 6, 1957, 4; Albert Brown, interview with author, Balboa Heights, RP, November 22, 2001. All official documentation supports the uprooting of the West Indian community of La Boca for safety reasons, though several former Zonians told me the constant traffic of blacks headed for La Boca through the white town of Balboa may have contributed to the company's decision.

65. For a description of ethnic conflict in La Boca during the construction and Third Lock Project, see "Your Town: La Boca," *Panama Canal Review*, June 4, 1954, 14–16. For its new transformation into a "gold town," see "La Boca: New Town Rising on Old Site," *Panama Canal Review*, March 6, 1959, 13.

66. For the 1946–49 origins of the School of the Americas and its mission, see Barber and Ronning, *Internal Security and Military Power*; Gill, *The School of the Americas*. For internal conflicts at the school, see "Incident Involving Ecuadorean and Peruvian Military Personnel on May 17, 1957," May 27, 1957, File 335: Investigation (Criminal Line of Duty), RG 338, NARA; "Altercation between Chilean and Argentine Cadets, November 12, 1962," November 24, 1962, U.S. Army Caribbean, File 335: Investigation, Criminal Investigations, RG 338, NARA; "Cadets Gang Up on RP Cop," *Panama American*, April 16, 1955; "Off-Limits Violations Reports," December 1, 1960, section 3; "Caribbean School Trainees Fight with Panamanian National Guard and Other Cadets," U.S. Army Caribbean, File 305: Off Limits Violations, July–December 1960, RG 338, NARA.

67. "Tireless Chinese Gardeners Provide Fresh Vegetables for the People of the Zone," *Panama Canal Review*, January 6, 1956; "Chinese Gardeners Keep Zone Housewives Well Stocked," *Panama Canal Review*, June 15, 1958. For U.S.-Chinese accommodation in Panama, see Sui, *Memories of a Future Home*, 113–35; Aihwa Ong, "On the Edge of Empires: Flexible Citizenship among Chinese in Diaspora, *positions* 1.3 (1993): 745–48.

68. For an overview of the U.S. military in Panama, see De Mena, *The Era of the U.S Army Installations in Panama*. For land area percentages, see *Annual Report of the Panama Canal Company and the Canal Zone Government 1968*, 147.

69. For insights into civilian-military hostility in the Canal Zone, see antagonistic letters in the Mailbox section of *Panama American*, February 17, 1946; July 11, 1946; July 26, 1946; September 9, 1946; May 5, 1950; July 15, 1950; July 22, 1950; July 27, 1950; July 29, 1950; July 8, 1953; July 13, 1953; July 18, 1953; March 5, 1965; also see "Los Zonians son los que deben irse dicen evacuados de Panama," *Panama Américana*, February 3, 1964, in which military dependents evacuated after the 1964 riots criticize Zonians.

70. In 1960, for example, out of a civilian population of 42,112, 30,623 lived in the Balboa District and 11,499 lived in the Cristobal District (*Annual Report of the Panama Canal Company and*

the Canal Zone Government, 1960, 34). Lucas Palumbo, retired U.S. high school teacher, interview with author, Piña, RP, December 21, 2001; Susan L. Stabler, "The Other Side: The Way It Is," *Panama Canal Review*, October 1, 1980.

71. Edgardo Tirado, retired CZ police officer, interview with author, Amador, RP, May 10, 2001; Captain Joseph Chamberlain, PanCanal pilot, interview with author, Piña, RP, December 22, 2001: "Cristobal High Baton Twirlers Gather for the Palm Bowl," *Spillway*, November 26, 1965.

72. Sue Stabler, retired school teacher, interview with author, Cardenas, RP, April 28, 2001. For Zone humor on this rivalry, see "You Know You're a CZ Brat If . . . ," www.czbrats.com. For travel notices between coasts, see Society News in *Panama American* and the *Star and Herald*, 1941–68.

73. Robert Taht, retired DOD worker, interview with author, Balboa, RP, April 29, 2001; Josephine Castro, retired PanCanal worker, interview with author, Sarasota, Florida, July 20, 2001.

74. *General Population Characteristics, Canal Zone 1970 Census*; Knapp and Knapp, *Red, White, and Blue Paradise*, 127–28; "Rodriquez's and Smith's Outnumber All Other Names on Panama Canal Rolls," *Panama Canal Review*, November 5, 1954.

75. For the best source of men's and women's social club activity in the postwar Zone, see *Panama Canal Review*, 1946–79; *This Month in Panama*, 1948–80; *Canal Record*, 1946–79. Some examples: "The Panama Reel and Rod Club's First International Marlin and Sailfish Tournament," *Panama Canal Review*, July 8, 1953, 9–22; "Panama Hunting among the Best," *Panama Canal Review*, May 1966, 20–22; "Skydiving Is Not for Daredevils," *Panama Canal Review*, September 12, 1962; "Atlantic Side Yachtsman Do Their Sailing in Blue Water," *Panama Canal Review*, July 3, 1959, 8–9.

76. May, *Homeward Bound*; Stoler, "Making Empire Respectable"; Stoler, "Sexual Affronts and Racial Frontiers"; Hyam, *Empire and Sexuality*.

77. Kennedy, *Islands of White*, 128–48; James Lonsdale, "Mau Maus of the Mind," *Journal of African History* 31 (1990): 393–421; James McDougal, "Savage Wars? Codes of Violence in Algeria, 1830s–1990s," *Third World Quarterly* 26 (2005): 117–31; "Ama-Zonians Kim, Becky, and Janice Gilliam at the Atlantic Imperial Equestrian Show," *Panama American*, February 3, 1968.

78. For a physical description of the Panama City–Canal Zone border in the early 1960s, I am indebted to Richard Koster, a novelist, journalist, and former U.S. Army Intelligence officer, for use of his unpublished manuscript on the 1964 Riots, and to Osvaldo Jordan Romeros, who walked with me along the Avenida de los Martires several times, pointing out the locations of various landmarks and describing those that are now gone.

79. Rodrigo Mendoza, retired Panamanian laborer, interview with author, Panama City, May 5, 2002.

80. The extensive photographic record of the 1964 Panama Riots provides the best images of Fourth of July Avenue and adjoining regions of the Panama-Zone border, Records Relating to the January 1964 Disturbances, Folder: Photographic Collection, RG 185, NARA. For borderland languages, see Alteager, *An Other Tongue*.

81. Thomas Carey, former Zonian, interview with author, Balboa, RP, May 15–17, 2001; *Canal Zone Code*, vols. 1–3.

82. See Canal Zone Maintenance Division budgets in the series *Annual Reports of the Governor of the Canal Zone*, 1904–51; *Annual Reports of the Panama Canal Company and the Canal Zone Government*, 1952–1979; "CZ Communities Are in a Fog When Spray Truck Makes Rounds," *Panama Canal Review*, July 2, 1954, 13. For high Zonian cancer rates, see Todd Robberson, "In Panama's 'Zone,' Fears Flourish," *Dallas Morning News*, October 14, 1999.

83. For the popularity of Panamanian food, see "Cocina Corner," a daily feature in the Zonian newspaper *Panama American*, 1940–65, which featured Panamanian recipes and cuisine; "Panamanian Dishes Tingle Taste Buds," *Panama Canal Review*, May 1966, 12–15. At Panama Canal Societies of Florida, Texas, and California reunions, retired Zonians revel in consuming and sharing their favorite Panamanian dishes.

84. Kenneth Underwood, retired CZ police officer, interview with author, La Boca, RP, May 5, 2001; Rex Raspberry, interview with author, Balboa, RP, March 6, 2001; Sue Stabler, interview with author, Cardenas, RP, April 28, 2001.

85. Rigoberto Cardenas, interview with author, Amador, RP, March 10, 2001.

86. William H. Pohl, retired CZ police officer, interview with author, Diablo, RP, April 18, 2001.

87. Panama officially switched to driving on the right on April 1, 1943, after a rash of military-civilian accidents. See "Panama Moves to U.S Traffic System," *Star and Herald*, April 2, 1943. For the taxi driver's quote, Poftirio Sánchez, interview with author, Panama City, February 23, 2001.

88. Monsignor Ignacio Martinez, Panamanian priest, interview with author, Panama City, March 12, 2001.

89. William Edwards, interview with author, Sarasota, Florida, November 27, 2001.

90. For scholarly analysis of the state's role in the deportment of bodies, see "Docile Bodies," in Foucault, *Discipline and Punish*.

91. Sam Edwards, Autoridad de Canal de Panamá archivist, interview with author, Balboa Heights, RP, November 22, 2001.

92. "Rioters Arraigned in Court," *Panama American*, December 5, 1959.

93. Edgardo Tirado, interview with author, Amador, RP, May 10, 2001. For identity and cultural conflicts along another contested border see Gonzales-Berry and Maciel, *The Contested Homeland*.

94. "Zone Court Warns Blind Beggar," *Panama American*, January 12, 1968.

95. *History of the Canal Zone Police*, 20, 33–35; "5 Agricultores Arrestados en la Zona," *Critica*, March 12, 1965; "Over 40 RP Men Nabbed for Cutting Timber," *Panama American*, March 18, 1965'; "Three More Tree Cutters Nabbed by CZ Cops," *Panama American*, March 25, 1965; "Water Routes Clear Again for Farmers," *Spillway*, December 24, 1964, 1, 4: George Wheeler, retired CZ police officer, interview with author, Piña, RP, December 21, 2001.

96. *Government of Canal Zone v. Jose Leocadio Meña*, Case no. 4857, June 3, 1958, District Court Records of the Canal Zone, RG 21, WNRC. For the tradition of rural squatters in Latin America, see Collier, *Squatter Settlements and the Incorporation of Migrants into Urban Life*.

97. Tirado, interview with author, Amador, RP, May 10, 2001. U.S. District Court for the CZ docket books, part of RG 21 in WRNC, contain hundreds of cases of Panamanians charged with vagrancy, trespassing, or loitering in CZ during the postwar era. For problems of ethnic laborers in other colonial states, see Bernstein, *Constructing Boundaries*; *General Population Characteristics, Canal Zone 1970 Census*.

98. For the Mango Wars, see "Young Mango Picker Convicted," *Panama American*, May 24, 1950; "Mango Fever," *Panama Canal Review*, June 12, 1952, 13–14. For "sport" involved in border policing, see Andreas, *Border Games*; Guidice, *Hands of Stone*, 21–34.

99. For a court case over deporting Panamanians from the Zone, see *Government of Canal Zone v. Fermin Jesus Gonzalez T.*, Case no. 76–20-c, December 15, 1978, District Court Records of the Canal Zone, RG 21, WNRC. For CZ police shoving Panamanian activists off the "U.S. sidewalks," see Noriega and Eisner, *America's Prisoner*, 19–22; Roberto Pérez, Panamanian engineer, interview with author, Panama City, June 1, 2001.

100. Antonio Stanziola, Panamanian businessman, interview with author, Panama City, March 23, 2001.

101. Donnan and Wilson, *Borders*, 100–105; Dinges, *Our Man in Panama*, 61–66.

102. "Panama to Fight Canal Commissary," *New York Times*, July 2, 1914; Major, "The Panama Canal Zone," 56–61; McCullough, *Path between the Seas*, 114–17; Leonard, "The Commissary in United States–Panamanian Relations."

103. For origins of Panamanian elites' business orientation as well as their agricultural holdings, see Figueroa Navarro, *Domino y Sociedad en el Panama Colombiano*; Szok, "La ultima gaviota." For the commissary-control provisions of the accords, see "1955 Treaty of Mutual Understanding," in Arosemena G., *Historia Documental del Canal de Panama*, 321–24.

104. Knapp and Knapp, *Red, White, and Blue Paradise*, 183–84; Donald Philips, retired Pan-Canal worker, interview with author, Balboa, RP, December 22, 2001.

105. Winston Bryant, retired PanCanal worker, interview with author, Ancon, RP, March 29, 2001. For inequality in gold and silver wages prior to the 1955 treaty, see "Summary of Number of Reports, Pertaining to the Causes of Dissatisfaction with the United States, in Panama and Suggestion for Improving Relations with Panama," Folder Panama Canal [March 1956–April 1960], White House Office, Dwight D. Eisenhower Library.

106. Earl Barber, interview with author, Balboa Heights, RP, November 22, 2001; Pablo Prieto, retired CZ police officer, interview with author, Balboa Heights, RP, April 25, 2001; James Reid, interview with author, Balboa, RP, April 30, 2001. For President Arias's boast to President Eisenhower that he could easily acquire U.S. liquor from friends in the Zone, see "Memorandum of a Conversation, Ambassador's Residence. Panama City," July 23, 1956, FRUS, 1955–57, 7: 278–79. For the commissary purchases of President Anastasio Somoza of Nicaragua, see "Nicaraguan President Somoza Visits the Canal Zone," *New York Times*, November 20, 1953.

107. Pablo Prieto, interview with author, Balboa Heights, RP, April 25, 2001.

108. For insight into the changing problem of drugs in the CZ, see Internal Security Report: "Growing Narcotics Problem in the Canal Zone," June 3, 1971, and "Inter-Agency Narcotics Team," July 28, 1972, Folder C/LAW 18: Narcotics vol. 1, Internal Security Office, RG 185, NARA; *History of Canal Zone Police*, 31–32. U.S. District Court for the Canal Zone criminal docket books, part of RG 21 records at WNRC, contain hundreds of cases of mostly Panamanian but also U.S. drug convictions in the Zone for the postwar period, with a marked increase of cases in the 1970s. For a contrary view on Vietnam-era military drug use, see Kuzmarov, *The Myth of an Addicted Army*.

109. "Statement of Lt. Col. James M. Krebs, Chief, Drug Policy Branch, Department of the Army," in *Alcohol and Drug Use in the Canal Zone*, H.R. 8471 and H.R. 10581, in *Panama Canal Oversight*, 253–58; Chief Olotebiliquina to Merrill, May 23, 1949, File 250.471, RG 338, NARA.

110. On easy access to drugs in Panama, Nina Kosik, retired DOD worker, Herman Wilkerson, retired PanCanal worker, Tom Carey, and Captain Tom McLean, PanCanal pilot, interviews with author, Balboa, RP, January 11, 2002; MacDonald, *Mountain High, White Avalanche*, 98–118; Walker, *Drugs in the Western Hemisphere*, 229–50. For National Guard involvement in drugs, see "Narcotics Control Action Plan and Country Enforcement Plan," December 12, 1972, Folder: Narcotics (Policy and General Correspondence), Panama Canal Company, Internal Security Office, RG 185, NARA.

111. Murillo, *The Noriega Mess*, 137–41, 381–88, 399–402.

112. Carter, *Keeping Faith*, 160–64. For an overview of the treaty and ratification fight, see LaFeber, *The Panama Canal*, 158–92; Moffett, *The Limits of Victory*. For negative Panamanian views, see Bernal, *Los tratados Carter-Torrijos*; Pérez-Venero, *Before the Five Frontiers*; Greene, "The Country with Five Frontiers."

113. Wheaton, *Panama Invaded*; Méndez, *Panamá*; Soler, *La Invasión de los estados unidos a Panamá*; Louis Henken, "The Invasion of Panama under International Law," *Columbia Journal of Transnational Law* 29 (1991): 293–317; Independent Commission of Inquiry on the U.S. Invasion of Panama, *The U.S. Invasion of Panama*; Lindsay-Poland, *Emperors in the Jungle*, 138–71; "The End of American Era in Panama," *Washington Post*, December 15, 1999.

Chapter 2: Race and Identity in the Zone-Panama Borderland

1. "Negro Rapes Young American Woman in Midnight Assault," *Panama American*, February 23, 1946.

2. "U.S. Woman Assaulted in Balboa," *Star and Herald*, February 23, 1946; "Engineer Employee Held as Suspect in Zone Rape Case," *Star and Herald*, February 26, 1946; "Criminal Assault Suspect Arraigned," *Star and Herald*, February 27, 1946.

3. "Criminal Assault," *Panama Tribune*, March 3, 1946. For Greaves's comments to his family, see "Rapist Sentenced to Fifty Years in CZ Pen," *Panama American*, April 2, 1946. Gardner's admonition from *Government of Canal Zone v. Lester Leon Greaves*, Case no. 3861, April 2, 1946, from Records Division, Autoridad del Canal de Panamá, Balboa Heights, RP.

4. Daniel G. Blackburn, "Why Race Is Not a Biological Concept," in Lang, *Race and Racism in Theory and Practice*, 3–26; *Census of the Canal Zone; Census of the United States and Outlying Regions, Census of the Canal Zone*, 1910, 29–31; *Manual of Information Concerning Employments for Service on the Isthmus of Panama*, Panama Canal Collection (PCC), Centro de Recursos Tecnícos (CRT), Balboa, RP; *The Blue Book of the Panama Canal*; Personnel Records, Panama Canal Department, Joint Board of Army and Navy, 1903–38, RG 225, NARA; Wade, *Race and Ethnicity in Latin America*, 15.

5. For examples of Manifest Destiny and Social Darwinism, see Senator Albert J. Beveridge's speech to the U.S. Senate, March 3, 1900, *Congressional Record*, 56th Congress, 1st Session, 1900, pt. 1, 704, 710–11; Hunt, *Ideology and U.S. Foreign Policy*, 44–91.

6. Lewis, *The West Indian in Panama*. For the plight of the "silver" Europeans in the CZ, see Donadio, *The Thorns of the Rose*.

7. Mack, *The Land Divided*; DuVal, *And the Mountains Will Move*. For Panamanian tolerance for interracial unions, see Felipe Juan Escobar, "Arnulfo y las razas minoritarias" (1940–41), in Mendoza, *Panamá*.

8. Hunt, *Ideology and U.S. Foreign Policy*, 56–57, 60–61, 66–67, 142. For frontier attitudes toward Panama, see McGuinness, *Path of Empire*, 73–77, 88–90, 123–46. For Zonian certainty that Panamanians could not run the Canal, see *Canal Record* 14 (December 1980): 34–35; Kris Kolesnik, "Panama Canal: The Aftermath," *Canal Record* 16 (September 1981): 14; Ted Scott, "Dateline 1984," *Panama American*, February 12, 1964.

9. For early racist attitudes toward West Indians, see Franck, *Zone Policeman 88*, 11–12, 37–38, 50, 85, 91, 128, 130–31, 167, 176, 193–94, 225.

10. For early Panamanian attitudes toward North Americans, see Blas Tejeira, *Pueblos Perdidos*. For U.S. reluctance to hire Panamanians, see "Native Workers Turned Away," *Star and Herald*, July 14, 1904.

11. "General Population Statistics, Canal Zone," in *1960 Census of U.S. Population*; "General Population Statistics, Canal Zone," in *1970 Census of U.S. Population*; Weber, *The Protestant Ethic and the Spirit of Capitalism*.

12. For a demographic breakdown of postwar Zonians, see "How Do Zonians Work and Play? This Is What They Have to Say," *Panama Canal Review*, February 5, 1954, 1, 15; "Where Do the Zonians Come From?," *Panama Canal Review*, December 3, 1954, 3; "Zonians Reduced

to the Averages," *Panama Canal Review*, March 3, 1961, 6, 7, 17; Clarence McConkey, *The Union Church of the Canal Zone, 1950–1992*, PCC, CRT, Balboa, RP; "Papal Rep Pleads for Parochial School in CZ," *Star and Herald*, September 26, 1949; "Why No Catholic School in the CZ?," Mailbox, *Panama American*, August 11, 1949. For the religious affiliation of the U.S. Canal Zone governors, see Cochez, *Las biografías breves del gobiernadors de la zona del canal*.

13. "Plans for Memorial 25 Years in the Making," *Panama Canal Review*, April 2, 1954; "In a Week-Long Program the Canal Zone Celebrates the Roosevelt Centennial," *Panama Canal Review*, October 3, 1958; "That Glorious Week," *Panama Canal Review*, December 5, 1958; Alejandro Rodríguez, Panamanian schoolteacher, interview with author, Curundu, RP, May 22, 2003.

14. For the 15 percent figure, see "Zonians Reduced to the Averages," *Panama Canal Review*, March 3, 1961, 6–7, 17; "Typical Zonian? Well, He Just Could Be You," *Panama Canal Review*, January 20, 1964, 3; Sam Edwards and Albert Brown, interview with author, Balboa Heights, RP, May 14, 2001.

15. "So Long Pal," Mailbox, *Panama American*, December 2, 1945.

16. For creole-penisulares conflicts, see Burkholder and Johnson, *Colonial Latin America*, 103, 184–85, 314; Cochez, *Las biografías breves del gobiernadors de la zona del canal*; George Wheeler, interview with author, Balboa, RP, January 12, 2008; Walter Boltin, retired Zonian postal worker, interview with author, Balboa, RP, December 12, 2002.

17. Philip Bonk, retired PanCanal engineer, interview with author, Balboa, RP, May 3, 2001. For the Zone's hiring more stateside professionals, see "Typical Zonian? He's Being Revised," *Spillway*, January 22, 1965, 3.

18. Walter Boltin, interview with author, Balboa, RP, December 12, 2001; Sue Stabler, interview with author, Cardenas, RP, June 5, 2001.

19. Walter Boltin, interview with author, Balboa, RP, December 12, 2001.

20. For the importance of these CZ town sites to Zonian identity, see articles on these communities in *Panama Canal Review*, 1953–56.

21. Carl Tuttle, retired PanCanal electrician, interview with author, Balboa, RP, June 2, 2002; Anne Tiblier, wife of PanCanal pilot Captain Tiblier, interview with author, La Boca, RP, August 18, 2008.

22. Barbara Jackson and Joanne Kent, Zonian wives, interview with author, Gamboa, RP, April 28, 2001; Henry Twohy, retired CZ police officer, interview with author, Balboa, RP, May 8, 2001; Bud Kelleher, retired PanCanal worker, interview with author, Balboa, RP, May 3, 2001.

23. Richard Koster, interview with author, Panama City, RP, May 14, 2001; Carl Posey, "The Bittersweet Memory That Was the Canal Zone," *Smithsonian*, November 1, 1991, 6; Pablo Prieto, interview with author, Balboa Heights, RP, March 10, 2002.

24. Edgardo Tirado, interview with author, Amador, RP, April 23, 2001. For the Klan that did exist in the CZ in the 1920s, see Haas, KKK, 59–63. For stereotypes of redneck Zonians, see Antonio Sucre, "Los Afortunados Zonians, Una Neuva Raza," *Panamá America*, May 8, 1958; cartoon in Weeks and Gunson, *Panama*, 27.

25. DuBois, *Danger over Panama*, 346–49: Ealy, *Yanqui Politics and the Isthmian Canal*, 82–92; Knapp and Knapp, *Red, White, and Blue Paradise*, 173–78; Norman A. Werner, "Remembering Bilgray's," *Panama Canal Review*, October 1, 1980.

26. Theresa Novey, Panamanian wife and businesswoman, interview with author, Panama City, April 12, 2001.

27. "Your New Zone Clubhouses and Theatres," PCC, CRT. For housing improvements from wooden to cinder block construction, see William Homa, U.S. construction contractor, interview with author, La Boca, RP, June 4, 2001; "Bids for Converting Atlantic Side Equipment

to 60 Cycles Will Be Advertised During August," *Panama Canal Review*, August 5, 1955; "First Domestic Appliances in Canal Zone Homes Converted to 60 Cycles," *Panama Canal Review*, July 6, 1956. For air-conditioning's debut in the Zone, see "Air Conditioning Booms in Zone—Is Pleasant—Needs Caution," *Panama Canal Review*, November 6, 1959; Knapp and Knapp, *Red, White, and Blue Paradise*, 42–44, 91–92, 179–81.

28. "Panama after Dark," "Carnivals and Fairs," and "Sports in Panama," *This Month in Panama*, November 1965. For background on night life, Art Pollack, PanCanal worker and musician, interview with author, Balboa, RP, June 3, 2001.

29. Zone officials in "Zonians Reduced to Averages," *Panama Canal Review*, March 3, 1961, claimed 20 percent of U.S. inhabitants spoke Spanish, but Panamanians and Zonians dispute this. Most place the number of fluent speakers at less than 5 percent. See also "So You Want to Learn Spanish?," *Panama Canal Review*, January 6, 1961, 10.

30. James Reid, interview with author, Balboa, RP, May 14, 2001.

31. For the U.S. obsession with racial separation, see Lamar and Thompson, *The Frontier in History*; Meyer, *As Long as They Don't Move Next Door*; McGirr, *Suburban Warriors*.

32. Panameño, "Geography Was God's Gift," Mailbox, *Panama American*, May 12, 1946.

33. Lt. Ecm (USNR), "Think This One Over," Mailbox, *Panama American*, December 12, 1945.

34. For changing attitudes toward race in postwar era, see Borstelmann, *The Cold War and the Color Line*; Von Eschen, *Race against Empire*; "J'Accuse," Mailbox, *Panama American*, September 28, 1946.

35. *McSherry Report on Housing and Labor Conditions in the Panama Canal Zone*, June 1, 1947, PCC, CRT. For resistance to report, see "Labor Conditions in the Canal Zone: Personnel Policy Board of Office of the Department of Defense," September 7, 1948, File 220.846/230–741, RG 338, NARA; "United States Government Labor Relations in the Panama Canal Zone," FRUS, 1948, 9: 682–83; W. Tapley Bennett, Memorandum of a Conversation, March 28, 1947, FRUS, 1947, 8: 950–53; Mehaffey to Wood, October 25, 1946, Labor: June–December 1946, PCC, Washington Office Subject Files, RG 185, NARA.

36. John O'Reilly, retired PanCanal worker, interview with author, Balboa, RP, February 12, 2002.

37. Dee Collins, "Agitated," Mailbox, *Panama American*, November 5, 1963; Ruth G. Stuhl, "What Record Shows on Sovereignty in the Zone," *Panama American*, November 5, 1963.

38. Fair Play, "Living Up to the Treaty," Mailbox, *Panama American*, February 20, 1956. "The unfortunate decision by the Canal Zone Administration in 1954 to circumvent the *Brown vs. The Board of Topeka, Kansas* decision handed down by the Supreme Court," and "The main concern of the local [Zone] administration is to maintain a segregated policy despite all the fancy nomenclatures such as 'United States Program' and 'Latin American Program,'" in Philips, Council of Latin American Communities to Rep. Leonor Sullivan, June 21, 1971, Folder: Schools, 1969–71, PCC, Washington Office Subject Files, RG 185, NARA. For continuing references to this deliberate policy, see Fleming to Javits, September 28, 1963, Subject: Segregation and Discrimination in the Canal Zone, Folder: Segregation, 1961–63, PCC, Washington Office Subject Files, RG 185, NARA; Memorandum: Canal Zone School, December 8, 1969, PCC, Washington Office Subject Files, RG 185, NARA.

39. For statistics on Zone school enrollments, including military, civilian, and Panamanian numbers, see DuBois, *Danger over Panama*, 224. For Panama's own racialist legacy, see Rout, *The African Experience in Spanish America*, 273–78; Andrews, *Afro-Latin America*, 137–41, 156–57, 185–89, 203–7.

40. Anderson, *Imagined Communities*, 3. For Panamanian hostility toward Zonians, see

American Mary, Mailbox, *Panama American*, May 5, 1958; Arthur Eggar, retired PanCanal worker, interview with author, Balboa, RP, May 11, 2001.

41. "C.Z. Hobby Clubs Urged to Register with New Employees," *Panama Canal Review*, November 2, 1951, 4.

42. For voluminous coverage of Zone clubs and associations in the postwar era, see *Panama Canal Review*, 1945–79; *Canal Record*, 1945–79; *Spillway*, 1945–79. These groups include the Balboa, Pedro Miguel, Gatun, and Cristobal yacht clubs, Gamboa and Summit Hill golf clubs, Balboa Rod and Reel Club, Tarpon Fishing Club, the San Juan and Los Rios Hunting Clubs, Diablo Spinning Club, Gem and Mineral Society, Diablo Camera Club, and various bottle, stamp, book, and butterfly collecting clubs. For the New York Yankees in Panama, see "Zonians Excited as Yankees Visit the Isthmus for Exhibition Series," *Star and Herald*, February 24, 1947; "Yankees Arrive in Style," *Panama American*, February 27, 1949. Panamanians also flocked to see the Yankees, who ironically were their favorite U.S. baseball team. (With the Panamanian ace relief pitcher Mariano Rivera on the team, Panama's love affair *con los yanquis* continues.)

43. "Hapless Husband Loses Job, Gets Clobbered by Wife," *Panama American*, May 5, 1956; "Wife Stabs Hubby Who Said Gravy Was Thin," *Panama American*, October 11, 1956; "Wife Asks for Divorce from Messy Mate Who Didn't Bathe," *Panama American*, May 18, 1956; "Pervert Inquiry Gets Go Ahead in the Senate," *Panama American*, May 24, 1950; "Estonian Woman Who Knows Soviet Horrors Tells Tale Locally," *Panama American*, February 17, 1952.

44. Jack Love, retired PanCanal worker, interview with author, Balboa, RP, May 11, 2001; Neil Waddell and Ed Cairns, "Identity Preference in Northern Ireland," *Political Psychology* 12 (June 1991): 205–13; A. M. Gallagher and S. Dunn, "Community Relations in Northern Ireland," in Stringer and Robinson, *Social Attitudes in Northern Ireland*.

45. For Zonian climatic health fears, see George Eugene, "Effects of the Tropics on the White Man Having Special Reference to Conditions in the Panama Canal Zone," January 1920, PCC, CRT; *Manual of Information Concerning Employments for Service on the Isthmus of Panama*. For employee vacation policy, see *Canal Zone Employee Handbook 1952*, PCC, CRT.

46. Tom Carey, interview with author, Albrook, RP, May 4, 2001; Knapp and Knapp, *Red, White, and Blue Paradise*, 46; Earle, *The Sack of Panamá*; "Just Played Pirates at Old Panamá," *Panama This Month*, June 1960 (memories of these youth events can also be found at www.zonebrats.com). For background on cayuco races of 1954, see Eric Jackson, "Scenes from the Cayuco Races Start," *Panama News*, April 13–26, 2003.

47. For emotions stirred by such activities, see Migdal, *Boundaries and Belonging*; Fried, *The Russians Are Coming!*; "Theater Guild Stars Shine," *Panama Canal Review*, April 12, 1958.

48. Notices for these brands are in the "Commissary Talk" section of the *Panama Canal Review*, 1945–69, CRT. For identity politics in postwar brand names, see Cohen, *A Consumer's Republic*.

49. Discussions of shortages, newly arrived items, prices of meat, canned vegetables, and clothing are in "News of Your Commissary Stores," a monthly feature in the *Panama Canal Review*, 1945–65, CRT, Balboa, RP. For Chinese gardens in the CZ, see "Chinese Gardeners Keep Zone Housewives Well Stocked," *Panama Canal Review*, June 15, 1958.

50. Benshoff and Griffin, *America on Film*; especially Clum, *"He's All Man!"* For motion picture stars, see "Panama Canal Clubhouse Theatres" section in the *Panama Canal Review*, 1941–79.

51. *Riff-Raff* (RKO, 1947) directed by Ted Tetzlaff. For *Riff-Raff* promotional tag lines, see *Panama American* and *Star and Herald*, November 28–December 30, 1947; Bragonier to Marshall, Subject: Local Dailies Add Their Voices to Mrs. De Jan's Protesting of RKO's "Riff Raff" as Injurious to Panama's Reputation, July 22, 1947, 819.4061, RG 59, NARA.

52. "Cunas Visit Zonians, Zonians Visit Cunas as Isthmian Good Neighbors Swap Calls,"

Panama Canal Review, October 2, 1953, 5; "Lock Operator and Wife Specialize in Wild Animal Buying and Training," *Panama Canal Review*, June 6, 1952, 6; "Madden Forest Preserve: A Jewel of a Jungle," *Panama Canal Review*, August 1970.

53. "Albrook Couple Want to Adopt 'Jungle Boy,'" *Panama American*, July 15, 1950; "Cristobal Student Missing in the Jungle Escapes Unscathed," *Panama American*, February 24, 1956; SCTV schedule for Tarzan Theatre listings in *Panama American* and the *Panama Canal Review*, 1955–68. "It's a Wonderful World for Boys," *Panama Canal Review*, July 5, 1957; on a similar theme, see "Of Birds, Babies, and a Boa," *Panama Canal Review*, May 5, 1961.

54. For the Zone's Bellamite structure, see Knapp and Knapp, *Red, White, and Blue Paradise*, 4–6, 30–34, 74–76. For the low rents and services deductions, see "New Employee Statement," *Spillway*, November 24, 1967, 4; George Gershow, retired CZ police officer, interview with author, Balboa, RP, May 19, 2001; Rex Raspberry, retired Gorgas Hospital nurse, interview with author, Balboa, RP, April 23, 2001; Daniel Cooper, retired U.S. Army sergeant, interview with author, Curundu, RP, August 3, 2002; "Mount Hope Printing Plant Ends Era of Commissary Books," *Panama Canal Review*, November 7, 1952.

55. For the CZ "socialist" lifestyle, see Posey, "The Bittersweet Memory"; Fed Up, "Keep Your Socialist Lifestyle," Mailbox, *Panama American*, April 30, 1951; Clarence McClonkey, "Leaving Never-Never Land," *Christian Century*, October 5, 1977, 869–71; "Socialism in Panama, a Historic Success," *Boquete Panama Guide*, April 19, 2011, http://www.boqueteguide .com/?p=6267; For examples of employee dismissals for "moral" offenses, see Folders on Employee Misconduct, PCC, Washington Office Subject Files, RG 185, NARA; "Governor Holds Meeting with Civic Councils," *Panama Canal Review*, January 1, 1954.

56. "1952 Brings Income Tax Problems to Forefront for Canal Zone Employees," *Panama Canal Review*, January 4, 1952, 7.

57. Knapp and Knapp, *Red, White, and Blue Paradise*, 99–116, 117–25; Tom Carey, interview with author, Balboa, RP, May 4, 2001; Nina Kosik, interview with author, Balboa, RP, November 8, 2001; Lucas Palumbo, interview with author, Piña, RP, May 10, 2002.

58. Rex Raspberry, interview with author, Balboa, RP, April 23, 2001; "WCTU Dept. (Gamboa Division)," Mailbox, *Panama American*, December 17, 1945; Joseph Chamberlain, interview with author, Piña, RP, May 10, 2002; Captain Anthony Tiblier, PanCanal pilot, interview with author, La Boca, RP, August 5, 2006. For more on pilot drinking, see Gaines and Mile, *Piloting the Panama Canal*; William Bliven, interview with author, Cardenas, RP, May 14, 2001; Richard Knowlton and Virginia Berridge, "Constructing Imperialism and Sobriety," *Drugs: Education, Prevention and Policy* 15.5 (2008): 439–50. For postwar U.S. drinking in a larger context, see Rotskoff, *Love on the Rocks*.

59. On Zonian proclivity for complaining, see "Second Generation Zonians" Mailbox, *Panama American*, May 6, 1956. For Zonians as perpetual gripers, see Biesanz and Biesanz, *People of Panama*, 77–78; Arthur Eggar, interview with author, Balboa, RP, May 11, 2001; William Hannah, interview with author, Balboa, RP, July 3, 2007. For Zonian hatred of the State Department, see William Bliven, retired PanCanal employee, interview with author, Cardenas, RP, May 14, 2001.

60. For "herrenvolk egalitarianism" in other colonial settings, see Frederickson, *White Supremacy*; Pattel-Gray, *The Great White Flood*; Rivett, *Immigration*

61. For Zonian "egalitarianism," see Knapp and Knapp, *Red, White, and Blue Paradise*, 117–25; Peter Moreland, U.S. shipping agent, interview with author, Piña, RP, January 5, 2006; Tom Carey, interview with author, Balboa, RP, May 4, 2002; George Gershow, interview with author, Balboa, RP, May 19, 2002.

62. Joseph Chamberlain, interview with author, Piña, RP, May 10, 2002; "Pilots in the Mak-

ing," *Panama Canal Review*, February 7, 1959, 8; Captain Tom McLean, interview with author, Margarita, RP, January 5, 2004.

63. Edgardo Tirado, interview with author, Amador, RP, April 12, 2001.

64. Biesanz and Biesanz, *People of Panama*, 231–35; Knapp and Knapp, *Red, White, and Blue Paradise*, 128–31, 140; "Zonians Reduced to the Averages," *Panama Canal Review*, March 3, 1961, 6. For the overall structure of CZ employment, see "Salary Increases and Job Classification Categories for Panama Canal Company and the Canal Zone Government, 1958," Roberts to Whitman, October 13, 1957, PCC, Washington Office Subject Files, RG 185, NARA; 1940 and 1979 workforce stats in Folder: Employee Work Force, January–June 1979, PCC, Washington Office Subject Files, RG 185, NARA.

65. For nationalist attitudes of Panamanian students, see Goldrich, *Sons of the Establishment*; Goldrich, *Radical Nationalism*. For an *interiorano* view of the CZ and Panamanian bourgeoisie, see Gudeman, *Relationships, Residence, and the Individual*; Osvaldo Jordan, Panamanian professor, interview with author, Chorrera, RP, April 12, 2001.

66. For U.S. racial categorizing of Panamanian defendants, see District Court Records of the Canal Zone, 1904–65, RG 21, WNRC. Authorities dropped racial categories after 1965. For French and British colonists' misreading of native reality, see Marston, *The Politics of Education in Colonial Algeria and Kenya*; Baussant, *Pieds-noirs*.

67. 1961 *Canal Zone Holiday Calendar*; Spencer, *Panama Folklore*; "Carnaval en la Via España," *Panamá América*, February 25, 1968; "9 Girls Seeking Crown as Queen of Atlantic Side Carnaval," *Spillway*, January 21, 1966; "Carnavales y Ferias," *Panama Canal Review en Español*, November 1965, 8–9, 22, 30–31.

68. Patricia Markun, "Panama's Dances Intrigue the Gringo," *Panama This Month*, March 12, 1962; "United States Participation in the Chorrera Fair," *Spillway*, May 6, 1966, 4; "Everybody's Doing It: Dig That Crazy Cumbia," *Panama This Month*, June 1960; "Canal Zone College Chorus Tours Chiriqui," *Spillway*, May 20, 1966, 4; Francisco Velásquez, retired Panamanian civil engineer, interview with author, Quarry Heights, Panama City, RP, May 13, 2001.

69. Pratt, *Imperial Eyes*, 201–8; McAlister, *Epic Encounters*, 16.

70. For exoticizing native cultures with local participation, see Renée Alexander Kraft, "¡Los gringos vienen! (The Gringos Are Coming!): Female Respectability and the Politics of Congo Tourist Presentations in Portobelo, Panama," *Transforming Anthropology* 16 (April 2008): 20–31. For a "tourist" view of foreign cultures, see Strain, *Public Places, Private Journeys*; José Menéndez Pereira, Panamanian lawyer, interview with author, Panama City, April 21, 2001.

71. Mary Louise Pratt, "Arts of the Contact Zone," 91 *Profession* (1991): 33–40; "Gringos Warmly Welcomed by Peasants of Panama," *This Month in Panama*, April 1957. Among Zonian archaeology enthusiasts embraced by Panamanians were Karl Curtis, Philip Dade, and Miles DuVal. Rabbi Nathan Witkin and Reverend William Willard also received kudos for their charitable work in the republic. Evelyn Rigby Moore helped the University of Panama organize its library, and Dean Glen Murphy of the CZ College recruited numerous working-class Panamanian students to his institution in the 1960s–1970s who later attended universities in the United States.

72. Knapp and Knapp, *Red, White, and Blue Paradise*, 126–27; Nina Kosik, interview with author, Balboa, RP, November 8, 2001; Biesanz and Biesanz, *People of Panama*, 234, 311–14. For insights into a broad range of interracial marriages, see Breger and Hill, *Cross-Cultural Marriage*; Romano, *Intercultural Marriages*.

73. John Morales, retired DOD worker, interview with author, Balboa, RP, May 5, 2002. For racism against Panamanians, Latin Americans, and mixed-race children, see Biesanz and Biesanz, *People of Panama*, 222–23, 311–14; Knapp and Knapp, *Red, White, and Blue Paradise*,

126–28, 156–59. For the plight of mixed-race peoples in a larger context, see DaCosta, *Making Multiracials.*

74. Frank and Angela Lee Azcarrga, retired PanCanal employees and business owners, interview with author, Panama, RP, August 15, 2004. For analysis of U.S.-Panamanian marriages in the early postwar period, see John Biesanz, "Inter-American Marriages on the Isthmus of Panama," *Social Forces* 29 (December 1950): 159–63; John Biesanz, "Adjustment of Interethnic Marriages on the Isthmus of Panama," *American Sociological Review* 16 (December 1951): 38–45; Clarence McNeece, retired PanCanal worker, interview with author, Balboa, RP, April 12, 2001.

75. "Johnson and Scales Arraigned in Panama for Lux Double Murder," *Panama American,* May 8, 1943.

76. Lloyd and Barbara Kent, retired PanCanal worker and wife, interview with author, Gamboa, RP, April 5, 2001.

77. "Johnson and Scales Had Plans for More Robberies," *Panama American,* May 12, 1943; Gil Ponce to Wilson, *Tribunal Superior Del Primer Distrito Judicial, Caso No. 31,* March 7, 1944, AMRE.

78. Brodie Burnham, "At the Crossroads," *Panama American,* May 11, 1943.

79. "RP Police Corner Escaped Killers on Isolated Coiba," *Panama American,* May 5, 1946; "Escaped Coiba Murderers Are Recaptured," *Star and Herald,* June 18, 1946.

80. "Carl Johnson, Charles Scales and Ringleaders Shot," *Star and Herald,* September 29, 1946; Lloyd Kent, interview with author, RP, April 30, 2001; "Coiba Island Killing Now Being Probed," *Nation,* October 3, 1946.

81. For fallen whites in Southeast Asia, see Stoler, "Sexual Affronts and Racial Frontiers"; "Elusive CZ Convict on the Loose Again," *Panama American,* February 24, 1950; "Escaped CZ Convict Found in Costa Rica," *Panama American,* July 19, 1950.

82. Canal Zone Police Memorandum: Chester Myers Investigation, April 19, 1950, Folder: Public Relations/Republic of Panama, 1950, PCC, Washington Office Subject Files, RG 185, NARA.

83. "Thirty Day Draft for Balboa Jail Volunteer," *Panama American,* May 16, 1956; "Loitering Nets 10 Day Jail Terms for U.S. Youths," *Panama American,* January 10, 1968; "Tourism," *Spillway,* July 16, 1964.

84. How much effect Zonians had on this resignation is debatable. See LaFeber, *The Panama Canal,* 131–32.

85. "Panamanian Flag to Fly beside U.S. Banner in Shaler Triangle," *State Department Bulletin,* October 10, 1960, 558–59; "Stars and Stripes Fly from 112 Staffs When CZ Celebrates a Holiday," *Panama Canal Review,* August 5, 1955, 10; "Kennedy-Chiari Communique on Flags in the Canal Zone," *Public Papers of the Presidents of the United States: John F. Kennedy,* 1962, 481–82.

86. I am indebted to Richard M. Koster for his generosity in loaning me his unpublished account of the 1964 uprising, written when he worked for the 4077th U.S. Army Intelligence Unit in Panama. Much of the background to the events of 1964 comes from the first section, "Long Week-end in Panama."

87. "Panama Crisis, 1964," National Security File, NSC Histories, Lyndon Baines Johnson Library; "Los Sucesos de Enero 1964," *Ministerio de Relaciones Extraneros: Memoria 1964,* vol. 1, AMRE; "Anatomy of a Riot," *Orbis* 22 (September 1964): 113. For a Zonian viewpoint, see "What Really Happened January 9, 1964 at the Flagpole?," *Spillway,* January 20, 1964.

88. For a balanced, insightful view of the riots, see McPherson, *Yankee No!,* 93–99; Alan L. McPherson, "From Punks to Geopoliticans," *Americas* 58.3 (2002): 395–418; for more of the Panamanian view, see "Testimony of Guillermo Guevara Paz," *Star and Herald,* January 14, 1964; "Agresión Pasa a Pasa," *La Hora,* January 12, 1964.

89. Johnson, *Vantage-Point*, 181–87.

90. Koster, "Long Week-end in Panama," 1. For the U.S. military's narrative of the riots, see "United States Southern Command Chronology of Events—January 7–January 12, 1964," 1–48, NSF Country Files, Panama, Lyndon Baines Johnson Library, also in Records Relating to the January 1964 Disturbances, RG 185, NARA. On Chiari's reaction, see Johnson, *Vantage-Point*, 186.

91. "Listo de Herido y Muerto en los Sucesos de Enero 1964, Numero 2," Relacciones entre Panamá y Los E.E.U.U. 1964, vol. 2, AMRE; "Critica la durez de los Zonians," El *Panamá-América*, June 9, 1964, 1.

92. "Zonians Should Leave Panama, Say Evacuated Military Families," *Panama American*, February 3, 1964; "Critica la durez de los Zonians," *Panamá Américana*, June 9, 1964.

93. Memorandum for CZ Governor: "The Meehan-Payne Lawsuit and Its Implications," March 3, 1964, Folder: Adverse Action and Appeal: Payne, and Meehan, Washington Office Subject Files, RG 185, NARA; Joaquín Beleño, "Patriotismo y traición," La Hora, February 12, 1964. For West Indian fears, see Conniff, *Black Labor*, 146.

94. Alfonso Chardy, "Panama's President Has His Brother Billy, Too!," *Miami Herald*, March 4, 1979.

95. "Arnulfo Se Caso Con Una Gringa De La Zona!," *Guerra*, May 2, 1964.

96. U.S. Embassy Panama to Rusk, Deptel No. 605, May 9, 1964, Subject: False Claim of Presidential Candidate's Marriage to SouthCom Commander's Daughter, Folder: Social Conditions Panama, January–June 1964, RG 59, NARA; "False Notice of Arnulfo Arias' Marriage to Jane O'Meara," *Panama American*, May 9, 1964. As an example of the intimacy between Panamanian elites and the United States, the son of Vice President Dominador Bazán was a cadet at West Point. See "Subject: Acceptance of Applicant Kaiser Bazán as West Point Academy Cadet," March 2, 1960, Folder: Panamanian Applicants for West Point, RG 349, NARA.

97. "Bishop McGrath Criticizes U.S. Actions," *Panama American*, January 13, 1964; "Bishop McGrath's Address to the American Society of Panama," August 22, 1962, NSC Country Files, Panama, Lyndon Baines Johnson Library; Monsignor Ignacio Martinez, interview with author, Panama City, March 12, 2001; Rodrigo Mendoza, interview with author, Panamá, RP, May 5, 2002.

98. Arosemena, *Fundacion de la nacionalidad panameña*; García, *Naturaleza y forma de lo panameño*; Soler, *Fundación de la nacionalidad panameña*; Barrios, *Identidad nacional*; Materno Vásquez, *Sobre el hombre cultural panameño*. For literature on the "black legend" of Panama's origins, see Biesanz and Biesanz, *People of Panama*, 155–56; Szok, "La ultima gaviota," 33, 42–43; Selser, *El Rapto de Panamá*. For a more recent and devastating analysis of the black legend of Panama's birth and continuing subservience to the gringos, see McPherson, "Rioting for Dignity," 221–25. For an equally critical yet balanced Panamanian view, see Barrios, *Identidad nacional*.

99. "Tropical Differential Now 15% for New Hires," *Spillway*, October 16, 1964, 1.

100. *Ministerio de Relaciones Exteriores: Memoria 1972*, 2: 12–14, AMRE; Rogers to Sayre, Subject: "Torrijos/Noriega Opinion Regarding Dual Citizenship of Persons Born in Canal Zone," November 15, 1972, Folder: Latin American Employee Groups and Unions, PCC, Internal Security Office, RG 185, NARA.

101. Richard Severo, "Canal Zone Is in an Identity Crisis as U.S. and Panama Haggle," *New York Times*, November 23, 1973; Tom Carey, interview with author, Balboa, RP, May 4, 2001. The so-called Insular Cases of the Supreme Court invalidated full U.S. citizenship to children born in "non-incorporated territory," such as the Canal Zone. See *Rasmussen v. United States* (1905). U.S. legislation in 1937 corrected this for offspring of one or more U.S. citizens who were

born in unincorporated territory. See Title 8 USC section 1403. Preoccupation over citizenship in the Zone continued into the U.S. presidential election in 2008, when critics of Senator John McCain questioned his right to run as a "natural-born citizen" since he had been born in 1936 in the CZ, not on U.S. soil.

102. For Torrijos's strategy in this period, see Escobar Bethancourt, Torrijos, 123–64; Alan Riding, "Is America Giving Away the Panama Canal?," Saturday Review, July 24, 1976. Saddam Hussein called the borderland state of Kuwait the nineteenth province (of Iraq) after his 1990 invasion.

103. Marvin Wainwright, retired PanCanal worker and construction contractor, interview with author, Balboa, RP, January 15, 2003. For an analysis of U.S. drug smuggling and consumption in Panama, see Ernest L. Abel, "Marijuana on Trial: The Panama Canal Zone Report," Substance Use and Misuse 17.4 (1982): 667–78; "Statement of Lt. Col. James M. Krebs, Drug Policy Branch, Department of the Army," in Alcoholic Use in the Canal Zone, H.R. 8471 and H.R. 10581, 253–58. For depression in the CZ in the 1970s, see Herman Wilkerson, interview with author, Balboa, RP, July 18, 2001.

104. Snowcraft to Ford, Subject: Panama Canal Labor Dispute, March 19, 1976, Presidential Handwritten File, Folder: Foreign Affairs, Panama Canal (2), Gerald R. Ford Library; Nina Kosik, interview with author, Balboa, RP, January 5, 2002; Knapp and Knapp, Red, White, and Blue Paradise, 135, 140, 211–15, 236–42; Clymer, Drawing the Line at the Big Ditch, 50–51, 103–5.

105. Knapp and Knapp, Red, White, and Blue Paradise, 258–61, 263–65. Zonians summed up their betrayal with a joke that harkened back to fantasies of simpler times. President Carter dies (a Zonian hope?) and meets President Truman at the pearly gates. "How are things going in the States?" Truman asks. "Well, the Iranians occupied our embassy and are holding all the Americans hostage," Carter replied. "You sent in the Marines, right?" "Well, no," Carter drawled. "And then the Russians invaded Afghanistan," Carter admitted. "Well, you sent in the 101st Airborne, right?" "No," Carter mumbled. "And then Castro sent over all his criminals and mental rejects to Florida as immigrants," Carter moaned. "Well, you blockaded them with the U.S. Navy, right?!" Truman glowered. "No," Carter replied sheepishly. "Jesus Christ, next you'll be telling me you gave away the Panama Canal!" Jorden, Panama Odyssey, 642; Major, Prize Possession, 354.

106. "Mood Grim in the Zone as the Treaty Passes," Star and Herald, April 19, 1978.

107. For "In Memoriam" notices, see Canal Record 13 (September 1979): 81.

108. For T-shirt photos, see Canal Record 14 (September 1980): 100; "Memorandum on Incidence of Psychiatric Disorders and Depression," Gorgas Hospital, Department of Occupational Health, Philips to Wilber, May 16, 1978, PCC, Washington Office Subject Files, RG 185, NARA; Rita Sosa, retired DOD schoolteacher, interview with author, Panama City, May 15, 2001; Lucas Palumbo, interview with author, Piña, RP, May 15, 2001.

109. "Sentimental Journey" dinner in Canal Record 13 (September 1979): 49–50.

110. "There's no people like Zone People / No matter where you go / Camaraderie, Nostalgia . . . / That's what we all do know!" Canal Record 11 (June 1979): 33.

111. Canal Record 13 (December 1979): 91.

112. For details of the controversy, see Canal Record 13 (March 1979): 17, 31. Most Zonians hold that the disinterring was done solely out of concern for grave maintenance and not future proximity to Panamanians of color or fear of desecration.

113. Even after 2000, many Americans continued to work on the Canal through the Autoridad de Canal de Panamá due ironically to Torrijos's granting of Panamanian citizenship to all the Zone-born in 1972. Though many could only speak a few words in Spanish, they remained

bona fide Panamanian citizens who could not be laid off to clear the way for the hiring of more Panamanians thanks to Torrijos's measure.

114. For new locations of these Zonian families and communities, their remembrances and experiences, see the Panama Canal Society at www.pancanalsociety.org, their publication, the *Canal Record*, and the Canal Zone Museum in Seminole, Florida.

115. For Canal Zone reunions, see *Canal Record*, August 1977, August 1979, August 1980, August 1981, August 1982. For the nostalgia they evoke, see Posey, "The Bittersweet Memory."

116. Lori Gibson, retired PanCanal employee, interview with author, Gamboa, RP, May 4, 2001.

Chapter 3: Race and Identity in the Zone-Panama Borderland

1. Albert Brown, interview with author, Balboa Heights, RP, October 23, 2001.

2. For borderland manifestations of race, identity, and nation, see Donnan and Wilson, *Borders*, 3–5, 57–62, 157–58; Baud and van Schendel, "Toward a Comparative History of Borderlands," 231–34.

3. Conniff, *Black Labor*, 5–6. For similar third-national labor strategies, see Tandon and Raphael, *The New Position of East Africa's Asians*; Look Lai, *Indentured Labor, Caribbean Sugar*; Robert B. Kent, "A Diaspora of Chinese Settlement in Latin America and the Caribbean," in Ma and Cartier, *The Chinese Diaspora*, 117–140.

4. The controversial 1941 Constitution was not invalidated until March 1, 1946; for critical analysis of the document, see Conniff, *Black Labor*, 98–104; Robinson, "Panama for the Panamanians"; Arauz et al., *La historia de Panamá en sus textos*, 2: 194–97.

5. For historical background on the West Indian experience, see Conniff, "The Rise and Decline of the West Indian Community in Panama"; Conniff, *Black Labor*, 16–40; Maurer and Yu, *The Big Ditch*, 108–20.

6. Oliver Senior, "The Colon People," *Jamaica Journal* 11–12 (1978): 43–49; LaFeber, *The Panama Canal*, 49–52; McGuinness, *Path of Empire*, 77, 82.

7. McGuinness, *Path of Empire*, 73–80; Frederick, "Colón Man a Come"; Barbara Jamison, "Promises Broken, Illusions Lost: Panama Diary," *Nation*, March 15, 1993; Lara Putnam, "To Study the Fragments/Whole," *Journal of Social History* 39 (June 2006): 412–37.

8. "The Roosevelt Medal," *Canal Record*, February 10, 1909; McCullough, *The Path between the Seas*, 492–502. For U.S. and West Indian death rates during Canal construction, see McCullough, *The Path between the Seas*, 501, 582; Greene, *The Canal Builders*, 130–34; Maurer and Yu, *The Big Ditch*, 119.

9. For analysis of the little known role of U.S. blacks in building the Canal, see Patrice M. Brown, "The Panama Canal: The African-American Experience," 121–26, PCC, CRT. For a description of the early "gold-silver" system, Conniff, *Black Labor*, 31–36.

10. For insight into the identity of West Indian Canal workers, see Lewis, *The West Indian in Panama*; Newton, *The Silver Men*.

11. Reginald Owen, retired PanCanal worker, interview with author, Panama City, April 12, 2001; Alberto Osborne, retired PanCanal worker, interview with author, Panama City, April 19, 2001; George Westerman, "Historical Notes on West Indians on the Isthmus of Panama," PCC, CRT.

12. For these and other Barbadian and Jamaican dishes, see Babb, *Cooking the West Indian Way*; Harris, *Sky Juice and Flying Fish*; Knapp and Knapp, *Red, White, and Blue Paradise*, 165.

13. For the obeah man's role in West Indian society, see Bryce-Laporte, "Crisis, Contra-culture, and Religion among West Indians in the Panama Canal Zone"; Fernández Olmos and

Paravisini-Gebert, *Sacred Possessions*. The quote on "obeah man" is from Earl Barber, interview with author, Balboa Heights, RP, November 11, 2001.

14. For a lexicon of *bajan* expressions, see Howard Clark, "Reflections," *Canal Record*, 12 (December 1978): 8; Collymore, *Barbadian Dialect*; http://www.bajanfuhlife.com/dictionary /index.html; Knapp and Knapp, *Red, White, and Blue Paradise*, 49–50. For scholarly analysis of bajan and pidgin languages, see Andersen, *Pidginization and Creolization as Language Acquisition*; Hymes, *Pidginization and Creolization of Languages*. Shorty and Slim (aka David B. Sietz and Alex Martin Reyes Salisbury) produced several CDs: *Mango Street* (1995), *Gone Platano* (1997), and *Tird One* (1999). Their website is www.shortyandslim.com.

15. Manuel Lowell Ocran, "El idoma inglés y la integración social de los panameños de origen afro-antillano al caracter nacional panameño," *Revista Nacional de Cultura* 15 (1976): 32–39. For problems of other English-speaking groups in the region, see Marshall, *English-speaking Communities in Latin America*.

16. For analysis of Panamanian perceptions of the West Indian community, see Marixa Lasso, "Race and Ethnicity in the Formation of Panamanian National Identity." For West Indians as *tío toms*, see Pernett y Morales, *Loma Ardiente y Vestida de Sol*, 107–9; Lidio Pitty, *Estacion de Navegantes*, 303–9; for resentments over West Indian-Panamanian dating and intermarriages, see Biesanz and Biesanz, *The People of Panama*, 223–25.

17. For West Indians and *Diablos Rojos*, see Peter A. Szok, "Jorge Dunn y la pintura popular," *La Prensa*, June 25, 2005.

18. The best study of Arnulfo is Conte-Porras, *Arnulfo Arias Madrid*. For the fear of a foreign cultural tidal wave in Panama, see Szok, "La ultima gaviota," 40–41, 44–49; and Felipe Juan Escobar, "Arnulfo y las razas minoritarias (1940–1941), in Alberto Mendoza, *Panamá*, 300–302.

19. Winston Williams, retired PanCanal worker, interview with author, Panama City, May 6, 2002.

20. Carlos Jordan Romeros, retired PanCanal worker, interview with author, Chorrera, RP, July 12, 2002. For Panamanian hostility toward West Indians and vice versa, see John Dorscher, "The People Caught in No-Man's-Land," *Tropic Magazine* (Miami Herald), December 12, 1976.

21. Arroyo, "Race Theory and Practice in Panama," 157.

22. Knapp and Knapp, *Red, White, and Blue Paradise*, 183; Arroyo, "Panama" Al Brown; Pérez Medina, *Historía de Béisbol Panameño*; Stewart, *Los Mejores Bateadores Del Béisbol Latino*.

23. Cecil Haynes, retired PanCanal employee, interview with author, Panama City, RP, August 21, 2002; "One Cent Brings Shame on Old-Timer," *Panama American*, March 20, 1946; Vincente Aaron Williams, interview with author, Balboa, RP, May 3, 2001.

24. Taunya Lovell Banks, "Colorism," and Trina Jones, "Shades of Brown," both in Johnson, *Mixed Race America and the Law*; Knapp and Knapp, *Red, White, and Blue Paradise*, 156–59; Lis-Beth Willis, "A Historiography of the Color Complex and Its Representation in Spike Lee's *School Daze*," MA thesis, University of Miami, 2001.

25. For Central American and U.S. perceptions of race and race mixing, see David Baranov and Kevin A. Yelvington, "Ethnicity, Race, Class, and Nationality," in Hilman and D'Agostino, *Understanding the Contemporary Caribbean*, 211–18; Roger N. Lancaster, "Skin Color, Race, and Racism in Nicaragua," *Ethnology* 30 (October 1991): 339–53; Bost, *Mulattas and Mestiza*; Sweet, *The Legal History of the Color Line*; David A. Hollinger, "The One-Drop and the One-Hate Rule, " *Daedalus* 134 (January 2005): 18–29.

26. Knapp and Knapp, *Red, White, and Blue Paradise*, 161–62. For the multiplicity of Latin American racial categories and the concept of *mejorar su raza*, see Baranov and Yelvington,

"Ethnicity, Race, Class, and Nationality"; Graham, *The Idea of Race in Latin America*, 3, 7–12, 39–43.

27. Justo Arroyo, "Race Theory and Practice in Panama," 152–63; Estelle T. Lau, "Can Money Whiten?," in Johnson, *Mixed Race America and the Law*.

28. For social banditry, see Hobsbawm, *Bandits*; Slatta, *Bandidos*; Joseph, "On the Trail of Latin American Bandits." Williams's biography is in File 55-K-1391, Part 1, Subject: Convict John Peter Williams, Panama Canal Executive Office Records, Balboa Heights, RP.

29. For the West Indian plight from the end of canal construction to the Depression, see Conniff, *Black Labor*, 64–78. For background on Williams's early life, see Suspect Description: John Peter Williams, June 10, 1920, File 55-K-1391, Panama Canal Executive Office Records.

30. Williams to MacIlvaine, May 1, 1918, File 55-K-1391, Panama Canal Executive Office Records. Also in the file is MacIlvaine's note to Williams of May 3, 1918, that backs up Koerner's version of events and rejects Williams's appeal and his request for another driving test.

31. For Williams's early associations with U.S. citizens, see Suspect Description: John Peter Williams, Canal Zone Police and Fire Division, June 10, 1920, File 55-K-1391, Panama Canal Executive Office Records.

32. Reginald Owen Lloyd, retired PanCanal worker, interview with author, Ancon, RP, February 12, 2002. For the role of emotion in history, see Kitayama and Markus, *Emotion and Culture*; Stearns and Lewis, *An Emotional History of the United States*.

33. For lists of massive quantities of women's jewelry that Williams stole, see Phillips, Memorandum for Chief, Canal Zone Police and Fire Division, November 26, 1920; for Williams's eventual acquisition of a CZ taxi license, see Suspect Description: John Peter Williams, June 10, 1920, both in File 55-K-1391, Panama Canal Executive Office Records.

34. For Williams's jungle lair, see "Burglars of Las Sabanas Located by Panama Police: In the Heart of the Woods," *Star and Herald*, June 6, 1920.

35. Some genealogists also claim the "Kid" was born William Henry Bonney. For literature on his life, see Jameson, *Billy the Kid*; Tatum, *Inventing Billy the Kid*.

36. For U.S. reporters' "jungle" obsessions regarding Williams, see "Captain Solis Returns to Panama Leaving Convict Hiding in the Bosky Jungle," *Panama American*, June 7, 1920; "Peter Williams and Cristobal Sampson Still Leading Police a Merry Chase through Jungleland," *Panama American*, June 8, 1920.

37. For banana tree anecdote, Albert Brown, interview with author, Balboa Heights, RP, February 10, 2002. Numerous older West Indians have similar stories relating to Williams.

38. For Williams as a bootlegger and refugee on U.S. bases, see Philips to Johannes, October 25, 1920; for CZ Police–Panama Police squabbling, see Johannes to Lamb, October 25 1920; for "monkey business," see Cooper to Kallay, October 12, 1920, all in File 55-K-1391, Panama Canal Executive Office Records.

39. For Williams's 1919 escape, see Johannes to Harding, September 24, 1919; Callaway to Chief of Panamanian National Police, November 5, 1919, both in File 55-K-1391, Panama Canal Executive Office Records. For examples of West Indian servant collusion in Williams's burglaries, see Phillips to Johannes, Charge Sheet: Fifth Count, January 7, 1921, Kallay to Johannes, Charge Sheet: Fifteenth Count, January 7, 1921, in File 55-K-1391, Panama Canal Executive Office Records.

40. For the significance of the obeah man in West Indian culture, see Bryce-Laporte, "Crisis, Contraculture, and Religion among West Indians in the Panama Canal Zone." For Williams's 1920 Wanted posters, see Johannes to Harding, November 26, 1920, File 55-K-1391, Panama Canal Executive Office Records.

41. Reginald Owen Lloyd, interview with author, Ancon, RP, February 12, 2002.

42. "John Peter Williams: El Robin Hood Panameño, Capitulo 26," *Más Para Todas*, March 20, 1978, 36–37; "Peter Williams Shot at Ancon," *Star and Herald*, February 14, 1922; "Burglars of Las Sabanas Located by Panama Police," *Star and Herald*, June 6, 1920.

43. "Peter Williams, Notorious House Breaker, Evades Capture by Zone Cops and Then Gives Himself Up," *Star and Herald*, December 10, 1920.

44. "Peter Williams, Notorious House Breaker, Evades Capture by Zone Cops and Then Gives Himself Up"; *Government of Canal Zone v. John Peter Williams*, February 17, 1921, Case nos. 1702–1731, District Court Records of the Canal Zone, RG 21, NARA. For treatment of the Williams family, see "Zone Will Cremate Williams' Body This Morning," *Star and Herald*, February 15, 1922.

45. For Williams's early pledge to escape, see Walston to Johannes, February 28, 1921, File 55-K-1391, Panama Canal Executive Office Records. For the warden's account of Williams's rescue of Carr, see Walston to Police Johannes, September 13, 1921, File 55-K-1391, Panama Canal Executive Office Records.

46. Kennedy, Memorandum for the Chief, February 14, 1922, File 55-K-1391, Panama Canal Executive Office Records. For the official description of Williams's escape, see Walston to Johannes, February 17, 1922, File 55-K-1391, Panama Canal Executive Office Records.

47. "Peter Williams Shot at Ancon," *Star and Herald*, February 14, 1922; Johannes, Memorandum for the Executive Secretary, February 14, 1922, File 55-K-1391, Panama Canal Executive Office Records.

48. Kooistra, *Criminals as Heroes*.

49. "Panama Bandit Died in Ancon Hospital without Regaining Consciousness," *Star and Herald*, February 15, 1922. For various interpretations of the subaltern in Latin American history, see Rodríquez et al., *The Latin American Subaltern Studies Reader*.

50. "Panama: A Nation without Heroes," in Krauss, *Inside Central America*, 244–97. For comments that Panamanians were *vendidos*, "sold ones," or "patria sellers" who had bargained away their sovereignty, see Biesanz and Biesanz, *The People of Panama*, 156; Szok, "La última gaviota," 42–43.

51. For a critique of U.S. media constructions of the 1989 invasion, see Johns and Johnson, *State Crime, the Media, and the Invasion of Panama*, 63–86.

52. "Pete's Brain Was above Par Said Experts," *Star and Herald*, February 16, 1922; Autopsy Report, John Peter Williams, Dr. Herbert C. Clark, February 15, 1922, File 55-K-1391, Panama Canal Executive Office Records.

53. D. E. Thompson to editor, *Star and Herald*, February 18, 1922.

54. "Zone Will Cremate Williams' Body This Morning," *Star and Herald*, February 15, 1922; Panama Canal Health Department, Certificate of Death for John Peter Williams, February 15, 1922, File 55-K-1391, Panama Canal Executive Office Records. For the silver bullet legend, Livingston Quinn, Joseph Braddock, Thompson Randolph, and Owen Winthrop, retired PanCanal workers, interviews with author, Panama City, April 10, 2002.

55. For folklore beliefs about Williams, I am indebted to Lindolph Leon Ashby III and Gilberto Alls, veteran bartenders at Elks Lodge 1414, in Balboa, RP. This theme of West Indian collective resistance and defiance in the face of U.S. power also pervades the conclusion of Williams's lone biography: Jurado, *John Peter Williams*, 172–76.

56. Angus Brown, retired PanCanal worker, interview with author, Gamboa, RP, January 28, 2001.

57. Sam Edwards, retired PanCanal worker and Autoridad de Canal de Panamá archivist, interview with author, Balboa Heights, RP, April 12, 2001.

58. For the cold war campaign against Local 713 and the United Public Workers of America, see Conniff, *Black Labor*, 112–16; Major, *Prize Possession*, 218–25. For the U.S. government's and popular media's war on Local 713, see "Double Standard," *Time*, June 23, 1947.

59. Africanus, "Segregation and Integration," Mailbox, *Panama American*, August 20, 1956; Stay in Yard, "Church Segregation," *Panama American*, August 25, 1956; Vincente Forbes, "No Somos Criollos, Somos Panameños Como Los Demás," *La Hora*, June 23, 1955.

60. "Washington Hotel Incident: Protest Mailed to Truman," *Panama American*, February 12, 1952; "Hotel Workers Strike over Discrimination," *Workman*, February 13, 1952.

61. "Granville Brown Protest Continues in Balboa," *Panama American*, June 8, 1956.

62. Lester Leon Greaves, retired PanCanal worker and convict, interview with author, San Miguelito, RP, January 12, 2004, and August 4, 2005.

63. In 1958 Kellogg Alton White, Lionel Smith, and Leslie Williams, leaders of the Panamanian Negro Improvement Association, formed the Committee for the Defense of Lester Leon Greaves. They wrote many letters to governors of the Canal Zone, including to Governor William A. Carter, December 7, 1961, File 55-K-2620, Records Division, Panama Canal Executive Office Records. For Powell's and the NAACP's support, see "NAACP Pledges to Study Means of Assisting in Lester Greaves Case," *Panama Tribune Sunday*, January 19, 1954; Powell to Seybold, February 12, 1956, File 55-K-2620, Records Division, Panama Canal Executive Office Records.

64. Beleño, *Los Forzados de Gamboa*.

65. Beleño, *Los Forzados de Gamboa*. For a Panamanian analysis of Beleño's work, see Mirna Miriam Pérez-Venero, "Raza, color, y prejuico en la novelistica panameña contemporanea de tema canalero," PhD diss., Louisiana State University, 1973.

66. For Beleño's background, see "Joaquín Beleno y la novela canalera, 1921–1988," *Revista Lotería* 373 (1988): 59–63. For the "tragic mulatto," see Beane, *The Characterization of Blacks and Mulattoes*. For classic tragic mulatto novels of nineteenth-century Cuba and descriptions of the "colonial black's" place in Panamanian society, see Castillero Calvo, *Los negros y mulatos en las historia social panameña*; Armando Fortune, "El esclavo negro en el desenvolviemiento económico del istmo de Panamá durante el descubrimiento y la conquista," *Revista Lotería* 228 (February 1975): 1–16; Faulkner Watts, "Perspectivos sobre el afro-panameño," *Revista Lotería* 234 (August 1975): 36–48.

67. Lester Leon Greaves, interview with author, San Miguelito, RP, January 12, 2004, and August 4, 2005.

68. Roberto Peñaloza, retired Panamanian laborer, interview with author, Curundu, RP, April 1, 2002. For West Indian opinions on Greaves's innocence, Angus Brown, interview with author, Gatun, RP, June 10, 2002; Albert Brown, interview with author, Corozal, RP, January 14, 2004. For Zonian viewpoints, Robert Taht, interview with author, Balboa, RP, May 11, 2001. For the complex issue of rape, sexual assault, and date or acquaintance rape, possibly involved in the Greaves case, see Cahill, *Rethinking Rape*, 109–42; Ward et al., *Acquaintance and Date Rape*; Hampel, *Viva Panama*, 109–10.

69. Fear of "de back ponch" was the most consistent story in all my interviews with older retired West Indians in Río Abajo and at Local 907, the Panamanian union headquarters in Ancon. No documentation exists to support this conspiracy theory in records of Gorgas Hospital. Cecil Haynes, interview with author, Panama City, August 11, 2002. Haynes opined that many older West Indians' quick deaths after retirement were more the result of overwork and age than any deliberate U.S. genocide.

70. Sylvester Linton, retired PanCanal worker, interview with author, Ancon, RP, June 7, 2001.

71. For silver schools' "transition" to Latin American schools, see Wilson et al., *Schooling in the Panama Canal Zone, 1904–1979*, 101–34, PCC, CRT. For "dumping" of West Indians into Panama after 1955, see Conniff, *Black Labor*, 117–19; Major, *Prize Possession*, 226–29.

72. "Panamanian Complaints over U.S. Racism in the Canal Zone," Memorandum to the Governor, February 22, 1959, PCC, Washington Office Subject Files, RG 185, NARA.

73. John Dorschner, "The People Caught in No-Man's-Land," *Tropical Magazine* (*Miami Herald*), December 12, 1976.

74. Quoted in Davis, "Panama," 21.

75. All of these Panamanian West Indian oral interviews are from the Voices of Our America Collection of Vanderbilt University, http://voicesamerica.library.vanderbilt.edu/voices.php.

76. For "false colonial consciousness," see Fanon, *The Wretched of the Earth*; Fanon, *Black Faces, White Masks*; Joane Nagel, "False Faces," in Davis, *Identity and Social Change*, 81–108.

77. Robert Newton, retired PanCanal worker, interview with author, Panama City, May 19, 2001.

78. Earl Barber, interview with author, Corozal, RP, August 15, 2006.

79. Owen Jeffries, interview with author, Panama City, May 20, 2001.

80. George Barnabas, retired DOD plumber, interview with author, Panama City, August 16, 2002.

81. For the origins of the black antidiscrimination crusade against the Elks Club in 1970–73, see Mabry to Mather, April 23, 1970, U.S. Southern Command, and Dichter to Hixon, February 20, 1971, Folder: Discrimination 1969–71, Washington Office Subject Files, PCC, RG 185, NARA; "Governor Orders Canal Zone Elks to Abolish 'Whites Only' Policy," *Panama Tribune*, February 20, 1971; Conley to Innis, "Permission to Demonstrate Granted," October 2, 1972, and Parker to Rogers, Subject: "Revocation of Elks' Land Leases," PCC, Internal Security Office, RG 185, NARA; Subject: Student Demonstrations at Paraiso High School, January 19–20, 1972, Folder: C/SCH Latin American Schools, PCC, Internal Security Office, RG 185, NARA.

82. For "Cholo" Omar, see Barry et al., *Inside Panama*, 14; "First Afro-Panamanian Student Admitted to the Canal Zone Junior College," *Spillway*, September 2, 1961; George W. Westerman, "School Segregation in the Panama Canal Zone," *Phylon* 15.3 (3rd Quarter 1954): 276–87; Phi Delta Kappa, *Schooling in the Panama Canal Zone*, 135–37.

83. "Sam Whyte Triangle to Be Inaugurated," *Spillway*, September 2, 1966, 4.

84. For the Panama Canal Company's and the CZ government's hostility toward and suspicion of militant West Indians, see Lewis to Quinn, Subject: Black Panamanian to Serve as Youth Advisor to Governor, January 20, 1974; Internal Security Paper, Subject: Moral, Legal, Political, and Racial Problems of the Latin American Communities in the CZ, December 19, 1972; Memorandum, District Police Chief, Cristobal, Subject: Study of the Latin American Communities, March 7, 1972; Walker to Sayre, Subject: Termination of Militant West Indian Radicals Employed by the Canal Zone, February 28, 1972, all in PCC, Internal Security Office, Washington Office Subject Files, RG 185, NARA.

85. Many rank-and-file members of Local 900 in Ancon confirm these widely held views, along with a sense of U.S. abandonment of the remaining West Indian Canal workers in Panama after December 31, 1999.

86. Museo de Afro Antillano de Panamá, Ciudad de Panamá, Calle 24 y Avenida Justo Arosemena, Barrio de Calidonia. For West Indian Canal commemorations, see Parker, *Panama Fever*, xx.

87. Desmond Williams, retired PanCanal worker, interview with author, Colón, RP, Au-

gust 15, 2009. One of the incongruities of conducting research in Panama was listening to so many Latin Panamanians denounce the Jim Crow system in the "old Zone," while so many West Indians, who actually suffered under its constraints, expressed a certain nostalgia for at least some elements of it: their old segregated townships, clubhouses, commissaries, athletic fields, churches, and sense of communitarian unity.

Chapter 4: Desire, Sexuality, and Gender in the Zone-Panama Borderland

1. "Two GIs Jailed in Balboa Face Charge of Rape," *Panama American*, April 18, 1955; *Government of the Canal Zone v. Vernon Omar Helton*, Case no. 4555, and *Government of the Canal Zone v. William Jerry Mitchell*, Case no. 4556, April 17, 1955, District Court Records of the Canal Zone, RG 21, Washington National Records Center; "Girl Says 268 Pound GI She Was with Tried to Rape Her," *Panama American*, April 23, 1955.

2. "Dos Soldados Norteamericanos Estan Arestado Para Violación de Panameñas," *La Hora*, April 18, 1955.

3. For centrality of desire in colonial settings, see Young, *Colonial Desire*; Stoler, *Race and the Education of Desire*. For TR's "desire" for Panama as object of his masculine obsessions, see Watts, *Rough Rider in the White House*, 114–22.

4. "Asesino al Club Unión," *Mundo Grafico*, July 15, 1939; "Madison Love Gunned Down by Ex-Lover at the Union Club," *Star and Herald*, July 15, 1939; Kathleen Moore Knight, "Death Came Dancing." *American Magazine* (New York), March 1940.

5. For similar U.S. efforts to regulate prostitution, see Bailey and Farber, *The First Strange Place*; Moon, *Sex among Allies*; Chapkis, "Power and Control in the Commercial Sex Trade," 181–202.

6. Johnson, *An American Legacy in Panama.*

7. Nagel, *Race, Ethnicity, and Sexuality*, 7–8.

8. Luibhéid, *Entry Denied*, x.

9. Luibhéid, *Entry Denied*, 77; Donnan and Wilson, *Borders*, 129–37.

10. Laurence, *The Social Agent*; McCormack, *Regulating Sexuality*; Costigliola, *Roosevelt's Lost Alliances*, 261–62, 266–67, 289.

11. *Codigo Penal de la República de Panamá*, 179.

12. "Packed CZ Court Hear Girl Tell of Fight, Rape," *Panama American*, April 27, 1955.

13. *Government of Canal Zone v. Vernon Omar Helton*, Case no. 4555, April 17, 1955, District Court Canal Zone, RG 21, WNRC.

14. "Helton Case Goes to Jury," *Panama American*, June 11, 1955. For anti-American reactions to U.S. military sex crimes in Asia, see Schirmer, *Sexual Abuse and Superpower Difficulties in the Philippines and Japan*.

15. For gendered constructions of Panamanian identity, see Alan McPherson, "Rioting for Dignity." For similar themes in both a U.S. and an international context, see Robert D. Dean, "Masculinity as Ideology: John F. Kennedy and the Domestic Politics of Foreign Policy," *Diplomatic History* 22 (Winter 1998): 29–62; Andrew Jon Rotter, "Gender Relations, Foreign Relations."

16. "Fourteen Year Minimum for Helton if Convicted as Charged," *Panama American*, June 11, 1955.

17. Beleño, *Los Forzados de Gamboa*, 146.

18. For additional Panamanian commentary on "gate girls," see Joaquín Beleño, "Proporciones Astronomicas," *La Hora*, June 14, 1955; Mario J. Obaldía, "Dolorosa Readidad," *La Hora*, July 6, 1955. For U.S. discussion of the "gate girl" problem at USO dances, see Chapin to Hol-

land, May 12, 1955, Panama Country File, Dwight D. Eisenhower Library; "Points of Friction with the Local Population," Harrington to Martin, February 14, 1957, FRUS, 1955–57, 7: 331–32. For U.S. screening of prostitutes among these women, see "Clementine Rangel Díaz, 19, Panamanian, Given 10 Days for Loitering at Ft. Kobbe Gate," Judge's Bench, Panama American, October 31, 1956.

19. For the honor-shame paradigm in Latin American sexuality, see Melhues and Stolen, Machos, Mistresses, and Madonnas; Johnson and Lipsett-Rivera, The Faces of Honor.

20. Memorandum: "Abandoned Children of U.S. Service Personnel in Panama," James to Philbin, January 4, 1962, Folder: Personnel: Community Relations, HUSCC, RG 349, NARA.

21. Thrush, interview with author, Panama City, July 16, 2002; Cooper, interview with author, Curundu, RP, August 4, 2003.

22. For differing cultural, gender, and sexual perceptions between Americans and Panamanians, see John Biesanz, "Inter-American Marriages on the Isthmus of Panama," Social Forces 29 (December 1950): 159–63; Biesanz and Biesanz, The People of Panama, 229–30, 311–14, 367–68; John Biesanz and Luke M. Smith, "Adjustment of Inter-American Marriages on the Isthmus of Panama"; Ramón Carillo and Richard Boyd, "Some Aspects of the Social Relations between Latin and Anglo-Americans on the Isthmus of Panama"; Knapp and Knapp, Red, White, and Blue Paradise, 126–27, 174–76.

23. "Dismissal Denied in Rape Case," Panama American, June 16, 1955. On Panama as a U.S. sexual playground, see Kenneth Underwood, interview with author, La Boca, RP, May 12, 2000; Prieto, interview with author, Balboa Heights, RP, May 12, 2001; Edgardo Tirado, interview with author, Amador, RP, April 23, 2001; Joseph "Jody" Chamberlain, interview with author, Piña, RP, December 21, 2001; Luke Palumbo, interview with author, Piña, RP, December 21, 2001; Ismela Ruiz, retired Panamanian maid, interview with author, Panamá, RP, November 12, 2001; Bianca Iglesias, retired Panamanian waitress, interview with author, Panama City, November 13, 2001; Roberto Murillo, retired Panamanian construction worker, interview with author, Curundu, RP, December 5, 2001.

24. Government of Canal Zone v. Vernon Omar Helton, Case no. 4555, April 17, 1955, District Court Records of the Canal Zone, RG 21, WNRC.

25. Government of Canal Zone v. Vernon Omar Helton.

26. Government of the Canal Zone v. Lester Leon Greaves, Case no. 3861, February 24, 1946, District Court Records of the Canal Zone, RG 21, NARA.

27. "Jury Finds Helton Guilty of the Lesser Crime of Battery," Panama American, June 12, 1955; Joaquin Beleño, "Propociones Astronomicas," in "Temas Aridos," La Hora, June 14, 1955. For an angry Panamanian critique of the Helton-Mitchell case, see Mario J. Obaldía, "Dolorosa Readidad," La Hora, July 6, 1955.

28. "Dismissal Denied in Rape Case," Panama American, June 16, 1955. For the CZ government's appeal to Vallarino, see Cazoria to McCormack, June 28, 1955, in Government of Canal Zone v. William Jerry Mitchell, Case no. 4556, April 17, 1955, District Court Records of the Canal Zone, RG 21, WNRC; "Sisters Firm in Decision," Sunday American, June 19, 1955; "Future a Mystery as Rape Charges Dismissed," Panama American, July 5, 1955. For dismissals or light sentences for GI rape, sexual assault, and murder of Panamanian women, see Pvt. Williams, 1942 rape of Severina Suarez (sixty days imprisonment); Cpls. Reed, Johnson, and Easley, 1954 rape of Juanita Rodriquez (case dismissed); Pvt. Arroyo-Gonzalez, 1953 sexual assault on Rufina Perez ($40 fine); Cpl. Calderno-Ramos, 1954 sexual assault and murder of Gladys Vasquez (case dismissed); Pvts. Linton and Anders, 1958 rape of Eufinia Olivarez (ninety days imprisonment); Joseph Wilson Fisher, 1958 rape case (ten-year sentence, five years suspended); Sgt. Willard Lee Brown, 1972 rape of Oderay Belucha (three-year suspended sentence), all in Files

250. 3 binders for the year listed, CID, RG 338 and CID, RG 349, NARA. For the importance of dignity in Panama, see Scranton, *The Noriega Years*, 16.

29. "800 Grabbed as RP Cops Spread Net over Vice Operations," *Panama American*, June 15, 1955; "El Problema de Moralidad" and "Congresso para Moralidad," El *Panama América*, June 13, 1955. "Panama Archbishop Beckman Bans Bathing Suits at Beauty Contests," *Star and Herald*, June 15, 1955; "Miss Panama Withdraws from Miss Universe Contest," *Panama American*, June 16, 1955.

30. Quoted in Allan Dodds Frank, "Everyone Wants Us," *Forbes*, February 23, 1987, 79.

31. Harrington, quoted in Hanson W. Baldwin, "Storm over the Panama Canal," *New York Times Magazine*, May 8, 1960.

32. "All these wayward children of the jungle ask is to be let alone to drift through life their own way" (Franck, *Zone Policeman 88*, 284–85).

33. Eisenmann, quoted in Guillermoprieto, *The Heart That Bleeds*, 232.

34. Gorgas, *Sanitation in Panama*; Burlingame, *Mosquitoes in the Big Ditch*; Goodman, "The Antivenereal Disease Campaign in Panama"; "Health Department of the Panama Canal Zone Report," *Social Hygiene* 5 (April 1919): 259–64.

35. "Dead Girl Linked to Dope Ring," *Panama American*, March 5, 1965; "Artista de Cabaret Asesinada!," *Critica*, March 5, 1965; "Histería Entre Artistas por el Caso de Roxana," *La Hora*, March 17, 1965.

36. "El Asesino Confeso!," *La Hora*, March 20, 1965; "Se Prohibe a Mujeres Estar Solas en las Cantinas," *Critica*, March 12, 1965.

37. Howarth, *The Golden Isthmus*, 164; McGuinness, *Path of Empire*, 36.

38. Guinn and Steglich, *In Modern Bondage*.

39. General Don Santiago De La Guardía, "Sobre el Problema de Prostitución en Panamá," *Revista Lotería* 4 (October 1919); Ward, *Imperial Panama*, 21–23.

40. McCullough, *The Path between the Seas*, 145–47.

41. Forbes-Lindsay, *Panama and the Canal To-day*, 16.

42. McCullough, *The Path between the Seas*, 560–61; Major, *Prize Possession*, 124, 130; Mack, *The Land Divided*, 532–35; Diaz Szmirnov, *Génesis de la Ciudad Republicana*, 85–90.

43. Von Muenchow, *The American Woman in the Panama Canal Zone*; Brewster, *3000 Bachelors and a Girl*; Parker, *Panama Canal Bride*; James, *Woman in the Wilderness*. The first comprehensive census of Panama in 1920 listed 1,053 prostitutes in the republic, but that date was seven years after the height of the U.S. construction period. Of these, 86 percent were Latin American or Caribbean women (*Censo de República de Panamá 1920*, 27).

44. Roe, *The Great War on White Slavery*; Major, *Prize Possession*, 136–41; Hector R Marín, "Puerto Ricans in Defense of the Canal," Quarry Heights, Canal Zone, 1948: GPO, PCC, CRT. For similar efforts at U.S. military regulation of Latin American prostitution in Puerto Rico, see Briggs, *Reproducing Empire*, 46–73; Guevara Mann, *Panamanian Militarism*, 56.

45. Hyman, *Particularidades de la Prostitución en Panamá*, 9–12.

46. For the role of chulas in Panamanian society, see Jordan Romeros, interview with author, Chorrera, RP, February 24, 2002; Joyce Isveth Mendoza, Panamanian accountant and APC worker, interview with author, Las Cumbres, RP, June 21, 2002.

47. For marinadas, see Carillo and Boyd, "Some Aspects of the Social Relations between Latin and Anglo Americans on the Isthmus of Panama." For Noriega's youthful memories of the marinadas, see Noriega and Eisner, *America's Prisoner*, 19.

48. For their detailed memories of World War II and their youth in Panama and the marinadas, I am indebted to José Miguel Moreno (b. 1914), former Panamanian ambassador to the United States and foreign minister of Panama; Rubén Dario Carles (b. 1920), former Pana-

manian minister of finance; retired CZ Police officers George Gershow (b. 1924) and Charlie Fears (b. 1915); and Rolando Liñares, a Panamanian American.

49. "Colón Mob Threatens Sailors Who Climbed Atlantic Side Statue," *Panama American*, February 4, 1950; Carillo and Boyd, "Some Aspects of the Social Relations between Latin and Anglo Americans on the Isthmus of Panama," 734.

50. "U.S. Service Personnel Complain of Scams and Assaults in Panama," *Star and Herald*, August 12, 1943.

51. "Disreputable Journalism," *Star and Herald*, August 25, 1945.

52. For a description of similar "bullring" brothel operations in World War II Honolulu, see Bailey and Farber, *The First Strange Place*, 102–5.

53. Hampel, *Viva Panama*, 74.

54. Palumbo, interview with author, Balboa, RP, January 8, 2004. For a description of legal prostitution in Panama in the 1940s and 1950s, see Biesanz and Biesanz, *People of Panama*, 367–68.

55. Happyland, Lido, Rialto, and Kelly's Ritz nightclub advertisements in *Panama America*, September 15, 1945. For descriptions of Panamanian nightclub fare in the World War II era, see advertisement sections of *Panama American* and *Star and Herald*, 1942–45; Linnea Angermuller, ed., "Jean Coffey's Memories of the Canal Zone," *History Items of the Canal Zone*, August 15, 2002, http://gozonian.org/memory030329.shtml; Knapp and Knapp, *Red, White, and Blue Paradise*, 174–75.

56. *Panama Lady* (RKO, 1939), directed by Jack Hiveley; *Panama Hattie* (Warner Bros., 1942), directed by Norman Z. McLeod; *Panama Sal* (Republic Pictures, 1957), directed by William Witney.

57. Hyman, *Particularidades de la Prostitutión*, 22–26, 35–36.

58. "Se Recontruye el Crimen del Hotel Estación," *Mundo Grafíco*, March 8, 1941; "Los Protagonistas del Crimen Pasional de Colón," *Mundo Grafíco*, September 12, 1942; "Probe of Rosita Lane Case Is Closed in Colon," *Star and Herald*, October 30, 1942; Courtney to Lane, Request for Death Records, July 10, 1946, 99 Files, RG 185, NARA; "Los Encantos de una Cabaretera Provocan Muerte de 3 Hombres," *Revista Más Para Todos*, July 3, 1978, 36–37; "Historía de 'La China,' la Mujer Fatal," *Revista Más Para Todos*, February 13, 1981, 15–17.

59. Jeffrey, *Sex and Borders*; Montgomery, *Modern Babylon?*; Charles Fears, retired CZ police chief, interview with author, Panama City, August 12, 2004; "Disreputable Journalism," *Star and Herald*, August 24, 1945.

60. For international aspects of U.S. military prostitution, see Enloe, *Bananas, Beaches, and Bases*; Enloe, *The Morning After*; Moon, *Sex among Allies*. For prostitution in European and Asian empires, see Hyam, *Empire and Sexuality*.

61. Bea Trap, "Housing, Mosquitoes, Rats, Streets—All Headaches for U.S. Health Officer in Panama," *Panama American*, November 30, 1947; "Spanish Films on Sexual Hygiene for U.S. Troops," August 11, 1951, File 330.011 (Character Guidance), RG 349, NARA.

62. U.S. Public Health Service, "Computations on Expenditure on Commercial Prostitution in Panama, 1945," in *The Venereal Disease Situation in the Panama Canal Zone and the New Control Program*, 32–35. For earlier efforts to control VD in Panama, see Dock, *Hygiene and Morality*. For examples of unit monitoring of VD in U.S. military in Panama, see "Venereal Disease Rates, 45th Reconnaissance Battalion," December 3, 1951, File 330.11, Headquarters U.S. Army Caribbean Command (HUSAC), RG 349, NARA; Armed Forces Disciplinary Control Board Panama Area: VD Statistics, May 15, 1973, File 330.11, Headquarters U.S. Army Caribbean Command (HUSAC), RG 349, NARA.

63. Subject: Off-Limits Restrictions, April 26, 1954, File 250.2, HUSAC, CID, RG 349.

64. Daniel Cooper, interview with author, Curundu, RP, July 23, 2002.

65. Wayne Bryant, retired U.S. soldier and DOD worker, interview with author, Balboa, RP, August 5, 2003.

66. Wayne Bryant, interview with author.

67. For midnight revues, see Tom McClain, interview with author, Balboa, RP, August 16, 2005; Lieutenant Colonel Bruce Gilhooly, interview with author, Storrs, Connecticut, November 12, 2003; Daniel Cooper, interview with author, Curundu, RP, July 23, 2002.

68. For Panamanian repression of illegal prostitution and vice, see "Secret Police Grab 26 in Gambling Den Raid," *Panama America*, September 9, 1945; "All Gambling to Be Government Operated in Panama," *Panama America*, March 8, 1946; "800 Grabbed as RP Police Spread Net," *Panama America*, June 15, 1955; "La Lucha contra los Delincuentes," *Panama American*, June 18, 1955; "En la actitud de E.E.U.U. Hacia Panama La Guardia Nacional Contra La Prostitución," *Panama America*, June 16, 1957; "RP Plans Crackdown on Illegal Artistas," *Panama American*, March 10, 1965; "Yepes contra la Prostitución," *Más Para Todos*, March 1, 1978; George Gershow, interview with author, Balboa, RP, April 15, 2002.

69. "250 Authorized Brothels in RP," *Panama American*, June 29, 1951.

70. "Girl Threatens Suicide to Avoid Being Deported," *Panama American*, September 29, 1945.

71. Bula, "Time Will Tell," Mailbox, *Panama American*, September 21, 1946.

72. "Panamanian Wife Speaks Out," *Panama American*, July 2, 1946.

73. Memorandum: "Off Limits Restrictions and Repression of Illegal Prostitution," January 1, 1947, File 333.5–337, Headquarters Panama Canal Department (HPCD), OPM, RG 338, NARA. For similar strategies in the British Empire, see Levine, *Prostitution, Race, and Politics*. For U.S. military-regulated prostitution in Asia, see Sturdevant, *Let the Good Times Roll*.

74. Balboan, "Sour Grapes Maybe, Huh?," Mailbox, *Panama American*, December 1, 1945; Lee Amberths, retired U.S. soldier, U.S. consulate investigator, and Autoridad de Canal de Panamá archivist, interview with author, Corozal, RP, January 15, 2005.

75. *Canal Zone Code*, 134–36.

76. Skip Burger, retired DOD worker, interview with author, Margarita, RP, January 15, 2005.

77. "Slight Girl Slights the Zone Again," *Panama American*, July 27, 1955; *Government of Canal Zone v. Doris Rud*, Case no. 5022, July 5, 1960, and Case no. 4863, July 1, 1958, District Court Canal Zone, RG 21, WNRC. For other Canal Zone prostitution cases, see "Larceny of $138 from Sgt. William I. Franklin by Panamanian Prostitute," July 28, 1947, File 333.5, HPCD, OPM, CID, RG 349, NARA; Summary of Testimony, Rita Bustamante: Vagrancy Charge, November 19, 1951, Panama Canal Executive Department, Police and Fire Division (PFD), 99 Files, RG 185, NARA; *Government of Canal Zone v. Maria de los Angeles Moreno*, Case no. 3374, July 5, 1962, District Court Records of the Canal Zone, RG 21, WNRC.

78. "Afternoon Raid Uncovers Girl in La Boca Closet," *Panama American*, January 25, 1956; *Government of Canal Zone v. Ira Benjamin Clark*, Case no. 2969, Violation of the Mann Act, September 20, 1949, District Court Records of the Canal Zone, RG 21, WNRC; *Government of Canal Zone v. Ruben Eastman*, Cases no. 61634 and 61635, Violation of the Mann Act, October 10, 1948, District Court Records of the Canal Zone, RG 21, WNRC; "Taxi Driver, 3 Girls Jailed for Vagrancy in 'Hustling' Case," *Panama American*, July 7, 1950; "Women and Three Men Jailed in CZ for Vagrancy," *Panama American*, September 25, 1950; "Happyland Show Girl Arrested for Trespassing on the Zone for Lewd Purposes," Judge's Bench, *Panama American*, December 13, 1952; "13 Year-Old Takes Stand in Balboa White Slavery Case," *Panama American*, May 15, 1951; "Woman Who Can't Keep Out of Zone Must Serve Term: 27-Year Old Vilma C. Haynes Had

7 Priors of Soliciting in the Zone," *Panama American*, February 7, 1955; "Clementine Rangel Díaz, 19, Panamanian, Given 10 Days for Loitering at Ft. Kobbe Gate," Judge's Bench, *Panama American*, October 31, 1956; Captain Dave Sherman, PanCanal pilot, interview with author, Diablo, RP, January 19, 2005.

79. "Elijah Bey, Negro GI from Ft. Clayton Arrested on Suspicion of Killing Roxana," *Panama American*, March 17, 1965; "CZ GI Accused Wife of Killing Bar Girl," *Panama American*, March 19, 1965.

80. "Clayton GI Admits Robbing Bar Girl," *Panama American*, March 18, 1965.

81. For analysis of the historic roots to Central American prostitutes' racism against black men, see Putnam, *The Company They Kept*, 76–111; Putnam, "The Work and Lives of Prostitutes during Costa Rica's Early Twentieth-Century Banana Booms," 31–32. For a similar phenomenon in the Tijuana borderland, see Hart, *Empire and Revolution*, 255, 367; Lloyd Thompson, "Syphilis in the Negro," *American Journal of Syphilis* 3 (July 1919): 385–86.

82. "Clayton GI Admits Robbing Bar Girl," *Panama American*, March 18, 1965.

83. "Zone GI Confesses to Killing Bar Girl," *Panama American*, March 29, 1965.

84. "Histería entre Artistas por el Caso de Roxana," *La Hora*, March 17, 1965; "Se Prohibe a Mujeres Estar Solas en las Cantinas," *Crítica*, March 12, 1965; "El Soldado Eliahu Bey: Porque le Escupió la Cara y lo Llamó Negro Mató a Roxana," *La Hora*, March 20, 1965; "El Asesino Confeso," *Crítica*, March 20, 1965; "El Cuchilo Con que Bey Mató a Roxana," *La Hora*, March 23, 1965; "Senala el Soldado Bey: Sólo la Muerte de Roxana Pudo Contrarrestar el Agravio que Esta le Causó," *La Hora*, March 26, 1965.

85. Monsignor Ignacio Martinez, interview with author, Panama City, March 12, 2002.

86. Albilio Mosquera, retired PanCanal worker, interview with author, RP, August 28, 2002.

87. Roberts to Danielson, Subject: "U.S. Army Marriages to Panamanian Undesireables," April 14, 1954, File 333.1 (Character Development), HUSAC, CID, RG 349, NARA; Lee Amberths, interview with author, Corozal, RP, January 15, 2005; Patrick O'Neill, interview with author, Balboa, RP, January 15, 2003; Miguel J. Moreno, interview with author, Panama City, April 22, 2001.

88. Lee Amberths, interview with author, Corozal, RP, January 15, 2005.

89. Lee Amberths, interview with author, Corozal, RP, January 15, 2005; Robinson to Brown, Report of Investigation, Subject: Miss Cleopatra Shields (stage name?), October 11, 1954, File 333.5, HUSAC, CID, RG 349, NARA.

90. Memorandum for the Police District Commander Cristobal, Subject: Marina Clothilde de Smitt, September 12, 1944, PFD, 99 Files, RG 185, NARA.

91. Lee Amberths, interview with author, Corozal, RP, January 15, 2005.

92. "Boquete: Retirees Paradise," *Panama News*, February 12, 2006; "Content to Watch the Bananas Grow, More Retirees Relocate to Panama," *New York Times*, April 11, 2006.

93. Lee Amberths, interview with author, Corozal, RP, January 15, 2005.

94. Un Panameño, "Reply: Gorgas Doctors," Mailbox, *Panama American*, January 5, 1956. For a larger perspective on regional domestic abuse, see Alméras et al., *Violence against Women in Couples in Latin America and the Caribbean*. Quote is from "Probe of Rosita Lane Case Is Closed in Colon," *Star and Herald*, October 30, 1942.

95. Report of the Provost Marshal, Ft. Amador, Daily Report of Unusual Incidents, Subject: Vasquez Murder, September 2, 1954, File 250.3, OPM, CID, RG 349, NARA. For further insights into Puerto Rican machismo, see Ramírez, *What It Means to Be a Man*, 7–42. For Latin American machismo in numerous countries, see Gutmann, *Changing Men and Masculinities in Latin America*.

96. Margarita Dulces Aldama, retired Panamanian waitress, interview with author, Panama City, RP, August 6, 2003.

97. "Family in U.S. Tries to Win Leniency for Bigamist," *Star and Herald*, June 20, 1942; Memorandum for Chief of Division, Subject: Aubrey Lee Conn's Marital Status, April 8, 1942, Panama Canal Zone Executive Department, PFD, 99 Files, RG 185, NARA; Subject: Marital Status of Walter Condrey, September 30, 1943, 99 Files, RG 185, NARA. For various Canal Zone bigamy cases, see Porter to Commander Special Troops, October 31, 1947, "Sgt. Harry K. Bjornberg Case," File 250.1, HPCD, Office of Adjutant General (OAG), RG 338, NARA; Mrs. Marion Rutherford to Colonel Matthews, August 9, 1948, "Sgt. Robert Keaton Rutherford Case," December 17, 1951, File 333.5, "Individual Investigations," U.S. Army Caribbean Command (USACC), OAG, RG 349, NARA; "Pvt. Virgil D. Corcoran Case," File 333.5, "Individual Investigations," U.S. Army Caribbean Command (USACC), OAG, RG 349, NARA.

98. March to Wiley, August 9, 1951, "Melva Esther Isaza Case," File 250.3, "Individual Investigations," U.S. Army Caribbean Command (USACC), OAG, RG 349, NARA. For similar examples of Latina bigamy cases in Panama, see Subject: Carmen Seldago Carsen's Attempted Bigamy, September 22, 1944, Panama Canal Zone Executive Department, PFD, 99 Files, RG 185, NARA.

99. Helen Escobar, Panamanian office worker, interview with author, Chorrera, RP, August 16, 2005.

100. "Wave of Child Support Attachments from Army Pay," *Stars and Stripes*, December 19, 1973; Bruce Lambert, "Abandoned Filipinos Sue U.S. over Child Support," *New York Times*, June 21, 1993; Francisco Herrera, interview with author, Panama City, August 22, 2003.

101. John MacTaggart, retired U.S. soldier and PanCanal employee, interview with author, Balboa, RP, August 21, 2002; Robert Wilkins, retired U.S. soldier, interview with author, Curundu, RP, July 28, 2002.

102. Miguel J. Moreno, interview with author, Panama City, April 22, 2001; William Jorden, oral history transcript, January 17, 1987, Lyndon Baines Johnson Library.

103. Mary Coffey, retired DOD secretary, interview with author, La Boca, RP, January 14, 2005.

104. Doug Williams, retired PanCanal lockmaster, interview with author, Piña, RP, December 22, 2001.

105. Jacinta Williams, retired U.S. secretary and wife of U.S. soldier, interview with author, Orlando, Florida, August 5, 2001.

106. Marbel Sánchez Guerra, Panamanian saleswoman and wife of retired Zonian, interview with author, Chorrera, RP, August 5, 2001.

107. Teresa Martínez Navarro, Panamanian government employee, interview with author, Chilibre, RP, August 12, 2006.

108. "Tivoli Hotel Embezzlement Blamed on Infatuation," *Panama American*, February 27, 1956.

109. Roberts to Brett, Subject: Recent Homosexuality Arrests, January 3, 1952, File 250.1(C) Misconduct, USACC, CID, RG 349, NARA. For the concept of "hegemonic masculinity" that informed much U.S. military behavior in Panama, see R.W. Connell and James W. Messerschmidt, "Hegemonic Masculinity"; Ramon Hinojosa, "Doing Hegemony: Military Men and Constructing Hegemonic Masculinity," *Journal of Men's Studies* 18.2 (2010): 179–94. For other imperial views on the importance of "martial masculinity," see Streets, *Martial Races*. For general heterosexual fears of "gay behavior," see Bergling, *Sissyphobia*. For differing views on male homosexuality in Latin America, and machista reactions against it, see Lancaster, *Life Is Hard*; Schifter, *Lila's House*, 37–58, 113–16.

110. *Government of the Canal Zone v. Philip Crosby*, Case no. 5029, October 14, 1960, conviction for "Infamous Crime Against Nature," District Court Records of the Canal Zone, RG 21,

WNRC; Affidavit by Deponent in Case against Lt. Paul K. Ceasar, November 13, 1956, File
333.5, USACC, CID, RG 349, NARA; Subject: Sodomy by Lieutenant David A. Pohl, Statement
of Lt. Paul K. Caesar, October 24, 1947, File 250.1, HPCD, OPM, RG 338, NARA; Neuropsychiatric Service, SU 7452nd, Certificate of Examination: Sgt. Leon W. Harker, November 27, 1947,
File 250.1, HPCD, OPM, RG 338, NARA.

111. Subject: James Waint, Panamanian, Charged with Sodomy on 2 U.S. Soldiers, September 17, 1947, File 250.1, USACC, CID, RG 338, NARA; Penn and Shoen Associates, *Homosexuality and the Military.*

112. Memorandum to the Assistant Chief of Staff, Subject: Alleged Homosexuality among
Enlisted Women, December 9, 1947, File 250.1(C), HUSCC, RG 338, NARA; "Clinical Record
of Stanton, Margaret, Pfc.," Complaint: Neuropsychiatric Observation for Alleged Sexual De-
viation, March 20, 1947, File 250.1, USACC, CID, RG 338, NARA.

113. Greaves, interview with author, San Miguelito, RP, January 5, 2004.

114. "WACs Dressed for the Occasion Will Get Their Men," *Panama American,* September
18, 1946. For rules on fraternization, see Women's Army Corps, *A Book of Facts about the WAC.*

115. "Suicide Hinted in Death of U.S. Woman Worker: Cited for Misconduct with Teen-
Aged Girl," *Panama American,* July 22, 1946.

116. Hyam, *Empire and Sexuality,* 34; Aldrich, *Colonialism and Homosexuality,* 188.

117. "The Male Animal," Mailbox, *Panama American,* July 30, 1948.

118. "Canal Zone Wolves," Mailbox, *Panama American,* July 24, 1948; Werewolf, "Sisters
under the Sun," Mailbox, *Panama American,* July 27, 1948.

119. "Gentleman Writes," Mailbox, *Panama American,* July 28, 1948.

120. Sally Sue, "Some Suggestions," Mailbox, *Panama American,* December 23, 1945;
U.S.-Bound AF Wife, "Keg of Dynamite," Mailbox, *Panama American,* February 17, 1956.

121. Franck, *Zone Policeman 88,* 29. For similar attitudes in another colonial setting, see
Georgina Gowans, "Gender, Imperialism and Domesticity," *Gender, Place and Culture* 8 (September 2001): 255–69; Alma Henderson, interview with author, Orlando, Florida, August 3,
2001.

122. I. Retch, "Strong Medicine," Mailbox, *Panama American,* September 25, 1956; BB, "He-
Man Hunter Speaks Up," *Panama American,* October 2, 1956. For more scholarly analysis of the
importance of guns and hunting to masculine imperial identities, see Mackenzie, *Empire of
Nature.* For hegemonic versus subordinate masculinity, see Mike Donaldson, "What Is Hegemonic Masculinity?"; Connell and Messerschmidt, "Hegemonic Masculinity."

123. For the strong Zonian identification with the U.S. military, see "A Christmas Message
from Governor Leber" (a tribute to the Zone-born serving in Vietnam), *Spillway,* December 22,
1967, 3–4; "U.S. Preparedness Briefing Monday on the Atlantic Side," *Spillway,* December 15,
1967, 1; "Amphibious Forces Ships Escorted through the Panama Canal During the Cuban
Missile Crisis," http://www.usshullassociation.org/DD945/Amphibious%20Ship%20List
/AmphibiousShipList.htm; "Canal Closed to Commercial Traffic for Missile Crisis in Cuba,"
Washington Post, October 22, 1962.

124. "Residents of Ancon Guard Fence for Security: Tensions Still High after Riot's Calm,"
Star and Herald, January 15, 1964.

125. Puzzled, "Re: She Chauffeurs," *Panama America,* September 6, 1945; Jane, Betty, and
Susie, "Whatcha Want—Eggs in Your Beer?," Mailbox, *Panama America,* July 2, 1946; "It's the
Women Again," Mailbox, *Panama America,* September 13, 1946; Tax Payer, "Five Buck Fever,"
Mailbox, *Panama America,* February 7, 1956.

126. "Governor's Wife Gives 2nd Get Acquainted Tea," *Panama American,* September 21,
1956. For other chauvinistically named dishes, see Graham, *Tropical Cooking in Panama;* U.S.

Medical Wives Society, *La Cocina de Panamá*; "CZ's Youngest Generals Preparing for Big Events," *Panama America*, May 14, 1951; "Canal Zone First Boys State Begins Six Year Program at Ft. Gulick," *Panama America*, June 13, 1955; "Generals and Admirals-for-the-Day Awarded by VFW," *Panama America*, May 17, 1955.

127. For U.S. women workers in the early days of the Zone, see Greene, *The Canal Builders*, 107–16, 226–66; "Nursing Has Come a Long Way Since the Days of Dorothy Dix," *Spillway*, March 18, 1964, 3.

128. "537 Women Will Lose Differential," *Spillway*, October 7, 1966, 1. By law, only one breadwinner per U.S. family could receive the differential, typically the husband since he earned more in most cases. This remained a source of resentment for many U.S. working wives for years.

129. "Editor's Note," Mailbox, *Panama American*, July 2, 1946; R. Dancer, "Resourceful Women," *Panama American*, March 31, 1950.

130. "New Maternity Leave Regulations," *Spillway*, January 5, 1968, 4.

131. "Attractive Gamboa Wife and Mother Is First Woman to Transit Canal in Cayuco," *Spillway*, July 10, 1948.

132. "Girl Bullfighter Here Tomorrow for Performance," *Panama American*, February 1, 1956; "Bette Ford Se Despidira con la Afición Del Istmo," *Panamá Américana*, February 1, 1956; Gus O'Shaugn, "Bette Ford, Story of a Lady Bullfighter," *Village Voice*, August 1955.

133. Mary Newland, "Republic's First Woman Cabinet Minister Successfully Combines Career and Femininity," *Panama American*, July 29, 1950. For conflicts and alliances between feminism and "femininity" in the region, see Emilie L. Bergmann (ed.), *Women, Culture, and Politics in Latin America*; "Panama Still Tensely Quiet: 375 Jailed, 4 Dead," *Panama American*, July 6, 1948. For King's views on the United States and Panama, see King, *La Problema de la Soberanía en las Relaciones entre Panamá y los Estados Unidos*; "Lack of Leaders Led to Riots—Thelma King," *Panama American*, June 20, 1966. For her daily column "Tribuna Publica," see "La Lucha Racial en Los Estados Unidos," *La Hora*, March 16, 1965; "Panameños Deportados de la Zona del Canal," *La Hora*, March 18, 1965.

134. Chris Skeie, retired PanCanal employee, interview with author, Balboa, RP, January 22, 2002; Sarah Chamberlain, daughter of PanCanal pilot, interview with author, Piña, RP, August 12, 2008.

135. Marvin Wainwright, interview with author, Balboa, RP, May 12, 2002; George Wheeler, interview with author, Piña, RP, December 23, 2002. For wife-swapping in colonial Kenya, see Fox, *White Mischief*.

Chapter 5: The U.S. Military

1. "El Soldado Relata el Bestial Asesinato de Niño de 20 Meses," *Panamá América*, November 26, 1956; "More Details of Rose's Atrocities in the Panamanian Papers," *Panama American*, November 27, 1956.

2. Okun, *The Early Roman Frontier on the Upper Rhine Area*.

3. Jamail, *Panama Canal Zone*, 27–30; LaFeber, *The Panama Canal*, 94–98.

4. For such images, see cartoons in editorial sections of *La Hora*, *Crítica*, and *El Día*, January 9–21, 1964. For a good account of who killed whom during the riots, see Eric Jackson, "The Beginning of the End of the Canal Zone," *Panama News*, December 28, 1999; "Inside Story of the Panama Riots," *U.S. News and World Report*, March 30, 1964.

5. Memorandum of a Telephone Conversation, O'Meara to Taylor, January 10, 1964, FRUS, 1964–68, 31: 771–72.

6. International Commission of Jurists, *Report on the Events in Panama*; "Panama's Case Falling Flat before International Jurists," *Miami Herald*, January 14, 1964. For analysis of the riot's postmortem and consequences, see McPherson, "Courts of World Opinion."

7. Enloe, *Bananas, Beaches, and Bases*; Enloe, *The Morning After*.

8. Osvaldo Jordan Romeros, interview with author, Diablo, RP, July 20, 2002.

9. Miguel J. Moreno, interview with author, Panama City, April 22, 2001. For Panamanian officials' preference for U.S. commanders over Zone authorities, see Harrington to Sowash, March 21, 1956, FRUS, 1955–57, 7: 267–68.

10. For Panamanian repulsion-attraction toward U.S. soldiers and culture, see Ealy, *Yanqui Politics and the Isthmian Canal*, 98–111.

11. "Los bases estadounidenses," *La Prensa*, December 25, 1991; "La presencía de los bases militares en Panamá," *La Prensa*, December 1, 1999; Gurdian Guerra, "Evolución histórica de la presencia militar norteamericana en Panamá," 360–421.

12. "Mother Tells How GI Beat 20 Month Old Son," *Panama American*, November 27, 1956; "Information re: medical treatment for dependent—Harold Frederick Rose," Wilson to Cox, February 17, 1957, File 250.3, "Correction and Punishment," USACC, OAG, RG 349, NARA; "Las Protestas de Los Negroes de Montgomery Continuan," *La Hora*, February 5, 1956.

13. "Asesinado por Su Padrastro con la Venia de Su Madre," *La Hora*, November 27, 1956; "Another Soldier Was Father of the Slain Boy," *Panama American*, November 28, 1956; "Ustedes lo Mataron" and "El Pecado de Ser Negrito," *La Hora*, November 27, 1956; "Declara Blanca María: Quien Mantiene A Mis Hijos?," *La Hora*, November 28, 1956; Subject: Exercise of Criminal Jurisdiction by Foreign Tribunals over U.S. Service Personnel Subject to Military Law, October 13, 1953, File 250.44, USACC, OAG, RG 349, NARA.

14. For cultural import of the cholita, see "Mi Cholita," in Vilanueva, *Música, Cantos y Danzas de Panamá*; Velasquez, *La pollera y la cultura interiorana de Panamá*, 51–57.

15. "El Niño Muriendose de Hambre y la Madre Bailando el Mambo," *La Hora*, July 2, 1955.

16. "Ahi Te Dejo Esa Vaina y Tiro A Su Hija Menor," *La Hora*, July 5, 1955; "El También es Panameño Abandonado!," *La Hora*, July 5, 1955; "Norbeta García Llega A Intervenir," *La Hora*, July 22, 1955. The final installment with the family posing in Chiriqui beneath the picture of President Remón is at "Asi Se Cerro Ese Capitulo Doloroso," *La Hora*, July 23, 1955. For Remón's ties to vice, see Pippin, *The Remón Era*, 6, 123–27.

17. Transcript of trial in Caribbean Command Teletype 6636, U.S. Army Caribbean to the Department of the Army, January 3, 1958, File 250.3, USACC, OAG, RG 349, NARA; also in "Rose Receives 20 Months for Manslaughter," *Star and Herald*, January 4, 1958.

18. "Diez Eventos Importantísimos de 1956," *La Hora*, December 31, 1956.

19. Medina, *Estimación de indicadores demográficos de la República de Panamá por el período 1950–1970*, 43–52; Weil et al., *Area Handbook for Panama*, 245–49.

20. Robert Thrush, interview with author, Panama City, July 16, 2002.

21. *Enlisted Man's Guide to Panama*; More and Jurey, *Panama in Your Pocket*; Subject: Orientation Regarding Proper Conduct in Republic of Panama, Goal: Respect for Panama, Panamanian Citizens, and the Panamanian Flag, June 24, 1954, File 250.1, HUSCC, RG 349, NARA; Wayne Bryant, interview with author, Balboa, RP, August 1, 2003.

22. U.S. *Army Caribbean Command Strategic Seminar 1954*, in PCC, CRT.

23. For U.S. policy toward African American troops in Panama, see Memorandum for Commander-in-Chief U.S. Headquarters Caribbean Command (USHCC), Subject: Negro Troops of United States Army on the Isthmus, January 14, 1942, File 291.2 (Race), RG 338, NARA; Belsi de Medina, U.S. consulate official, interview with author, Panama City, May 12, 2002; Xiomara de Robleta, interview with author, Quarry Heights, RP, June 3, 2001; Fulvia

Sucre, Panamanian secretary and wife, interview with author, Quarry Heights, RP, June 4, 2001.

24. Major, *Prize Possession*, 13–33; Conniff, *Panama and the United States*, 24–52; Lindsay-Poland, *Emperors in the Jungle*, 14–25.

25. Mack, *The Land Divided*, 211–35; Mellander and Mellander, *Charles Edward Magoon*, 16–26, 38–42; Conn and Fairchild, *The Western Hemisphere*, 413–15; De Mena, *The Era of U.S. Army Installations in Panama*, 7–54; Morris, *Guarding the Crossroads*, 128–63.

26. Gill, *School of the Americas*, 23–89; "School of the Dictators," *New York Times*, September 28, 1996; Mary McGrory, "Manuals for Murderers," *Washington Post*, September 26, 1996.

27. Johnson, *An American Legacy in Panama*; Johnson, *A History of the Quarry Heights Military Reservation*, 56–68; Lindsay-Poland, *Emperors in the Jungle*, 195–98.

28. For an overview of the U.S. hemispheric mission in Panama in the 1970s–1980s, see Black, *Sentinels of the Empire*; Morris, *Guarding the Crossroads*, 59–83.

29. Pearcy, *We Answer Only to God*, 109–32; LaFeber, *The Panama Canal*, 90–94; Vergara, *Acuerdos militares entre Panamá y los Estados Unidos*, 83–89; Acosta, *La influencia decisiva de la opinión pública en el rechazo del convenio Filós-Hines de 1947*, 48–57. For Panamanian resistance to the U.S. presence, see Gurdian Guerra, *La presencia militar de los Estados Unidos en Panamá*, 59–71.

30. For a comparative study in the Philippines, see Linn, *Guardians of Empire*.

31. Richard J. Levine, "The Good Life: Canal Zone Duty Is Nice for U.S. Military but Criticism Mounts," *Wall Street Journal*, January 10, 1974.

32. Charles Martin, "Ready at the Ninth Parallel," *Army Digest* 58 (March 1970): 25–28; "Budget Knife Threatens Southcom," *Star and Herald*, January 11, 1974. For military sporting events, see "U.S. Panama Team Wins '57 Golf Tournament" and "1957 Panama Area Armed Forces Boxing Tournament Begins," *Buccaneer*, November 21, 1957. For cross-national competitions, see "MP All-Stars Set Softball Series with Panama National Guard," *Buccaneer*, June 9, 1961; "Panama All-Stars Five Blisters Kobbe Stars," *Buccaneer*, April 28, 1961. For U.S. officers' anger over bad behavior at cross-national sports competitions, see "Subject: Personal Conduct at Sporting Events," McCarr to All Ranks, February 1, 1955, File 250.1, USACC, RG 349, NARA.

33. Report of the Inspector General, Subject: "Problems at Fort Kobbe," January 23, 1958, Folder 196, File 331.7, OPM, RG 349, NARA.

34. Juan Jiménez-Ramírez, retired U.S. soldier, interview with author, Curundu, RP, August 2, 2002.

35. Karl Marsden, retired U.S. soldier, interview with author, Curundu, RP, January 14, 2003.

36. For Rousenvell's attacks on military, see *Panama American*, July 4, 7, 12, 1935. For U.S. military suicides in the Zone, see "DRUI: Lieutenant Rudolph Wiedeman's Suicide Attempt," February 5, 1947, File 250.1, HPCD, OPM, RG 349, NARA; Criminal Investigation Report: Murder and Suicide, March 5, 1948, File 210.86, Folder: Joseph H. Sierer, HUSAC, OAG, RG 349, NARA; Investigation: Self-Inflicted Wound of Pvt. Charles G. Erskine, April 10, 1956, File 331.5, RG 349, NARA; "DRUI: Sgt. Charles W. Harding's Suicide Attempt," November 25, 1952, File 250.3, HUSAC, Adjutant General Report (AGR), RG 349, NARA.

37. For U.S. military atrocities in Panama during World War II, see "Zona Del Canal: Incidentes entre Soldados del Ejército de los Estados Unidos y ciudadanos panameños," vol. 17, bk. 2, 1941–49, AMRE; "Agreement between the United States and Panama for Leasing Defense Sites in Panama," FRUS, 1942, 6: 577–619.

38. "Army Police Arrest 4 Suspects in Armed Robbery of RP Bar," *Panama American*, February 21, 1950.

39. National Police of Panama Investigation, Charge: Armed Robbery, June 5, 1952, File 335, OAG, RG 349, NARA; Record and Recommendation: Court Martial for Armed Robbery, June 24, 1952, File 250.3, Adjudication and Punishment, File 335, OAG, RG 349, NARA.

40. "Clayton GI Admits Robbing Bargirl," *Panama American*, March 18, 1965.

41. "Three Missing Men in 'Hired' Cayuco Back from Taboga," *Panama American*, June 12, 1951; "GI Robs Car, Steals Maid Too," *Star and Herald*, January 19, 1958.

42. Fulvia Sucre, interview with author, Quarry Heights, RP, June 9, 2001.

43. For GI-caused traffic deaths in postwar Panama, see "Manslaughter Charge Filed against GI Who Struck Farmer," *Panama American*, March 10, 1950; Report of Investigation—Military Police, Offense: Manslaughter, Involuntary, Subject: Spc 3 James N. Mitchell, Victim: 11-year-old Enelda Ricoy-Baptista, March 15, 1956, USCC, OAG, File 331.5, RG 349, NARA; "Manslaughter Count Brought against Gulick GI," *Panama American*, June 7, 1956; "2 Marines Detained in Death of Panamanian in Cerro Azul," *Panama American*, February 14, 1957; "Car Kills Panamanian Woman in Balboa" (Pfc. Eugene William Roberts was driving), *Panama American*, March 13, 1965; "Zone Soldier to Serve RP Manslaughter Rap: Cpl. Alfred Pickett Killed Popular Panamanian Sports Figure, Adam Gordon in March 1966 Predawn Crash," *Panama American*, January 11, 1968; "19 Year Old RP Girl Injured in Accident with GI Companion," *Panama American*, February 17, 1950; "GI Pleads Guilty to Manslaughter of RP Girl," *Panama American*, October 17, 1956. In this last case Pfc. Jimmy Ray Williams received a suspended sentence after agreeing to pay the family of his eighteen-year-old date, Ofelía Caiedo, $200 for the death of their daughter. For a highly prejudiced Zonian critique of Panamanian driving, see "Hard and Heavy, 'Alto!' (Stop!)," Mailbox, *Panama American*, December 31, 1945; Report on Improvement Record for U.S. Motor Accidents, December 12, 1978, Washington Office Subject Files 1960–79, PCC, RG 185, NARA.

44. For U.S. concerns, see "Points of Friction with the Local Population," in Harrington to Martin, February 14, 1957, FRUS, 1955–57, 7: 331–32; Pearcy, *We Answer Only to God*, 109–32; Luis Guagnini, "La Guardía Nacional," *Revista Tareas* 40 (October–December 1977): 67–82.

45. Subject: Enlisted Men's Behavior in Panamanian Night Court, August 12, 1957, File 250.1, HUSCC, OAG, RG 349, NARA.

46. "Arrest of Pfc. Aguirre-Delgado," March 19, 1954, File 250.3, Daily Report of Unusual Incidents, USACC, OPM, RG 349, NARA. For reference to Pfc. Romero, see Memorandum for Assistant Chief of Staff—GI, Subject: Improper Conduct of Military Police, November 29, 1947, USACC, OPM, File 335.5, RG 338, NARA.

47. "Five Soldiers, 4 Others Involved in Brawls over Past Week-end," *Panama American*, September 17, 1950; Enrique Silvio, interview with author, San Miguelito, RP, April 14, 2002.

48. *Government of the Canal Zone v. Gerald David Thomas, Gustave Edward Smith, and Melvin Charles Alloway*, August 27, 1950, Case no. 3015, District Court Records of the Canal Zone, RG 21, WNRC.

49. Memo: "Final Investigation of Report on Assault on Sgt. Melber," June 16, 1947, File 250.01, Daily Report of Unusual Incidents, HPCD, OPM, RG 338, NARA; "Soldado de E.E.U.U. Deputado Asaltado Por Soldado Yanki," *La Hora*, June 6, 1947.

50. Karl Marsden, interview with author, Curundu, RP, July 22, 2003. For some of the vast literature on these masculinity concepts, see Messerschmidt, "Engendering Gendered Knowledge."

51. "Violaciones de Ley 79—Articulos 186–189," República de Panamá, Contoloría General de la República, *Estadística Panameña* 25–29 (October 1968–October 1972); Torrijos Herrera, *La Batalla de Panamá*, 113.

52. Subject: Mistreatment of U.S. Citizens, Sayre to Tack, January 11, 1972, Expediente

No. 1048–6, Asuntos Varios, 1972, La Zona Del Canal, bk. 4, AMRE; "Complaint of Assault," July 26, 1953, File 250.3, HUSAC, OPM, RG 349, NARA; "Army Refers to Increase in Assaults and RP Incident Reports," *Panama American*, October 18, 1963; Rex Raspberry, interview with author, Balboa, RP, May 12, 2001.

53. For historical connections between the U.S. military and the Panamanian National Guard, see Harding, *Military Foundations of Panamanian Politics*, 11–23; Arosemena, "El Cuerpo de Policía Nacional," 503–48.

54. "U.S. Army, RP Guardsmen Convene to Combat Crime," *Star and Herald*, January 5, 1956; "Guardsmen and GIs Work Together," *Buccaneer*, December 17, 1961; "RP Guardsmen Shoots Hoodlum Chased by GI," *Panama American*, March 22, 1965; "General Torrijos y la Guardia Nacional: Nueva Actitud Hasta Soberania Nacional," *Más Para Todos*, November 23, 1971; Silvio, retired National Guardsman, interview with author, San Miguelito, RP, April 14, 2002.

55. "U.S. Relief Team Extends Services in Disaster Area," *Buccaneer*, June 10, 1960; "Panamanian Kids to Be Entertained by MPs, Infantry," *Buccaneer*, December 19, 1958; "Solders Lend Helping Hand to Little Panamanian Girl," *Buccaneer*, December 6, 1957; "Best Soldiers Selected for Interior Aid Tour," *Buccaneer*, May 24, 1957; "Servicemen Take Time Machine Excursion to San Blas Islands," *Buccaneer*, March 14, 1958; "Contributions Continue for Needy of Marañón," *Buccaneer*, October 28, 1960.

56. "Benefits to Panama from U.S. Military Presence in the Canal Zone," *Spillway*, February 17, 1964, 3–4. For U.S. aid during the El Chorrillo fire, see "6 Dead, 500 Homeless in Chorrillo Fire Catastrophe," *Panama American*, February 27, 1950; "Distraught Fire Victims Aided by Samaritan Shore Patrol at the Limits," *Panama American*, February 28, 1950; "Army Units, RP Organs Continue to Aid Fire Victims," *Panama American*, March 2, 1950. For the San Miguel fire, see "Army Aids Fire Victims," *Buccaneer*, January 24, 1958; "Army Provides Aid to Panama Fire Victims," *Buccaneer*, January 17, 1958; "Zone Military Bring Health and Happiness to Darien Village" and "GI Santas Used Jeeps, Trucks and Plane to Bring Joy to Kiddies in Interior," *Panama American*, January 6, 1965.

57. "Operation Friendship Underway—Gen. Bogart," *Buccaneer*, July 15, 1960; "Army Cage Team Helps Interior Town Raise Funds for New Church," *Buccaneer*, October 14, 1960; "Ft. Davis Platoon GIs Helping Hand to Needy Family," *Buccaneer*, November 12, 1961; "79th Army Band Presents Concert at Panama School" and "Ft. Amador Wives Design and Make Dolls for Panamanian Children," *Buccaneer*, September 23, 1960; "Post Adopts Children's Hospital" and "GIs Take 95 Panamanian School Kids on Zoo Trip at Ft. Sherman," *Buccaneer*, August 26, 1960. For a more critical view of Operation Friendship, see Knapp and Knapp, *Red, White, and Blue Paradise*, 112–18.

58. "Operación Amistad Entre Generales: Bogart y O'Meara," *Panama América*, March 4, 1964; Estéban Moscoso, retired Panamanian bus driver, interview with author, Ancon, RP, January 14, 2002.

59. Andrew Richards, retired U.S. soldier, interview with author, Ft. Myers, Florida, August 12, 2001.

60. "Subject: Trial of Sailor for Refusal to Pay Legal Debt," February 6, 1958, File 250.3, Daily Report of Unusual Incidents, HUSAC, OPM, RG 349, NARA; File 250.3, HUSAC, OPM, RG 349, NARA; Subject: Failure to Pay Legal Debt," April 10, 1948, File 230.82, Daily Report of Unusual Incidents, HUSAC, OPM, RG 349, NARA. For gun incident, see December 27, 1954, File 250.3, Daily Report of Unusual Incidents, HUSAC, OPM, RG 349, NARA. For classic "Failure to Pay a Legal Debt" case involving insolvent GI and local taxi driver, see April 12, 1954, File 250.3, Daily Report of Unusual Incidents, HUSAC, OPM, RG 349, NARA.

61. "Soldier Pays Fine for Bottle Attack on Parked Chiva," *Panama American*, September 3, 1945.

62. Julío de Vargas, retired Panamanian taxi driver, interview with author, Ancon, RP, April 22, 2003; José Guevara E., interview with author, Panama City, January 19, 2002.

63. For ethnic and racial divisions within armies, see Enloe, *Ethnic Soldiers*.

64. Marín, "Puerto Ricans in Defense of the Canal," PCC, CRT. For other examples of "colonial armies," see Killingray and Omissi, *Guardians of Empire*.

65. Memorandum for Chief of Staff, Subject: Visit of the Department of the Army, November 15–17 inclusive, November 21, 1950, File 334–342, HUSAC, OAG, RG 349, NARA. For studies of Puerto Rican soldiers' alleged genetic inferiority that informed such racist attitudes among white U.S. commanders, see Goodman, "Genital Defects and Venereal Disease among Porto Rican Draft Troops"; Goodman, "Skin Diseases among the Porto Rican Troops"; Goodman, "Ulcerating Granuloma of the Pudenda."

66. Morris, *Guarding the Crossroads*, 68–82, in PCC, CRT. For early twentieth-century racial theories, see McFerson, *The Racial Dimension of American Overseas Colonial Policy*, 1–50, 79–98, 117–38; Stepan, *The Hour of Eugenics*; Hector R. Marín, "Puerto Ricans in Defense of the Canal," 1948, 5–7, PCC, CRT.

67. Morris, *Guarding the Crossroads*, 82.

68. "Utilization of Puerto Rican Manpower," September 19, 1955, File 312.1, HUSAC, Office of the Adjutant General, RG 349, NARA.

69. "Military Force Levels—Panama," Gaither to Harrington, December 30, 1959, HUSAC, RG 349, NARA; Robert Thrush, interview with author, Panama City, August 12, 2002; José Torres-Rivera, retired U.S. soldier, interview with author, Curundu, RP, August 4, 2002.

70. The U.S. Army's 470th Military Intelligence Group in CZ employed numerous Puerto Rican Americans, some in high positions of responsibility, such as Efraín Angueira, a G-2 liaison officer with the National Guard in the 1960s and the 1970s, and his superior, Armando Parada. For Angueira's and Parada's roles in the U.S.-Panamanian intrigues, see Koster and Sánchez, *In the Time of the Tyrants*, 77, 113–15, 125, 130, 136, 278; R. M. Koster, retired U.S. officer and novelist, interview with author, Panama City, June 9, 2001.

71. Roberto Cruz, former U.S. soldier and PanCanal employee, interview with author, Balboa, RP, July 21, 2005; Jimenez-Ramirez, interview with author, Curundu, RP, August 4, 2002; Rolando Sterling Arango, interview with author, Albrook, RP, April 22, 2001.

72. Xiomara de Robleta, director of Foreign Ministry Archive, interview with author, Quarry Heights, RP, May 12, 2001.

73. "Knifed Girl Had Refused to Marry Her Soldier Killer," *Panama American*, July 11, 1953; "Puerto Rican Soldier Used Commando Knife in Slaying," *Panama American*, July 12, 1953. For Puerto Rican GI crimes in Panama, see "Criminal Activity among U.S. Troops in Panama," April 7, 1960, File 250.1, Office of the Adjutant General, RG 349, NARA; "3 Ft. Davis GIs Held after Pfc's Death," *Panama American*, October 31, 1956.

74. Porter to General Crittenberger, quoted in Lindsay-Poland, *Emperors in the Jungle*, 57. Lindsay-Poland also details the U.S. military's use of Puerto Rican troops as "medical guinea pigs" for numerous chemical gas experiments during World War II (57–59).

75. "65th Commander Applauds His Guitar Plucking Troops," *Panama American*, June 24, 1951; "Puerto Rican Vets of Korea Going Home with Grim Stories," *Panama American*, May 19, 1951; "Army Reinstates 37 Puerto Ricans: Courtmartialed and Sentenced to 5 Years Hard Labor for Refusing to Advance in Korea," *Panama American*, July 14, 1953. For the 65th Regiment's experience in Korea, see Harris, *Puerto Rico's Fighting 65th US Infantry*.

76. For a study of World War II language training in Puerto Rico, see Collazo, *Guerra y*

educación; "Utilization of Puerto Rican Manpower," September 19, 1955, File 312.1, HUSAC, OAG, RG 349, NARA. For problems of bilingualism in Puerto Rico, see Cafferty and Rivera-Martínez, *The Politics of Language.*

77. Criminal Investigation Report, "Assault with a Deadly Weapon," January 10, 1951, File 333.5, HUSAC, OAG, RG 349, NARA.

78. Criminal Investigation Report on Pfc. Medina, "Attempted Murder on Firing Range," November 13, 1951, File 250.1, HUSAC, OAG, RG 349, NARA.

79. Enrique Torres-Rivera, retired U.S. soldier, interview with author, Curundu, RP, August 4, 2002.

80. Porter to Sibert, July 21, 1950, File 334–342, USACC, OAG, RG 349, NARA; "Subject: Enlistment of Negroes," File 291.2–311.4, USACC, OAG, RG 349, NARA; Panamanian quote from Pedrias, *Memorias 1945*, 113, AMRE; Subject: Friction between Military Personnel and Canal Zone Employees—Charges of Racism, December 12, 1956, Whitman to Potter, PCC, Washington Office Subject Files, RG 185, NARA.

81. "Psychotic Soldier Holds 100 at Bay," *Panama American*, August 15, 1953. Subject: Pvt. Angel Ramos Incident and Arrest, August 18, 1951, USACC, CID, RG 349, NARA.

82. Southern Command, Synopsis of Events, January 1964, RG 185, NARA; Cruz, interview with author, Balboa, RP, July 23, 2002. This is borne out in all Reports of Unusual Incidents from Caribbean Command records 1947–63, in which Puerto Rican soldiers figure prominently in Army crime data.

83. Methvin, "The Anatomy of A Riot," 479–88; International Commission of Jurists, *Report on the Events in Panama*, 16–34; "Slain Soldier's Body Returns from Panama," *New York Times*, January 16, 1964; Subject: Arrival of Widow of S/Sergeant Luis Jiménez-Cruz, January 17, 1964, and for $25 charge see Vance to Blauwkomp, January 31, 1964, both in Folder: CO 232 Panama, 1/12/64–1/31/64, Lyndon Baines Johnson Library; "Servicemen Survivors Fund Contributions Now Total $4200," *Spillway*, January 27, 1964, 1.

84. For the postwar Puerto Rican nationalist movement in 1964, see Vientós Gastón, *Comentarios a un ensayo sobre Puerto Rico*; Flores, *Divided Borders*; Ramón Modena, retired U.S. soldier, interview with author, Curundu, RP, August 4, 2002; Jordan Romeros, interview with author, Corozal, RP, July 17, 2002.

85. Brett to Cabot, Subject: Additional Colored Enlisted Naval Personnel to the Canal Zone, April 17, 1943, also referred to in detail in Murray to Lansing, April 11, 1947, and in "Participation of Negro Troops in the Post-war Military Establishment," May 23, 1945, all in File 291.2, HPCD, OAG, RG 338, NARA; Goytía to Hull, Subject: Negro Troops of United States Army on the Isthmus, January 14, 1942, File 291.2 (C) Race, HPCD, OAG, RG 338, NARA; "Subject: Enlistment of Negroes," McCarr to Sterling, May 14, 1950, File 291.2 (C) Race, HPCD, OAG, RG 338, NARA.

86. To C/S from G1, September 1, 1950, File 291.2–311.4, HPCD, OAG, RG 338, NARA.

87. President's Committee on Equal Opportunity in the Armed Forces, *Equality of Treatment and Opportunity for Negro Military Personnel Stationed within the United States.* For the decline in U.S. military morale during and after the Vietnam War, see Loory, *Defeated*, 39–57; Moser, *The New Winter Soldiers*; Paul L. Savage and Richard A. Gabriel, "Cohesion and Disintegration in the American Army," in Hixson, *Military Aspects of the Vietnam Conflict*, 120–56; "Subject: Activities of Black Militant Serviceman in L.A. Communities," April 19, 1972, Internal Security Office, PCC, RG 185, NARA; "Black GIs to Protest CZ Racism This Sunday," *Panama American*, November 14, 1972; "5 GIs Hurt in Racial Clash at Fort Davis in Canal Zone," *New York Times*, May 30, 1974.

88. Subject: "Protest against Discrimination at Canal Zone Elks Clubs," October 25, 1971,

PCC, Washington Office Subject Files, RG 185, NARA; Innis to Conley, October 2, 1972, PCC, Washington Office Subject Files, RG 185, NARA; "Fallo contra los Elks en la Zona," *Estrella de Panamá*, September 10, 1973, in Expediente no. 102, "Discriminación Racial En La Zona Del Canal," AMRE.

89. "Asilados como miembros de una fuerza armada extranjera," *Matutino*, May 11, 1971; "Servicemen Claim Bias," *Washington Post*, May 13, 1971.

90. "3 GIs Defect to Panama," *Panama American*, May 5, 1971.

91. "Panamá Concede Asilo a Tres Miembros de Ejército de Los E.E.U.U.," *La Hora*, May 11, 1971.

92. For the plight of African American service personnel in the Vietnam War, see Westheider, *Fighting on Two Fronts*; Mullen, *Blacks in America's Wars*; "Deserter GIs Prefer Panama to U.S.," *Panama American*, May 10, 1971.

93. "2 USA Investigators Arrested in Panama," *Star and Herald*, May 11, 1971; "Pentagon Dazed by Kidnapping Charge in RP," *Star and Herald*, May 12, 1971.

94. For the official U.S. version of the alleged kidnapping attempt, see U.S. Military Personnel in Custody in Panama, Meeting of the Panama Review Committee, May 18, 1971, Internal Security Office, PCC, RG 185, NARA. For the Panamanian reaction, see "La Cancillería Protestara al Embajada de E.U. por Intención de Secuestrar a los Asilados," *La Hora*, May 11, 1971; Restrepo, "Otra Agresion," in "Vox Populi Vox Dei" column, *Matutino*, May 12, 1971; Opiña, "Otro Lado de La Moneda," *Matutino*, May 12, 1971.

95. "Raw Deal, 3 Defectors Say," *Washington Star*, May 13, 1971. For a historical context to the African American dissent on the Vietnam War, see Harrison, "Impact of the Vietnam War on the Civil Rights Movement in the Midsixties," in Hixson, *The Vietnam Antiwar Movement*, 97–115; Restrepo, "Otra Agresion," *Matutino*, May 12, 1971. For the U.S. State Department confusion over the incident, see Subject: Panama Grants Asylum to Three American Soldiers, Rogers to Sayre, May 11, 1971, and embassy's reply, Subject: Two U.S. Servicemen Accused of Kidnapping Attempt, May 11, 1971, both in Internal Security Office, PCC, RG 185, NARA.

96. "GI Refugees Expecting Word from Lawyer," *Star and Herald*, June 22, 1971.

97. "Reporte de la Oficina del Ministro de Juicia," *Crítica*, May 21, 1971.

98. Colonel Lawrence Liberty, retired U.S. officer and businessman, interview with author, Balboa, RP, April 12, 2002.

99. For an overview of U.S. military–civilian relations, see Feaver, *Armed Servants*. For military base–civilian relations, see Dardia et al., *The Effects of Military Base Closures on Local Communities*. For the perennial complaint over military dual use of Zone facilities, see Joe Civilian, "Is This the Only Worry You've Got?," Mailbox, *Panama American*, February 7, 1945; Mr. Fly in Your Ointment, "Beware, Beware," Mailbox, *Panama American*, September 27, 1945.

100. Straight Shooter, "Stirring Up Trouble," Mailbox, *Panama American*, July 8, 1953.

101. Ex-Civilian 30 Year Soldier, "And an Upper Cut to the Jaw," Mailbox, *Panama American*, May 5, 1950.

102. Ft. Clayton Wife, "Unfair Tally," Mailbox, *Panama American*, July 31, 1950.

103. Disgusted GI, "Griping Civilians," Mailbox, *Panama American*, January 13, 1951.

104. Joe from Ft. Gulick, "Come to Sunny Panama," Mailbox, *Panama American*, July 21, 1951.

105. Nina Kosik, interview with author, Balboa, RP, August 11, 2003.

106. Wayne Bryant, interview with author, Balboa, RP, August 1, 2003.

107. For the early borderland nexus of contamination, disease, and sexuality, see Orenstein, "Sanitary Inspection of the Canal Zone"; Goodman, "The Antivenereal Campaign in Panama."

108. Kurt Buttelmann, former Zonian youth and current U.S. businessman, interview with author, Piña, RP, July 28, 2003.

109. Tom Carey, interview with author, Balboa, RP, April 14, 2001; Buttelman, interview with author, Piña, RP, July 28, 2003.

110. Tom Carey, interview with author, Balboa, RP, April 14, 2001.

111. For an overview of the 1964 riots see LaFeber, *The Panama Canal*, 105–9. For a multiperspective analysis, see McPherson, *Yankee No!*, 77–117. For Panamanian aid to stranded Americans, see "Panamanians Helped Many U.S. Neighbors," *Spillway*, January 20, 1964, 2. Some nine thousand American civilians and dependents, many of them businesspeople, lived in Panama in 1964, two-thirds in the transit cities and one-third in David, Boquete, and the interior. Some two thousand fled into the Zone following the riots. See "Here's How to Help Evacuees in the CZ," January 27, 1964, 1, and Memorandum for the Department of State: U.S. Embassy Survey of American Residents in Panama, 1964, December 12, 1964, PCC, CRT.

112. "The Zonians Must Go, Say Evacuees of Panama," *Panama American*, February 3, 1964; "Women Tell of Panama Escape," *Miami Herald*, January 21, 1964.

113. "Women Tell of Panama Escape," *Miami Herald*, January 21, 1964.

114. Hector Bienvenido Trujillo, "La Zona y los Zonietas," *Panama América*, February 21, 1964.

115. For military families' reluctance to socialize in Panama, see Nina Kosik, interview with author, Balboa, RP, January 6, 2004. Kosik is a third-generation Zonian who worked for the military and thus had a foot in both camps. For a comparative study of U.S. military interracial marriages, see Yuh, *Beyond the Shadow of Camptown*. For the cross-national social life of the American business "colony" in Panama, see James Reid, U.S. businessman, interview with author, Balboa, RP, May 12, 2001; *Gringo Gazette* (publication of the American Society, which boasted scores of Panamanian members), 1939–79.

116. Nina Kosik, interview with author, Balboa, RP, January 6, 2004. For white business and home owners' reactions to the 1960s race riots, see Sugrue, *The Origins of the Urban Crisis*, 209–58; Horne, *Fire This Time*, 283–89, 312–16.

117. Daniel Cooper, interview with author, Curundu, RP, August 10, 2002; LaFeber, *The Panama Canal*, 158–62, 170–82, 184–87; Knapp and Knapp, *Red, White, and Blue Paradise*, 211–24; Jorden, *Panama Odyssey*, 258–71; Robert Taht, interview with author, Balboa, RP, May 4, 2001.

118. Johns and Johnson, *State Crime, the Media, and the Invasion of Panama*; Mark Cook and Jeff Cohen, "How Television Sold the Panama Invasion," *Extra!*, January–February 1990, http://www.chss.montclair.edu/english/furr/panamainv.html; Marixa Lasso, Panamanian professor, interview with author, Panama City, August 26, 2003.

119. Grisela Carrera, Panamanian wife of retired U.S. soldier, interview with author Chorrero, RP, August 19, 2004; Mercedes Anchieta, Panamanian ex-wife of retired U.S. soldier, interview with author, Chilibre, RP, January 7, 2004.

Chapter 6: Crime and Resistance in the Borderland

1. *Canal Zone Code*, 528.

2. Guha, *Elementary Aspects of Peasant Insurgency*; Eric R. Wolf, "Facing Power—Old Insights, New Questions," in Vincent, *The Anthropology of Politics*; Genovese, *Roll, Jordan, Roll*.

3. Albert Brown, interview with author, Balboa Heights, RP, March 12, 2002.

4. Keegan, *The Mask of Command*; Stephen Heathorn, "How Stiff Were Their Upper Lips";

Lincoln, *Authority*; and Albert Brown, interview with author, Balboa Heights, RP, March 12, 2002.

5. Pearce, *Crimes of the Powerful*; J. G. Murphy, "Marxism and Retribution," in Duff and Garland, *A Reader on Punishment*, 44–70; Solzhenitsyn, *The Gulag Archipelago*.

6. *Webster's Encyclopedia Unabridged Dictionary of the English Language* (New York: Gramercy, 1996), 476.

7. For other examples of white colonial thievery and punishment of native "crime," see Hochschild, *King Leopold's Ghost*.

8. Vivian, "The 'Taking' of the Panama Canal Zone." For anti-Americanism in Panamanian textbooks, see de Calzadilla and Martínez, *Educación cívica*; King, *La problema de soberanía en las relaciones entre Panamá y los Estados Unidos de América*.

9. For the structure of Spanish colonial society in Panama, see Figueroa Navarro, *Domino y Sociedad en el Panamá Colombiano*; Soler, *Panama*. Some scholars would argue this U.S. racial hierarchy was imposed earlier than 1904, during the railroad construction days of 1850–55.

10. For oligarchy's strategy of blaming the Zone for its own failures, see LaFeber, *The Panama Canal*, 100; McPherson, *Yankee No!* 86, 97–99; Rudolf, *Panama's Poor*, 19–27.

11. For the Panamanian oligarchy's obsession with fences, gates, and security, see Subject: Fence along the Fourth of July Avenue, Parker to Rogers, August 1, 1972, Folder C/REP/6B Panama-U.S. Relations, Internal Security Office, RG 185, NARA. For crime in Latin America and its class and race ramifications, see Frühling, *Crime and Violence in Latin America*; Aguirre and Buffington, *Reconstructing Criminality in Latin America*; Salvatore et al., *Crime and Punishment in Latin America*.

12. For conditions in the Carcel Modelo, see Wilbert, *Finding Freedom in Panama*; "Visita del Presidente Chiari a Coiba," *Revista Guardia Nacional*, November 3, 1960. For prisons in the interior, see "Panamanian General Inspects David's Jail," *Panama American*, February 6, 1968 (which describes the six giant cells or pens that held two hundred prisoners, with three toilets, two of them functioning). For National Guard human rights abuses during the Torrijos-Noriega years, see Koster and Sánchez, *In the Time of the Tyrants*; Murillo, *The Noriega Mess*; Janson Pérez, *En Nuestras Propias Voces*.

13. *History of the Canal Zone Police*, 2; Major, *Prize Possession*, 139; "Diogenes Can Stop Looking," *Panama American*, April 18, 1951; Disgusted, "There Must Be Reasons," Mailbox, *Panama American*, February 2, 1952; "'Atlantickled and Gratified' Is Song of New Cristobalites," *Panama American*, May 11, 1951.

14. Goethals, *Government of the Canal Zone*, 11; *Canal Zone Code*, 120.

15. Bray, *The Common Law Zone in Panama*, 94–122; *Canal Zone Code*; Greene, *The Canal Builders*, 196, 267–77.

16. Bray, *The Common Law Zone in Panama*, 73–75, 88–90.

17. *History of Canal Zone Police*, 2, Greene, *The Canal Builders*, 287–301.

18. *History of Canal Zone Police*, 6.

19. *History of Canal Zone Police*, 2–4; Conniff, *Panama and the United States*, 75.

20. *History of Canal Zone Police*, 5–9; Greene, *The Canal Builders*, 267–68, 288–89, 293–95, 297–93, 309–22.

21. LaFeber, *The Panama Canal*, 33–36; Fishel, *The End of Extraterritoriality in China*; Scully, *Bargaining with the State from Afar*, 21–80.

22. Quoted in Urgate and Rippey, *Destiny of a Continent*, 146.

23. LaFeber, *The Panama Canal*, 63–65; Vega Méndez, *El Panameñismo y su doctrina*, 41–69.

24. "Lux Murder Case," File 19/4631, "99" Files, RG 185, NARA.

25. *History of Canal Zone Police*, 9.

26. *Annual Report of the Governor of the Panama Canal*, 1921, 45; "The Yanqui Legal System in the Canal Zone," in Ealy, *Yanqui Politics and the Isthmian Canal*, 92–108.

27. For conflicts between the two legal systems, see Shay, "The Panama Canal Zone."

28. *Canal Zone Code*; *Codigo Penal de la República de Panamá*.

29. Panamanian nationalists cited United Nations Bureau of Social Affairs, *Freedom from Arbitrary Arrest, Detention, and Exile*. For illustrative deportation cases, see *Government of Canal Zone v. Juan De La Cruz Perez*, October 18–21, 1949, Case no. 2974; *Government of Canal Zone v. Juan Jose Rosas*, February 23, 1950, Criminal Case no. 2985; *Government of Canal Zone v. Victor Manuel Belmejo*, May 3, 1955, Case no. 4554; *Government of Canal Zone v. Clarence Best*, January 21, 1958, Criminal Case nos. 3270, 3256, all in District Court Records of the Canal Zone, RG 21, WNRC.

30. For parole as social control, see Simon, *Poor Discipline*.

31. *Government of the Canal Zone v. George Bailey*, November 5, 1957, Case nos. 4801, 4802, 4803, District Court Records of the Canal Zone, RG 21, WNRC.

32. *Canal Zone Code*; *Codigo Penal de la República de Panamá*; Greene, *The Canal Builders*, 73–121, 196–98, 287–301.

33. Lucas Palumbo, interview with author, Balboa, RP, March 4, 2002.

34. *Government of Canal Zone v. Winston Eddrington Piggot*, October 18–21, 1949, Case no. 2972, District Court Records of the Canal Zone, RG 21, WNRC.

35. *Washington Post*, February 15, 1974.

36. Franck, *Zone Policeman 88*, 6, 313.

37. For Panamanian critiques of the Zone's exploitation, see Castillero Reyes, *Historia de Panamá*; Alfaro, *Medio Siglo de relaciones entre Panamá y Los Estados Unidos*. Of 1,620 cases in which the defendants spoke up (examined in District Court Records of the Canal Zone 1950–79, RG 21, WNRC), I found 132 cases in which they voiced a political protest.

38. *Government of Canal Zone v. Virgilio Gaytan Rodriquez*, July 31, 1959, Case no. 4968, District Court Records of the Canal Zone, RG 21, WNRC.

39. *Government of the Canal Zone v. Roberto Bayliss*, May 2, 1961, Case no. 5001, District Court Records of the Canal Zone, RG 21, WNRC.

40. *Government of the Canal Zone v. Federico Cascante Gonzalez*, December 1, 1959, Case no. 4978, District Court Records of the Canal Zone, RG 21, WNRC.

41. *Government of Canal Zone v. Alfred Jerome*, November 7, 1961, Case no. 5112, District Court Records of the Canal Zone, RG 21, WNRC.

42. Pre-sentence Report in *Government of Canal Zone v. Henry Williams H. (Hooker)*, October 10, 1964, Case no. 5906, District Court Records of the Canal Zone, RG 21, WNRC.

43. Estadisticas economicas, la provincia de Colón, *Panamá en Cifras* bk. 16, 1964, 4: 173–75.

44. *Government of Canal Zone v. Carlos Antonio Franklin Stewart*, August 26, 1960, Case no. 5032, District Court Records of the Canal Zone, RG 21, WNRC.

45. *Government of Canal Zone v. Virgilio Gaytan Rodriquez*, July 31, 1959, Case no. 4968, District Court Records of the Canal Zone, RG 21, WNRC.

46. For crime and arrest statistics, see *Annual Report of the Governor of the Panama Canal*, 1943, 95–97; 1946, 81–84. For rising crime rates, see *History of Canal Zone Police*, 21, which notes an increase in crimes during the war years, from 3,151 arrests in 1938 to 7,735 arrests (the majority of them Panamanians) in 1946. For the conviction rate of 81 percent in 1960, see Memorandum: Rising Crime in the Canal Zone, January 6, 1961, Folder D-E-P CLAS January 1961, Box 37, Internal Security Office, RG 185, NARA.

47. *History of Canal Zone Police*, 81–84.

48. For crime statistics in Panama and Latin America in this period, see Fajnzylber et al.,

Determinants of Crime Rates in Latin America. For poor Latin American economic performance in the 1950s, see Rabe, *Eisenhower and Latin America*, 64–99; Withers, *The Economic Crisis in Latin America*.

49. *Annual Report of the Governor of the Panama Canal*, 1946, 1966; LaFeber, *The Panama Canal*, 78–79, 81–84, 98–99, 102, 103–7, 116–21.

50. "Panamanian Girl Given Year Jail Term for Clothesline Theft," *Panama American*, July 12, 1946; "Thirteen Year Old Gets 30 Day Sentence for Clothes Theft" and "Zone Detective Had His Blue Jeans Stolen," *Panama American*, May 10, 1950; "Three Youngsters Sentenced to Jail for Petty Offences," *Panama American*, July 24, 1950; "14 year old Francisco Thomas stole two pairs of trousers from a clothes line in Ancon, 30 days. . . . Seymour Apola, 13, stole 2 blankets"); "Clothesline Theft Gets Second Sentence" and "Another Clothesline Theft in Ancon," *Panama American*, July 29, 1950; "Julio Martinez Charged with Stealing Laundry Basket and Clothing," Judge's Bench, *Panama American*, September 19, 1950; "Clothesline Theft Ends in Arrest: $500 Bail Set," *Panama American*, October 18, 1956; "2 Sentenced in T-Shirt Theft," Judge's Bench, *Panama American*, October 23, 1956; "Gladys Castillo, 19, Panamanian, Theft of Clothing off Clothesline," Court News, *Star and Herald*, January 7, 1961; *Government of Canal Zone v. Julio Santamaria*, Balboa Magistrate Court Case 131212, June 30, 1957, District Court Records of the Canal Zone, RG 21, WNRC.

51. Cooper, interview with author, Curundu, RP, August 10, 2002.

52. "RP Bandit Caught, Embassy Employees Recover Goods," *Panama American*, August 1, 1956; "CZ Beach Swimmers Lose Clothes until Boy Nabbed," *Panama American*, May 23, 1955; Cooper, interview with author, Curundu, RP, August 4, 2002.

53. "Theft of Police Garb Nets Jail Sentence for Two," *Panama American*, September 28, 1946; "Two CZ Cops Victims of Theft," *Panama American*, February 5, 1950.

54. "Fined $25 for Theft of Ballerina Shoes," *Panama American*, March 8, 1950; "Panama Man Held for Cash Box Theft at Pedro Miguel Club," *Panama American*, September 26, 1950; "He Wanted to Sleep Warm, He Will," *Panama American*, January 25, 1951 ("Carlos Antonio Stewart, 17, stole an Army blanket—15 day jail sentence"); Judge's Bench, *Panama American*, February 1, 1952 ("Augustín Vásquez, 20, stole rubber hose 20 days in jail; Christine Valderrama, 20—15 days for stealing a dress; Eulogio Pérez, 36, Panamanian, fined $25 for stealing $1.08 gallon of acetone from Paint Shop"); "Ancon Theft Case Bound Over to District Court: Oscar Carrington, 26, Panamanian Stole Canvas Tarpaulin," *Panama American*, February 17, 1952; "CZ Police Hunt for Thief Who Pilfered June Core's Silver," *Panama American*, February 29, 1952; "Ancon Purse Snatcher Gets 2 Years in Gamboa," *Panama American*, April 18, 1954; "MPs Follow Thieves' Paint Trail through Jungle," *Panama American*, May 7, 1955; "Purse Snatching Try Brings RP Man before Balboa Bar," *Panama American*, May 19, 1955; "Bolivar Ramon Stole 47 Rolls of Scotch Masking Tape," Judges Bench, *Panama American*, April 9, 1956; "Ft. Amador Janitor Guilty of Purse Theft at Office Party," *Panama American*, January 6, 1956; "Deportee Who Broke Probation by Theft Sent to Gamboa," *Panama American*, August 3, 1956 ("Roy Gunther stole three lengths of garden hose"); "RP and CZ Police Work Closely to Foil Purse Snatchings," August 20, 1956; "20 Year Old Bicycle Thief Gets 15 Days," *Panama American*, August 21, 1956.

55. Olmedo De Leon, Panamanian maintenance worker, interview with author, Cardenas, RP, April 17, 2001.

56. For examples of this kind of theft, see "Eric A. John Stole 30 lbs of Sugar from Corozal Sales Store," Judge's Bench, *Panama American*, December 12, 1945; "Two Panama Youths Seized in Commy Milk Burglary," *Panama American*, March 30, 1946; *Panama American*, February 12, 1952 ("Jose Manuel Zapata, guilty of stealing $100 bag of rice—$10 and 10 days"); *Panama American*, February 1, 1952 ("Pedro Manuel Alvarez, 41, stole a can of peaches valued

at 40 cents—10 days in jail"); "Theft of Candy, Comic Books Puts RP Man in Jail," *Panama American*, August 3, 1956; "Boy, 19, Jailed for Stealing Ham at Rodman," *Panama American*, February 20, 1956; "Cigarette Theft Nets 20 Day Sentence," *Panama American*, April 29, 1956; "Ex-Con Nabbed by CZ Cops," *Panama American*, May 9, 1956 ("'Bugsy' Clarence Drakes caught with package containing 5 cans of sausage"); "Pork Chop Thief Returns," *Panama American*, July 5, 1956; "RP Man Stole 51 Cents of Chopped Ham from La Boca Commissary," *Panama American*, October 23, 1956. For Panamanian women's participation in these thefts, see "Fined in Theft of Ham, Lotion, Hazel Boyd Scott, 54," *Panama American*, July 8, 1955; "Bag of Groceries Falls Out of Skirt, Woman Fined $50," *Panama American*, July 14, 1955; "Woman Burglar Gets Six Months for Theft of Change Purse," *Panama American*, February 17, 1956.

57. Olmedo De Leon, interview with author, Cardenas, RP, April 17, 2001. For the document that most closely matches De Leon's recollections, see Memorandum: Theft of U.S. Army Officer's Family Bicycle, CID Report, August 12, 1960, File 250.3, Daily Report of Unusual Incidents, OPM, RG 349, NARA. In this incident, the officer was a colonel, not a general, and the report read, "An investigating team and National Guard liaison proceeded to the border, where the culprits were apprehended."

58. Jack Love, retired PanCanal worker, interview with author, Balboa, RP, April 22, 2001.

59. For bridge theft, see *Government of Canal Zone v. Jose De La Cruz Pinzon V. (Vega) and Isidoro Rodriquez S. (Santos)*, Case no. 76–92-B, July 14, 1976, District Court Records of the Canal Zone, RG 21, WNRC. "Bird Trappers Arrested: Second Case of Bird Trapping in Less Than a Week," *Panama American*, September 17, 1945. For yacht theft, see *Government of Canal Zone v. Alejandro Azael Moreno*, Case no. 4820, February 4, 1958, District Court Records of the Canal Zone, RG 21, WNRC; "RP Boys Steal CZ Guinea Pigs from Board of Health Laboratory," *Panama American*, April 30, 1955. For toilet theft of an entire latrine, see *Government of Canal Zone v. Demetrio Antonio and Rafael Guerrero Fox*, Case no. 3009, July 18, 1950, District Court Records of the Canal Zone, RG 21, WNRC. For theft of Christmas trees and decorations, see *Government of Canal Zone v. Tomas Mendoza C. (Catuy)*, Case no. 11314, November 27, 1976, Cristobal Magistrate Court, RG 21, WNRC.

60. "Panama Dogs That Cross Boundary after August 1 Will Get the Works," *Panama American*, July 26, 1953; "12 Year Old Boy Stole Coconut from C.Z.," Judge's Bench, *Panama American*, January 29, 1951; "Young Mango Picker Convicted of Battery against Tree Owner," *Panama American*, May 24, 1950; "Talkative Loiterer Nabbed by Police at Balboa Court—Panamanian Parrot," *Panama American*, May 18, 1955; "Cars, Drivers, Dogs, Vendors and Peddlars—All Are Licensed by Canal License Section," *Panama Canal Review*, August 7, 1953, 8.

61. "Police on the Look-out for Panamanian Bill Splitters," *Panama American*, November 15, 1947; "Bill Splitters Strike Again," *Panama American*, March 16, 1953; Sayre to Tack, October 3, 1971, PCC, Washington Office Subject Files, RG 185, NARA.

62. For Protective Services annual loss reports, see Public Order and Protection Sections of the *Annual Reports of the Governor of the Canal Zone*, 1945–51; *Annual Reports of the Panama Canal Company and the Canal Zone Government*, 1952–79.

63. For a classic case involving military theft of machine guns and tires for sale in Panama, see *Government of the Canal Zone v. Edward Joseph Devinney, David Narciso Lewis, and Jack Joseph Powell*, Case no. 5143, January 19, 1962, District Court Records of the Canal Zone, RG 21, WNRC.

64. Wayne Bryant, interview with author, Balboa, RP, August 12, 2002. Winston and Marlboro brand cigarettes in particular, as well as U.S.-brand whiskey and U.S.-favored scotch, held more cachet for Panamanians than local Istmeño cigarettes and local rums.

65. Herman Wilkinson, interview with author, Balboa, RP, May 2, 2002; George Gerchow, interview with author, Balboa, RP, May 9, 2002.

66. Maria Carazo, Nicaraguan Panamanian high school teacher, interview with author, Panama City, January 12, 2005; Memorandum: Theft of Railroad Crane and On-going Investigation, November 14, 1966, Folder: Equipment Inventory, Internal Security Office, PCC, Washington Office Subject Files, RG 185, NARA.

67. Russell Goedjea, U.S. businessman in Panama, interview with author, Pedro Miguel, RP, March 23, 2002.

68. Belsi de Medina, interview with author, Panama City, May 1, 2007.

69. For preoccupation with servants in colonial societies, see Kennedy, *Islands of White*, 140–43; Stoler, "A Sentimental Education." For servant and employee theft, see Henry, *The Hidden Economy*.

70. Peggy Roberts, wife of Zonian club manager, interview with author, Daytona Beach, Florida, August 14, 2002.

71. For examples of Zone servant theft, see "14 Year Old Panamanian Girl Charged with Stealing Mistress's Wedding Ring," Judge's Bench, *Panama American*, July 22, 1948; "CZ Maid Guilty on Theft Charges," *Panama American*, June 1, 1951; *Panama American*, February 17, 1952 ("Christine Valderrama, 20—15 days for stealing a dress"); "Maid Guilty, Took Skirt," *Panama American*, April 2, 1956; "Servant Found Guilty of Theft of Employer," *Panama American*, May 14, 1956; "Fined in Theft of Ham, Lotion, Hazel Boyd Scott, 54," *Panama American*, July 8, 1955; "Theft of Radio Nets Jail Term," *Panama American*, January 20, 1968.

72. For racial, urban, and rural components in Panamanian servant hiring, see Carazo, interview with author, Panama City, February 23, 2001.

73. "Housewife, Cop Find Stolen Garments at Jungle Hideout," *Panama American*, February 22, 1952.

74. *Government of Canal Zone v. Harmodio Cedeno C. (Cerda)*, February 6, 1962, Case nos. 5136, 5137, 5138, 5139, 5140, 5141, District Court Records of the Canal Zone, RG 21, WNRC.

75. For examples of Panamanian criminals seeking refuge in Gamboa, see *Government of Canal Zone v. Federico Zapata*, May 2, 1958, Case no. 4794, District Court Records of the Canal Zone, RG 21, WNRC; *Government of Canal Zone v. Harmodio Cedeno C. (Cerda)*, February 6, 1962, Case nos. 5136, 5137, 5138, 5139, 5140, 5141, District Court Records of the Canal Zone, RG 21, WNRC.

76. *Government of Canal Zone v. Julio Tunon Dominquez*, October 17, 1961, Case no. 3370, District Court Records of the Canal Zone, RG 21, WNRC.

77. Herman Wilkinson, interview with author, Balboa, RP, May 2, 2002.

78. For the importance of power and communication cables to the U.S. military, see Colonel Fox, Memorandum: Cable Theft Problem, December 13, 1954, File 250.3, HUSAC, CID, RG 349, NARA.

79. For an overview of cable theft and its consequences, see Memorandum: Cable Theft, December 29, 1952, OAG, RG 319, U.S. Army Adjutant General Command Reports, NARA.

80. "Coordinated Efforts of Canal Organization Make for a Perfect Royal Visit to the Zone," *Panama Canal Review*, December 4, 1953; Memorandum: Communications Problems During Royal Visit, Robertson to McBride, November 6, 1953, File 335.5, HUSAC, RG 349, NARA. For other examples of postwar cable theft, see "Cable Thieves Get Penitentiary Terms," *Panama American*, February 5, 1952; Judge's Bench, *Panama American*, February 8, 1952 ("Aristedes González and Augustin Gill charged with cutting a power cable belong to Panama Canal Company"); "Cable Thieves Get 18 Months in Jail," *Panama American*, July 5, 1955; "Youths with Copper Cable Arrested by CZ Police," *Panama American*, May 23, 1956.

81. *Government of Canal Zone v. Joseph Nathaniel Rawlins*, November 20, 1951, Case no. 3049, District Court Canal Zone, RG 21, WNRC.

82. *Government of Canal Zone v. Tirill MacFadden Haynes*, November 29, 1955, Case no. 4511, District Court Records of the Canal Zone, RG 21, WNRC.

83. Judge Crowe and Zone Acting District Attorney J. Morton Thomas discussed this difficulty of guarding "power towers out in the jungle" during a case against Juan Gomez; see "Confession Nets One Year for C.Z. Wire Thief," *Panama American*, August 7, 1956.

84. *Government of Canal Zone v. Federico Zapata*, May 2, 1958, Case no. 4794, District Court Records of the Canal Zone, RG 21, WNRC.

85. Memorandum for Chief of Staff, U.S. Army Caribbean Command, April 12, 1951, File 250.3, Daily Report of Unusual Incidents, OAG, RG 349, NARA; *Government of Canal Zone v. Lester Livingston Harding*, March 23, 1950, Case no. 2989, RG 21, WNRC.

86. "Ancon Purse Snatcher Gets Two Years in Gamboa: Judge Hancock Is Determined to Break Up the Fad of Purse-snatching," *Panama American*, April 18, 1954.

87. For Crowe's cool before Panamanian rioters, see Affidavit: Guthrie F. Crowe, August 14, 1964, Records Relating to the January 1964 Disturbances, RG 185, NARA.

88. "A Bird's Tale: A Crowe Sends Sparrows to Prison," *Star and Herald*, April 5, 1958; *Government of Canal Zone v. Jose Felix Fuella*, November 5, 1957, Case nos. 4804, 4547, District Court Records of the Canal Zone, RG 21, WNRC.

89. For the moral instruction of the U.S. project in Panama, see Knapp and Knapp, *Red, White, and Blue Paradise*, 3–4; Greene, *The Canal Builders*, 37–74, 224; Parker, *Panama Fever*, 249–52; Mellander Mellander, *Charles Edward Magoon*.

90. For a brief overview of Greaves's case, with a telling headline, see "Negro Rapes Young American Woman in Midnight Assault," *Panama American*, February 25, 1946. For the Burling murder case, see "U.S. Court Will Try Vernal Watson for the Murder of Frank Burling," *Panama American*, January 20, 1968.

91. Please, Justice, "Justice, He Says," Mailbox, *Panama American*, June 30, 1951; "Ed. Note," *Panama American*, June 30, 1951.

92. Perplexed, "Comparative Justice," Mailbox, *Panama American*, September 21, 1956.

93. "Trial of C.Z. Churchman Continues," *Panama American*, August 21, 1956. For the color and class bias of criminal prosecution within U.S. legal culture, see Russell, *The Color of Crime*.

94. One headline on the bizarre case was "Pedestrian Hit by Drunken Driver Caused Her Own Death," *Panama American*, May 5, 1956.

95. "Manslaughter Charge: Gatun Lock Guard Accused of Killing Colón Woman," *Panama American*, July 3, 1956; "Gatun Lock Guard Fined $100 for Not Reporting Accident," *Panama American*, July 5, 1956.

96. "Battery on Zone Cop Is Third Similar Case in June," *Panama American*, July 20, 1955. This article details the dismissal of assault charges against a Panamanian, Herbert St. Louis, that Judge Altman termed "a technical charge and therefore next door to false arrest."

97. "Judge Throws Army Case Out of Court," *Panama American*, December 28, 1945.

98. E.O.M., "An Open Letter to Judge Crowe," Mailbox, *Panama American*, June 29, 1956.

99. Viva Lovelady, "Tired and Mad," Mailbox, *Panama American*, February 17, 1956.

100. For Panama, "Standards of Law and Conduct," Mailbox, *Panama American*, February 24, 1956.

101. Rouke and Chazarreta, *A Theory of Personalismo*; Strickon and Greenfield (eds.), *Structure and Process in Latin America, Patronage, Clientage, and Power Systems*.

102. William Cecil Fergusson, retired PanCanal worker, interview with author, Ancon, RP, May 21, 2001.

103. Herman Wilkinson, interview with author, Balboa, RP, May 2, 2002.

104. "Canal Zone Penitentiary: Historical Sketch," in *History of Canal Zone Police*, 40–41. For inmate statistics, see George, "Perspectives on the Canal Zone Penitentiary."

105. George, "Unfolding of a Correction Community: the Canal Zone Penitentiary," 25, PCC, CRT.

106. Beleño, *Los Forzados de Gamboa*; Hardy, "Canal Zone Penitentiary"; Teeters, *Penology from Panama to Cape Horn*, 62–68.

107. For the disciplinary system at Gamboa, see Meyer, *Manual for Inmates of the Canal Zone Penitentiary* (Meyer was the warden). For comparative literature on prison systems in Latin America, see Salvatore and Aguirre, *The Birth of the Penitentiary in Latin America*.

108. For U.S. trends in penology leading to the model prison movement see Pisciotta, *Benevolent Repression*.

109. Meyer, *Manual for Inmates*, 4–5.

110. A sample menu at Gamboa in 1947—Breakfast: bacon, eggs, ham, toast, jam, butter, coffee; Dinner: pork chops, mashed potatoes, apple sauce, gravy, bread pudding, creamed peas, bread, ice cream, coffee; Supper: cold meat, potato salad, baked beans, cheese, bread, jam, iced tea—is in Bea Thrapp, "Canal Zone Penitentiary: Spic and Span Corrective Institution, Work Farm," *Panama American*, November 9, 1947. Henry Twohy, interview with author, Balboa, RP, March 14, 2002.

111. For recidivism rates, see Warden Trout, interview with the author, in George, "Perspective on Conflict"; George, "Perspectives on the Canal Zone Penitentiary," 7–8. For similar failures in rehabilitation at model prisons in the United States, see Allen, *The Decline of the Rehabilitative Ideal*.

112. For "political consciousness" of Panamanian prisoners, see George, "Interim Rehabilitation Program for Canal Zone Penitentiary," in "Perspectives on the Canal Zone Penitentiary," 3–4. For Israeli and Northern Ireland prison systems as comparisons, see Human Rights Watch, *Prison Conditions in Israel and the Occupied Territories*; Ryder, *Inside the Maze*.

113. *Government of Canal Zone v. Harmodio Cedeno C. (Cerda)*, February 6, 1962, Case nos. 5136, 5137, 5138, 5139, 5140, 5141, District Court Records of the Canal Zone, RG 21, WNRC.

114. Carlos Menendez, Panamanian laborer, interview with author, Curundu, RP, June 2, 2002.

115. "Panamanian Shot in Leg after Stabbing Attempt at Gamboa," *Panama American*, September 4, 1945; Hardy, "Canal Zone Penitentiary," 14–20. For some examples of postwar escapes from Gamboa, see "Zone Policeman Apprehends Fleeing Panamanian Prisoner," *Panama American*, July 10, 1948; "Elusive CZ Convict on the Loose Again," *Panama American*, February 24, 1950; "Escaped CZ Convict Found in Costa Rica," *Panama American*, July 19, 1950; "Patient CZ Cop Gets His Man after Three Months," *Panama American*, April 13, 1956; "Recaptured Con Faces Zone Grand Larceny Rap," *Panama American*, January 12, 1968; *Government of Canal Zone v. Fabían Emilio Faundez R. (Rampolla)*, Case no. 76–169-B, October 29, 1976, District Court Records of the Canal Zone, RG 21, WNRC.

116. For Zoot Suit caper, see Hardy, "Canal Zone Penitentiary," 16. "Tainted Meat Scare at Gamboa," *Star and Herald*, February 29, 1960; "Gamboa Escapee Says He Was Only Chasing a Rabbit," *Panama American*, October 4, 1956; "Penitentiary Guard for 42 Years: Brought 'Em Back If They Escaped," *Panama Canal Review*, July 3, 1953, 11.

117. *Annual Report of the Governor of the Panama Canal*, 1964, 123–24; 1965, 125; 1967, 129.

118. "Disturbance at Gamboa under Control," *Star and Herald*, February 12, 1974; Frank Dupree, interview with author, Taboga, RP, May 4, 2002.

119. Lloyd Kent, interview with author, Gamboa, RP, April 4, 2001; Vincente Arron Williams, interview with author, Ancon, RP, May 3, 2001; Joanne Kent, interview with author,

Gamboa, RP, April 4, 2001; Anthony Stanziola, interview with author, Panama City, March 21, 2001. For a hostile Panamanian view of CZ Police that still lingers, see "La Leyenda Negra de la Policía de la Zona del Canal," *Siglo*, February 27, 2005; Hampel, *Viva Panama*, 162.

120. Noriega and Eisner, *America's Prisoner*, 22.

121. "Rude Policemen," Mailbox, *Panama American*, July 24, 1950.

122. Judge's Bench, *Panama American*, September 5, 1956 ("Guillermo Barrios fined $10 for parking more than 12 inches from the curb at Balboa Gasoline Station"). For a good commentary of CZ Police's traffic harassment, see Zonian Ted Wilber's "More Notes on Resentments," Believe Me column, *Star and Herald*, April 24, 1982.

123. This summons so infuriated the Panamanian bus company's owner that he took his complaint all the way to the U.S. consulate in Colón. See Sean M. Kelly, Memorandum: American Consulate in Colón, August 22, 1960, Lot Files, 1960–64, Central America and Panama, Folder: C.Z. Government / Panama Canal Company 1960, RG 59, NARA.

124. Richard Koster, interview with author, Panama City, May 14, 2001.

125. Don Philips, interview with author, Balboa, RP, April 24, 2001; Rex Raspberry, interview with author, Balboa, RP, March 27, 2001.

126. Wayne Bryant, interview with author, Balboa, RP, April 25, 2002; John Morales, interview with author, Balboa, RP, May 5, 2001; "The Canal Zone Police Association Take Care of Their Own," *Panama Canal Review*, January 1, 1954, 6; José the Mechanic, "Well Paid Police," Mailbox, *Panama American*, July 14, 1950.

127. Edgardo Tirado, interview with author, Amador, RP, May 12, 2001; Pablo Prieto, interview with author, Balboa Heights, RP, May 21, 2001; *Annual Report of the Panama Canal Company / Canal Zone Government*, 1959, 115.

128. Lorena Riba, Panamanian archivist, interview with author, Balboa, RP, May 11, 2002.

129. Diana Diaz de Novey, Panamanian businesswoman, interview with author, Panama City, April 12, 2001.

130. Sanderson to Davies, March 14, 1961, Complaint Folder: January–March 1961, Internal Security Office, Box 11, RG 185, NARA.

131. "New Assault Charges Are Filed against Two Panamanian Youths," *Panama American*, July 25, 1946; "Wild Night Rider Ends Up in CZ Court after Chiva Assault," *Panama American*, August 1, 1950; "Chiva Driver Draws 30 Days for Wild Escape Bid," *Panama American*, April 13, 1951.

132. "CZ Policeman Hit While Attempting to Nab Loiterer," *Panama American*, June 16, 1955; "Battery on CZ Cop: Third Similar Case in June," *Panama American*, July 20, 1955; *Government of Canal Zone v. William Gordon*, August 2–5, 1955, Case no. 4574, District Court Records of the Canal Zone, RG 21, WNRC. For Zonian anger over light sentences for assaults, see "Penalties for Socking Cops," Mailbox, *Panama American*, July 25, 1955.

133. "Canal Zone Hands Out Stiff Penalties for Commissary Violations," *Panama American*, September 17, 1956; "CZ Cop and Commissary Inspector Injured by Mob," *Panama American*, January 19, 1961.

134. "Panamanian Pulled Gun on Cop, Three Years in Gamboa," *Panama American*, February 17, 1956.

135. *Government of Canal Zone v. Charles Anthony Somerville Reid C. (Carter)*, September 5, 1967, Case no. 5622, District Court Records of the Canal Zone, RG 21, WNRC.

136. *Government of Canal Zone v. Pedlecador Clemente Caparossa C. (Cargill)*, June 6, 1967, Case nos. 5617–5227, District Court Canal Records of the Zone, RG 21, WNRC. While undoubtedly the most famous, Caparossa was not the only Panamanian "cop-fighter" of the late 1960s; see "RP Man Jailed for Hitting CZ Officer," *Panama American*, February 10, 1968.

137. *Annual Report of the Panama Canal Company and Canal Zone Government*, 1961, 117–18.

138. "Gov. Warns Residents: Disrespect for the Law Is on the Rise," *Star and Herald*, January 13, 1961.

139. *Annual Report of the Panama Canal Company / Canal Zone Government*, 1952, 105.

140. *Annual Report of the Panama Canal Company and the Canal Zone Government*, 1955, 105; *History of Canal Zone Police*, 23; *Annual Report of the Panama Canal Company and the Canal Zone Government*, 1958, 127.

141. *Annual Report of the Panama Canal Company / Canal Zone Government*, 1959, 115; Olmedo De León, interview with author, Cardenas, RP, May 20, 2001; *Annual Report of the Panama Canal Company / Canal Zone Government*, 1959, 115.

142. *Annual Report of the Panama Canal Company / Canal Zone Government*, 1964, 118–19. For comparisons on the hiring of black and minority officers and their effects on policing in the United States, see Moss, *Black Political Ascendancy in Urban Centers*.

143. For Canal Zone uneasiness over joint patrol policy, see *History of Canal Zone Police*, 34. For arrest statistics, see *Annual Report of the Panama Canal Company and the Canal Zone Government*, 1972, 146; 1978, 147. For the start of joint patrols, see "Joint RP-CZ Police Patrol?," *Star and Herald*, November 19, 1975; Raul Castillo, retired National Guardsman, interview with author, Panama City, August 21, 2003.

144. For arrest statistics, see *Annual Report of the Panama Canal Company and the Canal Zone Government*, 1970, 126, 138; 1971, 134–35, 146; 1979, 125, 144.

145. For Torrijos's internationalist strategy and relations with students, see Ropp, *Panamanian Politics*, 95–108; Harding, *Military Foundations of Panamanian Politics*, 127–54.

146. For percentages of offenses being served at Gamboa in the mid-1970s, see Raymond A. George, "Unfolding of a Correctional Community: The Canal Zone Penitentiary," 99, 1977, PCC, CRT. "Thousands Invade Balboa Police Station for Take-over Ceremony," *Star and Herald*, April 2, 1982.

147. Randolph Owen Stewart, interview with author, Colón, RP, February 12, 2002.

148. William Prohl, interview with author, Diablo, RP, April 12, 2001; Panameño, "Get a Load of This!," Mailbox, *Panama American*, March 8, 1961; Donnan and Wilson, *Borders*, 143–45.

Epilogue

1. Tucker and Hendrickson; *Empire of Liberty*; Hinderaker, *Elusive Empires*; Sanford, *Manifest Destiny and the Imperialism Question*; Merk, *Manifest Destiny and Mission in American History*; Johannsen, *Manifest Destiny and Empire*.

2. For different notions of U.S. empire, see May, *Imperial Democracy*; Dubofsky and Theoharis, *Imperial Democracy*; Lundestad, "'Empire by Invitation' in the American Century"; Lundestad, *Empire by Integration*; Musicant, *Empire by Default*; Steel, "The Accidental Empire." For recent critical assessments of U.S. imperialism, see Judis, *The Folly of Empire*; Buchanan, *A Republic, Not an Empire*; Grandin, *Empire's Workshop*; Johnson, *The Sorrows of Empire*; Allen, *America's Enlightened Imperialism*.

3. De Souza, "Notas acerca del a situación socio-politica de Panamá."

4. In 1971 Zone authorities demolished the Tivoli Hotel rather than transfer it to Panama, partly out of fear that General Torrijos might turn this grand symbol of Zonian majesty into a "museum of American imperialism." Scott, *Americans in Panama*, 43; "Stars and Stripes Fly from 112 Staffs When Canal Zone Celebrates a Holiday," *Panama Canal Review*, August 5, 1955, 10.

5. Upegui R., "Nostalgia for the Old Club Unión of Casco Viejo (Panamá)," *Lingua Franca*, February 28, 2009.

6. "Subject: Women Employment Discrimination Cases," Report of the Equal Opportunity Office, January 3, 1971, Folder: Status of Women, 1964–71, PCC, Washington Office Subject Files, RG 185, NARA.

7. Rodrigo Mendoza, retired Panamanian laborer, interview with author, Panama City, May 5, 2002.

8. Lutz, *The Bases of Empire*; Hugh Gusterson, "Empire of Bases," *Bulletin of Atomic Scientists*, March 10, 2009; Valdés Sánchez, *Cuba y los Estados Unidos*; Gobat, *Confronting the American Dream*; Langley and Schonoover, *The Banana Men*; Welsome, *The General and the Jaguar*; Renda, *Taking Haiti*; Calder, *The Impact of Intervention*. For equally important economic enclaves in this era, see Catherine C. Legrand, "Living in Macondo," in Joseph et al., *Close Encounters of Empire*; Grandin, *Fordlandia*.

9. Rosenberg, *Spreading the American Dream*; de Grazia, *Irresistible Empire*; Conniff, *Panama and the United States*, 80.

10. For an introduction to and definition of microsocieties, see Cowan and Strickland, *The Legal Structure of a Confined Microsociety*.

11. José Miguel Alemán, foreign minister of Panama (1999–2004), speech given at the conference Transferring the Panama Canal: Passage to a New Millennium, Williams College, October 21, 1999.

12. Ealy, *Yanqui Politics and the Isthmian Canal*, 89–91; Alfaro, *Diccionario de Anglicismos*.

13. Robert E. Terrill, "Colonizing the Borderlands: Shifting Circumference in the Rhetoric of Malcolm X," *Quarterly Journal of Speech* 86.1 (2000): 67–85; "The Panama Canal: A 'White Elephant,'" *St. Petersburg (Florida) Times*, September 6, 1977.

14. "The Unknown Zonians," *Spillway*, January 27, 1964, 2; Arendt, *Eichmann in Jerusalem*.

15. Emily S. Rosenberg, "Considering Borders," in Hogan and Paterson, *Explaining the History of American Foreign Relations*, 176.

16. "Records, Records, More Records," *Spillway*, October 16, 1964, 3.

17. For Panamanian disrespect accorded to CZ governor Seybold, see Harrington to Sowash, March 21, 1956, FRUS, 1955–57, 7: 267–68.

18. John Major, "Wasting Asset"; Martin B. Travis and James T. Watkins, "Control of the Panama Canal, an Obsolete Shibboleth?," *Foreign Affairs*, May 1959.

19. Migdal, *Boundaries and Belonging*.

20. Richard Broggi, retired PanCanal electrician, interview with author, Taboga, RP, August 4, 2002; Edgardo Tirado, interview with author, Amador, RP, April 23, 2001; Rolando Sterling Arango, interview with author, Albrook, RP, April 22, 2001; "Memo: Request for Deputy Thelma King to visit her son in the United States," U.S. Embassy Panama to Rusk, No. 757, March 2, 1962, Central Decimal File, 819.14/11–960 RG 59, USNA; for analysis of King's many contradictions, see Don Bohning, "She Aids Panama Reds But Is Not One of Them," *Miami Herald*, June 6. 1965.

21. Ong, *Flexible Citizenship*, 4, 15–16, 26.

22. Mendoza, interview with author, Panama City, May 5, 2002.

23. Many Panamanians were dissatisfied with the long, drawn-out nature of the Carter-Torrijos Treaty in 1977 that stretched the transfer out for two decades; the failure of the United States to clean up environmental damage on Zone bases; and especially the bloody U.S. invasion in 1989, which stemmed in part from a particularly galling amendment to the treaty, the DeConcini Reservation, which appears to grant the United States the right to use "military force in the Republic of Panama, to reopen . . . or restore operations of the Canal as the case may be."

Bibliography

Archives and Manuscript Collections

United States

Department of the Army, U.S. Army Military History Institute. Carlisle Barracks, Carlisle, Pennsylvania
Dwight D. Eisenhower Library, Abilene, Kansas
Georgetown University Library, Washington, D.C.
Gerald R. Ford Library, Ann Arbor, Michigan
Harry S. Truman Library, Independence, Missouri
John F. Kennedy Library, Boston
Library of Congress Manuscript Division, Washington, D.C.
Lyndon Baines Johnson Library, Austin, Texas
National Archives and Records Administration, College Park, Maryland
Nettie Benson Library, University of Texas, Austin
Operational Archives, Naval Historical Center, Washington Navy Yard, Washington, D.C.
Panama Canal Museum, Seminole, Florida
Washington National Records Center, Suitland, Maryland

Panama

Archivo de Recuerdos de la Autoridad del Canal de Panamá, Corozal
Archivo del Ministerio de Relaciones Exteriores, Quarrry Heights, Panama City
Archivo Ricardo J. Alfaro, Panama City
Archivo Nacional, Panama City
Biblioteca de le Direccion de Estadística y Censo, Panama City
Biblioteca Nacional, Panama City
Centro de Recursos Tecnícos, Biblioteca de la Autoridad del Canal de Panamá, Panama City
Instituto Nacional de Cultura, Panama City
Museo Afroantillano, Panama City
Museo Del Canal Interoceano De Panamá, Panama City
Panama Canal Executive Office Records, Balboa Heights
Universidad de Panamá, Biblioteca Interamericana "Simon Bolivar," Instituto del Canal y Estudios Internacionales, Panama City

Published Works

Aardweg, Gerard J. M. van den. *On the Origins and Treatment of Homosexuality: A Psychoanalytic Reinterpretation*. New York: Praeger, 1986.

Acosta, David. *La influencia decisiva de la opinión publica en el rechazo del convenio Fílos-Hines de 1947*. Panama City: Editorial Universitaria, 1993.

Adelman, Jeremy, and Stephen Aron. "From Borderlands to Borders: Empires, Nation-States, and the Peoples in between in North American History." *American Historical Review* 104 (June 1999): 814–41.

Aguirre, Carlos A., and Robert Buffington, eds. *Reconstructing Criminality in Latin America*. Wilmington, Del.: SR Books, 2000.

Akenson, Donald Harman. *God's Peoples: Covenant and Land in South Africa, Israel, and Ulster*. Ithaca, N.Y.: Cornell University Press, 1992.

Aldrich, Robert. *Colonialism and Homosexuality*. London: Routledge, 2003.

Alfaro, Ricardo J. *Diccionario de Anglicismos*. Madrid: Editorial Gredos, 1964.

———. *Medio Siglo de relaciones entre Panamá y los Estados Unidos*. Panama City: Imprenta Nacional, 1959.

Allen, Francis A. *The Decline of the Rehabilitative Ideal: Penal Policy and Social Purpose*. New Haven: Yale University Press, 1981.

Allen, William Dangaix. *America's Enlightened Imperialism: Essays on Our Cultural Relations with India, Philippines, China*. Peking, China: San Yu Press, 1933.

Alleyne, Mervyn C. *Construction and Representation of Race and Ethnicity in the Caribbean and the World*. Kingston, Jamaica: University of the West Indies Press, 2002.

Alméras, Diana, et al. *Violence against Women in Couples: Latin America and the Caribbean. A Proposal for Measuring Its Incidence and Trends*. New York: United Nations, 2005.

Alteager, Alfred. *An Other Tongue: Language and Ethnicity in the Linguistic Borderlands*. Durham: Duke University Press, 1994.

Amnesty International. *Israel and the Occupied Territories: Mass Arrests and Police Brutality*. New York: Amnesty International, 2000.

Andersen, Roger W., ed. *Pidginization and Creolization as Language Acquisition*. Rowley, Mass.: Newbury House, 1993.

Anderson, Benedict. *Imagined Communities: Reflections on the Origins and Spread of Nationalism*. New York: Oxford University Press, 1983.

Anderson, Malcolm. *Frontiers: Territory and State Formation in the Modern World*. Cambridge, U.K.: Polity Press, 1996.

Andreas, Peter. *Border Games: Policing the U.S.-Mexico Divide*. Ithaca, N.Y.: Cornell University Press, 2000.

Andrews, George Reid. *Afro-Latin America, 1800–2000*. New York: Oxford University Press, 2004.

Annual Report of the Panama Canal Company and the Canal Zone Government, 1952–1979. Balboa Heights, CZ: GPO, 1952–1979.

Annual Reports of the Governor of the Panama Canal. Balboa Heights, CZ: GPO, 1904–51.

Arauz, Celestino Andrés, et al. *La historia de Panamá en sus textos*, vol. 2: *1903–1968*. Panama City: Editorial Universitaria, 1999.

Arendt, Hannah. *Eichmann in Jerusalem: A Report on the Banality of Evil*. New York: Viking Press, 1963.

Arias, Harmodio. *The Panama Canal: A Study in International Law and Diplomacy*. London: P. S. King and Son, 1911.

Arias Calderon, Ricardo. "Panama: Disaster or Democracy?" *Foreign Affairs* 66 (1987–88): 328–47.

Arosemena, Justo. *Fundacion de la nacionalidad panameña.* Caracas, Venezuela: Biblioteca Ayacucho, 1982. 1st ed., 1855

Arosemena, Carlos A. "El Cuerpo de Policía Nacional." In *Panamá: 50 Años de República,* ed. Rodrigo Miro. Panama City: Imprenta Nacional, 1953.

Arosemena G., Diogenes A. *Historia Documental del Canal de Panama.* Panama City: Universidad de Panamá, 1962.

Arroyo, Eduardo. *"Panama" Al Brown 1902–1951.* Madrid: Alianza Editorial, 2007.

Arroyo, Justo. "Race Theory and Practice in Panama." In *African Presence in the Americas,* ed. Carlos Moore et al. Trenton, N.J.: Africa World Press, 1995.

Babb, Dalton. *Cooking the West Indian Way.* Oxford, U.K.: Macmillan Education, 1986.

Bailey, Beth, and David Farber. *The First Strange Place: The Alchemy of Race and Sex in World War II Hawaii.* New York: Free Press, 1992.

Baker, Jim. *Crossroads: A Popular History of Singapore and Malaysia.* Tarrytown, N.Y.: Marshall Cavendish, 2010.

Baldwin, Hanson. "Con: The Panama Canal—Sovereignty and Security," AEI *Defense Review,* no. 4 (1977): 12–34.

Bannon, John Francis. *The Spanish Borderlands Frontier 1513–1821.* Albuquerque: University of New Mexico Press, 1974.

Barbara, Augustin. *Marriage across Frontiers.* Philadelphia: Multilingual Matters, 1989.

Barber, Willard F., and C. Neale Ronning. *Internal Security and Military Power: Counter-insurgency and Civic Action in Latin America.* Columbus: Ohio State University Press, 1966.

Barrios, Presciliano. *Identidad nacional: Fantasía y verdad.* Panama City: Instituto Nacional de Cultura, 1993.

Barry, Tom, et al. *Inside Panama.* Albuquerque, N.M.: Interhemispheric Press, 1995.

Baud, Michiel, and Willem Van Schendel. "Toward a Comparative Approach to Borderlands." "*Journal of World History* 8 (Fall 1997): 211–42.

Baussant, Michèle. *Pieds-noirs: Mémoires d'exils.* Paris: Stock, 2002.

Beane, Carol Anne. *The Characterization of Blacks and Mulattoes in Selected Novels from Colombia, Venezuela, Ecuador, and Peru.* Berkeley: University of California Press, 1980.

Beleño, Joaquín. *Curundu.* Panama City: Impresora Nacional, 1958.

———. *Los Forzados de Gamboa.* Panama City: Impresora Nacional, 1960.

———. *Luna Verde.* Panama City: Impresora Nacional, 1955.

Belkin, Aaron, and Geoffrey Bateman, eds. *Don't Ask, Don't Tell: Debating the Gay Ban in the Military.* Boulder, Colo.: Lynne Rienner, 2003.

Belknap, Michael R. *Integration of the Armed Forces.* New York: Garland, 1991.

Bell, Shannon. *Whore Carnival.* Brooklyn, N.Y.: Autonomedia, 1995.

Beluche Mora, Isidro. *Acción Comunal: Surgimiento y estructuración del nacionalismo panameño.* Panama City: Editorial Condor, 1981.

Benshoff, Harry M., and Sean Griffin. *America on Film: Representing Race, Class, Gender, and Sexuality at the Movies.* Malden, Mass.: Blackwell, 2004.

Bergling, Tim. *Sissyphobia: Gay Men and Effeminate Behavior.* New York: Southern Tier, 2001.

Bergmann, Emilie L., ed. *Women, Culture, and Politics in Latin America: Seminar on Culture and Feminism in Latin America.* Berkeley: University of California Press, 1990.

Bernal, Miguel Antonio. *Los tratados Carter-Torrijos: Una tradición histórica.* 2nd ed. Panama City: Ediciones Revistas, 1985.

Bernardi, Daniel, ed. *Classic Hollywood, Classic Whiteness.* Minneapolis: University of Minnesota Press, 2001.

Bernstein, Deborah. *Constructing Boundaries: Jewish and Arab Workers in Mandatory Palestine*. Albany: State University of New York Press, 2000.

Biesanz, John. "Cultural and Economic Factors in Panamanian Race Relations." *American Sociological Review* 14 (1949): 772–79.

———. "The Economy of Panama." *Inter-American Economic Affairs* 6 (1952–53): 3–28.

———. "Race Relations in the Canal Zone." *Phylon* 11 (1950): 23–30.

———. "Social Forces Retarding Development of Panama's Agricultural Resources." *Rural Sociology* 15 (1950): 148–55.

———. "Uncle Sam on the Isthmus of Panama: A Diplomatic Case History." In *The Caribbean: Contemporary Trends*, ed. Alva Wilgus. Gainesville: University of Florida Press, 1953.

Biesanz, John, and Mavis Biesanz. *The People of Panama*. New York: Columbia University Press, 1955.

Biesanz, John, and Luke M. Smith. "Adjustment of Inter-American Marriages on the Isthmus of Panama." *Sociological Review* 16 (December 1951): 76–80.

———. "Panamanian Politics." *Journal of Politics* 14 (1952): 386–402.

———. "Race Relations in Panama and the Canal Zone: A Comparative Analysis." *American Journal of Sociology* 57 (1951): 7–14.

Biesanz, John et al., eds. *Materiales para el estudio de la clase media en la America Latina*. Vol. 4. Washington, D.C.: Unión Panamericana, 1950.

Black, Jan Knippers. *Sentinels of the Empire: The United States and Latin American Militarism*. New York: Greenwood Press, 1986.

Blanco, Tómas. *El prejuicio racial en Puerto Rico*. Río Piedras, Panama: Editorial Universitaria Universidad de Puerto Rico, 1985.

Blas Tejeira, Gil. *Pueblos Perdidos*. Panama City: Editorial Universitaria, 1995.

The Blue Book of the Panama Canal. Balboa Heights, Panama: GPO, 1916.

Borstelmann, Thomas. *The Cold War and the Color Line: American Race Relations in the Global Arena*. Cambridge: Harvard University Press, 2001.

Bost, Suzanne. *Mulattas and Mestizas: Representing Mixed Identities in the Americas*. Athens: University of Georgia Press, 2003.

Bourgois, Philippe I. *Ethnicity at Work: Divided Labor on a Central America Banana Plantation*. Baltimore: Johns Hopkins University Press, 1989.

Bray, Wayne D. *The Common Law Zone in Panama: A Case Study in Reception*. San Juan, Puerto Rico: Inter-American University Press, 1977.

Breger, Rosemary, and Rosanna Hill, eds. *Cross-Cultural Marriage: Identity and Choice*. New York: Berg, 1998.

Brennan, Denise. *What's Love Got to Do with It? Transnational Desires and Sex Tourism in the Dominican Republic*. Durham: Duke University Press, 2004.

Brewster, William. *3000 Bachelors and a Girl: or Panama Manhunt, the Romance of a School Teacher in the Canal Zone*. Balboa, Panama: Canal Zone Library, 1938.

Briggs, Laura. *Reproducing Empire: Race, Sex, Science, and U.S. Imperialism in Puerto Rico*. Berkeley: University of California Press, 2002.

Brock, Rita Nakashima, and Susan Brooks Thistlethwaite. *Casting Stones: Prostitution and Liberation in Asia and the United States*. Minneapolis: Fortress Press, 1996.

Bryce-Laporte, R. S. "Crisis, Contraculture, and Religion among West Indians in the Panama Canal Zone." In *Blackness in Latin America and the Caribbean: Social Dynamics and Cultural Transformations*, ed. Norman E. Whitten Jr. and Arlene Torres. Vol. 1. New York: Free World Press, 1995.

Buchanan, Patrick J. *A Republic, Not an Empire: Reclaiming America's Destiny.* New York: Regnery, 2013.

Buchanan, Allen, and Margaret Moore, eds. *States, Nations, and Borders: The Ethics of Making Boundaries.* New York: Cambridge University Press, 2003.

Burke, Peter. "History as Social Memory." In *Memory: History, Culture, and the Mind,* ed. Thomas Butler. New York: Oxford University Press, 1989.

Burkholder, Mark A., and Lyman L. Johnson. *Colonial Latin America.* New York: Oxford University Press, 2004.

Burland, Cottie A. *The Exotic White Man: An Alien in Asian and African Art.* New York: McGraw-Hill, 1968.

Burlingame, Roger. *Mosquitoes in the Big Ditch: The Story of the Panama Canal.* New York: John Winston, 1952.

Cabán, Pedro A. *Constructing a Colonial People: Puerto Rico and the United States, 1898–1932.* Boulder, Colo.: Westview Press, 1999.

Cafferty, Pastora San Juan, and Carmen Rivera-Martínez. *The Politics of Language: The Dilemma of Bilingual Education for Puerto Ricans.* Boulder, Colo.: Westview Press, 1981.

Cahill, Ann J. *Rethinking Rape.* Ithaca, N.Y.: Cornell University Press, 2001.

Calder, Bruce J. *The Impact of Intervention: The Dominican Republic During the U.S. Intervention 1916–1924.* Princeton, N.J.: Markus Wiener, 2006.

Campoamor, Ramón. *El Personalismo: Apuntes para una Filosofía.* Madrid: La Cátedra de Metafísica, la Universidad de Madrid, 1855.

Canal Postal Service. *Canal Zone Postage Stamps, 1961–1979.* Mount Hope, CZ: GPO, 1979.

Canal Zone Code. Balboa Heights, Panama: GPO, 1961.

Canal Zone Information Office. *The Panama Canal, Fiftieth Anniversary: The Story of a Great Conquest.* Mount Hope, CZ: GPO, 1964.

Carabaza, E., and M. de Santos. *Melilla y Ceuta: Las últimas colonias.* Madrid: Talasa, 1992.

Carew, Rod, with Ira Berkow. *Carew.* New York: Simon and Schuster, 1979.

Carillo, Ramón, and Richard Boyd. "Some Aspects of the Social Relations between Latin and Anglo Americans on the Isthmus of Panama." *Boletín de la Universidad Interamericana de Panamá* 2 (1945): 703–84.

Carter, Jimmy. *Keeping Faith: Memoirs of a President.* New York: Bantam Books, 1982.

Castillero Calvo, Alfredo. "El esclavo negro en el desenvolviemiento económico del istmo de Panamá durante el descubrimiento y la conquista." *Revista Lotería* 228 (February 1975): 1–16.

———. *Los negros y mulatos en las historía social panameña.* Panama City: Impresora Panamá, 1969.

Castillero Reyes, Ernesto J. *Historia de Panamá.* Panama City: Imprenta Nacional, 1955.

———. *Raices de las independencía de Panamá.* Panama City: Edición de la Academia Panameña de la Historia, 1978.

Caufield, Sueanne, et al., eds. *Honor, Status, and Love in Modern Latin America.* Durham: Duke University Press, 2005.

Censos Nacionales, 1940–1980. Panama City: Contraloría General de la República, 1942–1982.

Census of the United States and Outlying Regions, The Canal Zone, 1912. Balboa Heights, Panama: GPO, 1912.

Chafer, Tony, and Amanda Sackur. *Promoting the Colonial Idea: Propaganda and Visions of Empire in France.* New York: Palgrave, 2002.

Chamberlain, M. E. *Decolonization: The Fall of the European Empires.* Malden, Mass.: Blackwell, 1999.

Chant, Sylvia, and Craske, Nikki. *Gender in Latin America*. New Brunswick, N.J.: Rutgers University Press, 2003.

Chapkis, Wendy. *Live Sex Acts: Women Performing Erotic Labor*. New York: Routledge, 1997.

———. "Power and Control in the Commercial Sex Trade." In *Sex for Sale: Prostitution, Pornography, and the Sex Industry*, ed. Ronald Weitzer. New York: Routledge, 2000.

Citino, Nathan J. "The Global Frontier: Comparative History and the Frontier-Borderland Approach." In *Explaining the History of American Foreign Relations*, ed. Michael J. Hogan and Thomas G. Paterson. New York: Cambridge University Press, 2004.

Clifford, Nicholas R. *Spoilt Children of Empire: Westerners in Shanghai and the Chinese Revolution of the 1920s*. Hanover, N.H.: Middlebury College Press, 1991.

Clum, John M. *"He's All Man!" Learning Masculinity, Gayness, and Love from American Movies*. New York: Palgrave, 2002.

Clymer, Adam. *Drawing the Line at the Big Ditch: The Panama Canal Treaties and the Rise of the New Right*. Lawrence: University Press of Kansas, 2008.

Cochez, Rolando, ed. *Las biografías breves del gobernadors de la zona del canal*. Balboa, Panama: Panama Canal Collection, 1995.

Codigo Penal de la República de Panamá. Panama City: Imprenta Nacional, 1963.

Cohen, Lizabeth. *A Consumer's Republic: The Politics of Mass Consumption in Postwar America*. New York: Vintage Books, 2003.

Cohen, Robin. "Cultural Diaspora: The Caribbean Case." In *Caribbean Migration: Globalised Identities*, ed. Mary Chamberlain. New York: Routledge, 1998.

Collazo, José. *Guerra y educación: La militarización y americanización del puertorriqueño durante la Segunda Guerra Mundial, 1939–1945*. Santo Domingo, Dominican Republic: Editora Centenario, 1998.

Collier, David. *Squatter Settlements and the Incorporation of Migrants into Urban Life: The Case of Lima*. Cambridge, Mass.: Center for International Studies, 1976.

Collymore, Frank A. *Barbadian Dialect*. Widley, St. Michael, Barbados: Barbados National Trust, 1970.

Conn, Stetson, and Byron Fairchild. *The United States Army in World War II: The Framework of Hemisphere Defense*. Washington, D.C.: GPO, 1960.

———. *The U.S. Army in World War II: Guarding the United States and Its Outposts. The Western Hemisphere*. Washington, D.C.: GPO, 1964.

Connell, R. W., and James W. Messerschmidt. "Hegemonic Masculinity: Rethinking the Concept." *Gender and Society* 19.6 (2005): 829–59.

Conniff, Michael L. *Black Labor on a White Canal: Panama, 1904–1981*. Pittsburgh: University of Pittsburgh Press, 1985.

———. *Panama and the United States: The Forced Alliance*. Athens: University of Georgia Press, 2001.

———. "Panama Since 1903." In *The Cambridge History of Latin America*, ed. Leslie Bethel. Vol. 7. New York: Cambridge University Press, 1990.

———. "The Rise and Decline of the West Indian Community in Panama." In *El Canal de Panamá en el Siglo XXI*. Panama City: CELA, CEAPSA, UP, UTP, USMA, Ciudad del Saber, 1998.

Conte-Porras, Jorge. *Arnulfo Arias Madrid*. Panama City: Litho Impresora Panamá, 1980.

Coombs, G. M. "The Panama Canal and Its Defense." *Contemporary Review* 161 (July–December 1942): 178–80.

Corber, Robert J. *Homosexuality in Cold War America: Resistance and the Crisis of Masculinity*. Durham: Duke University Press, 1997.

Costigliola, Frank. *Roosevelt's Lost Alliances: How Personal Politics Helped Start the Cold War.* Princeton: Princeton University Press, 2012.

Cowan, Thomas A., and Strickland, Donald A. *The Legal Structure of a Confined Microsociety.* Berkeley: University of California Press, 1965.

DaCosta, Kimberly. *Making Multiracials: State, Family, and Market in the Redrawing of the Color Line.* Stanford: Stanford University Press, 2007.

Daley, Mercedes Chen. "The Watermelon Riot: Cultural Encounters in Panama City, April 17, 1856." *Hispanic American Historical Review* 70 (February 1990): 85–108.

Dardia, Michael, et al., *The Effects of Military Base Closures on Local Communities: A Short-Term Perspective.* Santa Monica, Calif.: Rand, 1996.

Darío Carles, Rubén. *La evolución de la policía de empleo y salarios en la zona del canal y el desarrollo económico de Panamá.* Panama City: Imprenta Nacional, 1976.

Darío Souza, Rubén, et al. *Panamá, 1903–1970: Nación-imperialismo. Fuerzas populares-oligarquía. Crisis y camino revolucionario.* Santiago, Chile: Talleres de la Sociedad Impresora, 1970.

Davis, Joseph E. *Identity and Social Change.* New Brunswick, N.J.: Transaction, 2000.

Davis, Darien J. "Panama." In *Afro-Central Americans: Rediscovering the African Heritage.* London: Minority Rights Group, 1996.

Davis, Raymond. "West Indian Workers on the Panama Canal: A Split Labor Market Interpretation." PhD diss., Stanford University, 1981.

Dawson, Graham. *Soldier Heroes: British Adventure, Empire, and the Imagining of Masculinities.* London: Routledge, 1994.

de Calzadilla, Diamantina, and Etna de Martínez. *Educación cívica.* Panama City: n.p., 1964.

DeCambell, Carolina, and Ofelia Hooper. "The Middle Class in Panama." In *Materiales para le estudio de la clase media en la América Latina,* ed. Theo Crevenna. Washington, D.C.: GPO, 1950.

DeConde, Alexander. *Ethnicity, Race, and American Foreign Policy: A History.* Boston: Northeastern University Press, 1992.

de Grazia, Victoria. *Irresistible Empire: America's Advance Through Twentieth Century Europe.* Cambridge, Mass.: Belknap Press, 2005.

de la Guardia, Roberto. "El fenómena de la esclavitud en la civilización panameña." *Hombre y Cultura* 2 (December 1972): 27–73.

De La Guardia, Santiago. "Sobre el Problem de la Prostitución en Panamá." *La Revista Lotería* 4 (October 1919). Reprinted in *La Revista Lotería* 89 (March 1958): 41–53.

De Mena, Delores. *The Era of U.S. Army Installations in Panama.* Ft. Clayton, Panama: USARO, 1996.

de Souza, Herbert. "Notas acerca del a situación socio-politica de Panamá." *Revista Tareas* 35 (1976): 1–27.

De Villiers, Marq. *White Tribe Dreaming: Apartheid's Bitter Roots as Witnessed by Eight Generations of an Afrikaner Family.* New York: Penguin, 1989.

D'Haen, Theo, and Patricia Krüs, eds. *Colonizer and Colonized: Conflicting Images and Representations.* Atlanta: Rodopi Press, 2000.

Diaz Espino, Ovidio. *How Wall Street Created a Nation: J. P. Morgan, Teddy Roosevelt, and the Panama Canal.* New York: Four Walls Eight Windows, 2001.

Diaz Szmirnov, Damaris. *Génesis de la Ciudad Republicana: Etorno, sociedad y ocio en la ciudad de Panamá.* Panama City: Agenda del Centenario, 2001.

Diener, Alexander, and Joshua Hagen. *Borderlines and Borderlands: Political Oddities at the Edge of the Nation-State.* Lanham, Md.: Rowman & Litttlefield, 2010.

Dinges, John. *Our Man in Panama: How General Noriega Used the United States and Made Millions in Drugs and Arms.* New York: Random House, 1990.

Dock, Lavinia L. *Hygiene and Morality: A Manual for Nurses and Others, Giving an Outline of the Medical, Social, and Legal Aspects of the Venereal Diseases.* New York: G. P. Putnam's Sons, 1910.

Donadio, William. *The Thorns of the Rose.* Panama City: Editorial Sibauste, 1999.

Donaldson, Mike. "What Is Hegemonic Masculinity?" *Theory and Society* 22.5 (1993): 643–57.

Donnan, Hastings, and Thomas M. Wilson. *Borderlands: Ethnographic Approaches to Security, Power, and Identity.* Lanham, Md.: University Press of America, 2010.

———. *Borders: Frontiers of Identity, Nation and State.* New York: Berg, 1999.

Dressler, David. *Practice and Theory of Probation and Parole.* New York: Columbia University Press, 1959.

Dubofsky, Melvyn, and Athan Theoharis. *Imperial Democracy: The United States Since 1945.* Englewood Cliffs, N.J.: Prentice-Hall, 1983.

DuBois, Jules. *Danger over Panama.* Indianapolis: Bobbs-Merrill, 1964.

Ducoff, Joseph Louis. *Human Resources of Central America, Panama, and Mexico, 1950–1980, in Relation to Some Aspects of Economic Development.* New York: United Nations Economic Commission for Latin America, 1960.

Dudziak, Mary L. *Cold War Civil Rights: Race and the Image of American Democracy.* Princeton: Princeton University Press, 2011.

Duff, Antony, and David Garland. *A Reader on Punishment.* New York: Oxford University Press, 1995.

DuVal, Miles. *And the Mountains Will Move: The Story of the Building of the Panama Canal.* Stanford: Stanford University Press, 1947.

Dzidzienyo, Anani, and Suzanne Oboler, eds. *Neither Enemies nor Friends: Latinos, Blacks, Afro-Latinos.* New York: Palgrave Macmillan, 2005.

Ealy, Lawrence. "The Development of an Anglo-American System of Law in the Panama Canal Zone." *American Journal of Legal History* 2 (1958): 283–303.

———. *Yanqui Politics and the Isthmian Canal.* University Park: Pennsylvania State University Press, 1971.

Earle, Peter. *The Sack of Panamá: Sir Henry Morgan's Adventures on the Spanish Main.* New York: Viking Press, 1982.

Edwards, Albert. *Panama: The Canal, the Country, and the People.* New York: Macmillan, 1913.

Eisenstadt, S. N., and L. Roniger. *Patrons, Clients, and Friends: Interpersonal Relations and the Structure of Trust in Society.* New York: Cambridge University Press, 1984.

Elkins, Caroline. *Imperial Reckoning: The Untold Story of Britain's Gulag in Kenya.* New York: Henry Holt, 2005.

Ellis, Lee. *Theories of Rape: Inquiries into the Causes of Sexual Aggression.* New York: Hemisphere, 1989.

Enlisted Man's Guide to Panama: Conduct Code for U.S. Army Personnel in Panama. Quarry Heights, CZ: GPO, 1939.

Enloe, Cynthia. *Bananas, Beaches, and Bases: Making Feminist Sense of International Politics.* Berkeley: University of California Press, 2000.

———. *Ethnic Soldiers: State Security in Divided Societies.* Athens: University of Georgia Press, 1982.

———. *The Morning After: Sexual Politics at the End of the Cold War.* Berkeley: University of California Press, 1993.

Enscore, Susan I., et al. *Guarding the Gates: The History of Ft. Clayton. Its Setting, Its Architecture, and Its Role in the History of the Panama Canal.* Champaign, Ill.: Engineering Research and Development Center, 2000.

Escobar, Felipe Juan. *Arnulfo Arias o el credo Panameñista, 1930–1940: Ensayo psico-patológico de la política panameña.* Panama City: Imprenta Nacional, 1946.

Escobar Bethancourt, Rómulo. *Torrijos: Colonia americana, no!* Bogotá: Carlos Valencia Editores, 1981.

Estadisticas Panameñas: Mujeres y Hogares, Vols. 5–39. Panama City: Contraloría General de la República, 1940–1979.

Estadisticas Panameñas: Estadisticas Economicas. Panama City: Contraloría General de la República, 1940–1979.

Fajnzylber, Pablo, et al., *Determinants of Crime Rates in Latin America: An Empirical Assessment.* Washington, D.C.: World Bank Publications, 1998.

Falcoff, Mark. *Panama's Canal: What Happens When the United States Gives a Small Country What It Wants.* Washington, D.C.: AEI Press, 1998.

Fanon, Frantz. *Black Skin, White Masks.* New York: Grove Press, 1967.

———. *The Wretched of the Earth.* New York: Weidenfeld-Black Cat, 1969.

Feaver, Peter D. *Armed Servants: Agency, Oversight, and Civilian-Military Relations.* Cambridge: Harvard University Press, 2003.

Fernández Olmos, Margarite, and Lizabeth Paravisini-Gebert, eds. *Sacred Possessions: Vodou, Santería, Obeah, and the Caribbean.* New Brunswick, N.J.: Rutgers University Press, 1997.

Fernós Isern, Antonio. "The White—and the Tropics." *Porto Rican Health Review* 1 (July 1926): 6–7.

Figueroa Navarro, Alfredo. *Domino y Sociedad en el Panamá Colombiano, 1821–1903.* Panama City: Editorial Universitaria, 1982.

Findlay, Eileen J. Suárez. *Imposing Decency: The Politics of Sexuality and Race in Puerto Rico, 1870–1920.* Durham: Duke University Press, 2000.

Fishel, Wesley R. *The End of Extraterritoriality in China.* New York: Octagon Books, 1974.

Flores, Juan, ed. *Divided Borders: Essays on Puerto Rican Identity.* Houston: Arte Público Press of the University of Houston, 1993.

Foley, Brenda Kathleen. "Image as Identity: Beauty Contestants and Exotic Dancers as Merchants of Morality." PhD diss., Brown University, 2004.

Forbes-Lindsay, C. H. *Panama and the Canal To-day.* Boston: L. C. Page, 1912.

Foucault, Michel. *Discipline and Punish: The Birth of the Prison.* New York: Vintage Press, 1995.

Fox, James M. *White Mischief: The Murder of Lord Erroll.* New York: Vintage, 1983.

Fox, Robert W., and Jerrold W. Huguet. *Population and Urban Trends in Central America and Panama.* Washington, D.C.: Inter-American Development Bank, 1977.

Franck, Harry A. *Zone Policeman 88: A Close Range Study of the Panama Canal and Its Workers.* New York: Century, 1913.

Frederick, Rhonda D. *"Colón Man a Come": Mythographies of Panamá Canal Migration.* Lanham, Md.: Lexington Books, 2005.

Frederickson, George. *White Supremacy: A Comparative Study in American and South African History.* New York: Oxford University Press, 1981.

Fried, Richard M. *The Russians Are Coming! The Russians Are Coming!: Pageantry and Patriotism in Postwar America.* New York: Oxford University Press, 1999.

Frühling, Hugo. *Crime and Violence in Latin America: Citizen Security, Democracy, and the State.* Baltimore: Johns Hopkins University Press, 2003.

Gaines, Charles, and Esther E. Mile. *Piloting the Panama Canal: Experience of a Panama Canal Pilot.* New York: Waters Club Press, 2001.

Gandásegui, H., Marco A. *Las clases sociales en Panamá.* Panama City: CELA, 1993.

———. *La democracia en Panamá.* Panama City: CELA, 1999.

García, Isaias. *Naturaleza y forma de lo panameño.* Panama City: Imprenta Nacional, 1956.

Geertz, Clifford. *The Interpretation of Cultures.* New York: Basic Books, 1977.

General Population Characteristics, Canal Zone 1960 Census. Washington D.C.: GPO, 1961.

General Population Characteristics, Canal Zone 1970 Census. Washington D.C.: GPO, 1971.

Genovese, Eugene. Roll, Jordan, Roll: The World the Slaves Made. New York: Vintage Books, 1976.

George, Raymond A. "Perspectives on the Canal Zone Penitentiary." MA thesis, University of Oklahoma, 1976.

———. "Perspective on Conflict: An Historical Overview of the Canal Zone Penal System." 1977, PCC, CRT.

———. "Unfolding of a Correctional Community: The Canal Zone Penitentiary," 1977, PCC, CRT.

Gill, Leslie. The School of the Americas: Military Training and Political Violence in the Americas. Durham: Duke University Press, 2004.

Gillis, John R., ed. Commemorations: The Politics of National Identity. Princeton: Princeton University Press, 1994.

Girman, Chris. Mucho Macho: Seduction, Desire, and the Homoerotic Lives of Latin Men. New York: Harrington Park Press, 2004.

Gobat, Michel. Confronting the American Dream: Nicaragua under U.S. Imperial Rule. Durham: Duke University Press, 2006.

Goethals, George W. Government of the Canal Zone. Berkeley: University of California Libraries, 1915.

Gold, Peter. Stone in Spain's Shoe: The Search for a Solution to the Problem of Gibraltar. Liverpool, U.K.: Liverpool University Press, 1994.

Goldrich, Daniel. Radical Nationalism: The Political Orientations of Panamanian Law Students. East Lansing: Michigan State University Press, 1962.

———. Sons of the Establishment: Elite Youth in Panama. Chicago: Rand McNally, 1966.

Gonzales-Berry, Erlinda, and David R. Maciel. The Contested Homeland: A Chicano History of New Mexico. Albuquerque: University of New Mexico Press, 2000.

Goodman, Herman. "The Antivenereal Campaign in Panama." Journal of Social Hygiene 5 (April 1923): 160–67.

———. "Genital Defects and Venereal Disease among Porto Rican Draft Troops." Journal of American Medical Association 72 (March 29, 1919): 907–13.

———. "Skin Diseases among the Porto Rican Troops." New Orleans Medical and Surgical Journal 72 (December 1919): 343–46.

———. "Ulcerating Granuloma of the Pudenda." Archives of Dermatology and Syphilis 1, n.s. 1 (1920): 151–69.

Gorgas, William O. Sanitation in Panama. New York: D. Appleton, 1915.

Gosnell, Jonathan K. The Politics of Frenchness in Colonial Algeria, 1930–1954. Rochester, N.Y.: University of Rochester Press, 2002.

Graham, Gladys R. Tropical Cooking in Panama: A Handbook of Tropical Foods and How to Use Them. Panama City: Panama American Press, 1948.

Graham, Richard, ed. The Idea of Race in Latin America, 1870–1940. Austin: University of Texas Press, 1990.

Grandin, Greg. Empire's Workshop: Latin America, the United States, and the Rise of the New Imperialism. New York: Henry Holt, 2006.

———. Fordlandia: The Rise and Fall of Henry Ford's Forgotten Jungle City. New York: Henry Holt, 2009.

Greene, Graham. "The Country with Five Frontiers." New York Review of Books, February 17, 1977.

Greene, Julie. *The Canal Builders: Making America's Empire at the Panama Canal.* New York: Penguin Press, 2009.

Griswold del Castillo, Richard. *World War II and Mexican Civil Rights.* Austin: University of Texas Press, 2008.

Guagnini, Luis. "La Guardía Nacional." *Revista Tareas* 40 (October–December 1977): 67–82.

Gudeman, Stephen. *Relationships, Residence, and the Individual: A Rural Panamanian Community.* Minneapolis: University of Minnesota Press, 1976.

Guevara Mann, Carlos. *Panamanian Militarism: An Historical Interpretation.* Athens: Ohio University Center for International Studies, 1996.

Guha, Ranajit. *Elementary Aspects of Peasant Insurgency.* Durham: Duke University Press, 1999.

Guidice, Christian. *Hands of Stone: The Life and Legend of Roberto Duran.* Wrea Green, U.K.: Milo Books, 2006.

Guillermoprieto, Alma. *The Heart That Bleeds: Latin America Now.* New York: Vintage Press, 1994.

Guinn, David E., and Elissa Steglich, eds. *In Modern Bondage: Sex Trafficking in the Americas: National and Regional Overview of Central America and the Caribbean: Belize, Costa Rica, Dominican Republic, El Salvador, Guatemala, Honduras, Nicaragua and Panama.* Ardsley, N.Y.: Transnational Publishers, 2003.

Gurdian Guerra, Reymundo. "Evolución histórica de la presencia militar norteamericana en Panamá." In *El Canal de Panamá,* ed. Juan Antonio Tack. Panama City: Instituto del Canal de la Universidad de Panamá, Editorial Universitaria, 1999.

———. *La presencía militar de los Estados Unidos en Panamá.* Panama City: Imprenta de la Universidad de Panamá, 1998.

Gutmann, Matthew C., ed. *Changing Men and Masculinities in Latin America.* Durham: Duke University Press, 2003.

Haas, Ben. KKK. Evanston, Ill.: Regency Books, 1963.

Hampel, John. *Viva Panama: A New Sea Level Canal.* Hudson, Fla.: Casananda, 1996.

Hanrahan, David. "Legal Aspects of the Panama Canal Zone—In Perspective." *Boston University Law Review* 45 (1965): 64–87.

Hanratty, Dennis M., ed. *Panama: A Country Study.* Washington, D.C.: GPO, 1989.

Harding, Colin. *Frontier Patrols: A History of the British South Africa Police and Other Rhodesian Forces.* London: G. Bell and Sons, 1937.

Harding, Robert C., II. *The History of Panama.* Westport, Conn.: Greenwood Press, 2006.

———. *Military Foundations of Panamanian Politics.* Somerset, N.J.: Transaction, 2001.

Hardy, Rufus. "Canal Zone Penitentiary." *Prison World* 21 (April 1946): 14–20.

Harkavy, Robert E. *Bases Abroad: The Global Foreign Military Presence.* New York: Oxford University Press, 1989.

Harris, Jessica B. *Sky Juice and Flying Fish: Traditional Caribbean Cooking.* New York: Simon and Schuster, 1991.

Harris, Louis. "Panama." In *Political Forces in Latin America,* ed. Ben Burnett and Kenneth Johnson. Belmont, Calif.: Wadsworth, 1968.

Harris, W. W. *Puerto Rico's Fighting 65th U.S. Infantry: From San Juan to Chorwan.* San Rafael, Calif.: Presidio Press, 1980.

Hart, John Mason. *Empire and Revolution: Americans in Mexico Since the Civil War.* Berkeley: University of California Press, 2002.

Hauser, William L. *America's Army in Crisis: A Study in Civil-Military Relations.* Baltimore: Johns Hopkins University Press, 1973.

Heathorn, Stephen. "How Stiff Were Their Upper Lips: Research on Late Victorian and Edwardian Masculinity." *History Compass* 2 (2004): 1–7.

Henriot, Christian. *Prostitution and Sexuality in Shanghai: A Social History, 1849–1949*. Cambridge: Cambridge University Press, 2001.

Henry, Stuart. *The Hidden Economy: The Context and Control of Borderline Crime*. London: Robertson,
1978.

Hershatter, Gail. *Dangerous Pleasures: Prostitution and Modernity in Twentieth Century Shanghai*.
Berkeley: University of California Press, 1997.

Hilman, Richard S., and Thomas J. D'Agostino, eds. *Understanding the Contemporary Caribbean*.
Boulder, Colo.: Lynne Rienner, 2003.

Hinderaker, Eric. *Elusive Empires: Constructing Colonialism in the Ohio Valley, 1673–1800*. Cambridge: Cambridge University Press, 1997.

History of the Canal Zone Police, 1904–1982. Balboa Heights, Panama: Panama Canal Collection,
1982.

Hixson, Walter L., ed. *Military Aspects of the Vietnam Conflict*. New York: Routledge, 2000.

———. *The Vietnam Antiwar Movement*. New York: Routledge, 2000.

Hobsbawm, Eric. *Bandits*. New York: Delacorte Press, 1969.

Hochschild, Adam. *King Leopold's Ghost: A Tale of Greed, Terror, and Heroism in Colonial Africa*. New
York: Houghton Mifflin, 1999.

Hogan, J. Michael. *The Panama Canal in American Politics: Domestic Advocacy and the Evolution of
Policy*. Carbondale: Southern Illinois University Press, 1986.

Hogan, Michael J., and Thomas G. Paterson, eds. *Explaining the History of American Foreign Relations*. New York: Cambridge University Press, 2004.

Horne, Gerald. *Fire This Time: The Watts Uprising and the 1960s*. Charlottesville: University Press
of Virginia, 1995.

Howarth, David. *The Golden Isthmus*. London: Collins, 1966.

———. *Panama: Four Hundred Years of Dreams and Cruelty*. New York: McGraw-Hill, 1966.

Howe, James. *A People Who Would Not Kneel: Panama, the United States, and the San Blas Kuna*.
Washington, D.C.: Smithsonian Institution Press, 1998.

Human Rights Watch. *Prison Conditions in Israel and the Occupied Territories*. New Haven: Yale University Press, 1991.

Hunt, Michael H. *Ideology and U.S. Foreign Policy*. New Haven: Yale University Press, 1987.

Hutton, Patrick H. *History as the Art of Memory*. Hanover: University of Vermont Press, 1993.

Hyam, Ronald. *Empire and Sexuality: The British Experience*. New York: St. Martin's Press, 1992.

Hyman, Lana Lois. *Particularidades de la Prostitución en Panamá*. Panama City: Universidad de Panamá Escuela de Ley, 1978.

Hymes, Dell, ed. *Pidginization and Creolization of Languages: Proceedings of a Conference Held at the
University of the West Indies, Mona, Jamaica, April, 1968*. Cambridge: Cambridge University
Press, 1971.

Independent Commission of Inquiry on the U.S. Invasion of Panama. *The U.S. Invasion of
Panama: The Truth Behind Operation "Just Cause."* Boston: South End Press, 1999.

Inés Robledo, Angela, and Yolanda Puyana Villamizar, eds. *Etica: Masculinidades y Feminidades*.
Bogotá: Universidad Nacional de Colombia, Centro de Estudios Sociales, 2000.

International Commission of Jurists. *Report on the Events in Panama, January 9–14, 1964*. Geneva,
Switzerland, 1964.

Irwin-Zarecka, Iwona. *Frames of Remembrance: The Dynamics of Collective Memory*. New Brunswick,
N.J.: Transaction Publishers, 1994.

Isaza Calderón, Baltazar. *Panameñismos*. Panama City: Biblioteca de Nacionalidad ACP, 1999.

Iván Zúñiga, Carlos. *El desarme de la Policía Nacional en 1916*. Panama City: Editorial Universitaria, 1973.

Jackley, John L. *A Study of the Impact of a New Panama Canal Treaty on the Non-DOD, U.S. Citizen Zone Resident, Prepared for the American Embassy Panama, June 10, 1976*. Donald Marquand Dozer Papers, 1893–1981, Hoover Institute Archives, Stanford University, Stanford, California.

Jaen Juarez, Omar. *La población del istmo de Panama: Estudio de Geohistoria*. Madrid: Agencia Española de Cooperación, 1978.

Jamail, Milton, ed. *Panama Canal Zone: Occupied Territory*. Panama City: Imprenta Nacional, 1973.

James, Joy. "U.S. Policy in Panama." *Race and Class* 32 (1990): 17–32.

James, Winifred L. *Woman in the Wilderness*. London: Chapman and Hall, 1915.

Jameson, W. C. *Billy the Kid: Beyond the Grave*. Lanham, Md.: Taylor Trade, 2008.

Janson Pérez, Brittmarie. *En Nuestras Propias Voces: Panamá Protesta, 1968–1989*. Panama City: Edición del Instituto de Estudios Políticos e Internacionales, 1994.

Jeffrey, Leslie Ann. *Sex and Borders: Gender, National Identity, and Prostitution Policy in Thailand*. Vancouver: University of British Columbia Press, 2002.

Johannsen, Robert W. *Manifest Destiny and Empire: American Antebellum Expansionism*. College Station: Texas A&M University Press, 1997.

Johns, Cristina Jacqueline, and P. Ward Johnson. *State Crime, the Media, and the Invasion of Panama*. Westport, Conn.: Praeger, 1994.

Johnson, Chalmers. *The Sorrows of Empire: Militarism, Secrecy, and the End of the Republic*. New York: Henry Holt, 2004.

Johnson, Kevin R. *Mixed Race America and the Law*. New York: New York University Press, 2003.

Johnson, Lyman L., and Sonya Lipsett-Rivera, eds. *The Faces of Honor: Shame, Sex, and Violence in Colonial Latin America*. Albuquerque: University of New Mexico Press, 2001.

Johnson, Lyndon Baines. *The Vantage-Point: Perspectives of the Presidency 1963–1969*. New York: Holt, Rinehart and Winston, 1972.

Johnson, Suzanne P. *An American Legacy in Panama: A Brief History of the Department of Defense Installations and Properties in the Former Panama Canal Zone*. Quarry Heights, Panama Canal Area: USARSO, 1995.

———. *A History of the Quarry Heights Military Reservation*. Balboa Heights, Panama: USARSO, 1996.

Johnson, Walton R., and D. Michael Warren, eds. *Inside the Mixed Marriage: Accounts of Changing Attitudes, Patterns, and Perceptions of Cross-Cultural and Interracial Marriages*. Lanham, Md.: University Press of America, 1994.

Jorden, William J. *Panama Odyssey*. Austin: University of Texas Press, 1984.

Joseph, Gilbert M., et al., eds. *Close Encounters of Empire: Writing the Cultural History of U.S.–Latin American Relations*. Durham: Duke University Press, 1998.

———. "On the Trail of Latin American Bandits." *Latin American Research Review* 25 (Winter 1990): 7–53.

Judis, John B. *The Folly of Empire: What George W. Bush Could Learn from Theodore Roosevelt and Woodrow Wilson*. New York: Scribner, 2004.

Jurado, Augustín. *John Peter Williams: El Robin Hood Panameño*. Panama City: Impresora Nacional, 1974.

Kaplan, Amy, and Donald E. Pease, eds. *Cultures of United States Imperialism*. Durham: Duke University Press, 1993.

Keegan, John. *The Mask of Command: Alexander the Great, Wellington, Ulysses S. Grant, Adolf Hitler, and the Nature of Leadership*. New York: Penguin Books, 1988.

Kemble, John Haskell. *The Panama Route, 1848–1869.* Berkeley: University of California Press, 1943.

Kennedy, Dane. *Islands of White: Settler Society and Culture in Kenya and Southeastern Rhodesia 1890–1939.* Durham: Duke University Press, 1987.

Kenworthy, Eldon. *America/Américas: Myth in the Making of U.S. Policy toward Latin America.* University Park: Pennsylvania State University Press, 1995.

Killingray, David, and David Omissi, eds. *Guardians of Empire: The Armed Forces of the Colonial Powers, 1700–1964.* New York: Manchester University Press, 1999.

King, Thelma. *La problema de la soberanía en las relaciones entre Panamá y los Estados Unidos.* Panama City: Ministro de Educación, 1961.

Kinsbruner, Jay. *Not of Pure Blood: The Free People of Color and Racial Prejudice in Nineteenth-Century Puerto Rico.* Durham: Duke University Press, 1996.

Kitayama, Shinobu, and Hazel Rose Markus, eds. *Emotion and Culture: Empirical Structures of Mutual Influence.* Washington, D.C.: APA, 1994.

Knapp, Herbert, and Mary Knapp. *Red, White, and Blue Paradise: The American Canal Zone in Panama.* San Diego: Harcourt Brace Jovanovich, 1984.

Kooistra, Paul. *Criminals as Heroes: Structure, Power and Identity.* Bowling Green, Ohio: Bowling Green State University Popular Press, 1989.

Koppes, Clayton R., and Gregory D. Black. *Hollywood Goes to War: How Politics, Profits, and Propaganda Shaped World War II Movies.* New York: Free Press, 1987.

Koster, R. M., and Guillermo Sánchez. *In the Time of the Tyrants: Panama, 1968–1990.* New York: Norton, 1990.

Kovuch, Karen. *Breaking Codes, Breaking Barriers: The WACs of the Signal Security Agency, World War II.* Ft. Belvoir, Va.: History Office, Office of the Chief of Staff, U.S. Army Intelligence and Security Command, 2001.

Kramer, Paul. *The Blood of Government: Race, Empire, the United States, and the Philippines.* Chapel Hill: University of North Carolina Press, 2006.

Krauss, Clifford. *Inside Central America: Its People, Politics, and History.* New York: Touchstone Books, 1992.

Kruse, Kevin M., and Stephen Tuck, eds. *The Fog of War: World War II and the Civil Rights Movement.* New York: Oxford University Press, 2012.

Kuzmarov, Jeremy. *The Myth of an Addicted Army: Vietnam and the Modern War on Drugs.* Amherst: University of Massachusetts Press, 2009.

LaFeber, Walter. *The Panama Canal: The Crisis in Historical Perspective.* New York: Oxford University Press, 1990.

Lamar, Howard, and Leonard Thompson, eds. *The Frontier in History: North America and Southern Africa Compared.* New Haven: Yale University Press, 1981.

Lancaster, Roger N. *Life Is Hard: Machismo, Danger, and the Intimacy of Power in Nicaragua.* Berkeley: University of California Press, 1994.

Lang, Berel, ed. *Race and Racism in Theory and Practice.* Lanham, Md.: Rowman and Littlefield, 2000.

Langley, Lester D. "Negotiating New Treaties with Panama: 1936." *Hispanic American Historical Review* 48 (1968): 220–33.

———. "The World Crisis and the Good Neighbor Policy in Panama, 1936–1941." *Americas* 24 (1967): 137–35.

Langley, Lester, and Thomas Schonoover. *The Banana Men: American Mercenaries and Entrepreneurs in Central America 1880–1930.* Lexington: University Press of Kentucky, 1995.

LaRosa, Michael, and Germán R. Mejía, eds. *The United States Discovers Panama: The Writings of*

Soldiers, Scholars, Scientists, and Scoundrels, 1850–1905. Lanham, Md.: Rowman and Littlefield, 2004.

Lasso, Marixa. "Race and Ethnicity in the Formation of Panamanian National Identity: Panamanian Discrimination against Chinese and West Indians in the Thirties." Paper presented at LASA Conference, Washington, D.C., September 6–8, 2001.

Laurence, Charles. *The Social Agent: A True Intrigue of Sex, Lies, and Betrayal Behind the Iron Curtain.* Chicago: Ivan R. Dee, 2010.

Leonard, Thomas. "The Commissary in United States–Panamanian Relations." PhD diss., American University, Washington, D.C., 1969.

Levine, Phillipa. *Prostitution, Race, and Politics: Policing Venereal Disease in the British Empire.* New York: Routledge, 2003.

Lewis, Lancelot. *The West Indian in Panama: Black Labor in Panama, 1850–1914.* Washington, D.C.: University Press of America, 1980.

Lidio Pitty, Dimas. *Estacion de Navegantes.* Panama City: Biblioteca de Nacionalidad ACP, 1999.

Lincoln, Bruce. *Authority: Construction and Corrosion.* Chicago: University of Chicago Press, 1994.

Lindsay-Poland, John. *Emperors in the Jungle: The Hidden History of the U.S. in Panama.* Durham: Duke University Press, 2003.

Linn, Brian McAllister. *Guardians of Empire: The U.S. Army in the Pacific 1902–1940.* Chapel Hill: University of North Carolina Press, 1997.

Lipman, Jana K. *Guantánamo: A Working-Class History between Empire and Revolution.* Berkeley: University of California Press, 2008.

Living and Working in the Canal Zone: A Booklet of Information for the Orientation of the U.S-Citizen Employees of the Panama Canal Company and the Canal Zone Government. Balboa Heights, Panama: GPO, 1958.

Locke, Hubert G. "The Color of Law and the Issue of Color: Race and the Abuse of Police Power." In *Police Violence: Understanding and Controlling Police Abuse of Force,* ed. William A. Geller and Hans Toch. New Haven: Yale University Press, 1996.

Look Lai, Walton. *Indentured Labor, Caribbean Sugar: Chinese and Indian Migrants to the British West Indies, 1838–1918.* Baltimore: Johns Hopkins University Press, 1993.

Loory, Stuart H. *Defeated: Inside America's Military Machine.* New York: Random House, 1973.

Luibhéid, Eithne. *Entry Denied: Controlling Sexuality at the Border.* Minneapolis: University of Minnesota Press, 2002.

Lundestad, Geir. *Empire by Integration: The United States and European Integration, 1945–1997.* New York: Oxford University Press, 1998.

———. "'Empire by Invitation' in the American Century." *Diplomatic History* 23 (Spring 1999): 189–217.

Lutz, Catherine. *The Bases of Empire: The Global Struggle against U.S. Military Posts.* New York: New York University Press, 2009.

Ma, Laurence J. C., and Carolyn Cartier, eds. *The Chinese Diaspora: Space, Place, Mobility, and Identity.* Lanham, Md.: Rowman and Littlefield, 2003.

MacDonald, Scott B. *Mountain High, White Avalanche: Cocaine and Power in the Andean States and Panama.* New York: Praeger, 1989.

MacGregor, Morris J., Jr. *Integration of the Armed Forces, 1940–1965.* Washington, D.C.: Center of Military History, U.S. Army, 1981.

Mack, Gerstle. *The Land Divided: A History of the Panama Canal and Other Isthmian Canal Projects.* New York: Knopf, 1944.

Mackenzie, John M. "The British Big-Game Hunting Tradition, Masculinity, and Fraternalism with Particular Reference to the 'Shikar Club.'" *Sports Historian* 20 (January–March 2000): 70–96.

———. *Empire of Nature, Hunting, Conservation, and British Imperialism.* Manchester: Manchester University Press 1990.

MacLaren, J. P. *A Brief History of Sanitation in Panama, 1513–1972.* Mount Hope, CZ: GPO, 1975.

Maier, H. G. "United States' Defense Rights in the Panama Canal Treaties: The Need for Clarification of a Studied Ambiguity." *Virginia Journal of International Law* 24 (1984): 287–322.

Major, John. "The Panama Canal Zone, 1904–1979." In *The Cambridge History of Latin America,* ed. Leslie Bethell. Vol. 7. New York: Cambridge University Press, 1990.

———. *Prize Possession: The United States and the Panama Canal, 1903–1979.* New York: Cambridge University Press, 1993.

———. "Wasting Asset: The U.S. Re-assessment of the Panama Canal, 1945–1949." *Journal of Strategic Studies* 3 (1980): 123–46.

Mann, Coramae Richey, et al., eds. *Images of Color, Images of Crime.* New York: Oxford University Press, 2006.

Marshall, Oliver, ed. *English-speaking Communities in Latin America.* New York: Palgrave-Mcmillan, 2000.

Marston, Elsa. *The Politics of Education in Colonial Algeria and Kenya.* Athens: Ohio University, Center for International Studies, 1984.

Materno Vásquez, Juan. *Sobre el hombre cultural panameño.* Panama: Imprenta Nacional, 1971.

Marthoz, Jean Paul. *Panama: La Malédiction du Canal.* Brussels: Lieu/Pl. Publication, 1979.

Martin, Carl. "Ready at the Ninth Parallel." *Army Digest* 58 (March 1970): 45–48.

Martínez, Oscar J. *Border Peoples: Life and Society in the U.S.-Mexican Borderlands.* Tucson: University of Arizona Press, 1994.

Maurer, Noel, and Carlos Yu. *The Big Ditch: How America Took, Built, Ran, and Ultimately Gave Away the Panama Canal.* Princeton: Princeton University Press, 2011.

May, Elaine Tyler. *Homeward Bound: American Families in the Cold War Era.* New York: Basic Books, 1988.

May, Ernest R. *Imperial Democracy: The Emergence of America as a Great Power.* New York: Harper and Row, 1973.

McAlister, Melani. *Epic Encounters: Culture, Media, and U.S. Interests in the Middle East.* Berkeley: University of California Press, 2001.

McCain, William. *The United States and the Republic of Panama.* Durham: Duke University Press, 1937.

McCleary, Richard. *Dangerous Men: The Sociology of Parole.* Beverly Hills, Calif.: Sage, 1978.

McClintock, Anne. *Imperial Leather: Race, Gender, and Sexuality in Colonial Conquest.* New York: Routledge, 1995.

McConkey, Clarence. *The Union Church of the Canal Zone, 1950–1992.* Balboa, Panama: Union Church, 1993.

McCormack, Leanne. *Regulating Sexuality: Women in Twentieth Century Northern Ireland.* Manchester, U.K.: Manchester University Press, 2011.

McCullough, David. *The Path between the Seas: The Creation of the Panama Canal, 1870–1914.* New York: Simon and Schuster, 1977.

McFerson, Hazel M. *The Racial Dimension of American Overseas Colonial Policy.* Westport, Conn.: Greenwood Press, 1997.

McGirr, Lisa. *Suburban Warriors: The Origins of the New American Right.* Princeton: Princeton University Press, 2002.

McGuinness, Aims. *Path of Empire: Panama and the California Gold Rush*. Ithaca, N.Y.: Cornell University Press, 2008.

McGuire, Phillip. *Taps for a Jim Crow Army: Letters from Black Soldiers in World War II*. Santa Barbara, Calif.: ABC-Clio Press, 1983.

McPherson, Alan L. "Courts of World Opinion: Trying the Panama Flag Riots of 1964." *Diplomatic History* 28 (January 2004): 83–112.

———. "Rioting for Dignity: Masculinity, National Identity and Anti-U.S. Resistance in Panama." *Gender and History* 19 (August 2007): 219–41.

———. *Yankee No! Anti-Americanism in U.S.–Latin American Relations*. Cambridge: Harvard University Press, 2003.

Medina, Vilma N. *Estimación de indicadores demográficos de la República de Panamá por el período 1950–1970*. Panama: Contraloría General de la República, 1973.

Melhues, Marit, and Kristi Anne Stolen, eds. *Machos, Mistresses, and Madonnas: Contesting Power of Latin American Gender Imagery*. New York: Verso, 1996.

Mellander, Gustavo A., and Nelly Maldonado Mellander. *Charles Edward Magoon: The Panama Years*. Rio Piedras, Puerto Rico: Editorial Plaza Mayor, 1999.

Méndez, Roberto N. *Panamá, 20 de diciembre de 1989, Liberación o Crimen?* Panama City: CELA, 1994.

Mendoza, Carlos Alberto, ed. *Panamá: Un Aporte a Su Historia*. Panama City: Corporación La Prensa, 2005.

Merk, Frederick. *Manifest Destiny and Mission in American History: A Reinterpretation*. Cambridge: Harvard University Press, 1995.

Messerschmidt, James W. "Engendering Gendered Knowledge: Assessing the Academic Appropriation of Hegemonic Masculinity." *Men and Masculinities* 15.1 (2012): 56–76.

Methvin, Eugene H. "Anatomy of a Riot: Panama 1964." *Orbis* 14 (Summer 1970): 463–89.

Meyer, A. O. *Manual for Inmates of the Canal Zone Penitentiary*. Balboa Heights, Panama: GPO, 1950.

Meyer, Leisa D. "Creating G.I. Jane: Sexuality and Power in the Women's Army Corps during World War II." In *Lesbian Subjects: A Feminist Studies Reader*, ed. Martha Vicinus. Bloomington: Indiana University Press, 1996.

Meyer, Stephen Grant. *As Long as They Don't Move Next Door: Segregation and Racial Conflict in American Neighborhoods*. Lanham, Md.: Rowman and Littlefield, 2000.

Migdal, Joel S., ed. *Boundaries and Belonging: States and Societies in the Struggle to Shape Identities and Local Practices*. Cambridge: Cambridge University Press, 2004.

Miller, Jennifer. "International Intervention—The United States Invasion of Panama." *Harvard International Law Journal* 31 (1990): 633–46.

Millett, Richard. "The Aftermath of Intervention: Panama 1990." *Journal of Inter-American Studies and World Affairs* 32 (1990): 1–15.

Missal, Alexander. *Seaway to the Future: American Social Visions and the Construction of the Panama Canal*. Madison: University of Wisconsin Press, 2008.

Moane, Geraldine. *Gender and Colonialism: A Psychological Analysis of Oppression and Liberation*. New York: St. Martin's Press, 1999.

Moffat, Alistair. *The Wall: Rome's Greatest Frontier*. London: Birlinn, 2009.

Moffett, George D. *The Limits of Victory: The Ratification of the Panama Canal Treaties, 1977–1978*. Ithaca, N.Y.: Cornell University Press, 1985.

Monroe, William G. *It Was Fun While It Lasted: The Memories and Musings of a Real American "Old-Timer."* New York: Greenwich, 1959.

Montgomery, Heather. *Modern Babylon? Prostituting Children in Thailand.* New York: Basic Books, 2001.

Moon, Katharine H. S. *Sex among Allies: Military Prostitution in U.S.-Korean Relations.* New York: Columbia University Press, 1997.

Mora, Isidro Beluche. *Acción Comunal: Surgimiento y estructuración del nacionalismo panameño.* Panama City: Editorial Condor, 1981.

More, Evelyn, and Dorothy Jurey. *Panama in Your Pocket: USO Guidebook.* Washington, D.C.: GPO, 1946.

Moreno, Humberto. *Las Bases Militares y el Desarrollo Nacional.* Panama City: CELA, 1996.

Morley, Samuel A. *Income Distribution Problem in Latin America and the Caribbean: The United Nations Report.* Santiago, Chile: ECLAC, 2001.

Morris, Charles. "The Panama Canal: 75 Years of Security History." *Security Management* 32 (September 1989).

Morris, Howard. "A Paternalistic Theory of Punishment." In *A Reader on Punishment,* ed. R. A. Duff and David Garland. New York: Oxford University Press, 1994.

Morris, Jan. "Panama: An Imperial Specimen." In *Destinations: Essays from Rolling Stone.* New York: Oxford University Press, 1980.

Moser, Richard R. *The New Winter Soldiers: G.I. and Veteran Dissent During the Vietnam Era.* New Brunswick, N.J.: Rutgers University Press, 1996.

Moss, Larry Edward. *Black Political Ascendancy in Urban Centers, and Black Control of the Local Police Function: An Exploratory Analysis.* San Francisco: R & E Research Associates, 1977.

Muldoon, James. *Identity on the Medieval Irish Frontier: Degenerate Englishmen, Wild Irishmen, Middle Nations.* Gainesville: University of Florida Press, 2003.

Mullen, Robert W. *Blacks in America's Wars: The Shift in Attitudes from the Revolutionary War to Vietnam.* New York: Pathfinder Press, 1973.

Munchow, Mrs. Ernest Ulrich von, ed. *The American Woman in the Panama Canal Zone.* Panama City: Star and Herald, 1916.

Murillo, Luis. *The Noriega Mess: The Drugs, the Canal and Why America Invaded.* Berkeley: Video Books, 1995.

Musicant, Ivan. *Empire by Default: The Spanish-American War and the Dawn of the American Century.* New York: Henry Holt, 1998.

Nagel, Joane. "Masculinity and Nationalism: Gender and Sexuality in the Making of Nations." *Ethnic and Racial Studies* 21 (March 1998): 242–69.

———. *Race, Ethnicity, and Sexuality: Intimate Intersections, Forbidden Frontiers.* New York: Oxford University Press, 2003.

National Security Files: The Crisis in Panama and the Dominican Republic, 1964–1968. New York: UPA, 1983. Microfiche.

Navarro, José-Manuel. *Creating Tropical Yankees: Social Science Textbooks and U.S. Ideological Control in Puerto Rico, 1898–1908.* New York: Routledge, 2002.

Newton, Velma. *The Silver Men: West Indian Labour Migration to Panama, 1850–1914.* Kingston, Jamaica: Ian Randle, 1984.

1961 Canal Zone Holiday Calendar. Balboa Heights, Panama: GPO, 1961.

Noriega, Manuel, and Peter Eisner. *America's Prisoner: The Memoirs of Manuel Noriega.* New York: Random House, 1997.

Okun, Marcia L. *The Early Roman Frontier on the Upper Rhine Area: Assimilation and Acculturation on a Roman Frontier.* Oxford: BAR, 1989.

Oliver, Mary Beth, and G. Blake Armstrong. "The Color of Crime: Perceptions of Caucasians' and African-Americans' Involvement in Crime." In *Entertaining Crime: Television Reality Pro-*

grams, ed. Mark Fishman and Gray Cavender. New York: Aldine Transaction Publishers, 1998.

Ong, Aihwa. *Flexible Citizenship: The Cultural Logic of Transnationality*. Durham: Duke University Press 1999.

Orenstein, A. J. "Sanitary Inspection of the Canal Zone." *Public Health Papers and Reports* 28 (1913): 65–76.

Ortner, Sherry, and Harriet Whitehead, eds. *Sexual Meanings: The Cultural Constructions of Gender and Sexuality*. Cambridge: Cambridge University Press, 1991.

Osgerby, Bill. *Playboys in Paradise: Masculinity, Youth and Leisure-Style in Modern America*. Oxford: Berg, 2001.

Padelford, Norman. *The Panama Canal in Peace and War*. New York: Macmillan, 1942.

Panama, Supreme Court of Justice. "The Republic of Panama against Wilbert L. Schwartzfiger: Involuntary Manslaughter." *American Journal of International Law* 31 (1927): 1822–27.

Panama Canal Oversight: Hearing before the Subcommittee on the Panama Canal of the Committee on Merchant Marine and Fisheries, House of Representative, Ninety-fourth Congress, First Session, November 18, 1975. Washington, D.C.: GPO, 1976.

Panamá en Cifras, Años 1936–1979. Panama City: Instituto Nacional de Estadisticas y Censo: Contraloria General de la República de Panamá, 1937–1980.

Parker, Elizabeth Kittredge. *Panama Canal Bride: A Story of Construction Days*. New Austin, Texas: Exposition Press, 1955.

Parker, Matthew. *Panama Fever: The Epic Story of the Building of the Panama Canal*. New York: Random House, 2007.

Parrish, James Robert. *The Tough Guys: Hollywood Masculine Icons*. New Rochelle, N.Y.: Crown, 1976.

Pattel-Gray, Anne. *The Great White Flood: Racism in Australia: Critically Appraised from an Aboriginal Historico-Theological Viewpoint*. Atlanta: Scholar Press, 1998.

Patterson, John. "Latin American Reactions to the Panamanian Revolution of 1903." *Hispanic American Historical Review* 24 (1944): 342–51.

Payson, Howard. *The Boy Scouts at the Panama Canal*. New York: A. L. Burt, 1913.

Pearce, Frank. *Crimes of the Powerful: Marxism, Crime and Deviance*. London: Pluto Press, 1976.

Pearcy, Thomas. *We Answer Only to God: Politics and the Military in Panama, 1903–1947*. Albuquerque: University of New Mexico Press, 1998.

Penn and Shoen Associates, Inc. *Homosexuality and the Military: A Sourcebook of Official, Uncensored U.S. Government Documents*. Upland, Pa.: Diane, 1993.

Pérez, Louis A., Jr. *On Becoming Cuban: Identity, Nationality, and Culture*. Chapel Hill: University of North Carolina Press, 1999.

Pérez, Victor Manuel, and Rodrigo Oscar de León. *El Movimiento de Acción Comunal en Panamá*. Panama City: Arte Tipográfico, 1964.

Pérez Medina, Ramón G. *Historía de Béisbol Panameño*. Panama City: Editorial Vista, 1994.

Pérez-Venero. Alex. *Before the Five Frontiers: Panama from 1821–1903*. New York: AMS Press, 1978.

Pernett y Morales, Rafael L. *Loma Ardiente y Vestida de Sol*. Panama City: Biblioteca de Nacionalidad ACP, 1999.

Phi Delta Kappa [Lowell C. Wilson, H. Lauren White, Michael E. Smith, and Charles L. Lattimer]. *Schooling in the Panama Canal Zone 1904–1979*. Balboa, Panama: self-published, 1980.

Pike, Frederick. *The United States and Latin America: Myths and Stereotypes of Nature and Civilization*. New York: Oxford University Press, 1994.

Pippin, Larry LaRae. *The Remón Era: An Analysis of the Decade of Events in Panama, 1947–1957*. Stanford: Stanford University Press, 1964.

Pisciotta, Alexander W. *Benevolent Repression: Social Control and the American Reformatory-Prison Movement.* New York: New York University Press, 1994.

Pizzurno Gelós, Patricia, and Celistino Andrés Araúz. *Estudios sobre el Panamá republicano, 1903–1986.* Bogotá: Manfer, 1996.

Plummer, Brenda Gayle, ed. *Window on Freedom: Race, Civil Rights, and Foreign Affairs, 1945–1988.* Chapel Hill: University of North Carolina Press, 2003.

Porras, Hernán. *Papel Historico de Grupos Humanos de Panamá.* Panama City: Biblioteca de la Nacionalidad, ACP, 1998.

Pratt, Mary Louise. *Imperial Eyes: Travel Writing and Transculturation.* London: Routledge, 1992.

Prescott, James R. *Political Frontiers and Boundaries.* London: Allen and Unwin, 1987.

President's Committee on Equal Opportunity in the Armed Forces. *Equality of Treatment and Opportunity for Negro Military Personnel Stationed Within the United States; Initial Report.* Washington, D.C.: GPO, 1963.

Price, A. Grenfell. "White Settlement in the Canal Zone." *Geographical Review* 25 (1935): 1–11.

Priestley, George. *Military Government and Popular Participation in Panama: The Torrijos Regime, 1968–1975.* Boulder, Colo.: Westview Press, 1986.

Procida, Mary A. *Married to the Empire: Gender, Politics, and Imperialism in India 1883–1947.* Manchester: Manchester University Press, 2002.

Public Papers of the Presidents of the United States: John F. Kennedy, 1962. Washington, D.C.: GPO, 1964.

Putnam, Lara. *The Company They Kept: Migrants and the Politics of Gender in Caribbean Costa Rica 1870–1960.* Chapel Hill: University of North Carolina Press, 2002.

———. "The Work and Lives of Prostitutes during Costa Rica's Early Twentieth-century Banana Booms." In *Centro de Investigaciones Históricas de América Central.* Paper prepared for the 12th annual meeting of LASA, Miami, March 16–18, 2000.

Quilliam, Daniel D. "Racial Peculiarities as a Cause of the Prevalence of Syphilis in Negroes." *American Journal of Dermatology and Genito-Urinary Diseases* 10 (1906): 277–79.

Rabe, Stephen G. *Eisenhower and Latin America: The Foreign Policy of Anticommunism.* Austin: University of Texas Press, 1988.

———. *The Most Dangerous Area in the World: John F. Kennedy Confronts Communist Revolution in Latin America.* Chapel Hill: University of North Carolina Press, 1999.

Ramírez, Rafael L. *What It Means to Be a Man: Reflections on Puerto Rican Masculinity.* New Brunswick, N.J.: Rutgers University Press, 1999.

Renda, Mary A. *Taking Haiti: Military Occupation and the Culture of U.S. Imperialism, 1915–1940.* Chapel Hill: University of North Carolina Press, 2001.

Richard, Alfred Charles. *The Panama Canal in American National Consciousness, 1870–1990.* New York: Garland, 1990.

Rivett, Kenneth. *Immigration: Control or Colour Bar?: Control or Colour Bar? The Background to "White Australia" and a Proposal for Change.* Melbourne, Australia: Melbourne University Press, 1962.

Robinson, William Francis. "Panama for the Panamanians: The Populism of Arnulfo Arias Madrid." In *Populism in Latin America,* ed. Michael L. Conniff. Tuscaloosa: University of Alabama Press, 1999.

Rodríguez, Ileana, et al., eds. *The Latin American Subaltern Studies Reader.* Durham: Duke University Press, 2002.

Roe, Clifford. *The Great War on White Slavery: or Fighting for the Protection of Our Girls.* Chicago: Roe and Steadwell, 1911.

Romano, Dugan. *Intercultural Marriages: Promises and Pitfalls.* Yarmouth, Me.: Intercultural Press, 2001.

Ropp, Steve. *Panamanian Politics: From Guarded Nation to National Guard.* New York: Praeger, 1982.

Rosenberg, Emily S. "Cultural Interactions." In *Encyclopedia of the United States in the Twentieth Century,* ed. Stanley I. Kutler. New York: Charles Scribner's Sons, 1996.

———. *Spreading the American Dream: American Economic and Cultural Expansion, 1890–1945.* New York: Hill and Wang, 1982.

Rotskoff, Lori. *Love on the Rocks: Men, Women, and Alcohol in Post–World War II America.* Chapel Hill: University of North Carolina Press, 2002.

Rotter, Andrew Jon. "Gender Relations, Foreign Relations, the United States and South Asia, 1947–1964." *Journal of American History* 81 (September 1994): 518–42.

Rouke, Thomas R., and Rosita A. Chazarreta. *A Theory of Personalismo.* Lanham, Md.: Lexington Books, 2004.

Rouquié, Alain. *The Military and the State in Latin America.* Berkeley: University of California Press, 1987.

Rousenvall, Nelson. *Life Story of "N.R." or 40 Years of Rambling, Gambling, and Publishing.* Panama City: Panama American, 1933.

Rout, Leslie B., Jr. *The African Experience in Spanish America, 1502 to the Present Day.* London: Cambridge University Press, 1976.

Rudolf, Gloria. *Panama's Poor: Victims, Agents, and Historymakers.* Gainesville: University of Florida Press, 1999.

Russell, Katheryn K. *The Color of Crime: Racial Hoaxes, White Fear, Black Protectionism, Police Harassment, and Other Macroaggressions.* New York: New York University Press, 1998.

Ryder, Chris. *Inside the Maze: The Untold Story of the Northern Ireland Prison Service.* London: Methuen, 2000.

Salvatore, Ricardo D., and Carlos Aguirre, eds. *The Birth of the Penitentiary in Latin America: Essays on Criminology, Prison Reform, and Social Control, 1830–1940.* Austin: University of Texas Press, 1996.

Salvatore, Ricardo D., et al., eds. *Crime and Punishment in Latin America: Law and Society Since Late Colonial Times.* Durham: Duke University Press, 2001.

Sánchez, Peter M. *Panama Lost? U.S. Hegemony, Democracy, and the Canal.* Gainesville: University Press of Florida, 2007.

Sands, William, and Joseph Lalley. *Our Jungle Diplomacy.* Chapel Hill: University of North Carolina Press, 1944.

Sanford, Charles L., ed. *Manifest Destiny and the Imperialism Question.* New York: Wiley, 1974.

Sanitation in the Canal Zone, Annual Report 1955. Balboa Heights, Panama: GPO, 1956.

Schifter, Jacobo. *Lila's House: Male Prostitution in Latin America.* Binghamton, N.Y.: Haworth Press, 1998.

Schirmer, Daniel B. *Sexual Abuse and Superpower Difficulties in the Philippines and Japan.* Durham, N.C: Friends of the Filipino People, 1996.

Schott, Joseph L. *Rails across Panama: The Story of the Building of the Panama Railroad, 1849–1855.* Indianapolis: Bobbs-Merrill, 1967.

Schoultz, Lars. *Beneath the United States: A History of U.S. Policy toward Latin America.* Cambridge: Harvard University Press, 1998.

Scott, James C. *Domination and the Arts of Resistance: Hidden Transcripts.* New Haven: Yale University Press, 1985.

———. *Weapons of the Weak: Everyday Forms of Peasant Resistance.* New Haven: Yale University Press, 1990.

Scott, William Rufus. *Americans in Panama.* Berkeley: University of California Libraries, 1913.

Scranton, Margaret E. "Dreams and Reality: Panama Canal, 1977 and 1997." In El Canal de Panama en el Siglo XXI. Panama City: CELA, CEAPSA, UP, UTP, USMA, Ciudad del Saber, 1998.

———. The Noriega Years: U.S.-Panamanian Relations, 1981–1990. Boulder, Colo.: Lynne Rienner, 1991.

Scully, Eileen P. Bargaining with the State from Afar: American Citizenship in Treaty Port China, 1844–1942. New York: Columbia University Press, 2001.

Seegel, Steven. Mapping Europe's Borderlands: Russian Cartography in the Age of Empire. Chicago: University of Chicago Press, 2012.

Selser, Gregorio. El Rapto de Panamá: De cómo los Estados Unidos inventaron un país y se apropriaron un canal. Buenos Aires: Editorial Alcándara, 1964.

Shaw, Carolyn Martin. Colonial Inscriptions: Race, Sex, and Class in Kenya. Minneapolis: University of Minnesota Press, 1995.

Shay, Martha Jane. "The Panama Canal Zone: In Search of a Judicial Identity." New York University Journal of International Law and Politics 9 (Spring 1976): 15–60.

Shipway, Martin. Decolonization and Its Impact: A Comparative Approach to the End of Colonial Empires. Malden, Mass.: Blackwell, 2008.

Siebert, Renate. Frantz Fanon: Colonialism and Alienation. Concerning Frantz Fanon's Political Theory. Benin, Nigeria: Ethiopia Publishing, 1974.

Silvestrini de Pacheco, Blanca. Violencia y criminalidad en Puerto Rico, 1898–1973: Puntes para un estudio de historia social. Río Piedras: Editorial Universitaria, Universidad de Puerto Rico, 1980.

Simbulan, Roland G. The Bases of Our Insecurity: A Study of the U.S. Military Bases in the Philippines. Manila, Philippines: BALAI Fellowship, 1983.

Simon, Jonathan. Poor Discipline: Parole and the Social Control of the Underclass, 1890–1990. Chicago: University of Chicago Press, 1993.

Slatta, Richard W., ed. Bandidos: The Varieties of Latin American Banditry. New York: Praeger, 1987.

Smit, Hans. "The Panama Canal: A National or an International Waterway?" Columbia Law Review 76 (1976): 965–88.

Smith, T. J., and J. Michael Hogan. "Public Opinion and the Panama Canal Treaties of 1977." Public Opinion Quarterly 51 (1987): 5–30.

Soler, Ricaurte. Fundación de la nacionalidad panameña. Caracas, Venezuela: Biblioteca Ayacucho, 1982.

———. La invasión de los estados unidos a Panamá. Mexico City: Siglo XXI Editores Mexico, 1991.

———. Panama: Nación y oligarchía, 1925–1975. Panama City: Ediciones Revistas Tareas, Imprenta Cervantes, 1976.

———. Pensamiento panameño y la concepción de la nacionalidad durante el Siglo XIX. Panama City: Imprenta Nacional, 1954.

Soler Torrijos, Giancarlo. La invasión de Panamá: Estrategias y tácticas para el nuevo orden mundial. Panama City: CELA, 1993.

Solzhenitsyn, Alexandr I. The Gulag Archipelago, 1918–1956: An Experiment in Literary Analysis. New York: Harper and Row, 1974.

Spencer, Phyllis. Panama Folklore. Panama City: InterAmerican Women's Club, 1948.

Stasiulis, Daiva, and Nira Yuval-Davis, eds. Unsettling Settler Societies: Articulations of Gender, Race, Ethnicity and Class. London: Sage, 1995.

Stearns, Peter N., and Jan Lewis, eds. An Emotional History of the United States. New York: New York University Press, 1998.

Steel, Ronald. "The Accidental Empire." In Writers and Issues, ed. Theodore Solotaroff. New York: New American Library, 1969.

Stepan, Nancy Leys. *The Hour of Eugenics: Race, Gender, and Nation in Latin America.* Ithaca, N.Y.: Cornell University Press, 1996.

Stephenson, Richard M., and Frank R. Scarpitti. *Group Interaction as Therapy: The Use of the Small Group in Corrections.* Westport, Conn.: Greenwood Press, 1974.

Sterling Arango, Rolando. *La Batalla de San Miguelito.* Panama City: Publipasa, 1999.

———. *La Insurrección de Colón.* Panama City: Publipasa, 1994.

Stewart, Mark. *Los Mejores Bateadores Del Béisbol Latino.* Hong Kong: 21st Century Books, 2002.

Stoler, Ann Laura. "Making Empire Respectable: The Politics of Race and Sexual Morality in 20th Century Southeast Asia." In *Dangerous Liaisons: Gender, Nation, and Postcolonial Perspective,* ed. Anne McClintock et al. Minneapolis: University of Minnesota Press, 1997.

———. *Race and the Education of Desire: Foucault's History of Sexuality and the Colonial Order of Things.* Durham: Duke University Press, 1995.

———. "A Sentimental Education: Native Servants and the Cultivation of Children in the Netherlands Indies." In *Fantasizing the Feminine in Indonesia,* ed. Laurie J. Sears. Durham: Duke University Press, 1996.

———. "Sexual Affronts and Racial Frontiers: European Identities and the Cultural Politics of Exclusion in Colonial Southeast Asia." In *Tensions of Empire: Colonial Cultures in a Bourgeois World,* ed. Frederick Cooper and Ann Laura Stoler. Berkeley: University of California Press, 1997.

Strain, Ellen. *Public Places, Private Journeys: Ethnography, Entertainment, and the Tourist Gaze.* New Brunswick, N.J.: Rutgers University Press, 2003.

Streets, Heather. *Martial Races: The Military, Race and Masculinity in British Imperial Culture, 1857–1914.* New York: St. Martin's Press, 2004.

Strickon, Arnold, and Sidney M. Greenfield, eds. *Structure and Process in Latin America, Patronage, Clientage, and Power Systems.* Santa Fe, N.M.: SAR Press, 2000.

Stringer, Peter, and Gillian Robinson, eds. *Social Attitudes in Northern Ireland: The First Report.* Belfast: Blackstaff Press, 1991.

Sturdevant, Saundra Pollock. *Let the Good Times Roll: Prostitution and the U.S. Military in Asia.* New York: New Press, 1993.

Sugrue, Thomas J. *The Origins of the Urban Crisis: Race and Inequality in Postwar Detroit.* Princeton: Princeton University Press, 1996.

Sui, Lok C. D. *Memories of a Future Home: Diasporic Citizenship of Chinese in Panama.* Stanford: Stanford University Press, 2007.

Sweet, Frank W. *The Legal History of the Color Line: The Rise and Fall of the One-Drop Rule.* Palm Coast, Fla., 2005.

Szok, Peter A. *"La ultima gaviota": Liberalism and Nostalgia in Early Twentieth-Century Panama.* Westport, Conn.: Greenwood, 2001.

Tandon, Yash, and Arnold Raphael. *The New Position of East Africa's Asians: Problems of a Displaced Minority.* London: Minority Rights Group, 1984.

Tatum, Stephen. *Inventing Billy the Kid: Visions of the Outlaw in America 1881–1981.* Albuquerque: University of New Mexico Press, 1982.

Taylor, Alan. *The Divided Ground: Indians, Settlers and the Northern Borderland of the American Revolution.* New York: Knopf, 2007.

Teeters, Negley K. *Penology from Panama to Cape Horn.* Philadelphia: University of Pennsylvania Press, 1946.

Theroux, Paul. *The Old Patagonian Express: By Train through the Americas.* Boston: Houghton Mifflin, 1979.

Thomas, J. Parnell. "Reds in the Panama Canal Zone." *Liberty* 25 (1948): 14–15, 47–54.

Thornhill, Michael T. *The Road to Suez: The Battle of the Canal Zone*. London: Sutton, 2006.

Torrijos Herrera, Omar. *La Batalla de Panamá*. Buenos Aires: Eudeba, 1973.

———. *La Quinta Frontera: Partes de la Batalla diplomática sobre el Canal de Panamá*. San Pedro Montes de Oca, Costa Rica: Ciudad Universitaria Rodrigo Facio, Editorial Universitaria Centroamericana, 1978.

Truett, Samuel. *Fugitive Landscapes: The Forgotten History of U.S.-Mexican Borderlands*. New Haven: Yale University Press, 2008.

Tucker, Robert W., and David C. Hendrickson. *Empire of Liberty: The Statecraft of Thomas Jefferson*. New York: Oxford University Press, 1990.

Turner, Domingo H. *Tratado fatal! (Tres esayos y una demanda)*. Panama City: Biblioteca de la Nacionalidad, ACP, 1999.

United Nations Bureau of Social Affairs. *Freedom from Arbitrary Arrest, Detention, and Exile: Yearbook on Human Rights, First Supplementary Volume*. New York, 1959.

Urgate, Manuel, and Rippey, James Fred. *Destiny of a Continent*. New York: Alfred A. Knopf, 1925.

U.S. Army, Caribbean Defense Command, Historical Section. *Acquisition of Land in the Panama Canal Zone*. Quarry Heights, Canal Zone, 1946.

———. *Control of Venereal Disease and Prostitution*. Quarry Heights, CZ: GPO, 1946.

———. *History of the Panama Canal Department*. 4 vols. Quarry Heights, Canal Zone, 1947.

———. *U.S. Army Caribbean Command Strategic Seminar 1954*. Quarry Heights, Canal Zone, 1954.

U.S. Medical Wives Society. *La Cocina de Panamá*. Balboa, Panama: GPO, 1968.

Valdés Sánchez, Servando. *Cuba y los Estados Unidos: Relaciones Militares, 1933–1958*. Havana: Editora Política, 2005.

Van Alstyne, Richard. "The Panama Canal: A Classical Case of an Imperial Hangover." *Journal of Contemporary History* 15 (1980): 299–316.

Vance, Cyrus. *Hard Choices: Four Critical Years in Managing America's Foreign Policy*. New York: Simon and Schuster, 1983.

Van Vleck, William C. *The Administrative Control of Aliens: A Study in Administrative Law and Procedure*. New York: Commonwealth Fund, 1932.

Vargas, Dalys. *Omar Torrijos Herrera y la Patria Internacional*. Panama City: Fundación Omar Torrijos, 2004.

Vega Méndez, Demóstenes. *El Panameñismo y su doctrina*. Panama City: Estrella de Panamá, 1963.

Velasquez, Joaquin. *La pollera y la cultura interiorana de Panamá*. Panama City: Impresora Nacional, 1963.

The Venereal Disease Situation in the Panama Canal Zone and the New Control Program. Quarry Heights, CZ: GPO, 1946.

Vergara, David. *Acuerdos militares entre Panamá y los Estados Unidos*. Chitré, Panama: Impresora Rios, 1995.

Vientós Gastón, Nilita. *Comentarios a un ensayo sobre Puerto Rico: "Puerto Rico, 1964: Un pueblo en la encrucijada de Roberto F. Rexach Benítez y Celeste Benítez."* San Juan, Puerto Rico: Ateneo Puertorriqueño, 1964.

Vilanueva, René. *Música, Cantos y Danzas de Panamá*. Panama City: Fornate Latino, 2000.

Vincent, Joan, ed. *The Anthropology of Politics: A Reader in Ethnography, Theory, and Critique*. Malden, Mass.: Blackwell, 2002.

Virgili, Fabrice. *Shorn Women: Gender and Punishment in Liberation France*. Oxford: Berg, 2002.

Vivian, James. "The 'Taking' of the Panama Canal Zone: Myth and Reality." *Diplomatic History* 4 (1980): 95–100.

Von Eschen, Penny M. *Race against Empire: Black Americans and Anticolonialism, 1937–1957*. Ithaca, N.Y.: Cornell University Press, 1997.

von Muenchow, Mrs. Ernst Ulrich, ed. *The American Woman in the Panama Canal Zone: From 1904–1916*. Panama City: Star and Herald, 1916.

Wade, Peter. *Race and Ethnicity in Latin America*. London: Pluto Press, 2010.

Walker, Samuel, et al. *The Color of Justice: Race, Ethnicity, and Crime in America*. Belmont, Calif.: Wadsworth, 2000.

Walker, William O., III. *Drugs in the Western Hemisphere: An Odyssey of Cultures in Conflict*. Lanham, Md.: Rowman & Littlefield, 1996.

Ward, Christopher. *Imperial Panama: Commerce and Conflict in Isthmian America, 1550–1800*. Albuquerque: University of New Mexico Press, 1993.

Ward, Sally K., et al., eds. *Acquaintance and Date Rape: An Annotated Bibliography*. Westport, Conn.: Greenwood Press, 1994.

Watts, Faulkner. "Perspectivos sobre el afro-panameño." *Revista Lotería*, August 1975, 36–48.

Watts, Sarah Lyon. *Rough Rider in the White House: Theodore Roosevelt and the Politics of Desire*. Chicago: University of Chicago Press, 2004.

Weber, Max. *The Protestant Ethic and the Spirit of Capitalism*. New York: Oxford University Press, 2010.

Weber, Cynthia. "Something's Missing: Male Hysteria and the U.S. Invasion of Panama." In *The "Man" Question in International Relations*, ed. Marysia Zalewski and Jane Parpart. Boulder, Colo.: Westview Press, 1998.

Weber, David J., and Jane M. Rausch, eds. *Where Cultures Meet: Frontiers in Latin American History*. Wilmington, Del.: SR Books, 1994.

Wedgwood, Ruth. "The Use of Armed Force in International Affairs: Self-Defense and the Panama Invasion." *Columbia Journal of Transnational Law* 29 (1991): 609–28.

Weeks, John, and Phil Gunson. *Panama: Made in the USA*. London: Latin American Bureau, 1991.

Weil, Thomas E., et al. *Area Handbook for Panama*. Washington, D.C.: GPO, 1972.

Weitzer, Ronald John. *Policing under Fire: Ethnic Conflict and Police-Community Relations in Northern Ireland*. Albany: State University of New York Press, 1995.

Welsome, Eileen. *The General and the Jaguar: Pershing's Hunt for Pancho Villa: A True Story of Revolution and Revenge*. New York: Little, Brown, 2006.

Westerman, George. "Gold vs. Silver Workers in the Canal Zone." *Common Ground* 8 (1948): 92–95.

———. *The West Indian Worker on the Panama Canal*. Panama City: Universidad de Panamá, 1951.

Westheider, James E. *Fighting on Two Fronts: African Americans and the Vietnam War*. New York: New York University Press, 1997.

Wheaton, Philip E. *Panama Invaded: Imperial Occupation versus the Struggle for Sovereignty*. Trenton, N.J.: Red Sea Press, 1991.

Whitten, Norman E., Jr., and Arlene Torres, eds. *Blackness in Latin America and the Caribbean: Social Dynamics and Cultural Transformations*. Bloomington: Indiana University Press, 1998.

Wilbert, William. *Finding Freedom in Panama: The True Account of the Experiences of an American Pastor in the Prisons of Panama*. DeBary, Fla.: Longwood, 2000.

Williams, Colin J., and Martin S. Weinberg. *Homosexuals and the Military: A Study of Less Than Honorable Discharge*. New York: Harper and Row, 1971.

Williams, William Appleman. *Empire as a Way of Life*. New York: Oxford University Press, 1980.

Wilson, Ruth Danenhower. *Jim Crow Joins Up: A Study of Negroes in the Armed Forces of the United States*. New York: Press of W. J. Clark, 1944.

Winant, Howard. *The World Is a Ghetto: Race and Democracy since World War II*. New York: Basic Books, 2002.

Withers, William. *The Economic Crisis in Latin America*. Glencoe, Ill.: Free Press of Glencoe, 1964.

Women's Army Corps. *A Book of Facts about the WAC: Women's Army Corps*. Washington, D.C.: GPO, 1944.

———. *73 Questions and Answers about the WAC*. Washington, D.C.: GPO, 1943.

Wucker, Michele. *Why the Cocks Fight: Haitians, Dominicans, and the Struggle for Hispaniola*. New York: Hill and Wang, 1999.

Yau, Julio. *El Canal de Panamá: Calvario de un Pueblo*. Madrid: Editorial Mediterráneo, 1972.

Young, Robert J. C. *Colonial Desire: Hybridity in Theory, Culture, and Race*. New York: Routledge, 1995.

Yuh, Ji-Yeon. *Beyond the Shadow of Camptown: Korean Military Brides in America*. New York: New York University Press, 2002.

Index

Italicized locators refer to illustrations.

class (*continued*)

in the Zone, 162–64; middle class, 95–96; middle class in Panama, 59; middle class in the Zone, 4, 7, 30, 80; and moral order in Panama, 130; multiclass clientele of brothels, 138; and nationalism, 13, 113; oligarchy and upper class in Panama, 14, 21, 45, 46, 106, 133, 175, 205–6; in Panama, 74, 79, 106; and Panamanian service workers around U.S. bases, 170; Panamanian working class, 40, 59, 74, 106, 108, 133, 135, 153; and participation in 1964 riots, 82; the poor in Panama, 10, 15, 18, 40, 47, 74, 82, 102, 106, 133, 135, 156, 166, 201, 202, 203, 205, 206, 216, 224, 222, 227, 228, 235, 236, 247, 248; and property advantages, 71; reaction by, to Roxana murder, 151; role of, in channeling U.S. sexual desires, 130, 133; segregation by, in Panama, 74–76; and status in the borderland, 247–48; stigma attached to gate girls, 133; support for retention of U.S. military bases in Panama, 171; upper-middle-class lifestyles, 32; and U.S. enlisted personnel, 130, 170–71; and U.S.-Panamanian marriages, 156–58; in U.S.-Panamanian social relations, 130; during World War II, 15. See also *rabiblancos*

Coco Grove, 209. See also sex and vice industries

Coco Solo Naval Base, 42, 97, 176

Codrington, Sewell, 181–82

Coiba Island penal colony, 81, 206

Cold Storage Plant (Cristobal), 211

Cold War, 20, 32, 37, 59, 61, 67, 71, 115, 147, 161, 176, 181, 252

Colombia, 12, 22, 87, 138, 139, 140, 176, 205, 232

Colombians, 8, 12, 28, 32, 42, 60, 79, 117, 131, 133, 149, 151, 152, 154, 201

Colón, 2, 3, 9, 11, 13, 14, 18, 20, 22, 24, 29, 31, 41, 48, 49, 57, 59, 82, 84, 95, 98, 102, 111, 114, 115, 126, 131, 133, 140, 141, 143, 144, 145, 147, 149, 168, 178, 179, 180, 191, 197, 206, 213, 216, 220, 227, 247, 253; Corridor, 39; Free Zone, 96; hospital, 16; map of, 97

colonialism (U.S.), 3, 123, 126, 134, 250, 253; British, 101; as demonic force, 10; internal, 205; neocolonialism in Cuba, 18; in Puerto Rico, 110; racial, 251

colons (French Algerian colonists), 76, 251

Communism, 116. See also Partido del Pueblo

"Concerned Brothers," 123, 192. See also African American soldiers in the borderland

concubinage, 6, 139, 166. See also sexuality

Conniff, Michael L., 3, 5, 94, 255n8, 256n8, 256n9, 256n17, 257n32, 260n60, 260n61, 271n93, 273n3–5, 273n9, 275n29, 277n58, 278n71, 289n24, 296n19, 305n9

Connor, "Bull," 63

"contact zones," 2, 78. See also encounters; Pratt, Mary Louise

Cooper, Daniel (Danny), 216

Coronado, 25, 206

Corozal Army Reservation, x, 42, 50, 91, 123, 176

crime in the borderland, 2, 7, 11, 24, 27, 44, 51, 59, 66, 71; arrests, 206, 214, 215, 237, 239, 240, 242; assault, 14, 87, 88, 93, 94, 118, 129, 130, 132, 135, 140, 166, 179, 190, 214, 215, 226, 227; bill-splitting, 218–19; blurred boundaries between work and crime, 222; burglary, 27, 109, 110, 111, 124, 210, 212–14, 215, 234, 235, 237; cable theft, 203, 223–24; against Canal Zone police officers, 236–37; Class I and Class II offenses in the Zone, 215; complaints in the Zone of coddling Panamanian criminals, 227–28; complexity of criminal alliances, 220, contraband (commissary and PX smuggling), 7, 11, 23, 42, 45–47, 203, 211, 219, 229, 236, 244, 249, 253; convictions, 214–215, 228; cost of, 219, 223, counterfeiting, 218; crime as resistance, 212, 213–14, 231–32, 237–38; crime in the Zone, 80–82, 229; crimes by U.S. military against Panamanians, 179–82, 185, 209; definition of crime, 205; denigration in the Zone of Panamanian criminals, 85, 207; effects of, on the Canal Zone, 242–44; felonies, 210, 223, 229, 241, 243; fraud, 87, 157–58, 215, 219; lack of violent crime in the Zone, 234; lar-

World War II, 14–15, 16, 33; urban, 169; U.S.-Mexican frontier, 96; and U.S. military, 202; Zone residents as "new frontiersmen," 162

Fuella, José Felix, 225

Galeta Island, 42, 176

Gamboa, 27, 28, 123; road gangs from the prison, 111. See also *Gamboa Road Gang*

Gamboa Penitentiary, 51, 81, 111, 116, 117, 158, 206, 208, 210, 211, 222, 225, 226, 229–32; black legend of, 229–30; composition of prisoners at, 229; drug smuggling at, 232; escape attempts from, 232; jurisdictional independence of, 229–30; "political prisoners" at, 231; recidivism rates at, 231; as refuge for Panama's poor, 222, 231; rehabilitative facilities at, 230–31; resistance at, 231–32; structural organization of, 230

Gamboa Road Gang (Los forzados de), 117

García, Dora, 173

García, Enrique, 143, 153–54

García, Norbeta, 173

Gardner, Bunk, 51, 154

Garvey, Marcus, 122

Gaskin, Ed, 115

"gate girls," 24, 133. *See also* sexuality; U.S. military

Gatún, 27, 32, 57, 114; dam, 223; lake, 41, 42, 93, 218; locks, 42

gender, 3, 5, 6, 138, 153, 156, 165, 227, 247; cross-gender themes of the counterculture, 166; declension of traditional gender roles, 163; gendered boundaries and constructions, 24–25, 32–33, 34, 118, 129, 130–31, 133–34, 166–67; gender divisions in U.S. military, 186; gendered hierarchies, 167; gendered images of Panama, 137, 175; gendered paternalism, 197; gender roles in the Canal Zone, 160, 161–62, 163; hegemonic masculinity, 159, 161, 183; machismo, 101, 153, 189; masculinity, 132, 158, 159, 174, 182; and separate housing, 159; subordinated masculinity, 161, 183

General-for-the-Day and Admiral-for-the-Day contests in the Zone, 200

Genovese, Eugene, 204, 205, 295n2

George, Ronald H., 111

Georgia, 98

Gibson (Kent), Lori, 92

Goethals, George W., 45, 55, 220, 296n14

González Manrique, Esteban, 144

Gorgas, William C., 137, 207, 281n34

Gorgas Hospital, 35, 50, 90, 183

Grant, Cary, 160

Grant, Gloria ("and her Giant Snake"), 142

Greaves, Lester Leon: as cause célèbre, 116–17, 136; claims to innocence, 116; legends and controversy surrounding his case, 118; rape case of, 50–51, 61, 86, 104, 111, 116–19. See also *Gamboa Road Gang*

Greene, Julie, 4, 273n8, 287n127, 296n15, 296n17, 296n20, 297n32, 301n89

Grut Azul, 39. *See also* prostitution

Guadeloupe, 95, 99

Guam, 169

Guatemala Coup of 1954, 161

Guerra, Vincente, 236

Guerrero, Rosa, 147

Guha, Ranahit, 204, 295n2

Hadrian's Wall, 2, 169

Haiti, 99, 248

Haitians, exotic nature of, for British West Indians, 99

Hall, Dale ("and her primitive Indian rhythms"), 142

Hampel, John, 118, 142, 144, 257n21, 277n68, 282n53, 302–3n.119

Hanan, John W., 109

Hancock, Joseph J., 211, 223, 224–25, 228

Happyland Nightclub, 15, 143, 143

Harding, Chester, 110

Harry, Gervaise W., 116

Hay, John, 12–13

Hay-Bunau-Varilla Treaty, 1, 144, 207

Hay-Herrán Treaty, 12, 22

Haynes, Cecil, 104

Haynes, Tirill, 224

Hays Censorship Code, 143

Haywood, Bill, 104

Helton, Vernon O., 128–29, 130, 132–33, 135–36

Helton-Mitchell rape case, 129, 130, 132, 136

274n26, 280n22, 291n57, 295n117, 301n89
Knights of Columbus, 54
Koerner, Charles F., 108
Korean War, 116, 135, 161, 171, 177, 178, 186, 187, 189, 190, 196
Kosik, Nina, 162, 200
Koster, Richard, 58, 84, 234, 259n56, 261n78, 270n86, 271n90, 292n70, 296n12
Kuna(s) Amerindians, 3, 5, 25–26, 34; and close association with Americans, 25–26; hostility toward Panama, 26; as marijuana smugglers, 47; "tribal justice" of, 47

La Boca, 27–28
LaFeber, Walter, 3, 255n8, 256n15, 256n16, 256n18, 258n40, 285n43, 263n112, 270n24, 273n6, 287n3, 289n29, 295n111, 295n117, 296n10, 296n21, 296n23, 298n49
La Hora, 136, 150, 172, 173
La Nación, 172
La Rocque, Gene, 177
Las Tablas, 76
Lee, Angela, 79
Lee, Spike, 105
Leocadio Meña, José, 41
Liberty, Larry, 195, 200
Local 713 (United Public Workers of America), 115
Local 900, 115, 116, 124
Local 907, 122, 124
Long, William, 236
Los Santos, 24, 179
lottery, 36, 49, 77, 175, 210
Love, Madison, 129
Luis Palma, Ana, 143
Lux Theatre Massacre, 80–81

Magoon, Charles Edward, 220
Major, John, 3, 255n8, 256n16, 257n22, 257n24, 257n25, 263n102, 272n105, 277n58, 278n71, 281n42, 281n44, 289n24, 296n13, 297n46, 305n18
Malcolm X, 122, 251, 305n13
Manifest Destiny, 52, 245
Margarita, 27, 31, 42, 57
Martie, Jessie, 237

Martínez, Boris, 21
Martínez, Oscar J., 19
Martinique, 95, 99; Martinicans, 107
masculinity. See gender
masks: of command, 204, 225; of false consciousness, 122; of servility, 204
Maurer, Noel, and Carlos Yu, 5, 273n5, 273n8
May, Elaine Tyler, 32
McCarty, Henry (alias "Billy the Kid"), 109, 114
McCullough, David, 4, 256n9, 263n102, 273n8, 281nn40–41
McGrath, Marco, 87
McNeece, Clarence, 80
McSherry, Frank, 62; report of (1947), 62, 266n35
Medina, José, 189
Meehan, Richard, 1964 C.Z. Police lawsuit of, 86
Melber, Adam, 182
Mendoza, Rodrigo, 36
Menéndez, José, 77
Mexicans, 245
Mitchell, William J., 128–29, 130, 132, 135, 136. See also Helton-Mitchell rape case
Missal, Alexander, 5
Montgomery bus boycott, 172
Morales, John, 79
Moreno, Miguel "Mike" J., 156, 171
Morgan, Henry, 67; Zonian identification with, 67, 164
Mount Hope Cemetery, 91
Mozambique, 88
Muñoz Marin, Luis, 190
música tipica, 36, 250
Myers, Chester, 82

nation, 118
Nasser, Gamal Abdel, 17
National Association for the Advancement of Colored People (NAACP), 117
National Party (South Africa), 61
Navajo Club, 139
Negueruela, Olga ("cute Cuban bombshell"), 142
New Cristóbal, 16, 41, 97, 207
New York Yankees, 65

Panama riots of January 1964, 8, 18–19, 22, 82–85, 151, 169, 185, 191, 198–200; evacuation of U.S. military dependents during, 198–99

Panama riots of November 1959, 17

Panama Sal (1957), 143

Panama Tribune, 96, 104

Panameñismo movement, 13, 209

Pan-American Highway, 14, 180

Paraiso, 27, 42, 114, 123, 225

Parker, David, 21

Partido del Pueblo, 238

Palau Lane, Rosita, 143, 153

Payne, Arthur (1964 C.Z. Police lawsuit of), 86

Pedro Miguel, 124; Locks, 42, 126; women's prison, 149

Peltier, Leo J., 81–82

Philippines, 15, 52, 169

Piggot, Winston, 211

Political Frontiers and Boundaries (James R. Prescott), 11

Porter, Cole, 143

Portobelo, 76, 138

post exchanges (PXs) on bases, 30, 46, 154, 155, 156, 201, 248; "Land of the Big PX," 153, 190; PX items as barter in the borderland, 154, 219; Zonian resentment over their exclusion from PXs, 195

Potter, William E., 116–17

Powell, Adam Clayton, 117

Pratt, Mary Louise, 77, 78, 269n69, 269n79

Prescott, Bobby, 104

Prescott, James R., 11–12, 256n12

Prieto, Pablo, 46, 235

Prohibition (1920–1933), 58, 59, 110

prostitution, 8–9, 14, 15, 19–20, 24, 36, 126, 131, 137; *artistas* as euphemism for, 15, 24, 133, 138, 147, 151; brothels in Panama, 3, 15, 19, 39, 40, 129, 133, 138, 139, 149, 150, 173, 180, 185, 197, 199, 248; in the Canal Zone, 148–49, 152; child, 136; *chulas* (procuresses), 139–40; crackdowns on, 146; during French construction, 138–39; guest-worker, 9, 139; layout and organization of brothels, 141–42; list of (in) famous brothels, 145; male prostitution, 131, 145, 146, 148; and the marinadas,

140–41; nationalities involved in, 8–9, 138, 151; numbers of, 147; origins of, in Panama, 138–40; pimps, 144, 149; reality of, in Panama, 144; restrictions on, during World War I, 139; U.S. and Panamanian regulation of, 144–45; in U.S. cinema, 142–43; in U.S.-Panamanian relations, 137; in World War II Panama, 14, 140–41

Pryer, Vernard, 193–95

Puerto Rican soldiers, in the U.S. Army, 8, 124; charges of cowardice during Korean War, 189; conflicts with Anglo and continental troops, 188–90; conflicts with Panamanians, 188–189, 191; as cultural mediators in the borderland, 187; discrimination against, by U.S. officers, 178; 189–90; deployments in World War II, 187; as intelligence assets in Panama, 188, 194; in the Korean War, 186, 187; machismo of, 154, 189; National Guard, 187; Panamanian attitudes toward, 175, 188–89, 191; violence by, against Panamanians, 154, 188–89

Puerto Rico, 154, 169, 177

Punta Paitilla, 16, 206

Putnam, Lara, 149, 273n7, 284n81

Quarry Heights Military Reservation, 18, 33, 35, 176

Queen Elizabeth II, 223

rabiblancos, 106, 133. *See also* class: oligarchy and upper class in Panama

rabicolorados, 133. *See also* class: Panamanian working class; class: the poor in Panama

race, 3, 5, 6, 33, 115, 129, 165, 201, 244, 246; Anglo-Saxonist race thinking, 52; categories of, 105–7; changes in attitudes on, after World War II, 60–63; *cholos blancos* (indigent whites), 79; *chombos*, 105, 112, 122; colorism in the borderland, 105–7; *costeños* (colonial blacks or *negros nativos*), 100–101, 106, 112; Darwinian theories of, 52; definitions of, 51–52; discrimination, 1, 27, 51, 52; and eugenics, 113; hierarchies of, in the borderland, 28, 52–53, 62, 65, 72–73, 106, 112, 121, 151, 204–5, 246; and identity, 3, 5, 50–54, 106, 181;

internal boundaries of, 26–28; and Joaquin Beleño's work, 117–18; and judicial outcomes, 136, 227; mixed-race offspring of the borderland (*panagringos* and *panahuchies*), 79–80, 100, 220; negritude and, 105; "one drop" rule of, in U.S. South, 79, 106; Panamanians views of race, 53, 107; *Plessy v. Ferguson*, 52; and prostitution, 138–39, 143, 149–50; racial caste system of Panama, 107, 205; racial divisions at Gamboa Penitentiary, 230; racial order, 43; radical black protest in the borderland, 122–23, 192–95; riots, 200; segregation of mixed-race couples and families in the Zone, 79, 246; segregation of schools and housing in Zone, 17, 26–28, 52, 62, 63–65, 102, 104, 114, 119, 123–24, 246; U.S. racial views of mixed-race Panamanians, 26, 52; in the U.S. military, 186–87, 190; and West Indians, 53, 93–94. *See also* McGrath, Marco; Panamanians; West Indians; Zonians

Radio Tribuna, 165

Rainbow City, 27, 114

Ramos, Ángel, 190

Ramsey, Fernando, 102

"Rappy Bait," 197. *See also* sexuality

Raspberry, Rex, 183, 234

Rawlins, Joseph Nathaniel, 223

Reagan, Ronald, 22

Red Scare, 238. *See also* Communism

Red Tank, 27

Reid, Charles Anthony, 237

Reid, James, 60

Remón, José Antonio, 16, 26, 46, 119, 123, 126, 146, 173; assassination of, and association with organized crime, 146–47; ownership of brothels and vice dens, 146, 173. *See also* Eisenhower, Dwight D.

Reserve Officers Training Corps (ROTC), 83, 200

resistance, 1, 3, 7, 168, 239, 244; against Canal Zone Police, 233–38; covert, 107; crime as political, 204, 212–13, 218; everyday forms of, 171; at Gamboa, 229–32; Panamanian images of, 132–33; squatting as, 43; vandalism as, 85; of younger politicized West Indians, 122–

23; within the Zone, 89. *See also* Gamboa Penitentiary; Panama Riots; Scott, James C.; Williams, John Peter

Rhodora, Jade ("The Rape of the Ape"), 142–43

Riba, Lorena, 235

Ridgway, Matthew B., 175

Riff-Raff (1947), 68

Río Abajo, 14, 24, 51, 98, 120, 121, 141, 146, 221

Rio Grande, 210

Río Hato, U.S. Airbase, 14, 15, 17, 21

Roberts, Peggy, 220–21

Robeson, Paul, 116, 122

Robinson, Jackie, 61

Robinson, Humberto, 104

Robles, Marco Aurelio "the Rifleman," 86

Rodman Naval Station, 176

Rodríquez, Adriana, 144

Rodríquez, Virgilio, 214

Roosevelt, Franklin D., 180

Roosevelt, Theodore, 38, 96, 97, 205, 220; Avenue, 50; Centenary in the Canal Zone, 55; Medal, 96

Rosales, Jesús, 194–95

Rose, Harold, 168–69, 172; child murder case of, 168–69, 172–74

Rosenberg, Emily, S., 252, 305n9, 305n15

Royo, Aristides, 86, 239

Royo, Ricardo, 86

Rud, Doris, 148

Saudi Arabia, 175

St. Lucia, 95

St. Mary's Church, 47; Catholic Parochial School, 47, 54

San Blas Islands, 25; "San Blas hotels," 142

San Miguel, 18, 34, 98, 216; fire of (1958), 184

Sánchez Salazar, Carmen "La China," 144

Sandinistas, the, 123

Santa Clara, 25, 42, 224

Santa Rosa, 41, 42

Scales, Charles Gordon, 80–81, 209. *See also* Lux Theatre Massacre

School Daze, 105

School of the Americas (formerly U.S. Army Caribbean School), 29, 176

Schmorleitz, Robert, 227
Scott, Edward "Ted," 53, 264n8
Scott, James C., 204
Scott, Muriel, 227
Semana Santa, 76
sex and vice industries, 6, 15, 19, 24, 39, 130, 138–41, 147, 177, 251; and contamination, 131, 137, 197, 207; erotic nightclub entertainment in Panama, 142; gambling and casinos, 32, 36, 40, 139, 141, 145, 179, 210, 247–49, and the marinadas, 140–41; "midnight revues" for GIs in Panama, 146; "Off Limits, Out of Bounds" establishments in Panama, 145–47; red zones and red-light districts, 14, 15, 35, 39, 131, 143, 147, 173, 178, 181; venereal disease, 145. See also prostitution
sexuality (in the borderland), 128, 130; definition of, 130; different mores of, 129–30, 133–35; failure to control, 130–31; frustration of some single Zonians, 160; homosexuality, 99, 131, 158–60, 228; lesbianism, 159–60; monitoring women's, 197; mores and practices, 129–31, 133–35; "rappy bait," 197; "sexual playground" for U.S. males, 135, 166, 177; taboos, 116; wife-swapping and swingers clubs, 89, 166. See also gender; prostitution; sex and vice industries
Sheridan, William, 132, 223
Silver City, 27
Singapore, 2
Smith, Gustave, 116, 182
Snake Pit Nightclub, 192
Socialism, 4, 69–11
Sothern, Ann, 143
South Africa, 43, 124; Nationalist Party in, 61
Southern Command. See U.S. military
Spaniards, 28, 54, 96, 245
sports, 31, 33, 65, 66, 250; baseball, 61, 65, 102, 104, 110, 126, 178, 187, 231; basketball, 59, 102, 178, 217; boxing, 43, 98, 102, 178, 187; cricket, 110; football, 63, 65, 66, 83, 197, 250; Major League, 251; New York Yankees in Panama, 65; Panama League, 65; segregated nature of, in Zone, 63, 104; Triple Crown horseracing, 102;

West Indian major league baseball players, 101–4
Stabler, Susan L., 31, 39, 56, 260–61n70
Star and Herald, 31, 66
Steele, William, 237
Stennett, Rennie, 102
Sterling Arango, Rolando, 188, 253
Stewart, Carlos Antonio Franklin, 213
Stoler, Ann Laura, 33, 262n76, 270n81, 279n3, 300n69
Stout, Hubert, 209
Suez Canal Zone, 2, 17, 89, 169, 172; crisis, 174

Tack, Juan Antonio, 88, 193. See also Kissinger-Tack Accords
Tatelman, Edward, 224
Texas, 90, 91
Thatcher Ferry, 16
Theatre Guild, 67, 161
This Month in Panama, 162
Thomas, Gerald, 116, 182
Tijuana (Mexico), 11, 96
Tirado, Carlos, 41, 252
Tirado, Edgardo, 58, 72, 235, 252
Tivoli Hotel (Guest House), 17, 21, 33, 157, 246
Tocumen Airport, 16
Torres-Rivera, Juan, 190
Torrijos, Omar, 21–22, 48, 112, 123, 178, 183, 193, 194, 202, 232, 239, 244; as a caudillo, 123; "Cholo" Omar, 124; exploitation of the Canal Zone fence, 21; opposition of, to the Zone, 21; racial liberalism and populism of, 123–24; as threat to Zonian identity, 87–89; Torrijosistas, 49, 256n5, 278n82, 290n51
transisthmian corridor, 2, 7, 10
Transístmica Highway, 14
Trujillo, Hector, 199

Ulster, 66, 131
unions, 59, 62, 89, 115, 124, 238, 251, 252
United Fruit banana operations in Panama, 15
United States, 1, 2, 6, 9, 13, 22, 25, 40, 72, 75, 81, 84, 91, 102, 105, 111, 119, 120, 125, 126, 130, 139, 142, 147, 154, 162, 175, 186,

Vallarino, Bolívar, 136
Vasquez, Gladys, 154
Veraguas, 24, 92
Verdugo, Elena, 143
Veysey, Victor, 89
Via España, 76, 194
Vietnam (War), 124, 161, 177, 192, 193, 195, 251, 253, 254; anti-Vietnam War protests, 193
Villa Amor, 39. *See also* prostitution
Volcán, 25

Wagner, Toby, 193–95
Watson, Eileen, 129
Watson, Vernal, 226
Wattino, Carlos, 194–95
Weapons of the Weak (Scott), 204
Webster, Ray, 104
Westerman, George, 96, 115
West Indians, 1, 5, 6, 7, 26–28, 34, 50–51, 62, 88, 94–96, 127; Afro Antillano Museum recognition of, 126; attempts to Hispanicize, 120; *bajun* dialect of, 99–100; baseball players in the major leagues, 102, 104; British emancipation of, 95; as *chombos*, 105, 112, 122; churches, 99; conflicts of, with Panamanians, 93–94, 101–2, 105, 120, 125–26; cultural identity of, 119–22; cultural influences on, 98; "de back ponch" fears of, 118–19; decline in canal workforce after 1951, 216; deaths and discrimination during construction, 96–97; diet of, 99; expulsion to Panama by U.S. officials, 27, 119, 124; "gold-silver" wage and segregation system of, 26–27, 52–53, 91, 97–98, 103, 172, 216; identity conflicts and transformations, 93–94, 119–22; influence of, on Panamanian culture, 101; influence on, of U.S. popular culture, 102; institutions and associations of, 99; leading families of (in Colón), 95–96; and Local 713, 115; obeah practices of, 99, 101, 110, 113–14; Panamanian hostility toward, 105, 112–13; Panamanian taxation of, 119; post–World War activism of, 114–16; radical protest of, 122–24; religious affiliations of, 98; resistance to assimilation, 26, 100, 120, 126; resistance to Jim

Crow and U.S. domination, 114, 116, 204, 211; silver towns of, 26, 27, 43, 102; Spanish language in schools after 1956, 119; as "third nationality" workforce, 94, 126; as *tío toms*, 101, 121; Torrijos' outreach to, 123–24; views by, of Canal Zone Justice, 228–29. *See also* Williams, John Peter
Wheeler, George, 56
Williams, John Peter, 107–14, 124; death of, 112, 114; escapes from the law, 110–11, 112; legend of, 110, 113–14; place in Panamanian history, 112–13; as "Robin Hood of the Canal Zone," 107, 114; social bandit role for West Indian community, 110–11; U.S. racial theories on, 113
Williams, Vincente, 105
Wolf, Eric R., 204, 295n2
women: abandoned, 155; advancements in employment for female Zone residents, 247; Ama-Zonians, 33, 34, 162, 164; British, 33; changing post–World War II role of, 162–65; Chilean, 32; Colombian, 8, 32, 60, 79, 133, 149, 151, 152, 154, 201; "decent-minded," vs. daring, 160, domestic violence against, 143, 153; Dominican, 8, 106, 151, 152; drawing GI support payments, 155; French, 33, 138; "gate girls," 24, 133; Haitian, 99; intermarriages with Panamanians, 156–57; intermarriages with U.S. citizens, 151–53, 156–57; mail-order brides during construction, 139; Mexican, 32; Panamanian, 10, 14, 19, 24, 25, 32, 37, 80, 82, 116, 128–33, 151, 152, 154, 201; in Panamanian garb, 76, 77; philanthropy of, during World War I, 13, 139, 248; prison, 148; rivalry among Panamanian and Zonian, 135, 160; society grand dames, 33, 162; U.S. women service personnel (WACs and WAVEs), 159; Venezuelan, 8, 32; Zonian, 32, 33, 65, 68, 135, 156; Zonian cotillion queens, 163; Zonian women's clubs, 162. *See also* gender
World War II, 1, 4, 7, 9, 10, 14–15, 16, 22, 24, 38–39, 61, 67, 97, 98, 129, 136, 139–40, 142–45, 147, 154, 159, 161, 163, 166, 174, 176, 179, 208, 212, 249, 250; "bonanza" in Panama, 15, 59, 80–81, 141; conflicting notions of race from post–World War II

social and institutional changes, 1, 5–6, 9, 29, 32–33, 39, 51, 54, 59, 60, 61, 114; fatalities, accidents, and injuries inflicted on Panamanians during, 179

Yalu River, 189
Young Men's Christian Association (YMCA), 54, 65; in Balboa, 148; in Cristobal, 182

Zapata, Federico, 224
Zone Liberation Organization (ZLO), 89
Zone-Panama borderland, 33–34, 35–37; anti-mosquito campaign in, 38; ceremonial encounters along, 76–78; criminal inhabitants of, 80–82; contraband smuggling along, 45–47; "crossing borders" along, 39–41; culture clash along, 33–38; drug use and trafficking in, 2, 7, 11, 19, 23, 36, 45, 47–48, 49, 66, 89, 143, 146, 165, 203, 229, 232, 239, 242, 249; emotional history of, 108; English-language newspapers in, 66; famous bars of, 59, 71, 173, 180, 182, 192, 246; famous nightclubs of, 142; identity crises in, 86–88, 93–95; income disparities in, 134, 157; "mango wars" of, 43; map of, 42; map of, on the Atlantic side (Colón), 97; map of, on Pacific side (Panama City), 35; popular U.S. culture along, 36–37; racial constructions in, 51–54, 93–95; religious identities in, 54; restrictions along, 43–45; service workers in, 74. See also Panama Canal Zone

Zonia, 15
Zonians, 1, 3, 5, 6, 24, 25, 34; as Afrikaners, 58; "Atlantic Side Syndrome" of, 30–31; "betrayal" of, by U.S. government, 74, 89–90; burial concerns over dead of, 91; as *colons*, 251; conflicts of, with U.S. military, 195–99; contested definitions of, 54–56; cooperation of, with U.S. military, 200; as creoles on the isthmus, 55–56; crime rates of, 71, 208, 211, 240–43; criminal Zonians, 80–82; decline in employment of, 16, 74; definition of, 54–55; drinking habits of, 58–59, 60, 71–72, 89, 148, 157, 159, 165; employee benefits of, 69–70; "fallen" Zonians, 79–80; family life of, 56, 66–67, 233; famous families of, 55; geographic identifications of, 57–58; hostility of, toward U.S. State Department, 72; identity of, 25, 51–53, 54–55, 57, 65–68; the jungle and U.S. identity of, 38–39, 69; knowledge of Panama vs. military dependents, 198; lodges and clubs of, 32, 54, 56, 59, 64, 65, 69, 73, 74, 85, 123, 247; lure of the "jungle" for, 38–39; nostalgia of, 6, 89, 90–91; "redneck," 58; as residents of the Raj, 195, 252; socialist identity of, 4, 69–71; social relations of, with Panamanians, 58–64, 74–76; U.S. hires, conflicts with, 56; "victimhood" of, 82, 87–89; workforce levels, 16. See also Panama Canal Zone
Zorn, Diane, 199
Zorn, James, 199